Making Mongol History

Making Mongol History

Rashid al-Din and the *Jami' al-Tawarikh*

Stefan Kamola

EDINBURGH
University Press

Edinburgh University Press is one of the leading university presses in the UK. We publish academic books and journals in our selected subject areas across the humanities and social sciences, combining cutting-edge scholarship with high editorial and production values to produce academic works of lasting importance. For more information visit our website: edinburghuniversitypress.com

© Stefan Kamola, 2019, 2021

Edinburgh University Press Ltd
The Tun – Holyrood Road
12 (2f) Jackson's Entry
Edinburgh EH8 8PJ

First published in hardback by Edinburgh University Press 2019

Typeset in 11/15 Adobe Garamond by
Servis Filmsetting Ltd, Stockport, Cheshire

A CIP record for this book is available from the British Library

ISBN 978 1 4744 2142 3 (hardback)
ISBN 978 1 4744 8387 2 (paperback)
ISBN 978 1 4744 2143 0 (webready PDF)
ISBN 978 1 4744 2144 7 (epub)

The right of Stefan Kamola to be identified as author of this work has been asserted in accordance with the Copyright, Designs and Patents Act 1988 and the Copyright and Related Rights Regulations 2003 (SI No. 2498).

Contents

List of Tables, Figures and Maps   vi
Preface   vii

1. Mongols in a Muslim World, 1218–1280   1
2. The Likely Course of an Unlikely Life, 1248–1302   28
3. Mongol Dynastic History, 1302–1304   59
4. New Projects of Faith and Power, 1304–1312   91
5. Remaking Mongol History, 1307–1313   121
6. Creating the Image of Rashid al-Din, 1312–1335   154

Epilogue: Rashid al-Din at the Court of Shahrokh   178

Appendix A   183
Appendix B   209
Bibliography   272
Index   305

Tables, Figures and Maps

Table 4.1	The *Collected Writings of Rashid*	113
Table B.1	Concordance of manuscripts of Rashid al-Din's historical works, by collection	266
Figure 5.1	The genealogical tree of Chinggis Khan, from manuscript K_2 64a	124
Figure 5.2	The genealogical tree of Chinggis Khan, from manuscript E_{11} 60a	125
Figure 5.3	The early and late genealogical trees of Dobun Bayan	126
Figure 5.4	Part of the genealogy of caliphs from the *Imperial Book*	128
Figure 5.5	The relationships between recensions of the *Blessed History*	135
Map 1.1	Sites of Ilkhanid history	x
Map 1.2	The dispensation of Chinggis Khan	5
Map 2.1	Ghazan's campaigns to Syria, 1299–1303	53

Preface

In 1836, Étienne Quatremère published *Histoire des Mongols de la Perse*, a portion of a dynastic history of the Mongols that had been written more than five centuries earlier. As an introduction, he attached a biography of the author of the work, Rashid al-Din, the doctor from Hamadan, and a description of his many and diverse works. Quatremère opens his study by declaring his goal: to rehabilitate the memory of a tireless civil servant and to compensate Rashid al-Din for the ingratitude of his contemporaries. In this, Quatremère succeeded admirably, assisted by the timely discovery of some of the most remarkable examples of early Persian book painting, which were also found in one of Rashid al-Din's historical works. Within a decade, scholars across Europe had seized on Rashid al-Din's historical writings as a key witness to Mongol history and to the emergence of book art in the Islamic world.

Close to two hundred years further on, not much has changed. Rashid al-Din's dynastic history remains invaluable for the study of the Mongol empire and his world history remains a landmark of early Persian book painting. Other biographies have followed on Quatremère's, but all of them highlight the same set of topics: the year of Rashid al-Din's birth; his relationship with his family's Jewish faith and choice to convert to Islam; his rise to prominence, writings, and fall from grace; and his ultimate execution at the hands of the Mongols who had employed him. Meanwhile, his dynastic history of the Mongols has been edited in full and in part, based on a set of widely recognised authoritative manuscripts.

This study attempts to step back from the prevailing approaches to Rashid al-Din's life and work, which unfolded across momentous historical changes in which he was intimately involved. His record of events, and the reports that others made of his activities during this period, reveal the anxieties of a society undergoing massive change and a court riven by factional conflict. To fix an exact course to Rashid al-Din's life, or to identify a single authoritative text for his Mongol history is to sacrifice a richness of incidental information imbedded in the heterogeneous, often conflicting historical record. This book looks at the life and work of Rashid al-Din through its unique textual witnesses, highlighting rather than resolving the discrepancies among our sources and exploring the motivations for authors and scribes to write and rewrite the story of the recent and distant past. The result, I hope, is a study of Rashid al-Din's life and historical writing that embraces the subjective nature of our sources, first and foremost those written by Rashid al-Din himself.

This book follows the course of Rashid al-Din's life, and so it might be called a biography. However, its main intent is not to definitively reconstruct one man's life and work, but rather to demonstrate certain historical processes that shaped and were shaped by that life. These include the rapid realignment of social and political identities in the Middle East during and immediately after the Mongol conquests; the forging of a cultural rapprochement between a foreign military ruling elite and indigenous cosmologies of faith, power, and historical time; and the sometimes very personal considerations that might lead a given author or scribe to put certain words on a page and not others.

As lonely as research can be, inquiry remains a social process, and there remain many to acknowledge for their contribution to this project. Joel Walker and Florian Schwarz led the graduate seminar in the winter of 2008 where I first encountered Mongol Studies and Rashid al-Din. Joel oversaw the dissertation on which this book is based with a wise and strategic eye that I continue to learn from. Having left the University of Washington while the project was still in infancy, Florian has offered periodic, insightful and constructive contributions, including a well-timed comment that there might in fact be an audience (of at least one) for a book that is half history and half manuscript study. In the wake of Florian's departure from Seattle, Charles Melville generously lent his support and expertise to the dissertation and in subsequent conferences and correspondences. Too many other scholars have weighed in along the way for me to list them here; I hope they might recognise the impact of their ideas as evidence of my respect for their contributions. The Society of Fellows at Princeton University was fertile ground in which to nurse the ideas of this book. During my time there, I benefitted from particularly timely interventions by Michael Cook, Mary Harper, Susan Stewart and Wendy Belcher.

Three others who deserve special mention for their sustained encouragement are Sheila Blair, Bruno De Nicola and Jonathan Brack. Sheila responded to a blind email from an anonymous graduate student almost a decade ago and has remained a source of wisdom, perspective and humour about all things related to Rashid al-Din. Bruno wrote a review of my dissertation that helped it gain some interested readership. Jonathan has provided regular and lively debate about many of the issues raised here. He also brought his own familiarity with the material to bear in reading an early typescript of the book, even as Anna Shields did the same from her perspective asking similar questions of the historiography of medieval China. Each of them offered characteristically astute observations, saving me from embarrassing factual errors and clumsy conceptual positions. I must insist on taking sole credit for all such that remain.

This study would have been impossible without access to the libraries and museums that preserve unique witnesses to the past. I owe a debt of gratitude to all the librarians and curators who have facilitated my research, especially Ursula Sims-Williams in London, Francis Richard in Paris, Olga Yastrebova and Olga Vasilyeva in St Petersburg, Alasdair Watson in Oxford, Katharina Kaska in Vienna, and Filiz Çakir Philip and Stephanie Allen in Toronto. Many others have helped me gain access to facsimiles of manuscripts I could not consult in person, particularly Hodong Kim, Christopher Atwood, Arham Moradi, Javad Abbasi, Farshideh Kounani and Abusad Islahi. Finally, I offer my sincere thanks to the Princeton University Committee on Research in the Humanities and Social Sciences, the Sharmin and Bijan Mossavar-Rahmani Center for Iran and Persian Gulf Studies, and the Board of Regents of the Connecticut State Universities, each of which provided funding for a different stage of research and writing. Judy Hanson at the Princeton Department of History quite spontaneously arranged office space for a former post-doc back in town for a month of frenetic writing in the summer of 2017, during which time an idea about a book turned into something like a book. Mia Karpov has weathered this project through its entire life cycle, which ought to be worth more than a brief mention at the end of a preface.

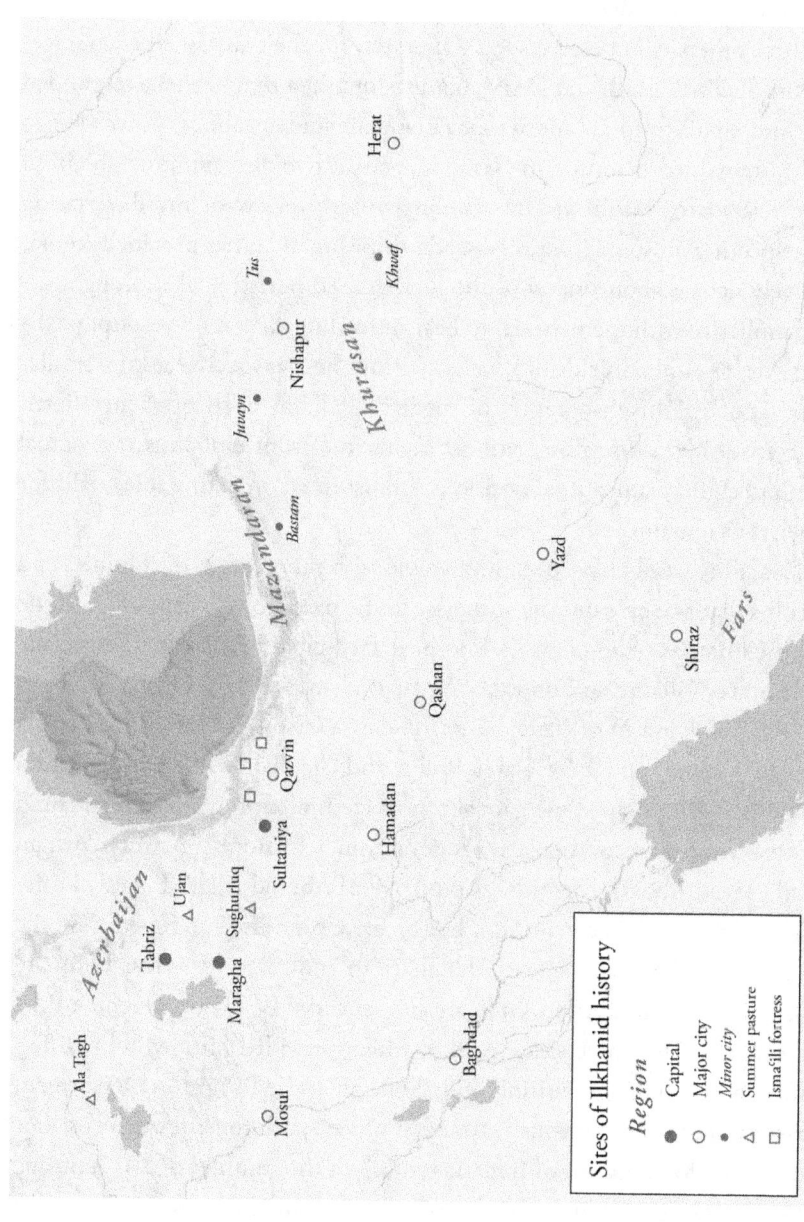

Map 1.1 Sites of Ilkhanid history. The late Ilkhanid capital Sultaniya also shows the site of the summer pasture of Qongqur-Oleng.

1

Mongols in a Muslim World, 1218–1280

On a July day in 1318, an elderly doctor and his teenage son faced execution on a charge of regicide. The doctor, Rashid al-Din from the city of Hamadan, had recently been the most powerful individual in the realm, an adviser to kings, patron of scholarship and charity, and author in genres as diverse as history, theology and natural philosophy. Thirty-six years earlier, he had attended the birth of the Mongol khan whom he was now convicted of poisoning. The relationship between the two had been so close that the khan, Oljeitu, had taken the same Muslim name, Ghiyath al-Din Muhammad, as Rashid al-Din's eldest son.

If Rashid al-Din was the pre-eminent statesman of the age, his accuser was a semi-literate *arriviste*, a jeweller-turned-politician named Taj al-Din 'Alishah, and he was motivated in his accusation by jealousy of his senior colleague's influence at court. According to a versified account of the execution written two decades later, Rashid al-Din watched a Mongol soldier behead his son and then spoke his final words. 'Tell 'Alishah,' he instructed the executioner, '"since your deeds have caused innocent blood to flow, the world will seek revenge from your soul. You shall gain nothing from this day. Nothing will come of it but this: that your tomb will be new and mine will be old."'[1] As predicted, 'Alishah enjoyed no lasting benefit from framing the senior statesman, and he is remembered – when he is remembered – as a footnote in a history largely written by and about Rashid al-Din, the doctor of Hamadan.

Rashid al-Din's death came exactly a century after another rash and momentous execution. In 1218, the city of Utrar – now in southern Kazakhstan – was subordinate to the shahs of Khwarazm. When the governor of Utrar ordered the massacre of a caravan of merchants from the realm of Chinggis Khan (d. 1227), and when Khwarazmshah Muhammad (d. 1220) failed to offer reparation for this act, they set in motion a series of Mongol invasions into southwest Asia.[2] In the decades following the massacre at Utrar, Chinggis Khan and his descendants brought the Islamic civilisation of Iran and Iraq to its knees. They then created a new political and cultural world, built on established Islamic norms and decorated with the scars of conquest and the trappings of transcontinental exchange.

This chapter traces the changing relationship between the predominantly Islamic society of the Middle East and the Mongol military elite that overran, occupied and finally came to rule over it. In the sixty years after Chinggis Khan's retributive raid against Khwarazmshah Muhammad, his descendants learned to appreciate the potential economic value of the Middle East. As they gradually built a state apparatus in the region, the Mongol elite faced a crisis of legitimacy, finding themselves ruling a foreign land that their predecessors had so violently plundered. At the same time, the experience of the Mongol invasions, culminating with the execution of the last 'Abbasid caliph in 1258, created a political vacuum within the indigenous society, as the familiar centres of power were swept aside by the new foreign occupying force.

To build and manage their state, and to celebrate their accomplishments in terms that the local population might accept, Chinggis Khan's descendants hired administrative professionals native to the eastern Islamic world. This first generation of scholar-bureaucrats took the first steps in normalizing the Mongols in the eyes of their subjects through scholarly and architectural projects. By 1280, the outline of a rapprochement had been sketched, to be filled out by later generations of administrators. These included a young Rashid al-Din, who was born into a Jewish medical family between waves of Mongol conquest. Such an individual could never have risen to the highest ranks of the state apparatus if it were not for the particular political culture of the new Mongol rulers and the often impromptu efforts of earlier scholar-bureaucrats to make sense of the Mongols in a Muslim world.

The Middle East in the Mongol Empire

Between 1219 and 1258, Mongol armies overran the lands of the Khwarazmshah and much of the eastern Islamic world in three waves.[3] Already at the onset of these invasions, the region faced a crisis of political leadership, as the Great Saljuq Empire disintegrated into a constellation of minor dynasties between Central Asia and the eastern Mediterranean. The family of Khwarazmshah Muhammad was one of several regional dynasties appointed as local governors by the Saljuqs. In the wake of their moribund patron dynasty, the Khwarazmshahs assumed *de facto* independence over the lands of Central Asia and eastern Iran. The decline of the Saljuqs was accompanied (and to some degree fuelled) by increased political activity of the Nizari Isma'ili 'assassins', who resisted Saljuq authority from fortified strongholds in the mountains of northern Iran and Syria. From these fortresses, they engaged in the political killings for which they are most famous. In Baghdad, the long-reigning 'Abbasid caliph al-Nasir (1180–1225) tried to capitalise on the Saljuq decline to reassert his own office as the central spiritual and secular authority in the Islamic world.

In short, on the eve of the Mongol invasions, political authority in the lands of the 'Abbasid caliphate was hotly contested. In particular, the antagonism between the emboldened caliph and the Khwarazmshah tilted towards open conflict. The massacre at Utrar precluded a decisive showdown, as the armies of Chinggis Khan descended on the cities of eastern Iran. Muslim accounts of the sudden appearance of Chinggis Khan's armies describe in apocalyptic terms these horsemen from the East and the butchery they committed against the cities of the Islamic world.[4] This reaction speaks to the destructive power of Chinggis Khan's campaign, but also to its sudden and seemingly capricious nature. Some cities were devastated while others were spared. In the end, after seven years of campaigning in western Asia, Chinggis Khan and his army disappeared back onto the steppe, leaving no occupying force to govern the region. Chinggis Khan had achieved his aim with the killing of the Khwarazmshah; the management of the lands of the caliphate was of little interest to him.

At the time of Chinggis Khan's death in 1227, the Islamic lands through which he had led his armies were still quite peripheral to the empire he had assembled. The most immediate Mongol-language source on the life of Chinggis Khan, the *Secret History of the Mongols*, describes the westward campaign primarily through the conflicts it engendered between members of the royal family and household. It leaves no impression that the Mongols were interested in anything more than some of the administrative talent that they acquired along the way.⁵ Chinggis Khan limited his direct accumulation of territory to the steppe areas that were of immediate use to his army of nomads. By contrast, the sedentary regions of the Middle East and China were at most sources of material and human plunder. Before his death, Chinggis Khan divided the steppe lands and nomadic people under his control among the members of his family, and particularly among the four sons by his chief wife, Borte.⁶ Chinggis Khan's youngest son, Tolui, took command of his father's central lands and army, while his older brothers inherited bands of territory expanding outward concentrically from the Mongol homeland.⁷ 'Ala' al-Din Juvayni describes the division of territories:

> To his eldest son, Jochi, he gave the territory stretching from the regions of Qayaligh and Khwarazm to the remotest parts of Saqsin and Bolghar and as far in that direction as the hoof of Tartar horse had penetrated. Chaghadai received the territory extending from the land of the Uyghur to Samarqand and Bukhara, and his place of residence was in Quyas in the neighbourhood of Almaligh. The capital of Ogedei, the heir-apparent, during his father's reign was his *yurt* in the region of the Emil and the Qobuq … Tolui's territory, likewise, lay adjacent thereto, and indeed this spot is the middle of their empire like the centre of a circle.⁸

Despite the fact that Chinggis Khan and his sons and generals had led armies deep into the Middle East and China, those regions are not described as part of his dispensation of territory. To the west, the portion of land allocated to his eldest son, Jochi, began with the territory of Khwarazm, but its outer boundary was left undefined, limited only by the expansionist capacity of the empire. Such an unbounded frontier invited further conquest westward along the Eurasian steppe belt, especially by the descendants of Jochi, who stood to gain control of the territory thus conquered. It also, however, laid the seed for conflict between the Jochids and other branches of the royal family over the question of who would control the significant resources of the Middle East.

In the years following Chinggis Khan's westward campaign all this was in the future, and the Middle East mattered little to the family of the Mongol conqueror. In the absence of direct Mongol governance, local political structures began to recover from the shock of the invasion. These included the

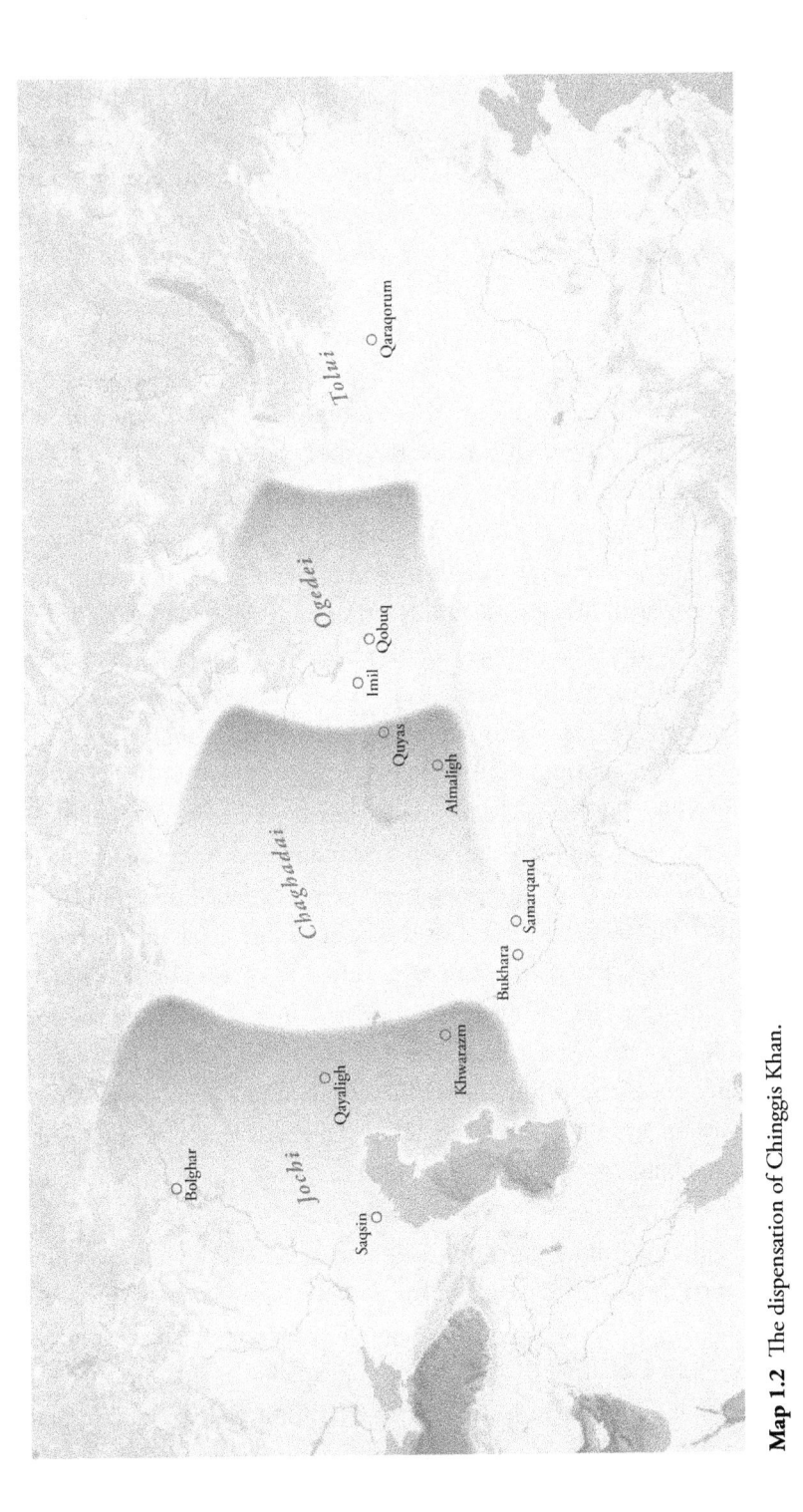

Map 1.2 The dispensation of Chinggis Khan.

'Abbasid caliphate in Baghdad, the network of Nizari Isma'ili fortresses, and the remnants of the state of Khwarazm, now led by Sultan Jalal al-Din (1220–31), son of Muhammad. Jalal al-Din had fled to India before Chinggis Khan and his army, and after the Mongols decamped for Inner Asia, he returned to reassert his father's claim to sovereignty in Central Asia and eastern Iran.

A Mongol army only returned to the Islamic world in 1231, when Chinggis' son and successor, Great Khan Ogedei (1229–41) dispatched an army under the command of the general (*amīr*) Chormaqun (d. 1241) to confront Jalal al-Din.[9] All major branches of the Mongol royal family, notably the families of the four primary sons of Chinggis Khan, contributed representatives and troops to this campaign. This was a signal that the occupation of these western lands was intended to benefit the entire empire, and not just one branch of the royal family. After hunting down Jalal al-Din and putting a definitive end to the state of Khwarazm, Chormaqun established a military occupation of the western conquered lands, headquartered on the rich pastures of Azerbaijan. From there, he led a series of campaigns to subdue the states of the Caucasus and Anatolia.

Only with Chormaqun's renewed campaign does the Mongol court seem to have woken up to the ample economic resources of the Middle East. Alongside the military occupation there developed an administrative apparatus to tap these resources. At the head of this apparatus there served a series of administrative appointees recruited from various sedentary and semi-sedentary peoples of Inner Asia who had already come under Mongol command: Uighurs, Qara Khitai and subjects of the defunct Khwarazmian state. Many of these individuals were loyal to Batu (d. 1256), Jochi's son and successor as ruler of the western steppe. As the senior figure among the many grandsons of Chinggis Khan, Batu enjoyed the distinction and honorific title of *aqa*, literally 'elder brother'. He never became Great Khan of the empire, but as a respected senior figure in the social dynamics of the ruling family, his opinion carried significant weight at the periodic *quriltai*s, the great meetings of royal and elite Mongols where major decisions were taken concerning imperial affairs, including the selection of Great Khans.

Because Batu inherited Jochi's patrimony to the western lands 'as far … as the hoof of Tartar horse had penetrated', and because he was uniquely respected among Chinggis Khan's descendants, he was largely successful, in the decade following Chormaqun's occupation, in extending his own influence over the emerging administration of the Middle East. His first deputy in this effort was a Khitan named Chin Temur (d. 1235), who had accompanied Chormaqun's campaign and who acted as the general's delegate in eastern Iran.[10] Meanwhile at Ogedei's court at Qaraqorum, on the steppes of Mongolia, Chin Temur's Khitan kinsman Yeh-lu Chu-ts'ai advocated maintaining the Chinese system for managing the agricultural lands that had come under Mongol administration with the fall of the Jin dynasty in 1234.[11] Chin Temur similarly approached his work in Iran with an eye towards maximising the agricultural and commercial potential of the subject region. His sensitivity to the management of sedentary populations, paired with a well-timed embassy to Qaraqorum, resulted in 1234 with him securing the right to establish a civil administration over the eastern Iranian provinces. This civil administration was independent from Chormaqun's military governorship in the far west. It drew on 'Abbasid and Khwarazmian precedents to lay the foundation for a Mongol-led bureaucratic government in the region.

From 1234, then, Mongol command in the Middle East was divided. Within the region itself, the main Mongol military occupation founded by Chormaqun continued to be based in Azerbaijan, while Chin Temur in the east of Iran developed a structure for civil administration. Chormaqun and Chin Temur were both dead within a decade, but others stepped into their places, perpetuating the division between the civil and military sides of the Mongol administration in the Islamic lands. The growth of a civil administration maps directly on the increased awareness among the Mongols of the region's economic potential. That awareness was also responsible for a growing rift between branches of the ruling Mongol family, and particularly between Batu Aqa and his cousins who held the title of Great Khan in Qaraqorum, over who would benefit from the Mongol occupation of the Middle East. This feud between the central Mongol court and the westernmost branch of the ruling family was a driving force in tearing the Mongol Empire apart. It resulted, by 1258, in the creation of a new dynastic Mongol state in the Islamic lands that had been of such little interest to Chinggis Khan.

Batu's Feud with Guyug

To staff his new civil administration, Chin Temur employed a number of bureaucrats who had formerly worked under the Khwarazmshahs. A group of such administrators had taken refuge in the eastern Iranian city of Tus, where they lived in hiding until the local residents surrendered them to Chin Temur. Among these fugitives was Baha' al-Din Muhammad Juvayni, scion of a family who had served Turkic dynasties in eastern Iran as early as the last great Saljuq, Sanjar (1118–57). Baha' al-Din himself had once served Khwarazmshah Muhammad, extending his family's experience with Turkic nomadic conquest dynasties. At the time of Chormaqun's invasion, however, he had been living as a private individual in his family's hometown of Juvayn, near Nishapur, before taking refuge in Tus.

When the residents of Tus handed Baha' al-Din over to Chin Temur, the Khitan governor took him into service and granted him the title of *ṣāḥib-diwān*, roughly 'treasury secretary'. By tradition, this title designated the foremost financial authority at court. Baha' al-Din may have gained it because of his family's long record of holding it under the Khwarazmshahs. Baha' al-Din retained this title until his death nearly two decades later, and while he does not seem to have exercised much formal responsibility during that time, he remained an influential adviser to the Mongol governors. By contrast, between 1230 and 1250 numerous individuals with various loyalties to one or another member of the Mongol royal family cycled through the administration of the Middle East. Of these, the most prominent held the title of *ulug bitikchi*, or Chief Secretary, a Turko-Mongol office that rendered the *ṣāḥib-diwān* largely redundant. Nevertheless, Baha' al-Din was a constant presence, if not a major actor, in the emerging civil government. His activity ultimately helped to shape the administration once the feuds within the royal family had been settled.

Chin Temur died in 1235, just a year after winning administrative autonomy from Chormaqun. In his place, Great Khan Ogedei appointed Nosal, an elderly Mongol general from the retinue of Batu Aqa. Nosal largely limited his activity to military affairs, leaving Chin Temur's ambitious deputy, the Uighur Korguz, also a dependant of Batu, to take active leadership over the civil administration. Nosal and Korguz were further assisted by another member of Batu's hereditary domain, the Khwarazmian secretary Sharaf al-Din, to whom the sources refer both by the Turko-Mongol title *ulugh bitikchi* and the corresponding Islamic title vizier. Meanwhile, Chormaqun's deputy in the military staff of Azerbaijan, Baiju, was also by all indications a representative of Batu's interests.[12] Thus, in the late 1230s, almost the entire senior administrative staff of the Mongol Middle East was filled by individuals dependent on the branch of the royal family headed by Batu Aqa. In 1240, Korguz managed to extend the administrative and fiscal jurisdiction that Chin Temur had won to cover the entire region of Chormaqun's military occupation. For a moment, it looked as if Batu had secured command over the Middle East away from the imperial centre headed by his uncle Ogedei.

The year 1241 marked a watershed in Mongol imperial history, and also in Batu's new-found monopoly over the administration of the Middle East. While his proxies had gained key positions in that region, Batu had since 1237 led a new Mongol military push into the lands of Russia and Eastern Europe.[13] Like Chormaqun's army, this one included troops beholden to each of the four main branches of the Mongol royal family. Most notably, at least one royal grandson from each branch participated in the endeavour. Batu, son of Jochi, led the expedition and was joined by Baidar and Buri, son and grandson of Chaghadai, Guyug and Qadan, sons of the Great Khan Ogedei, and Mongke and Bochek, sons of Tolui.[14] Over the course of the campaign, a rift opened between the cousins Batu and Guyug. The latter paired his arrogance as the son of the Great Khan with a tendency towards cruelty. Guyug's lineage posed a threat to Batu's authority, until Mongke intervened and convinced his uncle Ogedei to allow Batu to discipline their cousin. The animosity this bred between Batu and Guyug had enormous consequences, and ultimately contributed to the Middle East slipping out of Batu's control.

Despite these quarrels, Batu's campaign continued into Europe. After annihilating the major forces protecting the edge of the Roman Christian world in near-simultaneous battles at Liegnitz and Mohi, the Mongol force crossed the frozen Danube River on Christmas Day 1241 and stormed into the Balkans in pursuit of the fugitive Hungarian King Bela. As one branch of the army sacked the royal palace at Esztergom, another lay siege to the city of Split in Croatia. There, the archdeacon, Thomas, described the appearance of the horsemen of the East in terms of the miraculous and divine, just as Islamic writers had characterised the initial campaign of Chinggis Khan in the Middle East.[15] Thomas and his contemporaries also echoed the Muslim witnesses to Chinggis Khan's invasion by expressing surprise at how suddenly the Mongol invasion ended. Batu and his cousins did not follow up on their successes with a further drive into Latin territory. Instead, as other Mongol armies had done, they withdrew into the steppe-lands of the Volga basin, leaving Archdeacon Thomas and the rest of Christian Europe as puzzled by the disappearance of the Mongol army as they had been shocked by its arrival. Such capricious ferocity inspired the Latin West to dispatch diplomatic and intelligence missions to learn about the new Mongol threat and how it might be defeated or at least redirected against the Muslim states of Egypt and Syria.[16]

Batu's withdrawal from Europe can be explained in many ways. As had been the case when Chinggis Khan withdrew from the Middle East, Batu's mission was complete. Further, Europe provide less pasturage for the Mongol horses than the Eurasian steppe, and climactic fluctuation may have made 1242 a particularly difficult year to campaign in the west.[17] Another factor was undoubtedly the death of his uncle, the Great Khan Ogedei, on 11 December 1241. With Ogedei's death, the attention of the Mongol Empire turned inward towards the central court at Qaraqorum, where a *quriltai* would select a new Great Khan. Ogedei had expressed his desire that a grandson of his by a junior wife be named as his successor. After his death, however, his senior widow, Toregene Khatun (1241–6), assumed the regency of the empire and began advocating for her own son Guyug to become the next Great Khan. Batu, well established in his family's western territories and no friend of Guyug after their experience on campaign, held his armies in Western Asia, refusing to participate in the election of the cousin who had acted so insolently when they had campaigned together.

As dowager empress and regent of the empire, Toregene began the process of reasserting central control over the Middle East away from Batu. She pursued this aim by appointing new civil and military administrators for the region.[18] In 1241, the same year that Ogedei died in Qaraqorum, Chormaqun and Nosal, both Mongol generals in the west, also died. This allowed the Uighur Korguz to consolidate greater executive control in his own hands, a process he further advanced by having the *ulugh bitikchi* Sharaf al-Din arrested. In the process of bringing his case against Sharaf al-Din to Qaraqorum, Korguz stopped at the Chaghadaid court in Central Asia, where he managed to insult and antagonise a member of that branch of the royal family. Around the same time, news of Ogedei's death arrived at the Chaghadaid court, throwing Korguz's case into confusion and compelling him to return to eastern Iran. Almost as soon as he arrived, he was arrested by representatives of the Chaghadaid court because of the insult he had caused during his stay in Central Asia. Unable to reach a suitable verdict in the case, the Chaghadaids referred Korguz to Qaraqorum. Now, however, instead of standing as a plaintiff before Ogedei, he appeared before Toregene as the accused. When she failed to render judgement in the case and sent it back to Central Asia, the Chaghadaids promptly convicted and executed the Uighur administrator for his insulting manner.

The execution of Korguz, alongside the deaths of Chormaqun and Nosal, left the highest ranks of the administration in the Middle East unstaffed. The Chaghadaid court was at that time led by Chaghadai's grandson and chosen heir Qara Hulegu and his wife Orghina Khatun, who appointed as governor of the Middle East one of their own courtiers, a Mongol of the Oyirad tribe named Arghun.[19] Arghun had been central both in the investigation of Sharaf al-Din and in the arrest of Korguz. He served as the chief executive officer of the Mongol government in the Middle East from 1241 until 1256. During that time, he established durable fiscal policies that helped to stabilise the region as a productive area of the Mongol Empire.[20]

At the time of Arghun's appointment, Sharaf al-Din was confirmed as *ulugh bitikchi* and Baiju was allowed to assume command over military operations in Chormaqun's position. Thus, the leading civil and military officials surrounding Arghun remained dependants of Batu, just as had been the case before the spate of deaths in 1241. On the face of it, Batu might have expected to enjoy continued influence in the region. However, the new governor Arghun began the process of stewarding the region away from the orbit of Batu and towards the seat of Mongol imperium at Qaraqorum. In 1246, when Guyug was finally enthroned as Great Khan, Arghun travelled to Qaraqorum to lavish the new ruler and his courtiers with gifts. Guyug had initially opposed Arghun's appointment, but the latter's display of loyalty to the new Great Khan won him confirmation in his position.

Once enthroned, Guyug continued along the path set by his mother Toregene in trying to reclaim direct imperial command over the Middle East. He dispatched a new commander in chief, Eljigidei, to replace Baiju and thus curb Batu's influence over ongoing military operations in Anatolia, Georgia and northern Syria. The escalating conflict between the estranged cousins nearly came to a head in 1248, when Guyug left Qaraqorum with an army, ostensibly on a tour of his Central Asian territories, but probably with the intent of confronting Batu directly. This campaign came to a halt when the alcoholic Great Khan died suddenly. Though he had reigned for only two years, Guyug had, through administrative appointments and the threat of direct military action, escalated the animosity between Batu and the central Mongol court. A climactic struggle was postponed by his premature death but it was not permanently averted.

The Toluid Coup

After Guyug's death, the empire again entered a regency, this time under Guyug's widow Oghul Qaimish (1248–51), pending the selection of a new Great Khan. As he had done in 1241, Batu interfered in the process without ever leaving his base in the western steppe. This time, however, his absence was not the main factor delaying the selection process. Guyug's reign had been so short, and his death so sudden, that there was no clear line of succession, and dissent broke out among the various princes and dependants of the family of Ogedei over who should take the throne. Rather than boycott this already troubled process, Batu assumed the role of kingmaker, calling a *quriltai* in 1251 to select the new Great Khan at Ala Qamaq, southeast of Lake Balkash and far from the imperial centre.

Though he had called the *quriltai*, Batu did not claim the imperial throne for himself. Instead, he offered it to his cousin Mongke, who had supported Batu's authority over Guyug while the cousins were on campaign together a decade earlier. In exchange for being elevated as Great Khan by Batu Aqa, Mongke recognised his elder cousin's claim over the contested territory of Chormaqun's conquests south of the Caucasus. Through this action, Batu had regained at a stroke what had slipped away from him over the previous decade. The new arrangement relied, however, on the continuing good graces of Mongke.

Batu Aqa had orchestrated Mongke's coronation, but the move was fiercely opposed by members of the family of Ogedei. Their case against Mongke was strong: he was not a descendant of the son whom Chinggis Khan had selected to rule and his coronation was held far from the traditional homeland of the Mongols. In response to this opposition, and to add legitimacy to his claim, Mongke called a second *quriltai* to be held on the Mongol steppe. He followed this second coronation with a thorough purge of the Ogedeid family, as well as those members of the family of Chaghadai who had supported Ogedeid claims to the title of Great Khan. A foiled attack on the second *quriltai* that had been planned by members of the Ogedeid family provided legal cover to present these purges as legitimate judicial proceedings. They put an effective end to any Ogedeid claim to the imperial throne, and the lands of Central Asia were redistributed among the members of the Ogedeid and Chaghadaid families who had acquiesced with Mongke's accession.

With the crowning of Mongke and the subsequent liquidation of the Ogedeid house, the immediate threat to Batu's hold over the Middle East was neutralised. However, over the next five years, Mongke and other members of the family of Tolui launched a new effort to win command of the Middle East away from the house of Jochi. As with Toregene's efforts in this regard, they accomplished their aim through strategic administrative appointments, replacing individuals from the Jochid-dependent region of Khwarazm with others native to the lands of eastern Iran that had not been explicitly allocated to any one of Chinggis Khan's sons. Central to this shift was the Oyirad governor Arghun, who had first pledged his loyalty to the central court at the coronation of Guyug.

During his long tenure as governor of the Mongol Middle East, Arghun increasingly came to rely on Baha' al-Din Juvayni, Chin Temur's honorary *ṣāḥib-dīwān*, marginalising other high-level Central Asian administrators in favour of this son of eastern Iran. When Arghun departed for Qaraqorum on the election of Guyug as Great Khan, he appointed two deputies to jointly manage the region in his absence. These were Baha' al-Din and the Mongol general (*amir*) Buqa. With him, he brought Baha' al-Din's son 'Ala' al-Din, signalling that the alliance between Arghun and the long-serving *ṣāḥib-diwān* was becoming a family affair.[21] Such durable alliances between families of Mongol governors and their Persian administrators became a marker of the Mongol state in the Middle East for the next century.

As Arghun returned to the Middle East, Baha' al-Din met him *en route* with a delegation and gifts of luxury items that he had commissioned to be made for the purpose. Such an act of obeisance and gift-giving accorded with the Mongol custom of *tikishmishi*, and with it the Iranian Baha' al-Din signalled his loyalty to Arghun. In 1248, Arghun again set out towards Qaraqorum to settle a dispute over the management of artisans at Tabriz, and this time he took with him his *ulugh bitikchi* Khwaja Fakhr al-Din Bihishti and his *ṣāḥib-diwān* Baha' al-Din, as well as the latter's son 'Ala' al-Din 'Ata-Malik.[22] This second embassy never reached Qaraqorum, perhaps because of Guyug's abrupt death – we are reminded of Korguz's ill-fated embassy, which was also cut short in a year when the Great Khan died – and the dispute was settled at the Chaghadaid court.

When Arghun once again set out for Qaraqorum in May 1252 after Mongke's coronation as Great Khan, he took 'Ala' al-Din 'Ata-Malik along as a personal secretary and appointed Baha' al-Din Juvayni as sole deputy in the Middle East.[23] Baha' al-Din's appointment by Chin Temur's two decades earlier was shaping up into another chapter of the family's long history serving conquest dynasties with roots on the steppes of Inner Asia. Both 'Ala' al-Din and his younger brother Shams al-Din performed long service in the government of the Mongols in the Middle East and, as discussed below, they helped direct the first round of efforts to mediate the cultural difference between the nomadic military elite and the indigenous bureaucratic and sedentary society.

Just as the Juvaynis and others in the Middle East were becoming familiar with the presence of the Mongol occupation, the Mongol court increasingly appreciated the economic importance of the Middle East as a part of the empire. Early in the reign of Ogedei, northern China and Turkestan had been designated as special imperial provinces, branch secretariats from which tax income was directed back to the central court, rather than to any of the regional courts led by other members of the royal family.[24] Eventually, Iran was added to this list, becoming a third main zone of imperial governance headed by Chin Temur's administrative apparatus.

In Qaraqorum in 1252, as in 1246, Arghun declared his administrative allegiance to the central court. Now, however, that court was held by a son of Tolui, rather than an Ogedeid. During this visit, the governor and the Great Khan planned a new tax structure for the region, bringing it again to the centre of the court's attention. In exchange for Arghun's loyalty, Mongke confirmed the Oyirad once again in his position. The main source for this reappointment, written by Arghun's personal secretary 'Ala' al-Din Juvayni, describes it as a continuation of Mongke's staffing decisions for northern China and Turkestan, indicating that the Middle East was by this point truly considered a third imperial province alongside the original two. Through the efforts of Chin Temur, Korguz and Arghun, the Mongol court had come to value southwest Asia in a way that Chinggis Khan had not, as a productive and important region within an increasingly bureaucratised empire.

Mongke's original recognition of Batu's claim over the Middle East was now untenable, and Toluid efforts began in earnest to wrest the region away from the Jochid house. An immediate justification for renewed imperial intervention in the Middle East was provided around the same time, as voices from the Middle East began calling for Mongol military assistance to stabilise the politics of the region. Among an otherwise anonymous 'group of plaintiffs' who gathered at the new Great Khan's court to complain about the activities of the Isma'ilis was a judge (*qāḍī*) named Shams al-Din from the city of Qazvin in northern Iran.[25] In early accounts of this episode, Shams al-Din conveys a sense of danger felt by the residents of Qazvin because of the recent rebuilding of Isma'ili fortresses. This rebuilding, according to Shams al-Din, allowed the followers of the Isma'ili imam to spurn Mongol efforts to control and tax the region. In fact, the people of Qazvin had long been embroiled in property disputes with the Isma'ilis, whose fortresses ringed the city on the north.[26] Shams al-Din was almost certainly representing local economic interests when he appealed to Mongke for renewed Mongol intervention, indicating that the population had come to see the Mongols as potential partners in their local politics. For his part, Mongke was open to the idea, not out of any desire to rescue the residents of one distant Iranian city, but because of the threat the Isma'ilis posed to the Mongol fisc.

The net result of the various meetings held at Qaraqorum in spring 1252 was a new military campaign, led this time by a member of the royal family.

Mongke dispatched his younger brother Hulegu (d. 1265) with an army to the west just as he sent another brother, Qubilai (d. 1294), to begin the long process of subjugating the Song dynasty of southern China. Later, after the campaign had been successful and Hulegu and his descendants were established as the new ruling dynasty in the Middle East, historians working for them, including Rashid al-Din, recast the motivations for this campaign, crediting it to Mongke's own genius or to an appeal by the Mongol general Baiju for assistance against the Isma'ilis and the 'Abbasid caliph in Baghdad.[27] At the time, however, the Mongol court was primarily concerned with preserving taxable economic activity. As a result, this new campaign took a very different tone than the smash-and-grab adventure of Hulegu's grandfather, Chinggis Khan.

Hulegu's campaign progressed slowly.[28] In summer 1252, he deputised a Mongol general, Ked Buqa, to proceed to Iran and begin the assault of the Isma'ili fortresses. Hulegu himself only left Qaraqorum with his main army in the winter of 1252/3 and moved gradually across Central Asia, arriving outside the village of Kish – the modern Shakhrisabz, south of Samarqand – in the final weeks of 1255. Here the Oyirad Arghun, who by now had served as governor of the Mongol Middle East for fourteen years, met Hulegu and performed *tikishmishi*, just as Baha' al-Din Juvayni had done for him a decade earlier. The pair spent a month feasting in Kish and another in Shaburgan, south of the Amu Darya. Hulegu then dismissed Arghun, who set off once more for Qaraqorum.

Arghun later returned to the Middle East bearing the honorific title *aqa*, and he continued to perform important judicial and military functions for Hulegu and his son and successor Abaqa (1265–82). The transfer of executive authority from him to Hulegu in 1256 inaugurated a new form of Mongol governance in the region, now led by a representative of the royal family and a brother of the Great Khan. As a marker of his relative position in the imperial governance, Hulegu adopted the title *ilkhan*, or 'subordinate khan'.[29] From his position on the lower Volga, Batu Aqa evidently did not initially see the presence of his royal cousin as a significant threat to his own authority over the Middle East. He contributed troops to Hulegu's campaign, perhaps thinking it would help to subdue the restive elements of a region largely under his own command. However, Batu died around the time that Hulegu crossed the Amu Darya, removing the strongest opposition to direct imperial and Toluid control of the Middle East. Subsequent months saw a rapid realignment of political authority in West Asia, the end result of which was the firm consolidation of Toluid control over the Middle East.

When Mongke received news of his cousin's death, he immediately appointed Batu's son Sartaq, who was living in Qaraqorum, to succeed his father as head of the Jochid family. Sartaq died *en route* to the Volga region to claim his title, and Mongke dispatched a delegation to invest Sartaq's son Ulaghchi, with Batu's wife Boraqchin to serve as regent to the young prince.[30] While Mongke was thus meddling in Jochid dynastic affairs, he was also intervening in dynastic policies in the central territories of the Mongol world, held by the members of the families of Ogedei and Chaghadai who had declared their support for him and thus escaped his purges. The net result of these meddlings was that there remained no mature Mongol ruler in command of any part of the fragmenting empire other than Mongke and his brothers Qubilai and Hulegu, who were busy expanding Mongol authority on both sides of Asia.

This situation changed when Ulaghchi died in the winter of 1257/8 and Batu's brother Berke assumed command of the family of Jochi. Berke's accession was likely the very scenario that Mongke had tried to prevent by appointing first Sartaq and then Ulaghchi. It posed a dual threat to the newly empowered Toluid imperial system. First, as Batu's brother, Berke was a mature and experienced leader; and, second, Berke had converted to Islam while in his youth. His accession to the head of the Jochid house created a new arena of potential conflict as Hulegu led his army into the heart of the Islamic world.[31] Berke came to the throne around the time that Hulegu was completing his triumph over the Isma'ilis and beginning a second phase of the campaign against 'Abbasid Baghdad. The Muslim Berke had managed to prevent a Mongol attack on Baghdad as long as his powerful brother was alive by appealing to Batu Aqa's filial seniority over both Mongke and Hulegu.[32] With Batu out of the way, Hulegu proceeded with his march against Baghdad, capturing the city in February 1258 and killing the last 'Abbasid caliph al-Musta'sim. This affront against the faith of Berke, now powerless to prevent it, added religious tension to the political coup that the Toluid brothers had executed in annexing the Middle East to their own family's demesne.

Having established a royal Toluid presence in a region that Chinggis Khan had largely neglected, but which later generations of Mongols had come to value as an essential source of revenue and resources, Hulegu's invasion put the lie to the myth of a unified Mongol Empire. After 1258, branches of the family of Chinggis Khan were at war with one another more often than they were not. When Mongke died the following year, the struggle for the position of Great Khan pitted Qubilai against his youngest brother Ariq Boqe, while each brother's allies among the Ogedeid and Chaghadaid members of the family waged a proxy war in Central Asia. In the west, the Mongol advance against Egypt was stopped in 1260 when the forces of the Mamluk sultanate of Egypt defeated Hulegu's deputy Ked Buqa at 'Ayn Jalut in Palestine (discussed in Chapter 6). The Mamluks, whose title means 'slave' because of their origins as Turkic slave soldiers from the western steppe, remained the main geopolitical adversary to the *ilkhans* for the next sixty years.[33] With the western advance stalled and the eastern Mongol world engulfed in conflict, the *ilkhan* Hulegu was left largely to his own devices to govern the lands of the former 'Abbasid caliphate.

Monuments of Ilkhanid Legitimacy

In order to govern a region ravaged by his grandfather and squabbled over by subsequent Mongol elites, Hulegu required a source of political legitimacy. He found this in the people that he hired to run his government and in the buildings that they helped him and Abaqa to build. The early years of the Ilkhanate was a period of state formation, as the nomadic horsemen of the steppe learned – or were at least presented as knowing – how to govern in the Islamic world. To support the Toluid assertion of direct command over the Middle East, Hulegu fixed his permanent capital at Maragha, on the high pastures of Azerbaijan. From there, the scholar-bureaucrats of eastern Iran began to build a Mongol state using cultural symbols familiar to the Muslim and Iranian population.

The region around Maragha was the same area where Chormaqun had established his military headquarters and the most suitable territory in the Middle East to support the herds of animals that accompanied the Mongol armies. Members of Jochi's family had used the area for winter pasture, and it was the most hotly contested stake in Jochid claims over the Middle East in later generations. By building his capital here, Hulegu marked his family's enduring presence and control. He also made a series of administrative appointments before the fall of Baghdad that alienated the Jochid family from the Mongol government of the Middle East. When he first assumed command of the region from Arghun in the winter of 1255/6, Hulegu gained the assistance of three individuals from the former governor's entourage. These were Arghun's son Gerai Malik, a Central Asian Muslim named Ahmad Bitikchi, and 'Ala' al-Din 'Ata-Malik Juvayni, son of Chin Temur's original ṣāḥib-diwān and frequent travelling companion of Arghun between Iran and Qaraqorum. The diverse origins of this group – one Mongol, one Central Asian and one Iranian – speaks to the potentially divided loyalties of the administrative apparatus under Arghun. In subsequent years, Hulegu concentrated leading administrative positions in the hands of prominent scholars and bureaucrats from eastern Iran. These individuals helped to turn Hulegu's new capital in Azerbaijan into an administrative centre and spearheaded the earliest efforts at an intellectual and cultural rapprochement with the new royal Mongol presence. As Iranians from the eastern provinces living and working in the western Iranian world, they also helped to strengthen an Iranian cultural identity that gave the Ilkhanate an internal cohesion – a kind of pre-modern nationhood – independent of Jochid or any other external sovereignty.

Several of the administrative appointees who came into Hulegu's service had previously lived and worked under the patronage of the Isma'ili imam Rukn al-Din Khurshah and joined their patron when he surrendered to Hulegu in early 1256. By far the most prominent of these was Nasir al-Din Tusi (d. 1274), the greatest philosopher of his generation.[34] Once in Hulegu's service, Nasir al-Din oversaw the building and staffing of the first great monument of Mongol patronage in the Middle East, an astronomical observatory and research institute at Hulegu's new capital of Maragha. Writing most of fifty years later, Rashid al-Din claims that it was Hulegu's idea to employ Tusi on this project, to avoid sending him to Qaraqorum, where Mongke was also eager to build a new observatory.[35] Tusi himself says only that Hulegu wanted an observatory, but that he and his staff chose where to build it.[36] These accounts might well both be true; taken together, they suggest that the decision to build an observatory on the high plains of Azerbaijan was a demonstration of permanence and political independence, a monument to Hulegu's claim over the region.[37]

In addition to founding the observatory at Maragha, Tusi served as Hulegu's vizier. He was also tasked with administering the many institutions chartered under Islamic endowment law (*waqf*). Such institutions were historically exempt from government interference, but Hulegu directed that Tusi was to receive 10 per cent of all proceeds to finance operations at the new observatory.[38] While it is not known exactly how much funding this provided, the rich materials and high level of craftsmanship evident in surviving observation instruments made at Maragha suggest that 10 per cent of the endowed property in the realm amounted to a sizeable sum.[39] It was, in any event, the first observatory to be funded by *waqf* revenue, but like so much from the early decades of Mongol rule it set a precedent for later Ilkhanid institutions. By the end of the thirteenth century, Hulegu's great-grandson Ghazan Khan had constructed a second observatory at Tabriz to be funded entirely by charitable endowments.

Nasir al-Din Tusi's main commission at the new observatory was to coordinate astronomical observations in order to create a new set of tables charting the movement of the visible planets across the field of fixed stars.[40] For this, he employed astronomers from across the Islamic world, and from as far away as China. Supporting their efforts served two purposes for the new *ilkhan* Hulegu. First, it tied him into a tradition of royal support for astronomy that was even older than Islam. The Persian Sasanians had been active patrons of astral sciences for both practical and ideological purposes, a pattern that the ʿAbbasid caliphs were quick to emulate.[41] Other dynasties had subsequently adopted astronomy as a central component of royal ideology. Most notably, the Saljuq sultan Malikshah (1072–92) had supported a major observatory at Isfahan, and figural imagery representing stars and planets became a central component of Saljuq-period visual culture.[42] Most immediately relevant to Tusi's experience, the Ismaʿili imams had been among the strongest supporters of scientific research in the thirteenth century, and Tusi would have had direct exposure to the science under their patronage before Khurshah's surrender to Hulegu. For the *ilkhan* to continue this pattern of support provided a point of continuity across the otherwise dramatic historical rupture caused by the destruction of the Ismaʿili and ʿAbbasid political order.

The other great service that the Maragha observatory and Tusi's new astronomical tables offered to Hulegu was a way to determine auspicious days for court ceremonies. This same concern probably motivated Qubilai's interest in having his own observatory at Qaraqorum. After Hulegu's death, his son Abaqa ascended to the throne on a date – 19 June 1265 – that was deemed to be auspicious by both shamans and astrologers.[43] Beyond the functional and ideological benefits that accrued to Hulegu through his support of the Maragha observatory, Tusi and his staff were responsible for major advances in the science of observation astronomy.[44] The tables they produced set a new standard in accuracy for observation. Nasir al-Din also gave his name to the so-called 'Tusi couple', which models planetary motion within a geocentric cosmology.

A second major architectural project that shows the contribution of Tusi and his fellow Persian bureaucrats to the royal ideology and iconography of the young Ilkhanate is a palace built for Abaqa at the royal Mongol summer camp of Sughurluq, between Lake Urmia and Hamadan. The site of the palace is an elevated mineral plateau, the accretion of a large calcinating thermal spring that forms a lake at its centre. This creates a dramatic setting for any building, and an easy point of reference for identifying the site as it changed in function over time. Under the Sasanians, the site was home to Azargoshnasp, the Zoroastrian fire temple of Azerbaijan particularly associated with the elite warrior estate.[45] In the centuries after the Arab conquest, a village called Shiz grew up among the ruins of this fire temple.[46] Despite the urbanisation of the site, two ninth-century geographers preserve the memory of its Zoroastrian connection. Ibn al-Faqih attributes the temple to the Kayanian Kay Khosrau, while Ibn Khurradadhbih relates a tradition by which Sasanian rulers, after their coronation at the Sasanian capital near Baghdad, performed a pilgrimage on foot to Azargoshnasp for a second spiritual investment at what was believed to be the site of Zoroaster's birth.[47] In the tenth century, Hasan 'Ali Mas'udi mentions Shiz in a list of fire temples, and the travelling poet Mis'ar b. Muhalhil notes its significance among the fire temples of pre-Islamic Iran.[48]

Mis'ar's work was known to and cited by later writers, including the late-Ilkhanid historian Hamd Allah Mustaufi (on whom, see Chapter 6), but in the centuries immediately after Mis'ar wrote, the memory of Shiz as the site of a fire temple disappears from geographic literature.[49] In place of the site's Zoroastrian origins, a new association grew up around the dramatic spring-side ruins in Azerbaijan. As early as the eleventh century, the Persian poet Qatran Tabrizi refers to Azargoshnasp as the Throne of Solomon (*takht-e soleimān*), by which it is still most commonly known.[50] This is part of a pattern in the western Iranian world during the Saljuq period, by which major pre-Islamic Persian monuments were reimagined as relics of Judeo-Islamic prophetic history. To the south, by the turn of the thirteenth century, the Salghurids of Fars had created a legitimising ideology for themselves as protectors of the legacy of Solomon, whom they credited with building the Achaemenid ruins at Persepolis.[51]

While western Iranian practice thus tended to situate ancient ruins in the context of Islamic prophetic history, the memory of Azargoshnasp as a Zoroastrian site was preserved in the historical writing of the eastern Iranian world, and particularly the *Shahnameh* of Abu'l-Qasim Firdausi (d. 1020).[52] The decoration of Abaqa's new palace employed elaborate tiles glazed with lapis and gold, replete with visual and textual references to the *Shahnameh*.[53] These tiles would have reminded visitors of the site's importance in the Iranian kingly tradition.

Of course, such references necessarily required knowledge of the *Shahnameh* to interpret and appreciate. Such intimate knowledge of Firdausi's poem and the Iranian heroic tradition was, at the time of the Mongol conquest, relatively rare in the western Iranian world. In the eleventh century, Qatran Tabrizi, already mentioned, had tried to popularise eastern Iranian literature in the west, but he was largely frustrated in this effort. Further west, members of the Saljuq family in Rum had begun taking the names of legendary Iranian kings from around the turn of the thirteenth century. One historian writing at that court in the late twelfth century, Muhammad b. 'Ali Rawandi, frequently cites the *Shahnameh*, but only in a limited way and for moralising purposes, suggesting that he had access to the text only through a collection of extracts prepared for the great Saljuq sultan Malikshah.[54] Other than Qatran and Rawandi, western Iranian writers largely ignored Firdausi's work.

By contrast, the practice of invoking pre-Islamic Iranian rulers as exemplars of kingly virtues had become popular among panegyric poets at the eastern Iranian courts of the Ghaznavids and Qara Khanids.⁵⁵ These two dynasties, centred in Afghanistan and Central Asia, respectively, straddled the lands of the Samanids, who held their court at Bukhara and for whose governor at Tus Firdausi had begun his epic work. As the Ghaznavids and Qara Khanids divided up the Samanid state between them in the late tenth and early eleventh centuries, both courts adopted the poetic images of individual pre-Islamic kings into their own programmes of legitimation and ideology.

As a result, the lands with the richest poetic memory of the pre-Islamic Iranian kingly tradition were precisely the lands that provided Hulegu with his leading administrative staff as he entered the Middle East. Chin Temur's decision to appoint Baha' al-Din Juvayni as *ṣāḥib-diwān* established a lasting governing alliance between the ruling Mongols and the scholars of eastern Iran, including the Juvayni family and Nasir al-Din Tusi. As discussed in Chapter 3, 'Ala' al-Din Juvayni was also the first historian to make systematic use of the *Shahnameh* in telling the story of the Mongol past. In terms of the visual language of the early Ilkhanid court, Tusi and the Juvaynis – and probably other eastern Iranian administrators, scholars and artists in their service – were instrumental in choosing to decorate Abaqa's new palace with scenes and verses from a distinctly Iranian historical tradition. Emblematic of the new Mongol state-building programme was the conflation of regional Iranian traditions, as eastern literature decorated a western Iranian site long associated with kingship.

In the half century following the shockwave of Chinggis Khan's retributive raid against Khwarazmshah Muhammad, Hulegu and Abaqa had created a military patrimony state with at least the partial consent and support of the conquered population. The political situation of the region – already muddy before the arrival of Chinggis Khan – was further complicated by the devastating disinterest with which he viewed the region, its cities and their population. Later Great Khans began to appreciate the financial potential of including the region within the Mongol Empire, but Hulegu's arrival in the region turned it into a state of its own, with a political cohesion and cultural identity derived largely from Iranian tradition. The permanence of this state, and its aspirations at legitimacy, were signalled by monuments rooted in the literature and science of the Perso-Islamic world, as created by a generation of administrators from the eastern regions of Iran.

For two decades, under the first two *ilkhan*s Hulegu and Abaqa, the sons of Baha' al-Din Juvayni directed the administration of the state from Tabriz and Baghdad. These years saw constant pressure on the frontiers of the Ilkhanid state, as Abaqa faced opposition in Central Asia first by the Chaghadaid Baraq and later by rebellious Mongol factions, and on the Syrian frontier by the Mamluk sultans of Egypt.[56] Between these border contests, and perhaps because of them, Abaqa's reign was a period of relative stability and prosperity for the Ilkhanate. As part of this, the period saw unprecedented levels of cooperation between top Persian and Mongol administrators.[57] Abaqa moved his capital to Tabriz, while Baghdad remained a key political, economic, and intellectual centre, a second city of the realm to manage the agricultural wealth of Mesopotamia. From Tabriz and Baghdad, and from Hulegu's original capital of Maragha, the Juvayni brothers and Nasir al-Din Tusi – all of them from the east of Iran – oversaw a series of cultural projects that invested the *ilkhan*s as legitimate sovereigns of the Perso-Islamic world. Their successors in the administration grew up under this arrangement. Among them was a young doctor from the western Iranian city of Hamadan, who soon found himself situated for a prominent career at the court of the new lords from the steppe.

Notes

1. Hamd Allah Mustaufi, *Ẓafarnāma*, p. 1451.
2. Bartol'd, *Turkestan*, pp. 393–9, extensively treats the massacre at Utrar and the difficulty of locating it within the course of diplomatic and commercial contacts between Khwarazmshah Muhammad and Chinggis Khan.
3. For a general narrative of these invasions, see Jackson, *The Mongols and the Islamic World*, pp. 71–93 and 125–51.
4. Cook, 'Apocalyptic Incidents'; May, 'The Mongols as the Scourge of God'.
5. de Rachewiltz, *The Secret History of the Mongols*, pp. 189–95.
6. For this division, see Jackson, *The Mongols and the West*, pp. 101–3; Allsen, 'Sharing Out the Empire'.
7. For a new view of how Tolui's name and allocation of territory suggest that Chinggis Khan considered him his successor, see Togan, 'Otchigin's Place'.
8. Juvayni, *Ta'rīkh*, vol. 1, pp. 31–2; translation slightly modified from Juvayni, *The History*, pp. 42–3.

9. On Chormaqun's activities in the west, see May, 'The Conquest and Rule of Transcaucasia'.
10. On Chin Temur and his role in the early Mongol administration, see Aubin, *Emirs Mongols*, pp. 12–14.
11. On Yeh-lu Chu-ts'ai, see de Rachewiltz et al., *In the Service*, pp. 136–75.
12. Jackson, 'The Dissolution', pp. 216–18.
13. On the Mongol invasion of Europe, see Jackson, *The Mongols and the West*, pp. 58–86.
14. Jackson, *The Mongols and the Islamic World*, p. 103.
15. Thomas, *History of the Bishops*, pp. 254–5, 278–81 and 302–5.
16. For texts and discussion related to these missions, see Dawson, *Mission to Asia*. A significant bibliography has developed around the question of Latin expectations concerning possible Mongol conversion. A good starting point for accessing this is Ryan, 'Christian Wives of Mongol Khans'.
17. May, 'The Conquest and Rule of Transcaucasia', p. 23; Büntgen and Di Cosmo, 'Climatic and Environmental Aspects'.
18. For the details of this battle for administrative influence, see Jackson, 'The Dissolution', pp. 198–200 and 212–20; Aubin, *Emirs Mongols*, pp. 11–17.
19. de Nicola, 'The Queen of the Chaghatayids', p. 114 and n. 47.
20. On Arghun, see Lane, 'Arghun Aqa'; Aubin, *Emirs Mongols*, pp. 151–7; Kolbas, *The Mongols in Iran*, pp. 121–89; Kamola, 'History and Legend', pp. 575–7.
21. 'Ala' al-Din mentions his own presence on this embassy: Juvayni, *Ta'rikh*, vol. 2, p. 248; Juvayni, *The History*, p. 512.
22. Juvayni, *Ta'rikh*, vol. 2, p. 250; Juvayni, *The History*, p. 513.
23. Juvayni, *Ta'rikh*, vol. 2, p. 256; Juvayni, *The History*, p. 519.
24. On the institution of the branch secretariat, see Buell, 'Sino-Khitan Administration', pp. 141–7; Allsen, *Mongol Imperialism*, pp. 100–8.
25. Juzjani, *Tabaqat-e Nasiri*, vol. 2, pp. 181–2; Juzjani, *Tabaqat-i Nasiri*, trans. Raverty, pp. 1189–97; Ibn al-Tiqtaqa, *Al-Fakhri*, p. 36; Rashid al-Din, *Jami' al-Tawarikh*, pp. 973–4.
26. Daftary, *The Ismā'ilis*, pp. 372–406.
27. Juvayni, *Ta'rikh*, vol. 3, p. 90; Juvayni, *The History*, p. 607; Rashid al-Din, *Jami' al-Tawarikh*, pp. 973–4.
28. For more detailed descriptions of Hulegu's campaign, see Boyle, 'Dynastic and Political History', pp. 340–51; Smith, 'Hülegü Moves West'.
29. This is the most common understanding of the title, though others have been proposed. For an overview of these, and for a discussion of the challenges

involved in understanding the meaning and use of the term, see Hope, 'Some Remarks'. Throughout this book, I adopt the term *ilkhan* out of deference to prevailing usage, though it was not consistently used among Hulegu's successors.

30. Juvayni, *Ta'rikh*, vol. 1, p. 223; Juvayni, *The History*, p. 268.
31. On Berke's conversion, see DeWeese, *Islamization*, pp. 83–5.
32. Jackson, 'The Dissolution', p. 224.
33. On the conflict with the Mamluks, see Amitai-Preiss, *Mongols and Mamluks*; Broadbridge, *Kingship and Ideology*; Amitai, *Holy War and Rapprochement*.
34. For general information about Tusi's life, and particularly his time under Isma'ili patronage, see Tusi, *Contemplation*; Dabashi, 'The Philosopher/Vizier'.
35. Rashid al-Din, *Jami' al-Tawarikh*, pp. 1024–5.
36. Boyle, 'The Longer Introduction', pp. 245–6.
37. For general information on the Maragha observatory, see Sayılı, *The Observatory*, pp. 189–93.
38. Sayılı, *The Observatory*, pp. 207–11.
39. On these instruments, see Carey, 'The gold and silver lining'.
40. A manuscript of these tables, the *Astronomical Tables of the Ilkhans (Zij-e Ilkhani)*, has been published in facsimile: Tusi, *Zij-e Ilkhani*. Boyle, 'The Longer Introduction' provides the text and translation of one version of the work's introduction.
41. Gutas, *Greek Thought*, pp. 45–52, 108–10.
42. On Malik Shah's observatory, see Sayılı, *The Observatory*, pp. 160–6. For examples of astrological imagery in Saljuq visual culture, see Canby et al., *Court and Cosmos*, pp. 200–13.
43. Wassaf, *Ketab-e Mostatab*, p. 53.
44. Saliba, 'Horoscopes and Planetary Theory', pp. 364–8.
45. On excavations of the temple, see Naumann, 'Die Ausgrabungen'. For a review of the site's history and the history of excavations there, see Huff, 'The Ilkhanid Palace'.
46. Minorsky, 'Roman and Byzantine Campaigns', pp. 254–8; Tirmidhi, 'Zoroastrians'.
47. Tirmidhi, 'Zoroastrians', pp. 272–4.
48. Tirmidhi, 'Zoroastrians', pp. 275, 277–80.
49. Minorsky, 'Roman and Byzantine Campaigns', p. 101.
50. Melikian-Chirvani, 'Le livre des rois, II', p. 39.
51. Melikian-Chirvani, 'Le royaume de Salomon', pp. 3–20; Melikian-Chirvani, 'The Light of Heaven and Earth', pp. 119–20. The Sasanians had earlier

associated this site with the legendary Iranian king Jamshid, so that Pasargadae is even now known as the throne of Jamshid (*takht-e jamshīd*).

52. Melikian-Chirvani, 'Le livre des rois, II', pp. 43–7; Melikian-Chirvani, 'Conscience du passé', pp. 149–56.
53. Melikian-Chirvani, 'Le livre des rois, II', pp. 82–122; Melikian-Chirvani, 'Conscience du passé', pp. 152–6, 163–5; Masuya, 'Ilkhanid Courtly Life', pp. 91–103.
54. Tetley, *The Ghaznavid and Seljuq Turks*, p. 34.
55. Melikian-Chirvani, 'Le livre des rois', pp. 9–27.
56. On the unrest in Central Asia, see Biran, *Qaidu*, pp. 23–30. On military conflict with the Mamluks, see Amitai-Preiss, *Mongols and Mamluks*; for its diplomatic manifestation during the reign of Abaqa, see Broadbridge, *Kingship and Ideology*, pp. 32–8.
57. See, for example, the relationship between Su'unchaq and the Juvaynis at Aubin, *Emirs Mongols*, pp. 22–4.

2

The Likely Course of an Unlikely Life, 1248–1302

To write a biography of Rashid al-Din is complicated, as it is for most any pre-modern individual, by a total lack of candid sources for his early life.[1] Without documentation of birth, residence, education and professional training, or other formative experiences, we have only the retrospective comments of writers who knew or at least knew of their subject after his rise to prominence. In the case of Rashid al-Din, this meant knowing an immensely rich and influential character, a driving force behind Ilkhanid politics and intellectual life, and a divisive figure in the court culture of the period. Individual authors' presentations of Rashid al-Din's early life reflect their involvement in the political and social concerns of their own time.

Rashid al-Din does us no favours in this respect. Despite writing the single most important history of the Mongol Empire and the early Ilkhanate, Rashid al-Din is almost silent about his own role in that history. Indeed, if Rashid al-Din's work was the only history of the Mongols to have survived, we would hardly know that he played any part in it. In his later theological works, Rashid al-Din offers more autobiographical material, and modern scholars have looked to these as the most authentic information on his early life.[2] As discussed in Chapter 4, however, those theological writings were part of a careful programme of self-representation, and so we must be just as cautious with them as we are with the assessments by other writers.

We are wise to question the authenticity of any account of Rashid al-Din's early life written after he had already become a central and polarising public figure, and Chapters 4 and 6 do exactly that. We can, however, still get a sense of how Rashid al-Din's early life unfolded by reading those same accounts against the backdrop of political and social history in the Middle East in the decades surrounding the Mongol invasion. This chapter takes such an approach, reading the textual evidence for Rashid al-Din's early life with an eye towards the communities, societies and geographies in which he lived. As the Mongols came to see the Middle East less as a land to plunder and more as a royal domain, they created new opportunities for the technocrats and statesmen of the region. In this new atmosphere, the son of a Jewish doctor from Hamadan was better situated for a prominent career at court than he would have been if born a few decades earlier under the last ʿAbbasid caliphs.

Rashid al-Din grew up in a unique political and cultural geography. As he came to prominence, his life followed some of the patterns set by previous ministers of the new Mongol state. A schismatic court atmosphere and the gradual adoption of Islam by the ruling Mongol elite created a need for a new ideology of rule. By 1300, Rashid al-Din was perfectly situated to contribute to creating just such an ideology.

From Hamadan to Maragha

Rashid al-Din mentions his family of origin in two places. In the dynastic history of the Mongols for which he is most famous, while describing the fall of the Ismaʿili fortresses to Hulegu, Rashid al-Din lists some of the scholars who changed loyalties from the deposed imam to the triumphant khan:

> And when right-heartedness was revealed and verified in Khwaja Nasir al-Din Tusi and in the children of Raʾis al-Daula and Muwaffaq al-Daula – who were famous as great physicians and whose origins were from the city of Hamadan – [Hulegu] ordered that they be paid full honours and that they be given donkeys in order that their family and household and dependants and they themselves, along with their property and servants and followers and companions might be transported down from there. They were brought into service, and to this day they and their children have constantly been and still are attendant and esteemed at the court of Hulegu Khan and his illustrious offspring.[3]

Rashid al-Din does not clarify that the Muwaffaq al-Daula mentioned here was his own grandfather and that the children who entered Hulegu's service would therefore have included his own father, 'Imad al-Daula. That connection emerges only when we read this passage alongside another from Rashid al-Din's later theological treatises. At the opening of a work written around 1308, the then sixty-year-old vizier introduces himself as

> Master of the Worlds, Lord of the Age, Great Minister, Manager of the Affairs of the World, Trustee of the Interests of the Race of Adam, Servant of the Men of the Sword and of the Pen, adorned with the thrones of the vizierate, arrayed with the pillars of state ... Sultan of the Viziers and Doctors and Scholars of Creation, Rashid al-Haqq wa al-Dunya wa al-Din Fazl Allah, son of the Chief, the Grand Lord, the Fortunate Sultan of Philosophers and Princes of the Age, 'Imad al-Daula wa al-Din Abu'l-Khayr, son of the Chief, the Late Lord Muwaffaq al-Daula Eli, the medical practitioner from Hamadan, the one known as Rashid the Doctor.[4]

By the time he wrote this second passage, Rashid al-Din enjoyed unrivalled influence at court, in part because of his earlier historical writing. He was the companion and adviser to the ruling sultan and he was busy creating an image of himself and his patron as an epochal duumvirate of political and spiritual authority, as discussed in Chapter 4. The titles he assigns to himself here suggest a supreme confidence in his place in the government and in the very order of the Islamic world.

The second passage just quoted reveals a very different Rashid al-Din than his earlier historical writing does. In the history, he is vanishingly demur, failing to mention his relationship to his own grandfather as Muwaffaq al-Daula makes a fleeting appearance on the stage of Mongol history. In the theological treatise, Rashid al-Din's importance is measured by the ages of creation. Both passages, however, mention two important factors about his family of origin: a connection to the city of Hamadan and a generational occupation with the science of medicine. These two facts, along with the family's Jewish background – which Rashid al-Din tellingly chooses not to reveal – offer a starting point for reconstructing his life in the turbulent political and social contexts of the thirteenth-century Middle East.

After Hulegu accepted the surrender of the Isma'ili fortresses in 1256, he moved his army south from the region of Daylam towards the 'Abbasid capital at Baghdad. For this new phase of the campaign, he relocated his headquarters from Qazvin to Hamadan, a crossroads city between Baghdad, Khurasan and Azerbaijan.[5] Medieval Arab geographers describe Hamadan as a prosperous city, though its high elevation (at 1850 metres above sea level) brought uncomfortably cold winters and the city's significance had mostly been overshadowed by the emergence of Baghdad.[6] Hulegu was not the only *ilkhan* to pass through Hamadan. Abaqa died there in 1282, and the city hosted royal armies and entourages beginning with the dynastic turmoil of 1295. After 1297, it was a regular stop on the royal transmigrations between the summer capitals of Azerbaijan and winter camps around Baghdad, a continuing tribute to the city's crossroads location.

Between Chormaqun's invasion in 1231 and that of Hulegu in 1256, Hamadan sat between three centres of political power: the capital of Sunni Islam at Baghdad; the insurgent political and religious power of the Ismaʿili strongholds clustered in northern Iran; and the Mongol military occupation of Azerbaijan. Rashid al-Din was born into a Hamadani family towards the end of this period, between 1247 and 1251.[7] This was exactly the period when renewed conflict between the Ismaʿilis and the citizens of Qazvin drove the judge Shams al-Din to visit Mongke in Qaraqorum and appeal for a new Mongol military intervention.

At some point, perhaps as a result of the early Mongol conquest or the subsequent political insecurity, Rashid al-Din's grandfather sought the protection of the Ismaʿili fortress of Maymundiz. By comparison, Nasir al-Din Tusi entered Ismaʿili patronage some time in or shortly after 1224, that is, immediately after the devastating first campaign of Chinggis Khan. When Muwaffaq al-Daula moved his family from Hamadan to Maymundiz, he left behind a thriving Jewish community. Benjamin of Tudela probably exaggerates when he numbers it at 30,000 souls around the year 1270.[8] However, at the beginning of the thirteenth century, this community was certainly large and well connected: its *yeshiva* was in contact with the major academies of Talmudic learning in Baghdad.[9] Depending on when the family moved to the protection of Maymundiz, Rashid al-Din may have been born under Ismaʿili sovereignty, but his family must have retained extensive ties with their city of origin.

Hulegu's decision to relocate his military headquarters to Hamadan on his way to confront the caliph provided the family of Muwaffaq al-Daula an opportunity to re-join the community they had left behind in their move to Maymundiz. However, once Hulegu had established his new political base in the north of Iran, at least some of the family relocated there, part of a general gravitation of scholars and professionals to the new Ilkhanid capital at Maragha. We have already met Nasir al-Din Tusi, whose observatory employed trained astronomers from as far away as China. The Jacobite bishop of Aleppo, Bar Hebraeus, spent much of the last years of his life rebuilding churches in northwest Iran, dying at Maragha in 1286.[10] What meagre evidence survives suggests that Rabbinic and Talmudic authorities in Baghdad also relocated to the new political centre on the pastures of Azerbaijan. The Jews of Baghdad had welcomed Hulegu's arrival as a reprieve from at least eighty years of persecution under the latter 'Abbasids, and the Exilarch had formally welcomed the *ilkhan* into the city.[11] After the fall of Baghdad, Talmudic activity there went into decline or even ended entirely. While direct evidence for the shift of Jewish authorities to the north is scant, we find traces of it, for example, in the fact that the Jewish Exilarch commissioned a copy of his genealogy to be copied in Tabriz in 1306.[12]

The greatest testimony to the relocation of scholars, religious leaders and others to the north during the early Ilkhanid period is the work of Ibn al-Fuwati (1244–1323), who served as librarian at Tusi's observatory. Over the next several decades, Ibn al-Fuwati also earned income by copying manuscripts for private clients, including the Exilarch's genealogy. Ibn al-Fuwati is most famous for a collection of biographies, in which he left a record of the type of individuals attracted to Maragha from the more established centres of political and intellectual activity.[13] At least two of Muwaffaq al-Daula's sons appear in Ibn al-Fuwati's biographical collection. Ibn al-Fuwati calls 'Imad al-Daula and his brother, 'highly respected physicians and philosophers'.[14] As with other physicians in the medieval Islamic world, 'Imad al-Daula passed his profession on to his son, the future Rashid al-Din who was probably originally known as Rashid al-Daula, a form of his honorific name consistent with those that had marked non-Muslim – and specifically Jewish – members of elite society for several centuries.[15]

After studying at the feet of his father and uncle while living in Maragha, Rashid al-Din travelled to the southern city of Yazd to study with two other prominent doctors there.[16] This stint in Yazd initiated a long relationship between Rashid al-Din and the elite of that city: he later intervened on their behalf at court and he married his children into their families.[17] He also made significant financial investments in Yazd: over half of the land holdings listed in the deed of endowment that Rashid al-Din drafted towards the end of his life were located in and around that city.[18]

By late in the reign of Abaqa, when Rashid al-Din was around the age of thirty, he had returned to the Mongol court in northern Iran. The most contemporary biographical account, written by one of Rashid al-Din's later political appointees, Nasir al-Din Munshi Kirmani, claims that the doctor came to the attention of the Mongol military elite during the reign of Abaqa (1265–82) and continued to rise in their trust under Abaqa's son, Arghun (1284–91).[19] As part of this growing familiarity with the Mongol elite, Rashid al-Din travelled with the royal court at least part of the time. In March 1282, just a month before Abaqa's death, while Arghun was governor of the eastern provinces, Rashid al-Din attended the birth of prince Arghun's son Khudabanda, the future Sultan Oljeitu (1304–16).

The ties that Rashid al-Din built to the households of Abaqa and Arghun Khan were, in his own testimony, crucial for establishing a relationship with later members of the dynasty, and particularly with Khudabanda Oljeitu.[20] Once on the throne, Oljeitu treated Rashid al-Din as a trusted family doctor as well as a political adviser. In 1304, Rashid al-Din stood as an advocate for Oljeitu's wife Qutlughshah in her marriage to the sultan, and he was subsequently entrusted with raising the royal couple's daughter.[21] In 1306, when Oljeitu led a campaign to subdue the region of Gilan, he dispatched Rashid al-Din to attend another wife who had fallen ill, and when Rashid al-Din was bed-ridden with gout, the sultan visited him personally.[22] Even before the dramatic events that brought Rashid al-Din to the highest levels of government service, he had thus forged a strong bond with one particular branch of the Ilkhanid royal family. Abaqa, Arghun and particularly the latter's sons Ghazan and Oljeitu knew and trusted Rashid al-Din. This situation recalls the personal trust that allowed Baha' al-Din Juvayni to rise to prominence under the Oyirad governor Arghun. It opened a path to the remarkable heights of wealth and influence that Rashid al-Din later enjoyed.

Factionalism and Conversion at the Ilkhanid Court

While Rashid al-Din moved into a position of trust among members of the Mongol elite, the administration of the Ilkhanate was growing increasingly factionalised. This had already begun as the sons of Baha' al-Din Juvayni took the reins of government. 'Ala' al-Din was appointed as governor of the former 'Abbasid capital Baghdad after Hulegu's previous appointment, 'Imad al-Din Qazwini, was executed for corruption in 1261.[23] Almost immediately, Juvayni was himself denounced and sentenced to death. This sentence was subsequently revoked, and 'Ala' al-Din's fortunes improved somewhat after 1262, with the outbreak of open hostilities between Hulegu and Berke. In that year, a number of Mongol and Persian officials were put on trial.[24] The exact reasons for these purges in the top levels of the government are not clear. Rashid al-Din only mentions that one of the condemned men, the astrologer Husam al-Din, was punished for having called Hulegu's invasion of Baghdad inauspicious. Some were flogged and others executed, including Hulegu's personal secretary, Sayf al-Din.

In Sayf al-Din's place, Hulegu appointed Shams al-Din Juvayni, the younger brother of the governor of Baghdad, as *ṣāḥib-diwān* at the central court.[25] However, even having his brother in such a prominent position did not protect 'Ala' al-Din from attack. He was again arrested in 1264 and only reinstated as administrator of Baghdad under the nominal governorship of the Mongol Sughunchaq, who was also given oversight over the perennially mismanaged province of Fars. In the late 1270s, the Juvayni brothers again came under attack, this time by one of Shams al-Din's own administrative appointees, Majd al-Mulk of Yazd.[26] Shams al-Din was arrested, but managed to secure his release by soliciting letters of support from his followers. 'Ala' al-Din was chained and beaten after promising under duress to pay an exorbitant fine to settle charges of embezzlement. Irrespective of the truth or falsehood of these charges, the episode reveals that high appointment in the Ilkhanid bureaucracy created opportunities for self-enrichment and attracted charges of the same.

Two aspects of this court drama are worthy of note, as they informed the course of the later Ilkhanid administration. First, as a result of his accusation, Majd al-Mulk was appointed co-vizier with Shams al-Din. This situation, namely, the division of the duties of vizier as a check against the abuse of power by a single individual, had a precedent as early as 1246, when the Oyirad governor Arghun jointly appointed Baha' al-Din Juvayni and Amir Buqa as his deputies, and more recently in 1264, when Sughunchaq took his position alongside 'Ala' al-Din as governor of Baghdad. The division of supreme administrative responsibilities became a hallmark of the Ilkhanid administration and a bane to Rashid al-Din later in his career. The practice of appointing two viziers was meant to prevent the undue concentration of state power (and wealth) in the hands of a single individual, but it too frequently crippled the apparatus of state by fuelling factional conflict.[27]

A second aspect of Ilkhanid court politics that becomes evident in Majd al-Mulk's charge against the Juvaynis is the formation of alliances between individual Persian administrators and members of the Mongol military elite. Thus, while Shams al-Din Juvayni retained the support of the powerful Sughunchaq, Majd al-Mulk advanced his accusations against the Juvaynis by bringing them to Amir Yesu Buqa Kuregen. Such alliances, paired with the institution of the dual vizierate, had the effect in later years of dividing the Ilkhanid court against itself along fault lines between factions, each of which included members of both the Persian civil and the Mongol military elites.[28] The distinction between military and civil government that had formed under Chormaqun and Chin Temur in the 1230s had been reshaped: each of the major factions at court in later years drew equally from the ranks of men of the pen and of the sword.

'Ala' al-Din Juvayni was still in custody and being transported to Abaqa's court for trial when word came of the *ilkhan*'s death. Abaqa had made his son and chosen heir, Arghun, governor of the eastern provinces during his reign. Arghun was an outspoken critic of the Juvaynis' influence, and his accession to the throne would certainly spell an end to the brothers' prominence. The Juvaynis won a respite, however, in the person of Teguder (1282–4), the eldest surviving son of Hulegu. When Teguder won the acclamation of the majority of princes and generals, Arghun deferred to his election as *ilkhan*. Teguder had converted to Islam before his accession and had taken the Arabic name Ahmad. On his accession, he immediately had 'Ala' al-Din Juvayni released from custody.

The election of a Muslim *ilkhan* brought a more visibly Islamic tenor to the court, as Mongol terminology for the institutions and offices of government were replaced by Persian and Arabic ones and churches and temples were transformed into mosques.[29] The influence of Islam on the Ilkhanid government was a natural consequence of the Persianate bureaucracy that the Juvaynis had cultivated, and Rashid al-Din himself probably converted during the final years of Abaqa's reign, when the Juvayni administration was fully in place. During those years, the renowned Shafi'i theologian Nasir al-Din Baydawi produced the first historical work that fit the Mongols into an Islamic historical framework, as described in Chapter 3. That work demonstrates an attempt to reconcile the foreign infidel dynasty with the Islamic faith that was in the 1270s reasserting itself as the religion of state. We know that Baydawi travelled to Tabriz at least once in 1279, and Rashid al-Din was evidently familiar with his historical writing.[30] We have no evidence that Baydawi made a direct personal influence on the young Rashid. However, in the late 1270s and early 1280s, it was becoming increasingly apparent that, despite the end of the caliphate, Islam was to continue as the dominant cultural expression of the government in a region of diverse religious communities. This impression could only have been strengthened with the rise of Ahmad Teguder to the position of *ilkhan*. In fact, the most explicit evidence we have about the dating of Rashid al-Din's conversion to Islam is testimony reported by Badr al-Din al-'Ayni that Rashid al-Din had converted at the age of thirty.[31] This would put the conversion exactly during the last years of Abaqa's reign.

Having a Muslim on the throne in the person of Ahmad Teguder seemed to signal a rapprochement between the dynasty and the culture of the majority of their subjects. It did not prevent Majd al-Mulk from renewing his attack on the Juvaynis. He accused Shams al-Din of having poisoned the late *ilkhan* Abaqa, a charge for which Majd al-Mulk was eventually found guilty of slander and executed in August 1282. In his wake, Arghun pursued the charges against the Juvayni brothers himself. While spending the winter of 1282/3 in Baghdad, Arghun demanded full repayment from 'Ala' al-Din of fines previously levied against him. This renewed attack reputedly drove 'Ala' al-Din to his death by an apoplectic fit.

Arghun's eventual accession in 1284 initiated a raft of targeted attacks against the Islamic bureaucrats that Tusi and the Juvayni brothers had cultivated. The end of his reign in 1291 ushered in another wave of violence against Jewish figures in the bureaucracy who had benefited from the earlier actions against Muslim administrators. In both cases, the attacks were the result of personal animus, not systematic pogroms. Each cycle of violence put the levers of state into the hands of a new court faction of Mongol military leaders and Persian administrators. At the time of Arghun's accession, Rashid al-Din was likely a recent convert to Islam, though as we will see the memory of his Jewish heritage remained with him. That he – and indeed, several other known Muslim and Jewish members of the early Ilkhanid administration including the children of the Juvayni brothers – survived these two periods of violence against the two faith communities with which he was identified shows just how unsystematic those purges were. It also suggests that his connection to Arghun's family protected him and presented a pathway for his rise in government service.

One of the first victims of the anti-Islamic reaction that accompanied Arghun's accession was the vizier Shams al-Din Juvayni, who was executed on 16 October 1284 near the town of Abhar, outside Qazvin. The execution had been stayed temporarily by the Jalayir Mongol Amir Buqa, who had long been a political patron of Shams al-Din but who had also supported Arghun's claim to the throne in 1282 and again in 1284.[32] In September 1284, even before the execution of Shams al-Din, Arghun transferred the vizierate to Buqa, which perhaps eased the latter's decision to allow Shams al-Din's execution to take place.[33] As vizier, Buqa promoted his own allies to positions of influence. Perhaps the most important of Buqa's appointments was his brother Aruq, who became the new governor of Baghdad. Once there, Aruq promoted and protected a number of individuals who had earlier worked for the Juvaynis, and he eliminated several of the collaborators who had helped to elevate the Jalayir brothers at the Juvaynis' expense. In one sense, the Mongol brothers Buqa and Aruq simply stepped into the positions of the Persian Juvayni brothers, without significantly disrupting the governing apparatus that their predecessors had assembled.

Over the first five years of Arghun's reign, this change in leadership devolved into a broader reaction against Muslim influence at court and the Islamisation of the Mongol ruling elite. The continuity that Buqa and Aruq maintained was soon challenged by conservative members of the Mongol military who were eager to purge the administration of its Islamic character. In part, this was due to a backlash against Buqa and Aruq themselves, whom other Mongols blamed for excessively consolidating power in their own hands. In the late 1280s, the *ilkhan* Arghun began to replace Buqa's allies in various positions, removing his agents at Tabriz, Kirman and Fars. In 1288, Arghun replaced Aruq as governor of Baghdad with another Mongol, Ordo Qiya. The latter had gained favour at court by promising to collect unpaid taxes from Iraq. In this effort, he was aided by Saʿd al-Daula al-Abhari, a Jewish doctor who had previously served as deputy governor in Iraq.

Saʿd al-Daula and Ordo Qiya quickly escalated the political purge of the remaining Juvayni administrative system and its new Mongol leadership by informing the Ilkhan Arghun of Aruq's extensive extortions from the imperial treasury during his term at Baghdad. Faced with these reversals, Buqa attempted a coup against Arghun in the name of Arghun's cousin, Prince Jushkeb. Jushkeb wanted no part of the plot, which he revealed to Arghun, triggering a swift and bloody end to Buqa and to much of his family and followers in the first months of 1289. These purges reached deep into the administration that Buqa had inherited from his former client Shams al-Din: by 1292, almost the entire administrative corps that the Juvaynis had cultivated under Abaqa had been rooted out of the Ilkhanid government.[34]

In addition to eliminating current staff, Arghun decreed that Muslims were no longer to serve in the administration.[35] This left a crisis of staffing, which Saʿd al-Daula was able to fill by drawing on family connections within the Jewish community of northern Iran. Having gained favour with Arghun Khan for his ability to refresh the imperial coffers with funds collected at Baghdad, Saʿd al-Daula increased his personal influence by limiting access to the *ilkhan* to the three sympathetic Mongol *amirs* he named as his deputies. Other members of the military elite were stripped of influence at court. Some of the most powerful were assigned to military and administrative posts in the outer regions of the state.

Saʿd al-Daula's term as vizier was short. Arghun subscribed to the teachings of alchemists, and his death may have been brought on by drinking potions meant to extend his life. Arghun's final sickness afforded disaffected Mongol *amirs* and Persian administrators the opportunity to discredit and execute Saʿd al-Daula and his deputies in March 1291. Saʿd al-Daula's Jewish heritage, and his practice of packing the government with other members of his religious community, meant that the resentment felt against him became a purge of his supporters at court and, more generally, of the Jewish populations of Iraq.

If Rashid al-Din had indeed converted to Islam in or around 1280, it helps to explain how he survived the purges against Jews in 1291. However, it would also have left him potentially vulnerable to the anti-Muslim actions of earlier in Arghun's reign. However, his relationship to the central court was more familial than it was professional, as he and his father had gained the trust of members of the Mongol elite because of their medical background, and not for their administrative experience. Rashid al-Din's role in the early Ilkhanate was not as an administrator in the corps built by the Juvaynis, but as a professional attendant at court, and so the actions against the followers of the Juvaynis missed him entirely. Rashid al-Din's path from his early medical training in Maragha to become the most trusted adviser of the khan ran through the camps of Arghun's family rather than the offices of the growing bureaucratic state. It is perhaps for this reason that he remains invisible in the early histories of the dynasty.

In the Service of Ghazan

By the last decade of the thirteenth century, Persianate bureaucrats and professionals were beholden to various Mongol royal and non-royal families, integrating into the household *keshig* structure of elite Mongol society. After Arghun's death, the Ilkhanid state faced a crisis of succession, and these households were deployed in a new conflict over the throne. Arghun's eldest son, Ghazan, was eighteen years old, but was occupied putting down an insurrection in Khurasan, where his father had appointed him as governor after taking the throne in 1284. The Mongols who had led the backlash against Saʿd al-Daula nominated Arghun's uncle Baidu as *ilkhan*, but their failure to act decisively allowed Arghun's brother Geikhatu, who had served as governor of Anatolia since 1284, to seize the throne. While the question of succession had been decided, the top administrative appointment remained unsettled until November 1292, when Geikhatu appointed Sadr al-Din Zanjani as vizier.[36]

Sadr al-Din has a largely negative reputation in the sources on the Ilkhanate, mainly because Rashid al-Din and others later vilified him. Nevertheless, this new vizier personified the institutional development of the Ilkhanid state and he almost managed to salvage the state finances from the stress that early Mongol tax exactions had placed on the regional economy. Sadr al-Din was born into a family of judges from Qazvin. Like Rashid al-Din, his arrival at the highest levels of the Ilkhanid administration was aided both by his education and by his home city's proximity to the Mongol royal camps in Azerbaijan. Indeed, after the cycles of violence that marked the reign of Arghun, Qazvin became a reservoir of talent for rebuilding the Ilkhanid administration, and numerous residents of that city rose to be prominent members of the government.[37] Sadr al-Din entered Mongol service when he was very young, joining the entourage of the Mongol Amir Taghachar, and he was active in the factional conflicts that toppled the Juvaynis, Buqa and Aruq, and Saʿd al-Daula in turn. Now that it was his turn to manage the state, he worked to differentiate the roles of Mongol and Persian elements at court and he rebuilt the state apparatus by making new appointments at all levels.

Over the course of the 1290s, Sadr al-Din was thrice appointed to the head of the Ilkhanid administration, first by Geikhatu from 1292 to 1294, and then twice during the early years of the reign of Ghazan Khan (1295–1304).[38] His first administration was a period of strong consolidation, in which he appointed new judges and fiscal agents. He also refloated the state treasury by reining in spending at the central court and by contracting out the revenue collection of Fars. In consolidating his own authority, he attracted rivals, but since the Ilkhan Geikhatu was more concerned with the pleasures of court life than its politics, Sadr al-Din had a free hand in deflecting these threats.

In the end, Sadr al-Din's downfall, and that of Geikhatu, was brought on by the mounting fiscal difficulties of the state, a circumstance that Sadr al-Din did not create and which his administrative reforms were not adequate to address. In desperation, he turned in autumn 1294 to Bolad Chingsang, a Mongol *amir* from China, who advised him on introducing a Chinese-style paper currency. The resulting state-issued bills were so closely modelled on the Chinese *chao* that they bore the same name and even Chinese text. The population refused to accept the bills even under pain of punishment, bringing market activity to a halt and forcing a recall of the paper currency, destroying the credibility of Sadr al-Din as vizier and of Geikhatu as ruler.[39]

Rashid al-Din turned forty around the time Geikhatu came to the throne. Nasir al-Din Munshi Kirmani states in his biographical entry on Rashid al-Din, that 'when Geikhatu Khan became padishah, the mark of authority came to him'.[40] This may refer to an official appointment or simply to his coming of age to hold senior office.[41] It was repeated several decades later by Sayf al-Din 'Aqili, and the continued lack of clarity on this question may have inspired Khwandamir's early sixteenth-century compromise position: that Geikhatu offered Rashid al-Din the position of vizier but the latter declined it.[42]

Another contemporary account offers an even more enticing suggestion about Rashid al-Din's presence at Geikhatu's court. In a fleeting episode in the continuation of Bar Hebraeus' world chronicle, a Jewish cook named Rashid al-Daula attempts to maintain Geikhatu's table at his own expense in the face of the mounting state fiscal crisis. When his resources run out, Rashid al-Daula is forced to flee the capital.[43] This steward could easily be Rashid al-Din, who, as a student of Galenic medicine, would have been aware of the effect of various foods on the body's humours and who elsewhere bears the Mongol title of *ba'urchi*, or cook, in the household structure of the Mongol court, the *keshig*.[44]

If the Jewish cook described here was in fact Rashid al-Din, it remains to explain why the chronicler identifies him as Jewish – going so far as to call him Rashid al-Daula – given that Rashid al-Din most likely converted to Islam a full decade and a half before the events being described. An explanation can be found by reading this episode within the context of the surrounding pages of the chronicle. It is preceded by an account of the vizierate of Sa'd al-Daula emphasising the conflict between religious communities that allowed Jews to rise to unprecedented positions of authority during Arghun's reign.[45] Early in this account, the chronicler tells how a group of Arabs framed the community of Armenian Christians by hanging a dead dog in front of their own mosque. This leads to the discovery of a plot among Muslims to simultaneously kill Sa'd al-Daula along with his appointee as governor of Baghdad and the governor of Mosul.

In this atmosphere of intra-communal violence, the chronicler states,

Jews like Saʿd al-Daula enjoyed unchecked political power. The episode of Rashid al-Daula attempting to maintain Geikhatu's table falls immediately after the introduction of Saʿd al-Daula, whose extravagance is said to have driven Tabriz to desolation. In this context of social disorder and factional conflict, Rashid al-Daula appears as just one more extravagantly influential Jew attempting to curry favour at court. If the subject of this episode is indeed our Rashid al-Din, already prominent at the court of Geikhatu in 1294, then the chronicler's larger narrative aim of discrediting Jewish courtiers provides an explanation for overlooking his conversion to Islam. Put simply, for the anecdote to work in the chronicle, its main figure must still be Jewish, regardless of historical reality.

Rashid al-Din gives us one other hint about his service before 1298. In describing events of that year (detailed below), he mentions that he and Amir Qutlughshah had been part of the same *keshig*, or household guard.[46] Qutlughshah was one of Ghazan's most trusted military supporters by 1290, and is mentioned as a confidant of Abaqa's family as early as the mid-1270s.[47] It is therefore likely that Rashid al-Din spent at least some time in Ghazan's retinue before the latter came to the throne. As already mentioned, Arghun had appointed Ghazan governor of Khurasan in 1284, continuing a pattern practised as early as the Achaemenid period of delegating a member of the royal family – and often a designated heir – to manage the distant eastern reaches of an empire centred in Mesopotamia and western Iran. In the decade after his appointment, Ghazan cut his teeth as a military and political leader by stemming local revolts and defending against invasions from the Chaghadaid Khanate of Central Asia.

The most important rebel that Ghazan faced during this time was the Mongol Amir Nauruz, the son of the last pre-imperial Mongol governor Arghun Aqa. In 1284, the Ilkhan Arghun sent Nauruz east as a mentor to the young prince Ghazan. Nauruz revolted in January 1289 out of fear of being caught up in the ongoing purges of Buqa's allies and associates.[48] For most of the next six years, during which time Saʿd al-Daula and Sadr al-Din Zanjani served successively at the head of the Ilkhanid administration and Geikhatu drove the imperial treasury to ruin, Nauruz waged a periodic rebellion against Ghazan from the frontier region between the Ilkhanid and Chaghadaid khanates.[49]

When Nauruz first went into open rebellion, Arghun sent additional forces to reinforce his son, including his uncle Baidu and Amir Nurin Aqa. With their aid, Ghazan achieved his first success against the rebels as early as spring 1289, when Nauruz fled to seek assistance from the Chaghadaid Qaidu Khan. Nauruz spent close to three years in the Chaghadaid realm, during which time Arghun Khan died. While Ghazan did not actively contest Geikhatu's accession in 1291, he used the abeyance of Nauruz's rebellion as an opportunity to consolidate his viceregal administrative apparatus based at his court in the east of the Ilkhanate. In the winter of 1291/2, Nauruz returned to Khurasan in active rebellion at the head of an army that Qaidu had provided. After raiding as far as Nishapur, he was defeated by Amir Qutlughshah in late summer 1292 and again put to flight.

Faced with the challenge of putting his army back on a war footing in the face of this renewed threat, Ghazan replaced his financial chief, Muʿin al-Din Mustaufi, with Saʿd al-Din Sawaji, who had joined his service in 1289 as part of the household of Amir Nurin Aqa. Saʿd al-Din received the unenviable assignment of finding provisions for the Mongol army without overburdening the already weary population of the war-ravaged eastern provinces. Apparently he succeeded in this task, as he was reappointed to it in the following year. In 1294, Ghazan called on Saʿd al-Din to negotiate the surrender of Nishapur, which had also risen in rebellion. In collecting tax revenue and negotiating the surrender of cities, Saʿd al-Din was engaged during these years in the very same activities that would occupy him and Rashid al-Din after Ghazan took the Ilkhanid throne.

Late 1294 and early 1295 saw three events that set the course of Ghazan's rise to the throne. First, Ghazan refused to comply with the order to circulate Sadr al-Din's new *chao* bills, on the excuse that a paper currency could not withstand the humidity of Mazandaran. At around the same time, Nauruz rendered his final submission to Ghazan, ending two years of continuous brigandage. Finally, early in 1295 and shortly after Nauruz's surrender, news arrived in the east that a rebellion against Geikhatu had brought the latter's uncle Baidu to the throne. Between 1289 and 1295, Ghazan had come of age, gained experience as a military leader, engaged Saʿd al-Din from the household of Nurin Aqa to run his administration, spurned the monetary policy of the central court, and made peace with his former mentor and adversary Nauruz, who again joined his circle of advisers. The new change in government at the central court provided him with an opportunity to lever the executive experience he had thus cultivated into his own claim for royal authority.

Ghazan responded to Baidu's seizure of power by launching a counter-coup aimed at taking the Ilkhanid throne.[50] During summer 1295, Baidu offered to divide the territory of the Ilkhanate between himself and Ghazan, recognising the *de facto* autonomy that Ghazan had established in the eastern provinces. Despite the encouragement of Amirs Qutlughshah and Nurin Aqa to accept this settlement, Ghazan rejected the offer and committed himself to seizing the western capitals. In this decision, he was encouraged by Nauruz. Prince Ghazan's deference to his one-time adversary was a source of resentment for Qutlughshah and Nurin, who had spent so much energy fighting against Nauruz. Nevertheless, in summer 1295 Nauruz emerged once again as the most influential voice among Ghazan's circle of *amirs*.

Nauruz's influence over Ghazan during his rebellion against Baidu is most evident in the prince's decision to convert to Islam. Later historical writing presents Ghazan's conversion to Islam as the defining moment of his career. As discussed in Chapter 3, Rashid al-Din's version of events provides a vision of Ghazan harbouring monotheistic sentiments since his youth, with conversion as just the formal recognition of a deep personal conviction. This conforms to Rashid al-Din's highly polished presentation of the *ilkhan* as the fulfilment of God's plan for Islam.[51]

Other sources make clear that political and military exigency – and not individual religiosity – directed Ghazan at this moment. These include a version of Ghazan's early life and reign written by 'Abd Allah Qashani and later inserted into Rashid al-Din's dynastic history of the Mongols, as discussed in Chapter 3.[52] Qashani prefaces Ghazan's decision to convert with the comment that 'the blessed countenance [Ghazan] consulted with the *amirs* and agreed that the expedience of warding off the enemy and suppressing the violence of foes should be pursued by whatever means so that the enemy might be brought to destruction and trampled into obscurity'.[53] In short, Ghazan's conversion to Islam was later depicted as the sincere wishes of an innately Muslim soul, but in its time it served an immediate political need. It certainly aligned the prince's cause with important factions in the Ilkhanid state, including the mostly Muslim civil administration but also a growing body of Mongol military leaders, many of whom had already converted to Islam.[54]

Immediately after his conversion, Ghazan received emissaries from Baidu, including Shaykh Mahmud Dinavari. According to Rashid al-Din's account, Shaykh Mahmud was evidently displeased with Baidu's support of Christian interests, and he transmitted messages of support for Ghazan from several disaffected *amir*s at Baidu's court. Prominent among these was Amir Taghachar, who had been instrumental in bringing Baidu to power but who chafed at having been assigned – probably in fearful recognition of his significant influence at court – to govern the distant province of Anatolia along with his Persian client, Geikhatu's discredited vizier Sadr al-Din Zanjani. By emphasising Shaykh Mahmud's role in facilitating the defection of some of the most powerful *amir*s in the Ilkhanate, Rashid al-Din draws attention to the instrumental role of Islam in Ghazan's rebellion and eventual victory. This point is strengthened when Baidu's capture and execution is followed immediately – even before Ghazan enters the Ilkhanid capital – with an edict directing the destruction of all Buddhist, Christian and Jewish places of worship in Tabriz, Baghdad and other cities.[55]

Baidu was executed on 4 October 1295, after which Ghazan took immediate measures to consolidate his control over the Ilkhanid state. These measures fit into two basic categories: first, he assigned extraordinary powers to Nauruz to stabilise the state in the wake of successive coups; and, second, he judiciously accommodated competing court factions in the new government. Ghazan appointed Nauruz as the head of the military, vizier, *amir* of the entire realm and, according to Wassaf, even granted him the viceregency (*niyābat*).[56] He also assigned his adviser to govern Khurasan to address a renewed Chaghadaid invasion across the frontier where Nauruz had once waged his own rebellion.[57] The former rebel general had assumed all the markings of heir apparent for the young *ilkhan*.

While Nauruz held an unprecedented level of authority alongside Ghazan, other individuals from previous administrations were retained in their positions, a departure from the pattern of purges that had marked moments of succession since the rise of Arghun. Sadr al-Din Zanjani, who had been Geikhatu's vizier and who had helped to secure the defection of Taghachar and others to Ghazan in summer 1295, was rewarded with the office of *ṣāḥib-diwān*, while the position of *ulugh bilikchi* fell to Sharaf al-Din Simnani, who had worked alongside Ordo Qiya and Saʻd al-Daula at Baghdad. Muʻin al-Din Mustaufi, who had preceded Saʻd al-Din as *ṣāḥib-diwān* to Prince Ghazan, was retained as *mustaufi al-mamālik*, a position he had previously held under Arghun.[58]

Despite these efforts to ensure stability and to accommodate various factions within the administrative elite, the first year of Ghazan's reign saw the earlier factionalism of previous years continue unchecked. Some of this was internal to the Mongol royal family, as Taraqai Kuregen defected to the Mamluks with a company of Oyirads.[59] Much of it, however, centred around the figure of Amir Nauruz, who continued to wield considerable influence over the young *ilkhan*. The persecutions against Jewish, Christian and Buddhist places of worship in the first days of Ghazan's reign was probably instigated by the headstrong *amir*, and not by the *ilkhan*, whose own conversion to Islam was too recent and politically motivated to inspire such dogmatic measures.[60]

Nauruz unleashed a storm of conflict in 1296 by promoting Baidu's vizier, Jamal al-Din Dastjirdani, as head of the administration in place of Sadr al-Din. The latter became increasingly exposed at court when his patron Taghachar was again dispatched as governor of Anatolia. Finding himself once more marginalised, Taghachar threw his support behind yet another Ilkhanid claimant, backing a grandson of Hulegu named Sogei as the latter made his own effort to seize the throne. Taghachar's support for Sogei finally undid Ghazan's patience with the inveterate kingmaker. In executing Taghachar but not his client Sadr al-Din, Ghazan asserted his independent authority, refusing to eliminate a powerful administrator whom Nauruz had sought to marginalise. Also in 1296, Ghazan put an end to the systematic religious persecutions that Nauruz had spearheaded. The latter also returned from his posting as military governor in Khurasan to the Ilkhanid court without being summoned, earning a rebuke from Ghazan and leading to widespread desertions among the eastern armies.

To replace Nauruz in the east, Ghazan deputed his brother Oljeitu, who had been born in Mazandaran under Rashid al-Din's attendance. Then, late in 1296, Sadr al-Din and Shaykh Mahmud jointly denounced Jamal al-Din

Dastjirdani, leading to the latter's prosecution and execution and the elevation of Sadr al-Din as ṣāḥib-diwān for the third time. This was a direct reversal of Nauruz's early appointment. His fall from favour was made complete early in the following year, when he came under suspicion for having conducted independent communication with the Mamluk court in Egypt. Rashid al-Din's account of these events reveals his own political position: he presents them as the actions of a vast bureaucratic conspiracy masterminded by Sadr al-Din. In this account, Sadr al-Din plants a series of forged letters in the baggage of Nauruz's associates in order to incriminate the *amir*. In Chapter 5 we will see how Rashid al-Din himself was accused of similar actions after consolidating his own hold on power years later. Such dramatised episodes may miss the historical truth but still show the Ilkhanid court to be a deeply factional society, where chancellery mischief could achieve political ends.

However much credence we give to accounts like that of the conspiracy of Sadr al-Din, the charges against Nauruz led him to flee to Herat, where he was captured and executed in summer 1297. By then, most of his family and associates had already been killed. By one reckoning, the purges surrounding the rebellion of Sogai and the fall of Nauruz resulted in the deaths of five Mongol princes, thirty-eight *amir*s and uncounted soldiers.[61] Even after such a thorough liquidation of real and potential political threats, one more round of factional conflict was in store before Ghazan could fully secure his reign. This was a series of events that led to the execution of the three-time vizier Sadr al-Din. One of the prime movers and beneficiaries of these events was the companion and doctor of the family of Arghun, Rashid al-Din of Hamadan. Since the fall of Sadr al-Din is the first episode in which Rashid al-Din becomes directly and undeniably involved in central court politics, he begins at this point to enter our sources on Ilkhanid history.

The Shadow Vizier

At the time of Ghazan's ascension, Rashid al-Din was nearly twice as old as the new *ilkhan*. He had risen in the esteem of various Mongol *amir*s and, most importantly, the family of Arghun Khan. He had also embraced Islam, a step that Ghazan also took during his struggle against his great-uncle Baidu. Rashid al-Din was a trusted confidant and had been allowed into the ruler's family and government. The Mamluk biographer Safadi calls Rashid al-Din

Ghazan's 'counsellor and kin and companion and confidant and doctor and cook, so that Ghazan only ate from Rashid al-Din's hands and the hands of his sons'.[62] At the end of Ghazan's successful bid for the throne, according to one account, Rashid al-Din was appointed as governor of the southern city of Yazd, where he already had ties and which flourished under his management.[63] Ghazan meanwhile appointed Sadr al-Din to the vizierate on two separate occasions: first, after his role in catalysing Ghazan's revolt and again in the lead up to the fall of Amir Nauruz. The final disgrace of Sadr al-Din in 1298 made space at the head of the government, into which Rashid al-Din stepped alongside Saʿd al-Din Sawaji, Ghazan's fiscal procurator from the early 1290s.

According to Rashid al-Din himself, less than six months after Sadr al-Din's third and final appointment as vizier, two men accused him of embezzlement.[64] Other sources do not mention these accusations, though they agree that Sadr al-Din fell from grace after failing to convince Ghazan with his own accusations against Rashid al-Din.[65] While Hamd Allah Mustaufi blandly accuses Sadr al-Din of harbouring guile, Rashid al-Din and Munshi Kirmani each report a dramatic court scene in which Sadr al-Din denounces Rashid al-Din before the *ilkhan*, who quickly rebukes him. Later, Sadr al-Din escalates his attack by claiming that Rashid al-Din had complained against the powerful Amir Qutlughshah. When Ghazan learns of Sadr al-Din's machinations, he sentences the vizier to death. Qutlughshah himself executes Sadr al-Din by the side of a canal, cutting the condemned man in half. The episode ends with the jejune comment that 'in the end, when [Sadr al-Din] got what he wanted, he derived no enjoyment from it'.

This account is particularly dramatic perhaps because of Rashid al-Din's personal involvement and his investment in its outcome. Just as parallels can be drawn to the lives of the Juvaynis and Saʿd al-Daula, Sadr al-Din's career provides a blueprint for Rashid al-Din's: he was a talented and ambitious administrator who tried to put the state on firmer footing after a period of dynastic instability and unsustainable fiscal policy. His death, as reported by Rashid al-Din, also provides an antetype for the narrative of Rashid al-Din's own execution almost exactly twenty years later: cut in half by a Mongol soldier on the outskirts of a city.[66] Rashid al-Din's account of the fall of Sadr al-Din is important in one other respect, though, as it is one of very few places in his history of the Mongols where he makes reference to himself. The narrative aim of his account is to emphasise his own innocence and the support he enjoyed from Ghazan Khan. It is in narrating the unwinding of this plot that Rashid al-Din mentions that he and Qutlughshah had served together in Ghazan's household guard. If Sadr al-Din came to prominence in the orbit of Amir Taghachar, Rashid al-Din probably could count Qutlughshah among his allies and sponsors in the shifting map of factional politics during the transitional period between the death of Abaqa and the rise of Ghazan Khan. In the end, Qutlughshah remained central to Ghazan's household, while Taghachar was ultimately expendable. The fates of the administrators tied to those two important *amir*s played out accordingly.

In place of Sadr al-Din, Rashid al-Din was appointed as deputy to the new vizier Saʿd al-Din Sawaji, performing the duties of chief minister alongside another head administrator in an often antagonistic relationship. As previously discussed, the division of chief administrative duties of the state had some precedent by this point. Before 1298, single individuals had wielded increasingly monolithic administrative power, which they solidified by packing the government with members of their own families and other partisans. Thus, Shams al-Din Juvayni, Amir Buqa, Saʿd al-Daula and Sadr al-Din had each buttressed his individual authority by appointing his relatives and assistants to administrative positions. The dual vizierate was probably a way for the Mongol royal family and military elite to put a check on such concentration of power in the hands of a single individual or family. Qubilai Qa'an had introduced a different solution to the same problem in China by appointing Mongol overseers to serve alongside the more influential positions in the Chinese bureaucratic system. That approach had also been tried in the Ilkhanate, as in the case of ʿAlaʾ al-Din Juvayni and Sughunchaq or Ordo Qiya and Saʿd al-Daula, each pair serving first in the administrative apparatus of the Ilkhanate's second city, Baghdad. Both approaches – the division of authority and the joint appointment of Mongol overseers – introduced significant inefficiencies into government, and were an inevitable source of factional conflict and resentment.

The division of responsibilities between Rashid al-Din and Saʿd al-Din (and later Taj al-Din ʿAlishah) was one phase in a gradual re-articulation of the difference between the offices of vizier and *ṣāḥib-dīwān*. The initial

Mongol appearance in the region had created a sharp rupture in established patterns of Islamic civil administration, a rupture that had only begun to heal in the earliest Mongol administrative structures of the 1230s.[67] As a result of the disturbed state of administrative practice and titulature, Rashid al-Din's contemporaries applied various titles to describe his work at court. These are largely anachronistic applications and hide the fact that, from 1298 until 1317, Rashid al-Din held a unique place in the administration of the eastern Islamic world, performing the duties of high office while retaining a special personal tie to his sovereigns that was based as much in his medical training as in his administrative activities. Despite, or perhaps because of, Rashid al-Din's close connections with the ruling family, there is significant ambiguity about what formal role he played in the central Ilkhanid administration. To recall an example cited already, Munshi Kirmani tells of the great confidence that the Mongol *amir*s placed in Rashid al-Din even before Ghazan's ascension, but he describes Rashid al-Din's relationship with Ghazan as one of a privy councillor and regional administrator, and not a dossiered minister.

Even after Rashid al-Din had assumed a leading role in the government, his official position remains difficult to pin down. Wassaf asserts quite clearly that the position of *ṣāḥib-diwān* fell to Saʿd al-Din, while Rashid al-Din took a position as his deputy.[68] Elsewhere, Wassaf again implies that Rashid al-Din was vizier alongside Saʿd al-Din during Ghazan's first campaign to Syria in the winter of 1299–1300, discussed below.[69] Contemporary Mamluk chronicles mention Rashid al-Din for the first time in the context of that campaign as a 'state counsellor' working alongside Saʿd al-Din during this first campaign into Syria.[70]

Other reports are not as explicit. Most notably, Rashid al-Din never once mentions his own appointment as vizier in his history of the Mongols, naming Saʿd al-Din alone as the new vizier in the immediate wake of Sadr al-Din's execution. In relating his efforts to negotiate the surrender of Rahba al-Sham in 1303, Rashid al-Din calls himself simply 'the physician', in contrast to Saʿd al-Din, whom he names as *ṣāḥib-diwān*.[71] In his theological writings, such as the one quoted near the beginning of this chapter, Rashid al-Din calls himself, among other things, 'Sultan of Viziers', though, as discussed in Chapter 4, his attitude about his role in the Ilkhanid state changed dramatically between the time he rose to administrative prominence and when he wrote those lines. Writing after the death of Rashid al-Din, Hamd Allah Mustaufi names Saʿd al-Din as vizier, but specifies that the actual work of managing the state remained in the hands of Rashid al-Din.[72]

Hamd Allah Mustaufi offers another piece of evidence for the role of Rashid al-Din by way of omission. His epic verse history of Islam and the Mongols, the *Book of Victory*, features prominently in Chapter 6. In it, Mustaufi divides his dramatic and poetic retelling of Ilkhanid history into sections dedicated to the administration of individual viziers. While the elevation and deaths of Sadr al-Din, Saʿd al-Din and ʿAlishah are each set apart with heading titles, no such structural elements mark the administration of Rashid al-Din as vizier.

Any attempt to rectify these conflicting reports about Rashid al-Din's formal appointment and responsibilities is probably bound to fail. They are a witness to the complex and shifting administrative structure of a young military patronage state, by which the Mongol *ilkhan*s distributed personal favour and sought to avoid the consolidation of administrative power in the hands of any one individual. While Rashid al-Din's title may not have matched the duties that he performed for Ghazan, he was unquestionably an important figure, probably the single most influential person at court. In this regard, the best parallel is probably to the figure of Bahaʾ al-Din Juvayni, who had served as *ṣāḥib-dīwān* to the early governors of the Mongol Middle East, even when that position did not carry any apparent official duty.

Ghazan's War in Syria

After the deaths of Nauruz and Sadr al-Din Zanjani, Ghazan's reign was dominated by a series of campaigns into Mamluk-controlled Syria, part of an ongoing effort to reverse the defeat suffered by Ked Buqa at ʿAyn Jalut in 1260. During these years of renewed war against the Mamluks, Ghazan adopted an expanding array of Islamic and Iranian markers of legitimacy into his self-identification as a ruler, while also preserving elements from Mongol tradition. The coincidence of renewed warfare and accelerated ideological innovation was not accidental. The Mamluks presented both a geopolitical and a rhetorical threat to the Ilkhanate, and the diplomatic correspondence between the two states is encrusted with challenges and assertions about each dynasty's relative legitimacy to rule in the Islamic world.[73] Between 1298 and 1302, Ghazan took several steps to present himself as a legitimate ruler according to various traditions.

After appointing Saʿd al-Din and Rashid al-Din to the head of the administrative apparatus in place of Sadr al-Din, Ghazan spent the winter of 1298/9 in and around Baghdad, including a visit to the shrine of ʿAli b. Abi Talib at Najaf. The region of lower Mesopotamia had been semi-independent from the central court for the first forty years of the Ilkhanate, but Ghazan invested heavily in the city of Baghdad, wintered and hunted in the area, and brought it under more direct control as part of his preparation for campaigns into Mamluk-held Syria.[74] This visit, and others like it by Ghazan and his brother Oljeitu, had significant influence on the two *ilkhans'* performance of kingship, inspiring building projects and a gradual embrace of Shiʿi sentiments, as discussed in Chapter 4.

In the summer after his visit to Baghdad, Ghazan held a *quriltai* at Ujan in northwest Iran, at which he proclaimed Oljeitu as his intended heir. Beyond securing his succession, Ghazan's choice to spend the summer at Ujan, where he had recently ordered the building of a new royal summer camp, was an opportunity to celebrate his father and grandfather's efforts to memorialise their reigns through monumental building.[75] Abaqa's palace is discussed in Chapter 1. His son Arghun had similarly undertaken significant building projects, which are discussed in Chapter 4. Ghazan's choice to continue this building programme demonstrates that, already by 1299, he recognised the importance of cultural patronage for securing his position and his lineage at the head of the dynasty and the region.

In Tabriz, in autumn 1299, Ghazan received news of Mamluk raids along the Euphrates frontier. That winter, he embarked on his first campaign into Syria.[76] For this first effort to invade Syria, Ghazan advanced west from Tabriz across upper Mesopotamia during the last months of 1299, when the more northerly summer pastures were inhospitable. Having sent Amir Qutlughshah ahead with the vanguard, Ghazan crossed the Euphrates in early December and fought and defeated the Mamluk forces at Wadi al-Khaznadar, near Hims, on the twenty-second of that month.[77] This was the only major field victory by the Mongol army over the Mamluks, and it resulted in the surrender of Damascus to Ghazan. When meeting with

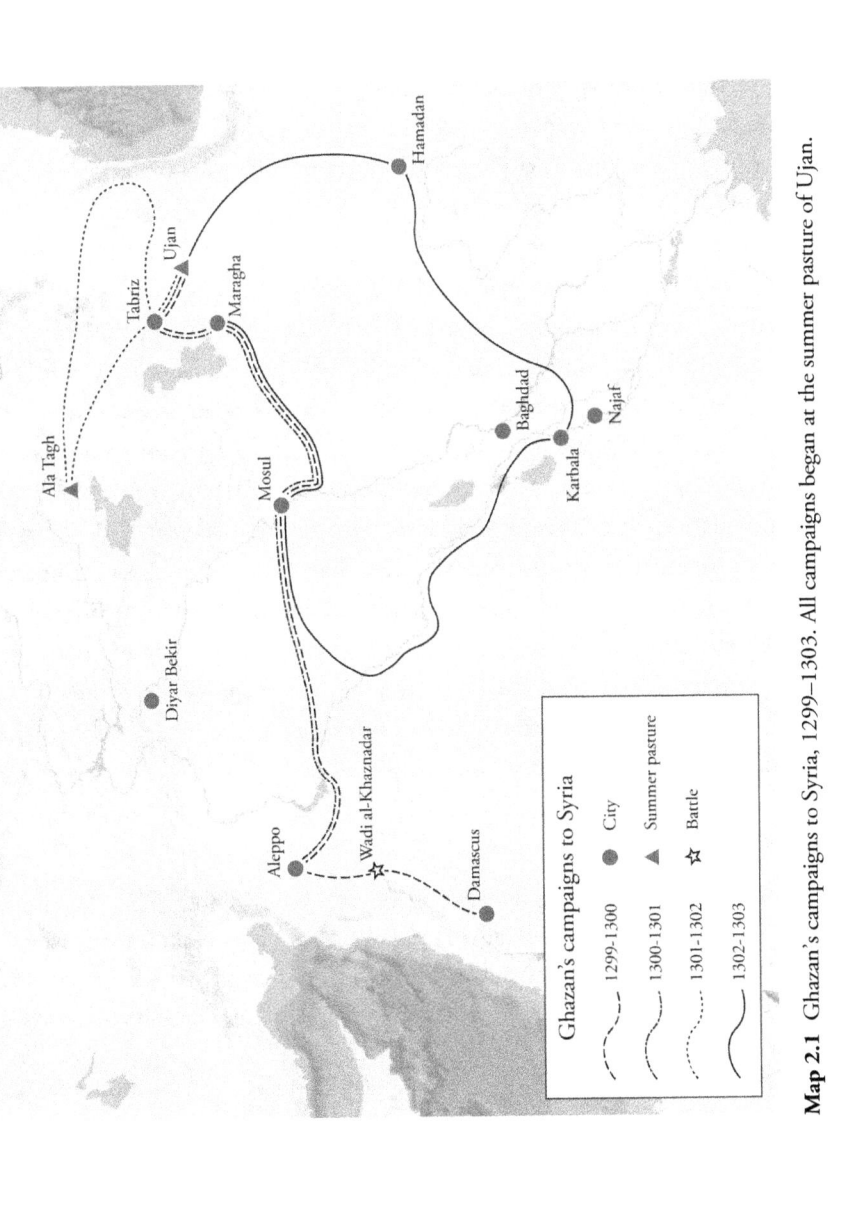

Map 2.1 Ghazan's campaigns to Syria, 1299–1303. All campaigns began at the summer pasture of Ujan.

the prominent residents of Damascus and communicating his victory to the Mamluk court, Ghazan struck an ideological tone that intentionally contrasted his own noble lineage from Chinggis Khan to the obscure origins of the slave-kings of Egypt.[78]

Ghazan returned from Damascus in spring 1300, leaving his top generals Qutlughshah and Chupan to oversee the Mongol occupation, which collapsed by late March in the face of local rebellion. After spending another summer and holding another *quriltai* at Ujan, Ghazan decamped for Syria in September 1300, again sending Qutlughshah ahead of the main force.[79] This second campaign halted around Aleppo from early November until early February, when Ghazan finally turned back because of heavy rains. He spent several months in a slow withdrawal from the Mamluk frontier. On his way back to his summer camp at Ujan, Ghazan also dispatched a letter to the Mamluk Sultan Qalawun, blaming the Mamluks for the ongoing conflict and accusing Qalawun of cowardice for having failed to confront Ghazan after the Mongols' victory at Wadi al-Khaznadar.[80] By spring 1301, Ghazan's efforts to campaign against the Mamluks had been stymied twice: first, by local resistance to an inadequate Mongol garrison in Damascus; and, second, by the elements. Better results were going to require a different approach, both strategically and in the formation of new expressions of legitimacy. In the latter respect, Ghazan's trusted physician and adviser Rashid al-Din would come to play a central role.

Notes

1. There have been several modern attempts to reconstruct Rashid al-Din's biography, beginning with Quatremère, *Histoire*, pp. i–lviii. Since then, extensive biographies have been assembled by Hoffmann, *Waqf*, pp. 53–98; Rajabzadeh, *Khwaja Rashid al-Din*, pp. 30–65; and more briefly by Krawulsky, *The Mongol Īlkhāns*, pp. 119–34.
2. Quatremère, *Histoire*, esp. p. v; Krawulsky, *The Mongol Īlkhāns*, pp. 119–34.
3. Rashid al-Din, *Jamiʿ al-Tawarikh*, pp. 990–1.
4. Rashid al-Din, *Lataʾif al-Haqaʾiq*, vol. 2, p. 2.
5. Rashid al-Din, *Jamiʿ al-Tawarikh*, pp. 993–4. For general information on Hamadan, see Barthold, *An Historical Geography*, pp. 129–32; Krawulsky, *Īrān*, p. 263; Fragner, *Geschichte der Stadt Hamadān*.

6. Yaʿqubi, *Les Pays*, pp. 72–3; al-Muqaddasi, *The Best Divisions*, pp. 348–9; Yaqut, *Dictionnaire*, pp. 597–608.
7. Various dates have been offered for the year of Rashid al-Din's birth. The year 1248 is the most commonly cited by modern scholars beginning with Quatremère, *Histoire*, p. v. A manuscript of Rashid al-Din's work not available to Quatremère gives slightly different information, which also seems somewhat more reliable. It would date his birth to between 1249 and 1251. For details, see Kamola, 'Rashīd al-Dīn', pp. 107–8.
8. Adler, *The Itinerary*, pp. 56–7.
9. Fischel, *Jews*, p. xxi n. 27.
10. For the life of Bar Hebraeus, see Takahashi, *Barhebraeus*, pp. 1–55.
11. Gil, *Jews*, pp. 239–31.
12. Gil, *Jews*, pp. 446, 465–7. Fischel, 'Azarbaijan', p. 6, considers it probable, though admittedly lacking documentation, that the seat of the Jewish Exilarchy moved from Baghdad to Tabriz with the transfer of political authority to the north.
13. For an overview on Ibn al-Fuwati's insight into Ilkhanid society, see DeWeese, 'Cultural Transmission'.
14. Ibn al-Fuwati, *Majmaʿ al-Adab*, vol. 4.2, pp. 719–20, no. 1043.
15. Fischel, *Jews*, p. 123 (citing Blochet); Netzner, 'Rashīd al-Dīn', pp. 122–3, naming Wassaf as a source but without providing a citation.
16. Jaʿfari, *Tarikh-e Yazd*, p. 92; Kateb, *Tarikh-e Jadid-e Yazd*, p. 134.
17. Afshar, 'Rashid al-Din Fazl Allah va Yazd', pp. 66–70. For more on this relationship and on how the elite of Yazd represent their ties to Rashid al-Din in telling the history of their city, see Mancini-Lander, 'Memory on the Boundaries of Empire', pp. 368–79; Mancini-Lander, 'Subversive Skylines'.
18. Hoffmann, *Waqf*, p. 65.
19. Kirmani, *Nasaʾim al-Ashar*, pp. 112–13.
20. Rashid al-Din, *Kitab al-Sultaniya*, Istanbul Nur Osmaniya MS. 3415, fol. 134a, cited in Rajabzadeh, *Khwaja Rashid al-Din*, p. 33 n. 2.
21. Qashani, *Tarikh-e Uljaytu*, pp. 8, 42. The daughter unfortunately died in his care.
22. Qashani, *Tarikh-e Uljaytu*, pp. 44, 195.
23. Safadi, *Kitab al-Wafi*, p. 78 no. 74.
24. Rashid al-Din, *Jamiʿ al-Tawarikh*, p. 1045.
25. Rashid al-Din, *Jamiʿ al-Tawarikh*, p. 1049.
26. Rashid al-Din, *Jamiʿ al-Tawarikh*, pp. 1110–15; Shabistari, *Talayahdaran*, pp. 193–200.

27. Lambton, *Continuity and Change*, pp. 55–7.
28. For a discussion of these factions in later decades, see Hoffmann, *Waqf*, p. 83.
29. Aubin, *Emirs Mongols*, p. 31.
30. For the influence of Baydawi's historical writing on that of Rashid al-Din, see Chapter 3.
31. Amitai-Preiss, 'New Material', p. 26.
32. Rashid al-Din, *Jami' al-Tawarikh*, pp. 1124–6, 1141–8.
33. Rashid al-Din, *Jami' al-Tawarikh*, pp. 1155–6.
34. Aubin, *Emirs Mongols*, p. 42.
35. Wassaf, *Ketab-e Mostatab*, p. 241.
36. Rashid al-Din, *Jami' al-Tawarikh*, pp. 1192–6.
37. Aubin, *Emirs Mongols*, pp. 25–8.
38. Ghazan's first appointment of Sadr al-Din to the head of the bureaucracy is only recorded in one version of the *Blessed History*, catalogued as the λ recension in Appendix B and discussed in Chapters 3, 5 and 6. While this was a late modification to the text, it adheres more closely to the court journals on which the narrative is based, and so is to be trusted in matters such as administrative appointments.
39. Rashid al-Din, *Jami' al-Tawarikh*, pp. 1197–9; Wassaf, *Ketab-e Mostatab*, pp. 270–5; Bar Hebraeus, *The Chronography*, pp. 496–7.
40. Kirmani, *Nasa'im al-Ashar*, p. 112.
41. On this latter interpretation, see Hoffmann, *Waqf*, p. 70.
42. 'Aqili, *Athar al-Wuzara'*, p. 285; Khwandamir, *Dastur*, p. 316.
43. Bar Hebraeus, *The Chronography*, p. 496.
44. On the connection of Galenic medicine and food, see Porman and Savage-Smith, *Medieval Islamic Medicine*, pp. 41–71. On the title of *ba'urchi*, see Allsen, *Culture and Conquest*, pp. 127–9.
45. Bar Hebraeus, *The Chronography*, pp. 487–91.
46. Rashid al-Din, *Jami' al-Tawarikh*, p. 1284.
47. Rashid al-Din, *Jami' al-Tawarikh*, p. 1208.
48. Rashid al-Din, *Jami' al-Tawarikh*, p. 1217; Wassaf, *Ketab-e Mostatab*, p. 314.
49. The career of Nauruz is one of the portions of Ilkhanid history most illuminated by 'Abd Allah Qashani's alternate history of the early career of Ghazan, discussed in Chapters 3, 5 and 6. The events related here are a collation of Rashid al-Din's main version and Qashani's: Rashid al-Din, *Jami' al-Tawarikh*, pp. 1226–67; Rashid al-Din, *Jami' al-Tawarikh* (ed. Alizada), p. 577–619. See also Wassaf, *Ketab-e Mostatab*, pp. 313–27.

50. On Ghazan's rebellion against Baidu, see Boyle, 'Dynastic and Political History', pp. 375–9.
51. On this, see Chapter 3, as well as Kamola, 'Beyond History'.
52. This is found in manuscripts of the λ recension, catalogued in Appendix B. It aligns with other contemporary accounts, as discussed by Melville, '*Pādshāh-i Islām*'. Brack, 'Mediating Sacred Kingship', pp. 327–38 definitively shows Qashani to be the author of this alternate narrative.
53. Rashid al-Din, *Jamiʿ al-Tawarikh* (ed. Alizada), p. 604.
54. Pfeiffer, 'Reflections', pp. 372–6.
55. Rashid al-Din, *Jamiʿ al-Tawarikh*, p. 1259.
56. Wassaf, *Ketab-e Mostatab*, p. 325.
57. Wassaf, *Ketab-e Mostatab*, p. 326.
58. Aubin, *Emirs Mongols*, p. 62.
59. Broadbridge, 'Marriage, Family and Politics', pp. 132–3.
60. Aubin, *Emirs Mongols*, pp. 62–3.
61. Wassaf, *Ketab-e Mostatab*, p. 329.
62. Safadi, *Kitab al-wafi*, vol. 25, p. 227.
63. Shabankara'i, *Majmaʿ al-Ansab*, p. 214. Kirmani, *Nasaʾim al-Ashar*, p. 112, mentions that he was put in charge of 'some of the provinces of the state' without specifying which ones.
64. Rashid al-Din, *Jamiʿ al-Tawarikh*, pp. 1283–5.
65. Kirmani, *Nasaʾim al-Ashar*, p. 112; Hamd Allah Mustaufi, *Tarikh-e Gozideh*, p. 604.
66. The general pattern of the vizier denounced by other bureaucrats and executed in disgrace is a narrative pattern in Persian historiography that stretches far beyond the Ilkhanate: Meisami, 'History as literature', pp. 42–52; Melville, 'The Historian at Work', pp. 73–80.
67. Lambton has called this a 'temporary break' in the larger continuity of the Perso-Islamic institution of the vizierate: Lambton, *Continuity and Change*, pp. 50–1.
68. Wassaf, *Ketab-e Mostatab*, p. 347.
69. Wassaf, *Ketab-e Mostatab*, p. 374.
70. Amitai-Preiss, 'New Material', pp. 28–9.
71. Rashid al-Din, *Jamiʿ al-Tawarikh*, p. 1311.
72. Hamd Allah Mustaufi, *Tarikh-e Gozideh*, p. 604.
73. Broadbridge, *Kingship and Ideology*, pp. 64–98.
74. Gilli-Elewy, *Bagdad*, pp. 99–118.
75. Rashid al-Din, *Jamiʿ al-Tawarikh*, p. 1324; Wassaf, *Ketab-e Mostatab*, p. 384.

76. On the first campaign, see Wassaf, *Ketab-e Mostatab*, pp. 371–81; Rashid al-Din, *Jami' al-Tawarikh*, pp. 1289–96; Boyle, 'Dynastic and Political History', pp. 387–9.
77. Amitai, 'Wādī 'l-Khaznadār'; Amitai, 'The Logistics'.
78. For a detailed discussion of the content and significance of this genealogical ideology, see Brack, 'Mediating Sacred Kingship', pp. 152–62.
79. On the second Syrian campaign, see Rashid al-Din, *Jami' al-Tawarikh*, pp. 1297–9; Boyle, 'Dynastic and Political History', p. 389.
80. Broadbridge, *Kingship and Ideology*, pp. 81–5.

3

Mongol Dynastic History, 1302–1304

After Ghazan's withdrawal across Mesopotamia in early 1301, it would be more than two years before the *ilkhan* again crossed the Euphrates River and marched into Mamluk territory. During that period, Ghazan cultivated a new hybrid political ideology that drew on Mongol, Islamic and Iranian precedent. As part of this new statement of royal authority, Ghazan began patronising new historical writing. This chapter traces the emergence of royally sponsored historiography in the Ilkhanate. The works that Ghazan commissioned were not the first historical works written under the *ilkhans*, but they were the first to respond to direct royal demands for a history that supported their claim to rule the eastern Islamic world. This effort culminated with the *Blessed History of Ghazan* (*Tarikh-e Mobarak-e Ghazani*) that Rashid al-Din composed for his patron in the early years of the fourteenth century.

New Approaches to an Old Problem

Rashid al-Din's narrative of Ghazan's slow retreat in 1301 draws three historical legacies together in Ghazan's performance as a ruler. He is at once portrayed as a reverent Muslim with a particular devotion to the partisans of 'Ali, a Mongol hunter and warrior, and a manifestation of the royal splendour of Sasanian kings. Having crossed the Euphrates on 2 February 1301, Ghazan visited the shrine to the martyrs of the Battle of Siffin and then spent three months in upper Mesopotamia. During this time, he engaged in hunting, reportedly performing a miraculous feat of archery, which Rashid al-Din explicitly compares with the legendary shot of the Sasanian Shah Bahram V Gur (421–38).[1] As part of that story, Bahram, acting on a request of his slave, Azada, strips a buck gazelle of his horns with a two-headed arrow and then pins another gazelle's head, foot and back together with a single arrow.

By comparison, Rashid al-Din tells us that Ghazan pierced all four feet and the body of an antelope using the distinctly Mongol type of arrow called a *tona*, leaving a total of nine wounds on the animal's body.[2]

Rashid al-Din's account of the following months describes a continuous escalation of activity aimed at bolstering Ghazan's legitimacy as a Muslim, Mongol and Iranian sovereign. However, at the time of the retreat itself, Rashid al-Din's work was still a couple years off. Ghazan would have to make one more failed attempt to invade Syria before trying a new approach – both in the invasion of Syria and in his choice of how to commemorate it. In early October 1301, he arrived at Ala Tagh, in the mountains of Azerbaijan. In other years, Ala Tagh had served as a summer residence, so this was an unseasonal visit. However, Ghazan had dispatched Qutlughshah to Diyar Bakr less than two weeks before arriving at Ala Tagh, but then recalled the general in early November and withdrew from Ala Tagh to the shores of the Caspian Sea. The pattern of sending Qutlughshah ahead in previous years, and the unprecedented act of moving to Ala Tagh in the autumn, suggest that Ghazan intended to invade Mamluk territory once more during the winter of 1301/2, trying an even more northerly route than the one he had taken in the previous two years.

Our sources do not tell us why Ghazan's new invasion never materialised. However, at the same time that this northerly campaign was floundering, a leading figure among the Shi'ite community of Iraq, Safi al-Din Muhammad Ibn al-Tiqtaqa, was taking shelter from heavy rains in the city of Mosul, on the upper Tigris River. While Ghazan withdrew towards the Caspian, Ibn al-Tiqtaqa began on 1 February to copy out an Arabic treatise combining a short essay on governance with a history of the caliphs from Abu Bakr (632–4) to al-Musta'sim (1242–58). Four months later, he dedicated the work to Mosul's governor, Fakhr al-Din 'Isa ibn Ibrahim, after whom it has come to be known as the *Fakhri*.[3] The *Fakhri* is a hybrid work, just one of series of texts from the late Saljuq world that describe the past in order to instruct their readers in proper behaviour and good governance.[4] Originally composed in Arabic, it was translated into Persian in 1323, a testament not only the work's popularity, but also to the gradual ascendance of Persian as a language of historical writing in the Ilkhanid period.[5]

Most of the historical information in the *Fakhri* is unoriginal, and much of it derives immediately from the universal history of Ibn al-Athir, who had written seventy years earlier for the previous Zangid lords of Mosul. When he writes about the *ilkhan*s themselves, Ibn al-Tiqtaqa generally accepts their legitimacy as sovereigns in the Islamic world: he portrays Hulegu as the 'just infidel' who deserves to rule by virtue of having defeated the corrupt political hierarchy of the late caliphate.[6] Elsewhere, he attributes to Ghazan a unique concern for the proper reverence of the Qur'an.[7] Ibn al-Tiqtaqa's most noteworthy contribution to the historical memory of the Mongols, however, is to depict them as ignorant of the importance of historical writing. Early in the *Fakhri*, he asserts that historical anecdotes and biographies constitute the most important field of study for rulers such as his patron, and he emphasises the significance of his own work as a teaching text. In contrast to this, he criticises the actions of 'ministers of old', who hid such didactic works from their sovereigns and who wrote in ornate chancellery prose in order to keep their patrons dependent on the administrative class.[8] Ibn al-Tiqtaqa advocates for an educated royalty, able to discern just action through their study of the past.

Ibn al-Tiqtaqa directs his disdain for the stylistic writing and the high-handed behaviour of ministers specifically against the historian and governor of Baghdad, 'Ala' al-Din 'Ata Malik Juvayni. He can perhaps be forgiven this antipathy: until 1281, Ibn al-Tiqtaqa's father had worked under the Juvaynis in the fiscal administration of the Ilkhanate, but then lost his life in a political struggle against 'Ala' al-Din.[9] Over the course of his text, Ibn al-Tiqtaqa accuses Juvayni of underappreciating the ruler's education and of misrepresenting aspects of Mongol royal culture, such as the scope of Chinggis Khan's hunting operations or the purpose of the Mongol system of postal relays.[10] Juvayni bears the harshest criticism for keeping his Mongol patrons in the dark about the didactic value of history, but Ibn al-Tiqtaqa reserves a share of blame for the *ilkhan*s themselves, claiming that they dismissed all scholarship not directly contributing to affairs of state.[11] This then offers an opportunity for the author to praise Fakhr al-Din and his family for having maintained a tradition of scholarship despite the bad example set by their new Mongol overlords.

In his criticism of the Mongols as poor students of history, Ibn al-Tiqtaqa echoes the sentiment of an earlier historian writing under an Inner

Asian nomadic dynasty. In the early to mid-twelfth century, Abu'l-Sharaf Jarbadhqani prepared a Persian translation of Muhammad ibn ʿAbd al-Jaffar al-ʿUtbi's history of Mahmud of Ghazna (998–1030), the *Kitab al-Yamini*. In the introduction of his translation, Jarbadhqani laments that the Saljuqs under whom he wrote had taken no interest in commissioning a history of their own dynasty. As a result, Jarbadhqani asserts, 'the memory of the Saljuqs ... will soon vanish, and their name will be erased from the rolls of the mind ... no one will remember them, and there will remain no memorial to their efforts'.[12] History has not entirely forgotten the Saljuqs, though we rely on perilously few contemporary sources for our basic narrative of their rule.[13] Notably, many of the most prominent writers of Saljuq history did not write at the dynasty's behest, but for one another.[14] A scholar-bureaucrat living under the Saljuqs could not expect much by way of royal patronage to record and preserve the events of recent history, but as a group, the class of scholar-bureaucrats maintained the practice of historical writing. Such an esoteric practice gave rise to the high chancellery prose that increasingly marks historiography from the period and which Ibn al-Tiqtaqa so despised.

A significant change to this pattern came just as Ibn al-Tiqtaqa was writing his critique of the Mongol rulers. Beginning in 1302, after his third failed attempt to invade Syria, Ghazan Khan undertook a major programme of historical patronage, commissioning narratives of the past that helped to articulate his family's claim to sovereignty. These works aimed to integrate the Mongols' nomadic Inner Asian heritage into Perso-Islamic traditions of historical thinking. This new project of ideology broadcast through historical writing became particularly important in light of the end of the Abbasid caliphate. As Ghazan reinvented the Ilkhanate as an Islamic state, the uncomfortable legacy of Hulegu as the killer of the last caliph had to be replaced by a more palatable story. As a result, the stylised chancellery prose of earlier historiography was tamed into a more concise and ideologically potent narrative demonstrating the role the Mongols were to play in the Islamic world. No work met this ideological challenge as effectively as the *Blessed History* of Rashid al-Din, but others contributed to it, creating an intellectual context in which to read that work.

Early Ilkhanid Historiography

Ibn al-Tiqtaqa's criticism of the *ilkhan*s as poor patrons of historical writing does not mean that no history was written in the first forty-five years of Ilkhanid rule, only that the new rulers took no direct role in supporting it.[15] Works such as the chronicles of Bar Hebraeus or of various Armenian authors served to reaffirm the collective identities of non-Muslim communities in the face of new political realities.[16] In Fars, where the Turkic dynasty of Salghurids governed as Saljuq appointees, a Zoroastrian apocalyptic tradition was updated, adding Chinggis Khan to a list including Alexander the Great and the Arabs, foreign invaders whose appearance brought new struggles for the Zoroastrian community of Iran.[17]

Historical writing also remained active among the community of Muslim bureaucrats working for the Ilkhanid state. They continued the practice of scholar-bureaucrats of the Saljuq period, who wrote histories for one another, despite their patrons' general disinterest in the genre. Such works were produced in the proximity of the new Mongol power, but did not involve direct royal patronage in the same way as the great building projects at Maragha and Azargoshnasp. Instead, they were written by and for the highly literate servants of the state. Between 1260 and 1284, at least three histories appeared from the pens of these scholar-bureaucrats. Viewed together, they reveal early efforts to incorporate the new Mongol rulers first into the narrative of Perso-Islamic history and then into the practice of cultural patronage that Ibn al-Tiqtaqa so valued, and they set the stage for Rashid al-Din's definitive history of the Mongol royal family.

Juvayni's History of the World Conqueror

The first Persian history produced under the *ilkhan*s had its roots in the Oyirad governor Arghun's repeated visits to Qaraqorum, as he helped to steward the Middle East away from Batu's sphere of influence and towards that of the central court. As discussed in Chapter 1, 'Ala' al-Din Juvayni, son of the long-serving *ṣāḥib-dīwān* Baha' al-Din, joined Arghun on three of these embassies. As a result of his visits to the central Mongol court, Juvayni writes, his friends and colleagues encouraged him to write a history of the rise of the Mongols.[18] Here at the beginning of the work, we already hear an echo of the situation under the Saljuqs, as scholar-bureaucrats inspired each other to continue the practice of writing about the past. The resulting work, the *History of the World Conqueror* (*Tarikh-e Jahangosha*), tells of the rise of Chinggis Khan and of his descendants through the time of Mongke and Hulegu, ending with the fall of the Isma'ili strongholds in 1256.[19] As part of this history, Juvayni offers a lengthy and sympathetic view of the Khwarazmian state that had suffered the brunt of Chinggis Khan's initial invasion. Coming from a family with a history of service to the Khwarazmshahs, Juvayni reveals his intimate knowledge of and nostalgia for the defunct state.[20]

The *History of the World Conqueror* is one of two works appearing at the dawn of the Ilkhanate that wrestle with the question of how to understand the presence of the Mongols within an Islamic society. The challenge facing Juvayni in this regard is made evident by comparing his work with a contemporary one written for the Ghurid sultan of Delhi, Nasir al-Din Mahmud (1246–66) by Minhaj al-Siraj Juzjani.[21] Named the *Nasiri Chapters* (*Tabaqat-e Nasiri*) after its dedicatee, Juzjani's work persistently condemns the Mongols as apocalyptic agents, come to destroy the civilisation of Islam.[22] For Juzjani, the only bright spot in the wasteland of Mongol history is the Jochid khan Berke, whose conversion represents a thin silver lining to the devastations of Chinggis Khan and Hulegu. By contrast, Juvayni lived and worked within the Mongol state, and had a vested interest in presenting it as a justifiable, if not an ideal political arrangement. He does not shy away from relating the devastation of Chinggis Khan's first invasion, but he casts that disaster as a form of punishment for the collective sins of Muslim society, a historical tonic, rather than an apocalypse. Juvayni is also willing to see merit in Mongol rulers, praising Ogedei's generous nature as Great Khan and emphasising Hulegu's more constructive activities when compared with those of Chinggis Khan.[23] He even offers an interpretation of traditional Mongol law (*yasa*) that casts it largely in accord with Islamic *shari'a*.[24]

Of greatest benefit to Islam, from Juvayni's perspective, was Hulegu's eradication of the heretical Isma'ili threat, and he ends his *History* with the fall of the strongholds of Alamut and Maymundiz. Juvayni's decision to omit the conquest of Baghdad may have been a simple matter of having to leave the work unfinished. He stopped writing soon after 1260, by which time Hulegu had appointed him governor of Baghdad. As he assumed administrative responsibilities, he may not have been able to continue his work, which shows itself in several places not to have received final editing.[25] Juvayni may, however, have had other reasons for not continuing his work through to the end of Hulegu's campaign. As he wrote, the fall of Baghdad was still very recent memory, and the shockwaves it sent through the Sunni community still reverberated quite loudly. The tentative steps that Juvayni takes to normalise the Mongol conquest would have been entirely undone if he rehearsed the cultural trauma marked by the end of the caliphate. By omitting this portion of Hulegu's campaign, Juvayni marks the fall of the Ismaʿilis as the beginning of a new historical moment. In Juvayni's work, the fall of the Ismaʿilis serves the same purpose that Berke's conversion does for Juzjani, ending the otherwise traumatic history of the Mongol conquests on a promising note. In a sense, each author in his own way accomplishes the same result as the updated Zoroastrian apocalyptic text, ending on an optimistic note for the ultimate salvation of the religious community to which the author belonged.

Besides rectifying the Mongol conquest with Islamic ideas about the fate of the community of believers, Juvayni draws extensively on Iranian historical traditions to illuminate his narrative. In particular, he frequently cites the *Shahnameh* of Abu'l-Qasim Firdausi, which also provided visual and textual decoration for Abaqa's palace at Azargoshnasp. The *Shahnameh* is a universal history of the Iranian world, stitching various Iranian heroic tales together into a contiguous narrative spanning from the legendary first man Gayumars up through the time of the Arab conquest.[26] In combining these tales, Firdausi gave them a cyclical pattern, in which the history of the Sasanian period (224–651) echoes that of the semi-legendary Kayanians.[27] Each of these great periods ends with an equally great conquest, the same conquests that so concerned the writers of Zoroastrian apocalyptic literature, namely, those of Alexander the Great and the Arab Muslims.

Firdausi's poetic epic was not immediately popular as a vision of history, even at the court of its dedicatee, Mahmud of Ghazna. Mahmud's court poet Farrukhi called the work 'a lie from end to end' and only scant references survive of the poem or its author from the first two centuries after it was written.[28] As mentioned in Chapter 1, the knowledge and use of Firdausi's text in western Iran was particularly limited on the eve of the

Mongol invasion, while the poem enjoyed some popularity among the court panegyricists of the eastern courts.

Juvayni, raised in this eastern Iranian intellectual milieu, is the first historian whose work engages the *Shahnameh* on a theoretical level by drawing the Mongols into the historical pattern that Firdausi had laid down. For Firdausi, the conquests of Alexander and the Muslims set the stage for new periods of historical greatness; his poem expresses confidence in the contemporary resurgence of Iranian dynasties and the New Persian language at the turn of the eleventh century. For Juvayni to refer so frequently to the *Shahnameh* draws his history into the historical perspective of Firdausi's epic: for Juvayni, the rubble of the Mongol conquest might become the foundation for a more unified and stable Iranian and Islamic community.

In addition to adopting Firdausi's pattern for the shape of history on a large scale, Juvayni deliberately cites the *Shahnameh* to juxtapose specific events from the recent past with episodes from the heroic Iranian tradition.[29] The *History of the World Conqueror*, like Abaqa's palace built just a few years later, surrounds the *ilkhan*s with reminders of a historical tradition that could be read as a model for their own state. Of course, the Mongols themselves were at this point probably unable to understand these Persian textual and visual cues for how to think about the passage of history. Juvayni, like his predecessors working for the Saljuqs, wrote primarily for others like himself, offering them a familiar lens through which to view the new lords of the eastern Islamic world.

Baydawi's New Historical Order

Even though Juvayni finished his *History of the World Conqueror* around the time that Hulegu appointed him as governor of Baghdad, the work is really a part of the events of the 1250s that brought Mongke to the position of Great Khan and Hulegu to the Middle East as a new sovereign presence. The work itself is dedicated to perpetuating the glory of Mongke, even though the Great Khan had no role in its production and likely did not even know about its existence. Juvayni's opportunity to travel to Qaraqorum and learn about the history of the young empire, and his subsequent position in the Ilkhanid administration, were shaped by his family's origins in the east of Iran. Growing up in that region, he would have gained an intimate knowledge of the *Shahnameh* and of the Khwarazmian state, and so it was only natural that he brought that background to bear on his history of the Mongols.

In subsequent decades, as Hulegu consolidated his control over the rest of the Iranian plateau and Mesopotamia, individuals from different regions and different backgrounds began to join the Ilkhanid administration. At the same time, dynastic histories began to focus on Hulegu's branch of the Mongol royal family, creating a uniquely Ilkhanid historiography. Beyond the families from Qazvin noted in Chapter 2, one significant political centre that sent representatives to the Ilkhanid court was Fars, where the Turkic Salghurid dynasty had ruled since seizing *de facto* independence from the weakening Saljuqs in 1148. Khwarazmshah Muhammad had captured and ransomed the Salghurid Sa'd b. Zangi (1198–1226) only a few years before Chinggis Khan's invasion, which came just in time to spare the Salghurids further setbacks at Khwarazmian hands. As a result, Sa'd's son, Abu Bakr (1226–60) willingly offered tribute to Ogedei, who reciprocated by bestowing on Abu Bakr the title of Qutlugh Khan and confirming the Salghurids as nominal governors of Fars.[30]

Recognition of Mongol suzerainty came with significant financial obligations and the acceptance of an administrative representative in Shiraz. Hulegu never needed to campaign in Fars to consider it part of his realm, and other *ilkhan*s kept out of the region as well. In 1263, Hulegu appointed a Salghurid princess, Abish Khatun, as governor, and a year later she was married to his son Mengu Timur, who thus became a royal representative for the dynasty in the south of Iran. After Mengu Timur's death in 1282, Abish Khatun was implicated in a local resistance effort to shed Mongol control. She was arrested and died in custody in Tabriz in 1286.[31]

Since Fars escaped the direct ravages of the early Mongol conquest, intellectual and cultural activity continued there unabated throughout the early Ilkhanid period. Most famously, the poet Sa'di (1292) took his pen name in honour of Abu Bakr b. Sa'd Qutlugh Khan, to whom he dedicated the first of his two major works, the *Bustan*. (Abu Bakr's son, also named Sa'd, was the recipient of Sa'di's other great work, the *Golestan*.) Another influential scholar from Salghurid Shiraz was the cleric and judge Nasir al-Din 'Abd Allah al-Baydawi (d. 1316?). He is most famous as an author of Qur'anic commentary and grammatical works, which tend to summarise and condense the works of earlier writers, rather than make original contributions to their respective fields. Of a similar nature is Baydawi's short historical work, the *Order of Histories* (*Nizam al-Tawarikh*).

Quite unlike Juvayni, who modelled his work on Firdausi's *Shahnameh* to include the Mongols in a cyclical model of Iranian history, Baydawi adds the Mongols to an expanding catalogue of non-caliphal dynasties. His model for this is the *Ornament of Accounts* (*Zayn al-Akhbar*) of Abu Saʿid ʿAbd al-Hayy Gardizi. Writing in the middle of the eleventh century for the Ghaznavid Sultan ʿAbd al-Rashid (1049–52), Gardizi compiled the history of Islam alongside that of the dynasties of Khurasan from the rise of Islam to the year 1041.[32] Following this pattern, Baydawi's *Order of Histories* tells briefly of the pre-Islamic Iranian past, followed by the story of Muhammad and the Rashidun, Umayyad and ʿAbbasid caliphs, and continues with the histories of the independent rulers of Iran from the Saffarids to the Khwarazmshahs. Baydawi then adds to these Iranian and Turkic dynasties a section on the *ilkhan*s.[33]

As is his practice with his theological and grammatical writings, Baydawi offers a condensed version of accounts from other texts, explicitly declaring his intent to abridge and explain the course of human existence as it has been recorded in 'reliable chronicles' so that it might have widespread benefit.[34] By presenting the *ilkhan*s alongside dynasties like the Samanids, Ghaznavids and Saljuqs that had previously been included in the Islamic historiographical tradition, Baydawi validates their rule, not necessarily as the epochal agents who initiate a new era of Iranian greatness, but as legitimate rulers in their own right. Already in Gardizi's work, this model of historical writing emphasised the transfer of authority between co-equally legitimate dynasties.[35] Baydawi simply adds the Mongols as one more iteration of the pattern.

Baydawi's aim in writing was not purely scholarly, but also had a professional motivation. He produced the first version of his work around 1279. Notably, it was neither commissioned by nor addressed to the Ilkhan Abaqa, whose energies were focused on the capital region of Azerbaijan and on various military conflicts on the Syrian and Central Asian frontiers. Instead, it was offered as a tribute to the Mongol Amir Sughunchaq, whom Abaqa had sent to Fars to investigate tax revenues.[36] Also in 1279, and perhaps in response to these blandishments, Sughunchaq attempted to have Baydawi appointed as chief judge of Fars, the same position that Baydawi's father had once held.

The *Order of Histories* was thus perhaps the first history written under the *ilkhan*s with the express purpose of securing political appointment, though this was not done by direct appeal to the *ilkhan*. At the end of his work, Baydawi praises Sughunchaq and Shams al-Din Juvayni for their generosity and justice. Baydawi says of Shams al-Din and his family that they were 'from among the hereditary lords of Khurasan, and during the time of former sultans, the binding and loosing of Khurasan was in their possession'.[37] Such a specific mention of Khurasan as the domain of the Juvayni family serves as a fitting homage to the influence of eastern Iranian scholar-bureaucrats at the central court during the reign of Abaqa. As a son of Fars, Baydawi worked to retain his own family's prominence in his home region, recognising that he now owed his position to foreigners, be they Mongol *amir*s or Khurasani scholars.

While acknowledging the importance of the eastern Iranian administrators who ran the state alongside the Mongol military elite, Baydawi introduces a specifically southern perspective that remained a distinct component of the genre of historical writing as it developed in subsequent centuries. This is most evident in his choice of which dynasties to include. The significance of including the Mongols has already been discussed. Baydawi also includes his own patrons, the Salghurids of Fars. Given his personal history, he was particularly well qualified to do this, and this is the most original section of the entire work. In addition to being of local interest, though, the Salghurids offer Baydawi a model of kingship against which to compare others, including the *ilkhan*s. The Salghurids consciously cultivated their own credentials as an Iranian and Islamic dynasty, in part through their association of Achaemenid ruins with the history of pre-Islamic Iran.[38] In this way, the choice to include them in the *Order of Histories* serves a parallel function to the rebuilding of the site of the Zoroastrian fire temple of Azargoshnasp as a royal palace. Both projects link the Mongols to the sites of pre-Islamic Iranian empires, real or imagined. While the tilework of Abaqa's palace, rich with visual and textual citations of the *Shahnameh*, recalls the Zoroastrian and Sasanian past, Salghurid memorialisation of the ruins of Pasargadae and

Persepolis emphasised their imagined association with both the Zoroastrian and the Judeo-Islamic prophetic traditions.

Fittingly for someone of Baydawi's legal training, his account of Salghurid history also emphasises the dynasty's credentials through numerous references to the Islamic institutions and clergy in their realm. Baydawi's Salghurids are exemplary patrons of the faith, just as Ibn al-Tiqtaqa portrayed Fakhr al-Din of Mosul two decades later. If Juvayni makes an effort to show that Mongol and Muslim societies are compatible, Baydawi actively solicits cultural patronage of religious scholarship by the Mongol *ilkhan*s and their *amir*s, and he looks ahead to the possibility of their conversion to Islam.

Mulla Qutb's Anonymous History

Another native of Fars who entered Mongol service in the early years of the Ilkhanate was Qutb al-Din Shirazi (1236–1311). He was a scion of the prominent Kazaruni family of physicians and had taken over his father's hospital position in Shiraz at the precocious age of fourteen.[39] Qutb al-Din came to Maragha originally to advance his medical studies. In this he was disappointed, but he soon became Nasir al-Din Tusi's most prominent student of mathematics. Over time he made significant contributions to the astronomical activities of the observatory, developing a new algorithm for modelling the movement of Mercury in the sky.[40]

Qutb al-Din also studied philosophy at Maragha, and several of Tusi's philosophical works survive in manuscripts copied by his student.[41] In his own later philosophical work, Qutb al-Din produced treatises on the nascent philosophy of Illuminationism, works that remain central to the Iranian philosophical tradition. Illuminationism had its origins in the work of Shihab al-Din Suhrawardi (1154–91), who began to articulate a radical gnostic theory of immediate and inspired cognition before his execution on the orders of Saladin.[42] In the very earliest period of the Mongol conquests, the prodigious mystical philosopher Ibn 'Arabi (d. 1240) developed the basic premises of Illuminationist thought, and Tusi's own work demonstrates some undeveloped features of this new philosophy.[43] Despite these early steps, Illuminationism was still only beginning to take formal shape by the late thirteenth century. Qutb al-Din's exposure to and development of this new strand of philosophy at Maragha suggests just how active that scholarly community was, producing works in fields far removed from the original mission of the observatory. That this happened at the hands of a teacher from eastern Iran and a student from the south further demonstrates how the new Mongol state began to break down regional circles of political patronage and create a unified Iranian intellectual space in which hybrid strands of Islamic theology and philosophy that had previously been suppressed as unorthodox and treasonous could flourish.

By 1282, Qutb al-Din was living in Anatolia, serving as judge of Siwas and Malatya, and preparing a commentary to the first chapter of the *Canon of Medicine* (*Qanun fi'l-Tibb*) by the eleventh-century doctor and philosopher Ibn Sina (980–1037). That was the year that Ahmad Teguder took the throne of the Ilkhanate, temporarily sparing the Juvaynis from the persecution they ultimately faced under Arghun. After coming to the throne, Teguder appointed Qutb al-Din to lead a delegation to Mamluk Cairo to announce the accession of the Muslim *ilkhan* as grounds to broker peace between the two states.[44] This peace was never achieved, in part because Ahmad Teguder's reign was so short, and when Arghun finally came to the throne in 1284, the project was abandoned.

Under these circumstances, and still in Anatolia, Qutb al-Din in 1286 copied out a manuscript containing a collection of short works, including treatises on Illuminationism and on conversion from Judaism to Islam, as well as several selections of poetry.[45] Tucked among these other works is a short historical text titled *Accounts of the Mongols* (*Akhbar-e Moghulan*).[46] In thirty-four short manuscript pages, the *Accounts* offer a brief dynastic history of the Mongols and *ilkhan*s from 1203 to the accession of Arghun in 1284. While technically anonymous, certain aspects of this text suggest that Qutb al-Din or someone close to him was responsible for it.[47]

The *Accounts* consist of a series of historical notes organised chronologically, but with no clear divisions between years or reigns.[48] The work preserves a large number of precise dates which, along with the title, suggests that its author had access to official court journals or records of events. It demonstrates a particular interest in and familiarity with the marital and blood relations between members of the Ilkhanid royal family and the highest stratum of the Mongol military elite. This same intimate knowledge of the ruling family and of daily affairs of court also marks the work of ʿAbd Allah

Qashani, discussed below and in Chapter 4. The narrative of the *Accounts*, inasmuch as there is one, is structured around the course of military campaigns and battles, including a uniquely detailed account of the siege of Isma'ili fortresses in 1256. This military history is punctuated by anecdotal accounts of events at court, including a dramatic telling of Majd al-Mulk's attacks against the Juvayni brothers.

Throughout the *Accounts*, events are dated using the Muslim *hijri* calendar, with the sole exception of the opening passage, which tells of Chinggis Khan's retreat to Lake Baljuna in summer 1203. The retreat to Baljuna marked the lowest point in Chinggis Khan's military career; after it, he rose from success to success to gain control over all the peoples of the steppe. This passage in the *Accounts* is dated according to the *hijri* calendar, as well as those of the Persians, Greeks, Uyghurs and Chinese. In one version of the astronomical tables prepared at Maragha, Nasir al-Din Tusi had used exactly the same synchronisation of calendars to date the Baljuna congress, marking it as the beginning of the Mongol Empire.[49]

The *Accounts* exhibit a keen awareness of military campaigns (including those in Anatolia where Qutb al-Din was living when he copied it), as well as dynastic affairs and the intellectual activities underway at Maragha. All of this suggests an author with direct access to the centre of Ilkhanid power and the documents and scholarship produced there: in short, someone very much like Qutb al-Din Shirazi. Whether Qutb al-Din was the work's author or he copied it from the notes of an otherwise unknown colleague, the *Accounts* reveal that court records existed of the events of early Ilkhanid history, though they may not have been particularly well organised. It also shows that, as a result of the work underway at Maragha, the events of Mongol history could be correlated not only to the calendar of the Islamic world, but also to those of other civilisations. Both of these circumstances – the existence of raw historical documents at the Ilkhanid court and the awareness and usability of foreign calendric traditions – bear directly on Rashid al-Din's later efforts to produce a more uniform narrative of the Mongols in the Middle East. It is, then, perhaps not surprising that the sole manuscript containing the *Accounts* bears the seal of the library that Rashid al-Din endowed late in his life as part of his own programme of cultural patronage (on which, see Chapter 4).

Whoever its author was, the existence of the *Accounts* confirms what has already been suggested by Baydawi's *Order of Histories*, namely, that, by the early 1280s, the Mongol *ilkhan*s had become the subjects of Persian dynastic historical writing. Furthermore, such writing could be based on court documentation and attuned to the internal politics of the dynasty. This was true even though the *ilkhan*s themselves were not yet involved in commissioning narrative histories. Furthermore, if Qutb al-Din was in fact the author of the *Accounts*, the work can be seen as having a professional motivation similar to Baydawi's. About a third of the text of the *Accounts* is dedicated to Arghun's revolt against Ahmad Teguder in 1284. Its effect is to justify the coup by portraying Ahmad Teguder as an inept ruler, suggesting that someone at Arghun's court, perhaps the *ilkhan* himself, was the intended recipient of the work. Qutb al-Din's previous involvement in broadcasting Ahmad Teguder's conversion to Islam and seeking peace with the Mamluks may have become a political liability after the rise of Arghun. In this light, the *Accounts* can be read as a political apology, showing its author to be a loyal supporter of the new regime.

Qutb al-Din Shirazi did enjoy further Mongol patronage, but mostly under Arghun's son Oljeitu Sultan (1304–16). By then, many of the Mongols in the Middle East, including the ruling family, had converted to Islam. In this earlier period, his decision to include the *Accounts* among the religious and philosophical tracts of his 1286 manuscript help us to understand how the Mongols gradually became the subject of Persian historical writing. It, along with Baydawi's *Order of Histories* and Juvayni's *History of the World Conqueror*, show a steady production of Mongol dynastic historiography under the early *ilkhan*s. However, as Ibn al-Tiqtaqa complains, those early *ilkhan*s had little use for these works. That changed, however, in the same year that Ibn al-Tiqtaqa wrote his *Fakhri*, as Ghazan regrouped for a new military and ideological challenge to the Mamluks of Egypt.

A New Historical Sensitivity

Ghazan spent the spring of 1302 hunting, as he had done after his failed campaign the previous year. This included time spent around the shore of the Caspian Sea catching swans and cranes. In his narrative of this activity, Rashid al-Din describes a Mongol hunt: an elaborate battue was constructed, by which animals could be funnelled into a confined space to be killed.⁵⁰ Hunting was not just a Mongol royal pastime, though. Sasanian art depicts similarly massive hunting expeditions as a marker of royal legitimation, analogous in its iconography to the pursuit of war. This hunting retreat and Rashid al-Din's elaborate description of it was perhaps intended in lieu of the aborted invasions of Mamluk Syria, and it ties Ghazan to both Mongol and Iranian ideas about successful military rulers. During this time, Ghazan wrote a letter to Pope Boniface VIII, which by its language appears to be just one entry in a larger correspondence on the possibility of a joint expedition against the Mamluks.⁵¹ As part of this letter, Ghazan recognises the pope's legitimacy as a sovereign power, showing that he was not above acknowledging foreign political entities, even if the Mongol and Islamic ideologies that he deployed in the service of his own reign were both fiercely totalising claims.

That summer, Ghazan held a *quriltai* at Ujan, which marked, as on earlier occasions, the ceremonial beginning of a new campaign into Syria. This time, however, rather than take either of the northern routes from previous campaigns, Ghazan turned south. During a processional advance through Iraq, Ghazan again engaged in a series of activities redolent with both Mongol and Islamic historical significance, projecting a particular image of himself as the embodied synthesis of these two traditions. At Ujan, he declared his own humility in the service of God and ordered the distribution of alms and recitations of scripture. Departing the Ilkhanid capital region, Ghazan travelled south, stopping to visit a shrine he had commissioned at Buzinjird and then at the site of a tree under which he had once camped while hunting down Nauruz and his family. On this later stop, according to Rashid al-Din, Ghazan listened to a story told by the Mongol envoy Bolad Chingsang about his royal ancestor Qutula, who had similarly achieved victory over an enemy after having supplicated God at a tree shrine.⁵²

A further episode from this tour into lower Mesopotamia illustrates the image that Ghazan projected of himself as a living synthesis of Mongol and Muslim tradition. 'Abd Allah Qashani reports the murder and cremation of a descendant of 'Ali during Friday prayers in Baghdad sometime during the *hijri* year 702, which began on 26 August 1302.⁵³ Though Qashani does not give a specific date for this event, the scope of his chronicle is narrowly limited to affairs in and around the royal court, suggesting that the murder took place while Ghazan was in the vicinity of Baghdad. Qashani reports that Ghazan reacted to the event by declaring religious tolerance for all Muslim sects, citing as his inspiration the precedent of both Muhammad and Chinggis Khan. Ghazan's respect for the biological descendants of the Prophet Muhammad suggests that he was already drawing a correlation between the genealogical tradition of Shi'i imams and Mongol ideas about the sanctity of royal blood. This signals a rapprochement between Muslim and Mongol ideas of authority and descent and an important step in the formation of a new model of Mongol kingship in the Islamic world.[54]

Ghazan proceeded through the region south of Baghdad, visiting at least one other shrine, ordering improvements to irrigation, and participating in several hunts along the way. During the whole time, he was engaged in extensive diplomatic correspondence with the rulers of Egypt, the Jochid Khanate and Byzantium. He crossed the Euphrates only in late January 1303 to visit the shrine of Imam Husayn at Karbala, finally arriving in early March at the island city of 'Ana. Here he spent about a week before proceeding against the Mamluk frontier post of Rahba al-Sham.

Beyond the ceremonial activities of his tour through lower Mesopotamia, Ghazan took a series of measures during the campaign of 1302/3 to mark the historical significance of his reign. One component of this was the inauguration of a new calendrical age, called the *khani* era, which was to be marked in solar years beginning on the spring equinox, the Persian New Year, of 1302. This was also the year that Ghazan is first recorded as commissioning literary works, including histories. At Ujan that summer, he granted Abu Sulayman Banakati the title King of Poets (*malik al-shu'ara*).[55] While the imperial camp was stopped at 'Ana in late winter 1303, Sa'd al-Din and Rashid al-Din introduced to the *ilkhan* Shihab al-Din 'Abd Allah al-Shirazi, a native to the southern province of Fars and former employee of the Salghurid dynasty there.[56] On his own initiative in previous years, Shihab al-Din had undertaken a continuation of the *History of the World Conqueror* of 'Ala' al-Din Juvayni, writing a three-volume work titled *The Allocation of Cities and Propulsion of Epochs* (*Tajziyat al-Amsar wa Tazjiyat al A'sar*).[57] Ghazan approved of the work and took Shihab al-Din under his patronage, later granting him the title Court Panegyrist (*wassaf al-hadrat*). From this title, he is most commonly known simply as Wassaf and his work as the *History of Wassaf*. Ghazan also instructed Wassaf to extend his historical chronicle to include his own reign, along with the life of Chinggis Khan.

Wassaf continued working on his history for another quarter of a century. The first three volumes that he presented to the *ilkhan* in 1302 contain events up to Ghazan's first invasion of Syria. The work demonstrates certain similarities with their model, the work of Juvayni, and with the later dynastic history written by Rashid al-Din. The *Allocation* serves, therefore, as a pivot point between the historical writing of scholar-bureaucrats in the late Saljuq and early Ilkhanid period and the more ideologically charged narratives that the *ilkhans* commissioned beginning with Ghazan.

Book One of Wassaf's *Allocation* picks up where Juvayni had left off, telling of the death of Mongke, the rise of his brother Qubilai as Great Khan, and the ongoing Mongol campaigns in China and the Middle East. This last includes an account of the sack of Baghdad, which Juvayni had been unable or unwilling to include, and it brings the story of the Ilkhanid dynasty through the reign of Arghun. The history of the Ilkhanate picks up late in Book Two with the end of Arghun's reign. Most of Book Two is given over to local concerns of southern Iran, including the history of the Salghurid dynasty. This marks a structural similarity with the second book of Juvayni's *History of the World Conqueror*, much of which tells the history of the Khwarazmshahs under which the author's family had served. Wassaf's account of Salghurid history is much longer and more detailed than the brief summary included in Baydawi's *Order of Histories*, offering significant information about Iranian political and administrative history during the early Mongol period. It remains our main source for Salghurid history.

In organising the narrative of his chronicle, Wassaf adapts into Persian several strategies from earlier Arabic historiography that later also appear in Rashid al-Din's writing. He periodically interrupts the main narrative of Ilkhanid history to tell the events of other courts, a strategy previously seen in the monumental *Epitome of the History of Prophets and Kings and Caliphs* (*Mukhtasar Ta'rikh al-Rusul wa'l-Muluk wa'l-Khulafa'*) of Tabari (839–923). Wassaf also inserts sections for miscellaneous events that do not fit in his main narrative, a practice with precedent in the *Perfect History* (*Kamil fi'l-Ta'rikh*) of Ibn al-Athir (d. 1233). Rashid al-Din later adopted both of these strategies in his dynastic history of the Mongols. Wassaf's extensive treatment of the Salghurids, meanwhile, provided a second historiographical precedent, alongside Baydawi, for including that dynasty in telling the history of the *ilkhans*' world.

Perhaps the most notable aspect of Wassaf's original work, both for its influence on Rashid al-Din and for the impression it must have made on Ghazan Khan, is his choice to end Book Three of the *Allocation* with a catalogue of Ghazan's building projects and reforms.[58] This turns the end of the *Allocation* into an elegy for Ghazan's reign. If Juzjani and Juvayni ended their histories of the Mongol conquest in ways that preserved a hopeful tone for the long-term survivability of Islam, Wassaf sees Ghazan's administrative and architectural projects as an appropriately optimistic finale in their own right. This made the *Allocation* an attractive object for the *ilkhan*'s patronage and an example of how historical writing could validate a ruler who struggled against enemy states, doubts over the sincerity of his conversion and the logistics of a military campaign.

Another historian who first received commissions under Ghazan was 'Abd Allah Qashani, a member of the prominent Shi'i Abu Tahir family of potters.[59] Qashani is most famous as the author of the only contemporary history of Oljeitu's reign, but several of his other works have survived.[60] These include a treatise on gemstones, which was originally dedicated to Rashid a-Din, as well as a collection of various histories that formed the basis for the world history that Rashid al-Din assembled for Oljeitu (discussed in Chapter 4). Qashani claims that Ghazan had commissioned this work under the title *Collected Histories* (*Jami' al-Tawarikh*), indicating that Ghazan was hoping to produce a broader historical narrative than just that of his family and its domain.[61]

One otherwise unattested work by Qashani that must have helped to secure him in Ghazan's favour has been only partially preserved in some manuscripts of Rashid al-Din's dynastic history of the Mongols.[62] The surviving portion of this work pertains to the early life of Ghazan Khan, up to and including his conversion to Islam and assumption of the Ilkhanid throne. Like Qashani's other writings, it shows him to be a professional writer, adept at the elaborate chancellery prose that marks the works of Juvayni, Wassaf and other scholar-bureaucrats from the late Saljuq milieu. From the text that has survived imbedded in manuscripts of Rashid al-Din's dynastic history, it appears that Qashani's work was a celebratory history, marking the definitive embrace of Islam by the Mongol dynasty.[63] It must have been completed before Ghazan's march through lower Mesopotamia, as Wassaf used it as a source in telling his own version of Ghazan's early reign, which forms part of the work that he presented to the *ilkhan* during that campaign.[64]

The *Blessed History of Ghazan*

The most famous historical work with roots in Ghazan's last and longest campaign is the dynastic history of the Mongols produced by his adviser Rashid al-Din, which was eventually titled the *Blessed History of Ghazan*.[65] Early in this work, Rashid al-Din mentions the *hijri* year 702 as the time of the composition of the work, a lunar year (26 August 1302–14 August 1303) corresponding to Ghazan's last campaign and the inaugural year of the *khani* era.[66] Elsewhere, Hamd Allah Mustaufi links the composition of the *Blessed History* directly to the first year of Ghazan's new calendar.[67] This was a new narrative, linked to a new historical era. The commission probably came, therefore, while Ghazan was preparing to enter Mamluk territory, either at his summer camp at Ujan or while wintering around Baghdad in 1302/3.

In his introduction to the *Blessed History*, Rashid al-Din outlines the work's origins and significance with a fairly generic justification for dynastic history. 'It is the custom of wise men and scholars,' he states,

> to make a record of important events, good and bad, of all periods, so that later they might be of benefit to their insightful descendants and progeny, and that the events of past centuries might be known in future times, and that by them the memory of famous kings and accomplished rulers might remain on the pages of time.[68]

To illustrate this point, Rashid al-Din offers the example of Mahmud of Ghazna, the memory of whose exploits were recorded for posterity by the poets Unsuri and Firdausi and the prose historian 'Utbi. It is to be remembered that Jarbadhqani voiced his concern about the Saljuqs being such poor patrons of historical writing in the course of translating 'Utbi's history of Mahmud of Ghazna.

Having stated the importance of dynastic history, Rashid al-Din presents the *Blessed History* specifically as an opportunity to clarify and preserve the history of the various nomadic people of Inner Asia, whom he designates under the general ethnonym 'Turk'.[69] Because of their nomadic ways, he states, the history of the Turks, and the differences among their various tribes – among which he counts the Mongols – had previously been unknown in the land of Iran.[70] The rise of Chinggis Khan and his descendants to rule over great swathes of Eurasia created a demand for knowledge about their history. Rashid al-Din criticises previous efforts to record the history of the Turks and Mongols, which he claims were imperfectly informed, a natural result of scholars working in an Islamic setting not having access to primary sources on their subject. Thus, while writing a dynastic history on the instruction of his Mongol patron, he insists that the work is for the benefit of the Islamic world, which had previously been misinformed about the Mongols who ruled it.

Rashid al-Din's concern for sources native to the subject culture of his history is evident also in his later historical works, discussed in Chapter 4.[71] However, he was not the first Muslim historian to make use of the historical traditions of the Inner Asian steppe: historians working under the Saljuqs had also incorporated that ruling family's own traditions of their dynastic origins.[72] At the heart of the difficulty in reporting on the Mongol past, Rashid al-Din explains, was the state of Mongol historical record-keeping until the time of Ghazan:

> Age by age, they have kept secure their true history in the Mongol language and script, without system or order, chapter by scattered chapter, hidden from the eyes of strangers or scholars. And they did not let anyone see or know about them, that they might understand and study them, until now, when the royal throne and crown of the land of Iran, which all the kings of the world long for, are ennobled by the blessed being of the Padishah of Islam, Sultan Mahmud Ghazan Khan, may his kingship last forever. Now, from his lofty high-mindedness he turned his blessed attention to it, so that it might be ordered and systematised. He issued a noble decree that the servant of the Ilkhanid state, the attendant on the benevolent lord, the author of this composition, Fazl Allah, son of Abu'l-Khair, known as Rashid, the doctor of Hamadan – God hold him straight and protect

him – collect the histories of origin and lineage of the Mongols and other Turks that resemble the Mongols, and arrange, chapter by chapter, their traditions and tales kept in their treasuries and entrusted to their *amir*s and royals.[73]

Rashid al-Din here highlights the unique opportunity of the moment, by which he was invited to organise and compile materials that had not been available to earlier historians of the Mongols. The passage reveals once more, alongside the evidence already provided from the work of Baydawi and Qutb al-Din Shirazi's 'anonymous' *Accounts of the Mongols*, that a historical tradition existed among the Mongols of the imperial period, even though little of it has survived in its original form.

Indeed, a rich variety of historical traditions circulated among Mongols in the early decades of the empire and were available to Rashid al-Din.[74] The most famous account of Mongol imperial origins is the *Secret History of the Mongols*, a semi-legendary account of Chinggis Khan's ancestors, his life and career, and the early reign of his son and successor Ogedei.[75] This is the only contemporary account of Chinggis Khan's life to survive in Mongolian, having been preserved in Chinese transliteration as a guide to Mongol language and culture for members of the Ming Dynasty diplomatic corps. After its rediscovery in the early twentieth century and translation into European languages in subsequent decades, some identified it as Rashid al-Din's source for early imperial history, since many of the same episodes are found in the two texts.[76] Differences between the *Secret History* and the *Blessed History*, however, point to a larger body of historical material that informed both texts, including chronicles and narratives, biographies and genealogies, wisdom sayings and other materials with mixed written and oral transmission. Christopher Atwood has recently published several pieces that shed enormous new light on this material through careful textual analysis of the *Blessed History* alongside extant Chinese and Mongolian texts.[77] Despite this range of sources, the only name that Rashid al-Din gives to his Mongol-language material is that of the *Golden Register* (*Altan Debter*). This term originally applied only to a limited genealogical account of the pre-Chinggisid Mongols, but following Rashid al-Din's example it has become a stand-in term for the entire collection of documents in diverse forms relating to the royal family and held by various members of the Mongol elite.[78]

In accessing and deciphering his Mongolian sources, Rashid al-Din was to have the assistance of 'wise and learned Chinese, Indians, Uighurs, Qipchaqs and others'.[79] Of all these specialists, as with the sources themselves, Rashid al-Din names only one: Bolad, a Mongol of the Dorben tribe whom Qubilai had sent to the Middle East in 1285 and who had remained there in the service of the *ilkhans*.[80] While in China, Bolad had been appointed to the rank of chancellor (*ch'eng-hsiang*), for which Rashid al-Din consistently refers to him as Bolad Chingsang. According to Rashid al-Din, Bolad Chingsang was a mine of information on Mongol tribal history and culture. However, as Christopher Atwood's recent dissection of Rashid al-Din's Mongolian sources has made clear, the Mongol historical tradition was far more diverse than the memory of one man. Presenting Bolad as he does as the great fount of Mongol tradition is symptomatic of Rashid al-Din's larger strategy in presenting his historical project, namely, to isolate and amplify the importance of individual sources and people, concealing a much more diverse reality. Besides doing this for Bolad Chingsang and the *Golden Register*, Rashid al-Din presents his patron Ghazan as the pinnacle of Islamic sovereignty and the *Blessed History* as the single most authoritative text on the Mongol dynasty. To a large extent this strategy has worked: Rashid al-Din and Bolad Chingsang have become a potent duumvirate in the imagination of modern scholars on the question of how Mongol history was transmitted.[81]

From a cacophony of voices, Rashid al-Din crafted a narrative that resonates both with well-established historiographical traditions of the Islamic world and with the more recent precedents established by his contemporaries at the Ilkhanid court. This is evident already in the introductory framing of the *Blessed History*. Even before describing the scattered Mongol sources for the work, Rashid al-Din opens the *Blessed History* with an account of the Judeo-Islamic patriarch Abraham, who instructed his children to record their descendants, so that the prophets, rulers and prominent individuals of later periods would know their place in a universal genealogical taxonomy of peoples.[82] This injunction establishes a clear measure for the legitimacy of rulers based on whether they had preserved a genealogical record. Establishing genealogical memory as a criterion for legitimacy served, among other things, to delegitimise the Mamluks of Egypt, who had been individually separated from their families and tribes of origin by their experience as slave soldiers.

Rashid al-Din next introduces his patron Ghazan Khan as the fulfilment of God's plan for Islam and then passes into his description of the composition of the *Blessed History*. Here he describes the failure of previous historians to record the Mongol past and the scattered state of their own historical record, as quoted above. This description of his process of gathering information, coming as it does after his introductory anecdote about Abraham, serves dual purposes. In addition to presenting what he would have us believe was his process in composing the work, Rashid al-Din casts the Mongols as the fulfilment of Abraham's injunction because they had preserved their history in writing, even if they had done so in a disorganised way and in secret from other groups. Put briefly, the Mongols appear already in the introductory to the *Blessed History* as rightful, if unintentional, heirs of the Abrahamic tradition.

Having completed his introductory remarks with the description of scattered Mongol sources, Rashid al-Din launches into the main text of the *Blessed History*. The first section is a history of the nomadic Turko-Mongol tribes of Inner Asia. After briefly describing pastoral nomadism, Rashid al-Din draws a comparison between the Arabs, who dwell in the deserted areas of the Middle East, and the Turks who have done the same on the Eurasian steppes.[83] These Turks, according to Rashid al-Din, all descend from the four sons of Dib Baqui, grandson of Noah through Japheth, who therefore provides a biological link between the Turko-Mongol genealogical traditions of the steppe and the Abrahamic traditions of the Judeo-Islamic world. This enhances the significance of Rashid al-Din's claim that the Mongols had adhered to the Abrahamic injunction to preserve genealogical records, as they are cast within the same human taxonomy descended from Noah as the Jewish, Muslim and Christian populations over which they ruled.

Rashid al-Din's actual description of the Turkic tribes begins with a brief narrative about Oghuz Khan, the legendary and eponymous ancestor of the confederacy of Turkic tribes which had burst into Islamic history under the leadership of the family of Saljuq three centuries earlier.[84] Rashid al-Din presents this legendary Turkic ancestor as a monotheist from birth, refusing to nurse until his mother rejects polytheism or to marry until he finds a bride who would follow him in his faith.[85] This insistence drives Oghuz into conflict with his relatives, the other descendants of Dib Baqui, creating an etiology for some of the broad divisions between groups of Turkic tribes. Rashid al-Din goes on to describe the various tribes of Turks, culminating with the clans of Mongols most closely related to the Borjigin of Chinggis Khan. In these descriptions, he mentions each tribe's traditional territories, how they joined Chinggis Khan's confederacy, and the names and notable deeds of members of each tribe up to his own time. This portion of the work presents the greatest opportunity for seeing through Rashid al-Din's working process. He continued to add information about the Turkic tribes as it became available, creating discrepancies within the work and between different versions produced over the course of several years. Some of these changes are described in Chapter 5.

The movement through the Turko-Mongol tribes towards that of the ruling Mongol family segues directly into the second section of the *Blessed History*, which narrates the lives of Chinggis Khan's ancestors over ten generations since the legendary ancestress of all the Mongols, Alan Qo'a. This section introduces the direct lineage of Chinggis Khan, and it begins to follow a consistent structure built around that lineage. For each member of the Mongol lineage beginning with Alan Qo'a, Rashid al-Din first narrates the members of his or her family and finishes with a genealogical tree showing his or her immediate descendants. The presentation of these genealogical trees changed over the course of the first decade after the *Blessed History* was written, as discussed in Chapter 5, but from the outset they play an integral role in establishing the genealogical coherence and significance of Chinggis Khan's family.

The accounts of Chinggis Khan's ancestors generally expand as they become more recent, so that significant historical narrative has been included in the sections on Chinggis Khan's three immediate forebears. By the time the narrative arrives at Chinggis Khan, it has assumed the pattern that will carry through the rest of the work, interspersing genealogical information and trees with narratives about the lives and careers of the Mongol royal family. The contents of the chapters dedicated to Mongol khans from Chinggis to Ghazan need not be summarised here, as they provide the raw material of this and any other study of Mongol history. In their basic format they are consistent with one another. Rashid al-Din divides the chapter (*dastan*) for each Mongol ruler into three sections (*qism*s): on the ruler's family, then on his career, and finally on miscellaneous events and anecdotes associated with him and his reign.

If we are to characterise the role of the three *qism*s of each *dastan* within the larger historical project of the *Blessed History*, we might say that the first (dealing with the ruler's family) lays out the genealogical connection between the members of the Mongol royal family. The second section outlines the main narrative of the history. The third section, then, creates an opportunity to present an essential portrait of each ruler's character and reign. Despite this consistency in formatting, the chapters on the different khans are of wildly different lengths. The chapters on Chinggis Khan and Ghazan Khan together make up more than 40 per cent of the whole *Blessed History*. This is due to the fact that their lives and careers are given the fullest treatment, but also because the third sections of these two chapters are among the most fully developed. For Chinggis Khan, this section contains twenty-seven anecdotes in a strange and non-idiomatic Persian that seems to have been rendered directly from Mongolian.[86] Most of these preserve Chinggis Khan's words and deeds, revealing his concern for order and propriety, honour, respect, sobriety and the care of the family, as well as the marks of a good ruler and commander (and in one instance, a good horse), and the efficacy of supplicating God. Set in the context of steppe life, these stories mark Chinggis Khan as the ideal nomadic ruler. Some have seen in them the core values of the legal system, or *yasa*, which Chinggis Khan is said to have left to his descendants.[87]

Among Chinggis Khan's sons, only Ogedei's character receives extensive treatment in this way. In a series of forty-eight anecdotes, Ogedei appears as merciful and generous to a fault, much as Juvayni had portrayed him in the *History of the World Conqueror*.[88] Right at the end of the work, Rashid al-Din gives another highly elaborated third section in his chapter on Ghazan Khan. In his header to this section, Rashid al-Din indicates that it was to contain two sub-sections: one of forty anecdotes, and the other of miscellaneous stories. Of these, only the forty anecdotes were ever completed. Even in this incomplete state, the third *qism* of the chapter on Ghazan Khan accounts for about 15 per cent of the total *Blessed History*. The forty anecdotes cover Ghazan's personal qualities, administrative reforms and building programmes. Taken together, they present an image of Ghazan as a devout monotheist (even before his conversion to Islam), just ruler and compassionate father of his state, the fulfilment of the ideological arguments running through the *Blessed History*.[89]

One of the attractions of the *Blessed History* to the modern student of Mongol history is its deceptively simple and unadorned style; Rashid al-Din claims to have written 'in clear wording so as to be easily comprehended by different minds'.[90] Just as Rashid al-Din focuses his description of sources on the *Golden Register* and Bolad Chingsang, here too he promises a simplified story of the Chinggisid royal family. Some of the minds he wanted to comprehend the text, no doubt, were members of the Mongol elite, to whom the work held the greatest interest but who were probably not versed in the high-register chancellery prose of other historical works from the Saljuq and Ilkhanid periods. Here again a precedent for Rashid al-Din's effort can be seen in the Saljuq period, as Nishapuri's *Saljuqnama* was written to be similarly accessible to the rulers whose history it preserved.[91] Behind that straightforward prose, however, Rashid al-Din's work delivers a powerful ideological message suited to Ghazan's effort to project an image simultaneously as a Mongol, Iranian and Islamic sovereign. Rashid al-Din goes far beyond Ibn al-Tiqtaqa's injunction that ministers should not hide the lessons of the past from their patrons. In his unadorned prose, he turns Ghazan into the proof of Mongol legitimacy in the Middle East. This central argument has continued to hold sway. As modern scholars study the Mongol Middle East, Ghazan's reign stands out as the most transformative phase of a dynamic period.

Notes

1. On the shot by Bahram V and its ramifications in art, see Ettinghausen, 'Bahram Gur's Hunting Feats'.
2. Rashid al-Din, *Jami' al-Tawarikh*, pp. 1298–9.
3. On the *Fakhri*, see Storey, *Persian Literature*, vol. 1, pt. 1, § 2 pp. 80–1; Storey and Bregel', *Persidskaya Literatura*, pp. 325–6; Ibn al-Tiqtaqa, *Al-Fakhri* (1997 edn, 1947 trans.). While copied and dedicated in 1301, the work may have been complete as much as two years earlier, as the latest anecdote included in it dates to the *hijri* year 698 (AD 1298–9).
4. For more on such works, see Peacock, 'Court Historiography', p. 345.

5. For the translation of the *Fakhri*, see Nakhjivani, *Tajarib*, with the date of translation at p. 3.
6. Ibn al-Tiqtaqa, *Al-Fakhri* (ed. Farhud and Mayu), pp. 23, 52, 74–5, 139–40.
7. Ibn al-Tiqtaqa, *Al-Fakhri* (ed. Farhud and Mayu), pp. 38–9.
8. Ibn al-Tiqtaqa, *Al-Fakhri* (ed. Farhud and Mayu), pp. 13, 20–1.
9. Ibn 'Inaba, *'Umdat al-Talib*, pp. 180–1.
10. Ibn al-Tiqtaqa, *Al-Fakhri* (ed. Farhud and Mayu), pp. 24–5, 59, 112.
11. Ibn al-Tiqtaqa, *Al-Fakhri* (ed. Farhud and Mayu), p. 25.
12. Jarbadhqani, *Tarjumah*, p. 9, translated by Meisami, 'Rulers and the Writing of History', p. 73.
13. For an overview of Saljuq historiography, see Meisami, *Persian Historiography*, pp. 141–280; Cahen, 'The Historiography'; Peacock, 'Court Historiography'.
14. Peacock, 'Court Historiography', pp. 333–6.
15. Aubin, *Emirs Mongols*, p. 23, has called this period a void in the historical record. See also Pfeiffer, 'Canonization', pp. 58–9.
16. On these works, and particularly the focus of Armenian sources on the potential benefit to the Armenian community of a Mongol alliance with the Latin Crusaders, see Luisetto, *Arméniens & Autres Chrétiens*, pp. 19–20, 23–6.
17. This text, the *Book of Jamasp the Sage* (*Ketab-e Hakim Jamasp*), is the subject of a separate study now in preparation. It is clearly based on the more widely known *Wisdom of Jamasp* (*Ahkam-e Jamasp*), which probably took shape just a few decades earlier.
18. Juvayni, *Ta'rikh*, vol. 1, pp. 2–3; Juvayni, *The History*, pp. 4–5.
19. On the *History of the World Conqueror*, in addition to the text and translation noted above, see Shabistari, *Talayahdaran*, pp. 165–205.
20. Jackson, 'Mongol Khans', p. 110; Fitzherbert, 'Portrait of a Lost Leader'.
21. Juzjani, *Tabaqat-e Nasiri* (1984 edition, translation of 1873).
22. Pfeiffer, 'Canonization', pp. 60–1.
23. Jackson, 'Mongol Khans', pp. 110–12.
24. Juvayni, *Ta'rikh*, vol. 1, pp. 16–25; Juvayni, *The History*, pp. 23–34; Aigle, 'Le grand jasaq', esp. at pp. 47–8.
25. Lane, *Early Mongol Rule*, p. 28.
26. The literature on the *Shahnameh* is vast. For a recent discussion of its historical and literary context, see Melville, 'The *Shahnameh* in Historical Context'; Abdullaeva, 'The *Shahnameh* in Persian Literary History'.
27. Melikian-Chirvani, 'Conscience du passé', pp. 135–7.
28. On the early lack of interest in the *Shahnameh*, see Tetley, *The Ghaznavid*

and Seljuq Turks, p. 5; Dabiri, 'The Shahnama'. The few mentions of the work in its first two centuries have been collected by Riyahi, *Sar Chashmah*, pp. 115–477.

29. Examples are given by Melikian-Chirvani, 'Le livre des rois, II', pp. 54–74; Melikian-Chirvani, 'Conscience du passé', pp. 137–49.
30. Wassaf, *Ketab-e Mostatab*, p. 156.
31. On the Salghurids, see Merçil, *Fars Atabegleri*; Bosworth, 'Salghurids'.
32. Gardizi, *The Ornament of Histories*. For the development of the model of Perso-Islamic universal history, see Kamola 'A Sensational and Unique Novelty'.
33. There are three editions of the *Order of Histories*, which differ from one another significantly. For a discussion of the various versions of Baydawi's work, see Melville, 'From Adam to Abaqa' (in two parts).
34. Melville, 'From Adam to Abaqa', pp. 75–6.
35. Meisami, *Persian Historiography*, pp. 66–79.
36. Melville, 'From Adam to Abaqa', pp. 81–3.
37. Baydawi, *Nizam al-Tawarikh*, p. 133.
38. Melville, 'From Adam to Abaqa', p. 83; Melikian-Chirvan, 'Le royaume de Salomon'.
39. For an overview of Qutb al-Din's life, see Walbridge, *The Science of Mystic Lights*, pp. 1–26; Wiedemann, 'Ḳuṭb al-Dīn Shīrāzī'; Chipman, 'A Tale of Two Doctors'.
40. Kennedy, 'The Exact Sciences', pp. 669–70, fig. 4 and pl. 16.
41. Pourjavady and Schmidtke, 'The Quṭb al-Dīn', pp. 280–4.
42. On Shihab al-Din Suhrawardi, see Ziai, 'Shihāb al-Dīn Suhrawardī'.
43. On Ibn 'Arabi, see Chittick, 'Ibn 'Arabī'. On Tusi's encounter with Illuminationism, see Ziai, 'The Illuminationist Tradition', pp. 470–3.
44. On this embassy in the context of Mongol–Mamluk diplomacy, see Broadbridge, *Kingship and Ideology*, pp. 38–44.
45. On this manuscript, see Pourjavady and Schmidtke, 'The Quṭb al-Dīn'.
46. For an overview of this work, see Lane, 'Mongol News'.
47. Takagi, '*Akhbār-i Mughūlān*', makes a similar argument, but in Japanese, and so I have only been able to consult the abstract. Any similarity between the argument presented here and Takagi's is coincidental.
48. The printed edition of the text, Afshar, *Akhbar*, inserts headings according to *hijri* years mentioned in the text, giving it the appearance of an inconsistent annalistic structure that does not match the manuscript.
49. Boyle, 'The Longer Introduction', pp. 250–1.

50. Rashid al-Din, *Jamiʿ al-Tawarikh*, p. 1302.
51. Mostaert and Cleaves, 'Trois documents'; Boyle, 'Ghazan's Letter'.
52. Rashid al-Din, *Jamiʿ al-Tawarikh*, pp. 1307–8.
53. Qashani, *Tarikh-e Uljaytu*, pp. 90–1.
54. Moin, *The Millennial Sovereign*, pp. 31–9, discusses the transposition of ideas of Chinggisid royal lineage onto those of spiritual succession from ʿAli across a broader timeframe.
55. Banakati, *Rawzat*, p. 465.
56. Wassaf, *Ketab-e Mostatab*, pp. 405–6, describes this audience, which he dates to Sunday 3 March 1303.
57. Wassaf, *Ketab-e Mostatab*. Joseph Hammer-Purgstall translated the work into German in the mid-nineteenth century, but only the first volume was published at that time. His full translations have recently been re-edited and published: Wentker, *Geschichte Wassafs*.
58. Wassaf, *Ketab-e Mostatab*, pp. 382–91.
59. Soucek, 'Abu'l-Qāsem ʿAbdallāh Kašānī'.
60. For more on Qashani's *oeuvre*, see Brack, 'Mediating Sacred Kingship', pp. 133–94, 322–44.
61. Qashani, *Zubdat al-Tawarikh*, pp. 3–4; Brack, 'Mediating Sacred Kingship', pp. 322–7.
62. These are the manuscripts of the λ recension in Appendix B. For more on this variant text, see Chapter 5, as well as Kamola, 'Rashīd al-Dīn', pp. 89–93; Brack, 'Mediating Sacred Kingship', pp. 137–46; Brack, 'Theologies of Auspicious Kingship', pp. 1155–8.
63. I owe a great deal to a sustained correspondence with Jonathan Brack, who has helped me to tease apart the relationship between Qashani's history of Ghazan's early life and Rashid al-Din's *Blessed History*. Brack was also the first to call Qashani's text a 'celebration history', which I adapt here.
64. For the relationship between Qashani and Wassaf on Ghazan's conversion, see Brack, 'Mediating Sacred Kingship', pp. 336–8.
65. Rashid al-Din, *Jamiʿ al-Tawarikh*, p. 32, omits the word 'blessed' from the title of the dynastic history, based on the reading of the main manuscript used for the edition (manuscript Z_{12} in Appendix B). As a result of this omission, Satoko Shimo has argued that the word 'blessed' was added to the work's title only after its initial composition: Shimo, 'Ghâzân Khan', pp. 106–8. Her argument is based on a larger theory that the ζ recension preceded others: Shimo, 'Ghâzân Khan'; Shimo, 'Three Manuscripts', p. 226. However, as demonstrated

in Chapter 5, the inclusion of images and the modifications to Chaghadai's family tree demand the ζ recension be a late version. Beyond manuscript Z_{12}, five others (manuscripts E_3–E_7) also lack the word 'blessed' in the title. However, other manuscripts from recensions prepared before and after the ε and ζ recensions include the term 'blessed', suggesting that it was always intended as part of the title. Manuscripts Z_{12} and the five manuscripts of ε seem to be outliers in this respect.

66. Rashid al-Din, *Jamiʿ al-Tawarikh*, p. 28. Elsewhere, Rashid al-Din refers to the *hijri* year 701 as 'last year': Rashid al-Din, *Jamiʿ al-Tawarikh*, p. 627.
67. Hamd Allah Mustaufi, *Ẓafarnāma*, p. 1414.
68. Rashid al-Din, *Jamiʿ al-Tawarikh*, pp. 32–3.
69. For a discussion of how the term 'Turk' became a general designation for all Inner Asian nomads in Ilkhanid and Timurid historiography, see Lee, 'The Historical Meaning'.
70. Rashid al-Din, *Jamiʿ al-Tawarikh*, pp. 33–4.
71. See also Pfeiffer, 'Canonization', pp. 62–4.
72. Peacock, 'Court Historiography', p. 354.
73. Rashid al-Din, *Jamiʿ al-Tawarikh*, pp. 34–5.
74. Allsen, *Culture and Conquest*, pp. 86–91, offered an early summary of this material, which Christopher Atwood has recently brought into much clearer light (see below).
75. For a translation, commentary and bibliography on the *Secret History*, see de Rachewiltz, *The Secret History of the Mongols*.
76. Scholars who have taken this position include Bayani, 'L'histoire secrète'; Krawulsky, *The Mongol Īlkhāns*, pp. 33–8.
77. Atwood, 'Rashīd al-Dīn's *Ghazanid Chronicle*', summarises more detailed analysis found in Atwood, 'Six pre-Chinggisid Genealogies'; Atwood, 'Chikü Küregen'; Atwood, 'Alexander, Ja'a Gambo'; Atwood, 'Pu'a's Boast'; and Atwood, 'The indictment of Ong Qa'an'.
78. For the latter use, see Allsen, *Culture and Conquest*, pp. 88–90. For the more limited understanding of the *Golden Register*, see Kim, 'A Re-examination'; Atwood, 'Six pre-Chinggisid Genealogies'.
79. Rashid al-Din, *Jamiʿ al-Tawarikh*, p. 35.
80. On Bolad, see Allsen, *Culture and Conquest*, pp. 63–80; Allsen, 'Biography of a Cultural Broker'.
81. See in particular Allsen, *Culture and Conquest*.
82. Rashid al-Din, *Jamiʿ al-Tawarikh*, pp. 23–6.

83. Rashid al-Din, *Jami' al-Tawarikh*, pp. 39–41.
84. Rashid al-Din's treatment of the story of Oghuz is more fully treated in Kamola, 'History and Legend', esp. pp. 565–8.
85. Rashid al-Din, *Jami' al-Tawarikh*, pp. 48–50.
86. Rashid al-Din, *Jami' al-Tawarikh*, pp. 581–91.
87. For an overview of the various views that have been expressed about the Mongol *yasa* and the challenges presented by this portion of the *Blessed History* and other sources, see Jackson, *The Mongols and the Islamic World*, pp. 113–16; Aigle, *The Mongol Empire*, pp. 135–45.
88. Rashid al-Din, *Jami' al-Tawarikh*, pp. 684–705; Juvayni, *Ta'rikh*, vol. 1, pp. 158–91; Juvayni, *The History*, pp. 201–36.
89. For more on how these forty anecdotes correspond to the overall ideological programme of the *Blessed History*, see Kamola, 'Beyond History'.
90. Rashid al-Din, *Jami' al-Tawarikh*, p. 37.
91. Peacock, 'Court Historiography', pp. 343–4.

4

New Projects of Faith and Power, 1304–1312

Ghazan did not live to see the *Blessed History* finished. Rashid al-Din continued in his position as adviser and administrator for Ghazan's brother and successor Oljeitu (1304–16). This included continuing his ideological work on behalf of the dynasty, though for his second patron this work took new forms. This chapter examines intellectual and architectural projects during Oljeitu's reign to show how the relationship between the new *ilkhan* and his elderly adviser changed the contours of Mongol Islamic sovereignty that had been sketched out during Ghazan's reign. Each component of Rashid al-Din's activity under Oljeitu has been the subject of recent study, including his activity as a patron of architecture and scholarship, his theological writings, and miscellaneous other scientific projects.[1] The aim of this chapter is to show how these diverse areas of activity overlapped with one another. In their intersection, they reveal a new ideological programme that cast Oljeitu as a truly universal ruler, beyond the scope of the hybrid Mongol–Iranian–Islamic ideology that marks Ghazan's reign.

Indicative of the new form of universal kingship that marks Oljeitu's reign is a change in titulature, as the new *ilkhan* presented himself as sultan, rather than simply as khan or padishah. Rashid al-Din propagated the new image of the sultan, but in doing so he was careful to include space for himself as Oljeitu's indispensable adviser and spokesman. Together, Oljeitu and Rashid al-Din modelled a particular form of sovereignty, in which the sultan's authority is proven, amplified, and reflected by the presence of the wise adviser at his side. This model of kingship had its roots in the Saljuq period, but assumed new significance in the Ilkhanate, when there was no caliph to countermand the authority of the sultan.

History after Ghazan

In Tabriz, in autumn 1303, preparations were underway for a new invasion of Mamluk Syria when Ghazan was struck with ophthalmia, perhaps just one symptom of a systemic infection. Chinese physicians cauterised the *ilkhan*'s wounds, and he left Tabriz at the end of October on a platform carried by Indian elephants, headed south to winter around Baghdad. After a slow and painful month, the royal entourage was forced by snow to set up winter camp in the fields of Azerbaijan, just southeast of Abaqa's palace at Sughurluq. According to Rashid al-Din, Ghazan, despite his ailing eyes, was still able to discern Muslims from Christians at sight and to deny the latter the benefit of his charity. He also issued an edict on the reformation of provincial taxes and investigated and passed judgement on the plotters of a failed coup in the name of his cousin Alafireng.[2] Even in Ghazan's final illness, Rashid al-Din portrays his patron through the overall ideological frame of the *Blessed History*: as a devout Muslim, lawgiver and legitimate scion of the Mongol royal family.

Ghazan died on 17 May 1304. His body was interred in the mausoleum he had commissioned as part of a large shrine complex in Shamb, a village on the western edge of Tabriz. His father, Arghun, had first developed the site and named it Arghuniya after himself. On this site, Ghazan ordered the construction of a mosque, schools, and various other charitable and scholarly institutions.[3] These were to be funded from the proceeds of 'that within the domain that was his by absolute legal right and his unfettered property, so that no slanderer might object'.[4] Rashid al-Din tells us that the idea for this new project, called the Gates of Piety (*abwāb al-birr*), came to Ghazan after he visited the shrines of saints in Khurasan and around Baghdad, including those of Beyazid Bastami and ʿAli b. Abi Talib.[5]

Dominating the new construction was the dome of Ghazan's tomb. It had been designed to surpass that of the Saljuq Sultan Sanjar in Merv, which was at the time the largest domed space in the world. In keeping with the presentation of his patron as an enlightened philosopher-king, Rashid al-Din tells us that Ghazan himself drew up the plans for this dome and even promised to provide light for its visitors. Asked by the workmen how many windows to leave in the dome, Ghazan answered, 'the light there should come from here, otherwise the accidental illumination of the sun in that place is of no benefit to anyone'.[6] These words recall those of the founder of Illuminationist philosophy, Suhrawardi al-Maqtul (d. 1191), for whom the 'accidental illumination' of physical light pales when compared with the spirit of an enlightened sage or ruler.[7] Ghazan's body was to continue conferring blessings on its visitors, just as the bodies of Beyazid and ʿAli were believed to do.

Five years before his death, Ghazan had designated his brother Khudabanda to succeed him. Rashid al-Din had known Khudabanda as long as anyone, having attended the prince's birth on the edge of the desert between Sarakhs and Merv on 24 March 1282. Writing of the event later, Rashid al-Din explained that the region had been suffering from prolonged drought, but that the prince's birth was accompanied by rain. From this miracle, the young Khudabanda acquired his second, more familiar name, Oljeitu, meaning 'blessing' in Mongolian.[8] When Oljeitu came to the throne, he was twenty-two years old, and Rashid al-Din was thirty years his senior. Throughout his time on the throne, Oljeitu relied on the elder statesman as a confidant and adviser, though Rashid al-Din's formal position at court is no clearer during this period than before. Just as Hamd Allah Mustaufi describes the situation under Ghazan in 1298, the historian Shabankaraʾi distinguishes between the 'title of the vizierate' (*nām-e vizārat*) held by Saʿd al-Din Sawaji, and the 'work of the state' (*kār-e mamlakat*), which fell to Rashid al-Din during this latter reign.[9]

The work of the state certainly included the ongoing economic management of the realm. It probably also included diplomatic assignments: in 1307, Rashid al-Din may have been involved in negotiations between Oljeitu and the leaders of Gilan to bring a politically acceptable end to the *ilkhan*'s ill-fated assault of the province, which had resisted Mongol sovereignty. Whatever his formal duties, Rashid al-Din continued to advise Oljeitu and to oversee the production of various scholarly and charitable projects. This put the sultan and his adviser in a cycle of patronage, by which Rashid al-Din created and presented projects to Oljeitu, who rewarded him with money and property to be reinvested in ever larger projects.[10] Rashid al-Din's activities as both patron and recipient of patronage resulted in the finest and most ostentatious examples of building and book art from the Ilkhanid period, but they also laid the groundwork for his fall from power.

Since Ghazan had died before the *Blessed History* was complete, Rashid al-Din presented the finished work to Oljeitu. In his account of the event, Rashid al-Din praises Oljeitu, claiming that, 'because the perfection of knowledge and perception and the fullness of wisdom and intuition is that of the Padishah, he laid out thorough corrections and an orderly arrangement' for the work.[11] Despite these contributions, and despite the fact that the work was completed during his reign, Rashid al-Din claims that Oljeitu insisted it continue to carry the name of its original patron, after whom it was titled the *Blessed History of Ghazan*.

The *Blessed History* was Rashid al-Din's first complete work. If it had been his last, he would be remembered as the author of the single most important source on the history of the Mongol Empire and the Ilkhanate. In subsequent years, however, he presented several additional works to his new sultan and patron. The first of these was a two-part history of the world, which came to be called the *World History* (*Tarikh-e 'Alam*). The first part of this work resembles an Islamic universal history in the form revitalised by Baydawi in the 1280s. It tells of the kings of ancient Iran and Judeo-Islamic prophets, then the life of Muhammad and the history of the caliphate to 1258, and finally a series of independent dynasties that had co-existed with the caliphate in the eastern reaches of the Iranian world. The second part reached far beyond the world of Islam, with sections dedicated to the Oghuz Turks, Chinese, Jews, Europeans and Indians.[12] In its intended form, this two-part world history was to be bookended by accounts of the life and reign of Oljeitu Sultan. Those portions of the work have not survived, but the intent to include them already marks the work's universalising ambitions. Rather than tack the history of Oljeitu onto the dynastic chronicle of the *Blessed History*, Rashid al-Din intended to begin and end the history of the world with the story of his patron. This plan, if completed, would have created a historiographical metonym of a world-embracing sovereign, whose life and reign could encompass the expanded horizons of human experience that the Mongol conquests had revealed.

The collection of summary histories in the second part of the *World History* has earned Rashid al-Din recognition as the 'first world historian'.[13] Several earlier historians in the Islamic world had included in their works sections on Europe, India and even China.[14] Rashid al-Din's *World History* stands apart from these earlier efforts not in the range of its coverage, but in its epistemological treatment. The tenth-century historian Masʿudi, for example, wrote about India and China, but primarily drew on sources from closer to home in doing so.[15] In the previous century, Yaʿqubi had included in his *History* information on the Chinese and Indians, but also on the Greeks and Romans, Babylonians and Egyptians, Yemenis and Syrians, Berbers and Turks.[16] For its geographical coverage, this might be considered the earliest world history in the Islamic tradition, though Yaʿqubi's aim throughout is to fit the various peoples of the world into a single universal pattern of history based on the assumption that Islam marked the theological perfection of human experience.[17]

Unlike these writers, who present the histories of other parts of Eurasia through an Islamic lens, Rashid al-Din retains his subjects' own historiographies, preserving ideas about the past and about the passage of time as they were understood among the people about whom he wrote. In this sense, his work is closer in spirit to that of the eleventh-century scholar Biruni, whose comparative chronology of various nations first examines the internal coherence of each culture's calendrical system before correlating it with the Muslim calendar.[18] Biruni was a main source of information for Rashid al-Din's history of India, but it seems he also offered an epistemological model for the treatment of foreign material in general.

In the end, Rashid al-Din's history did still aim to subsume these foreign histories under a single overpowering cultural force, but that force was his patron, the Ilkhan Oljeitu, rather than the historical finality of Islam. By allowing the historical traditions of the Jews, Indians and others to speak for themselves alongside one another, Rashid al-Din created a chronological cacophony. Oljeitu's story stood outside this mélange – outside history itself. The *World History* emphasises the world, rather than history: it presents a geographically universal vision of Oljeitu as a patron and sovereign.

Qashani's Claim

The cosmopolitan character of the Ilkhanid realm had greatly expanded the awareness of the Islamic world to foreign societies, and the *ilkhans*' capital city of Tabriz facilitated the gathering of information about the people and histories of distant lands. Not only did Tabriz attract emissaries from other Mongol realms, it also served as a destination and a crossroads for travellers, pilgrims and merchants.[19] After Ghazan had built his shrine complex at Shamb, he instructed that the surrounding area be urbanised, creating the new city of Ghazaniya, where merchants from Anatolia and Europe could unload their cargo and set up shop.[20] Along with these westerners, merchants and envoys from the eastern reaches of the Mongol world brought information about their lands of origin. As Chapter 5 will show, this exposure to foreign ideas about the past and how to present it inspired Rashid al-Din to introduce significant changes into the *Blessed History of Ghazan*. Before that happened, it provided the raw material for a new type of world history. The *World History* that Rashid al-Din presented to Oljeitu was the final result of this, but the path to that end had been blazed by another scholar at the Ilkhanid court.

As mentioned in Chapter 3, Ghazan's patronage of historical writing included the employment of 'Abd Allah Qashani. In addition to a celebratory narrative of Ghazan's rise to the throne that has been included in some manuscripts of the *Blessed History*, Qashani prepared for Ghazan a collection of histories of various peoples from across time and across the Eurasian continent. To this assortment of historical narratives, Qashani applied the title *Collected Histories* (*Jamiʿ al-Tawarikh*).[21] It was to include the histories of the 'Turks and Tajiks, Indians and Jews, China and Khotan and Manzi (Southern China), the Franks and Christians and Muslims and Zoroastrians, the Arabs and Persians, the regions of the East and the West'.[22]

Most of Qashani's collection of Eurasian histories survives in only a single manuscript.[23] After a section on Perso-Islamic history, it includes the histories of the Ismaʿilis, various minor dynasties contemporary to the ʿAbbasids, the Saljuqs and Salghurids, then the histories of Christian Europe, India, the Oghuz and other Turks, China, and the Jews. These largely correspond to Qashani's list of contents quoted above, though they are not bound in the order that he names them. Qashani's list is not ordered as a table of contents, but rather according to the conventions of chancellery prose: individual items in the list are grouped according to category and then made to rhyme, giving this pseudo-table of contents a literary flair. It is, therefore, not easy to tell what order Qashani intended for these sections. In the single manuscript that includes them, they are gathered individually, separated by leaves of heavier paper. They could just as easily be rearranged into any order.

At the opening of several sections, Qashani makes reference either to the commission to write the *Collection* or to his process of doing so. Unfortunately, the opening pages of several sections have been lost, and with them any further information about his sources or method. From the surviving passages, we can gain some insight into the early life of the work. Qashani's description of Ghazan's commission, including the title *Collected Histories* and the list of histories it included, is found near the beginning of his history of the Isma'ilis, which was a later addition to the work.[24] Qashani also mentions the royal interest in the *Collected Histories* at the beginning of his histories of India and China. In the former, he tells how Hulegu and all his tribe were Buddhist when they came to Iran, and that they attracted to their service scholars and monks from Turkestan, India, Kashmir, Tibet and from among the Uighur.[25] These enjoyed special privilege at court, at the expense of Muslim scholars, until Ghazan came to the throne, converted to Islam and denounced the beliefs of the Buddhists. Nevertheless, he selected the monk Kamalashri to convey the history of India.

In the introduction to his history of China, Qashani mentions Ghazan's particular interest in having such a history included in the *Collected Histories*.[26] He goes on to explain how the opportunity for such a history presented itself in the persons of two Chinese scholars named Litaji and Kamsun, who were trained in medicine, astronomy and the history of China. These two, Qashani tells us, summarised a history of China that had been written by three monks. (For more on this source, see section II.I in Appendix A.) Here more than anywhere, we see the impact that Mongol dynastic contacts across Asia had on the intellectual life of Tabriz, as the scholars and scholarship of China were available to be included in this new collection of histories.

The introduction to this *Collected Histories* has been lost from the manuscript that contains Qashani's histories of the various people of Eurasia. However, a second fragmentary manuscript survives, containing only the Perso-Islamic history from the beginning of the work, including its introduction.[27] Here we learn that Qashani modified his *Collected Histories* at some point after Oljeitu's rise to the throne, as he praises the latter *ilkhan* instead of his original patron.²⁸ Furthermore, Qashani tells us that in the interim between the two versions of the *Collected Histories*, he had prepared a second, concise history covering just the Iranian and Islamic world. The fact that he describes this second work in the introduction of the *Collected Histories* is evidence that he returned to and revised his original work at a later date. As part of his revised introduction, Qashani writes that, having composed for the *Collected Histories* the history of the seven regions of the world (*iqlim*, from the Greek *klima*),

> he wanted a history of the fourth clime, which is the cream of the seven climes, the choicest of the four inhabited climes, containing the lives of the rulers and sultans of the distant past and the sovereigns of the land of Iran and the lives of kings and prophets and caliphs of every age since Adam – peace be upon him – until the end of the period that was the lunar year 700 by Muslim reckoning.²⁹

Thus, after completing the original *Collected Histories*, Qashani turned his attention to a work specifically focused on the so-called fourth clime, namely, the region of Iran and Iraq. This basic structure matches a well-established genre of Perso-Islamic universal histories looking back to the monumental early tenth-century *History of Prophets and Kings* of Abu Jaʿfar al-Tabari. Based on Qashani's description of this second, shorter work, it has come to be known as the *Cream of Histories* (*Zubdat al-Tawarikh*).³⁰ Qashani then evidently replaced the Perso-Islamic history of his original *Collected Histories* with this new *Cream of Histories*: in the fuller surviving manuscript of the *Collected Histories*, the section on the history of Islam begins with the header, 'Part Two of the *Cream of Histories*'.³¹

Besides its inclusion in manuscripts of the reworked *Collected Histories*, Qashani's *Cream of Histories* has survived in a single manuscript copied in August 1317.³² This manuscript contains a Perso-Islamic universal history that is effectively identical to the one found in the revised *Collected Histories*, covering from the beginning of time through to the end of the ʿAbbasid caliphate. Unlike the larger collection, however, this stand-alone *Cream of Histories* includes a colophon that clearly indicates that it was intended to end with the ʿAbbasid history, and not to include the various other histories from the *Collected Histories*. From these three related manuscripts, we can reconstruct Qashani's early career as a historian. Having written a *Collected Histories* for Ghazan, he prepared a second work, containing a history of the pre-Islamic Iranian world and the history of Muhammad and the caliphate. At some point during Oljeitu's reign, he revisited his original *Collected Histories*, inserting praise for the new *ilkhan* and a description of his earlier compositions and replacing the beginning of his *Collected Histories* with his new *Cream of Histories*.

Meanwhile, Rashid al-Din presented his own version of a history of the world to Oljeitu on Friday, 14 April 1307.[33] This work, the *World History* (*Tarikh-e 'Alam*), is conceptually very similar to Qashani's *Collected Histories*: it begins with a Perso-Islamic universal history and then offers a series of discreet histories of various dynasties and people. Several of these latter histories are only slightly modified from those contained in Qashani's *Collected Histories*. For example, Rashid al-Din's history of China also includes the description of how Litaji and Kamsun summarised a history of China written by three monks. However, in Rashid al-Din's rendition, this process occurred under Oljeitu's direction, and not Ghazan's. Rashid al-Din also inserts before this episode a discussion of Nasir al-Din Tusi's employment of Chinese astronomers at the Maragha observatory. Besides these superficial changes, much of Rashid al-Din's history of China, as well as several other sections of his world history, are identical or near to identical copies of Qashani's work.

A full comparison of these two world histories goes beyond the scope of this study, but it is evident that they are part of the same process of preparing a world history for the *ilkhan*s, and that Qashani's *Collected Histories* was certainly the major source for Rashid al-Din's *World History*. Of course, since the only surviving copy of Qashani's histories of the people of Eurasia comes from his reworked later version of the *Collected Histories*, we may never know if he modified his own work to match Rashid al-Din's *World History* in order to substantiate his claim as the rightful author of both. One place where Rashid al-Din unabashedly reused Qashani's material is in the Perso-Islamic portion of his *World History*. Here he appropriated Qashani's *Cream of Histories* in its entirety for the opening sections of his own work. The only differences evident between the *Cream of Histories* and copies of the Perso-Islamic section of Rashid al-Din's *World History* is the addition of a few section headers in the latter. The marks of Rashid al-Din's appropriation are evident in surviving manuscripts of his *World History*: where Rashid al-Din's text transitions to the history of Muhammad and the caliphs, it preserves Qashani's header for 'Part Two of the *Cream of Histories*'.[34]

Rashid al-Din did introduce certain modifications into the material he appropriated from Qashani. Beyond short textual additions such as the mention of Chinese astronomers working at Maragha, he also applied an overall order to the work. In Rashid al-Din's treatment, the *World History* begins with the Perso-Islamic history taken from Qashani's *Cream of Histories* and then proceeds through a series of Iranian dynasties contemporary to the 'Abbasids. Only then does he transition to the histories of other parts of Asia, expanding outward from the Islamic world to the foreign. The order of these various sections is clearly indicated in a table of contents he included with the work, and brief passages at the end of some sections indicate a transition to the next. This intentional ordering of sections is in contrast to Qashani's *Collected Histories*, which seems to have been exactly that: a scrapbook of various histories of dynasties and people, with little overall structure applied to it. Missing are almost all of Qashani's descriptions of how the histories came to be written, as well as any mention of Qashani as the work's original author.

At some point after Rashid al-Din presented his *World History* to Oljeitu, it and the earlier *Blessed History* were combined as two volumes of one larger historical collection. Rashid al-Din called this compendium of dynastic and world histories the *Collected Histories*, appropriating Qashani's title alongside his work.[35] Despite Qashani's central role in preparing the material that became the more famous *Collected Histories*, Rashid al-Din received the recognition and reward attached to the project. Qashani tells us that this reward was substantial: half a million dinars from the state treasury, as well as property estate yielding an additional 200,000 dinars annually.[36]

In response to what he viewed as the appropriation of his work, Qashani launched an attack against Rashid al-Din in his later *History of Oljeitu*. This attack is based in the pernicious question over Rashid al-Din's sincerity as a Muslim given his Jewish origins. This accusation became one of the abiding sites of contention in discussions of Rashid al-Din's life and character in later centuries, and Qashani is its first great agitator. In two places in his *History of Oljeitu*, Qashani states his claim to have written the *Collected Histories*.[37]

In each instance, he begins by mentioning Rashid al-Din's presentation of the *Collected Histories* and the rich reward he received for it. Qashani then laments the fact that he, the rightful author, has not received any part of this reward, and ends with a passage of verse that emphasises the great favour that Rashid al-Din realises from the theft of Qashani's work.

As elsewhere in Qashani's writing and in Persian prose historiography, the use of verse here sets the episode apart from the main narrative and invests it with a moralising charge. Each time Qashani relates this episode, he specifically references Rashid al-Din's Jewish heritage, first by mentioning a band of 'degenerate Jews' who assisted Rashid al-Din, and later by casting the moralising verse into the voice of a group of Jewish clients of Rashid al-Din, whom the vizier had taught – and by implication, paid – to disavow the truth of the work's authorship. By invoking the religious community of Rashid al-Din's birth to cast doubt on his loyalty and moral integrity, Qashani establishes a literary trope presenting Rashid al-Din as a revanchist Jew. As discussed in Chapter 6, he would again take this approach in criticising Rashid al-Din's later activities at court.

Among modern scholars, Edgard Blochet was the first to recognise the similarities between Qashani's work and Rashid al-Din's *World History*. In his 1910 *Introduction* to Rashid al-Din's history, he gives full credence to Qashani's claim to authorship of the work.[38] Blochet's claim attracted the attention of Vasilii Bartol'd, who wrote a review of Blochet's *Introduction*. As part of this review, Bartol'd summarily dismisses the idea that Qashani might have written the *Collected Histories*. Bartol'd's argument rests on the idea that only someone with the prominence and court access that Rashid al-Din enjoyed could have possibly written with the kind of detail found in the *Blessed History* about the history of the Mongol ruling family.[39] This critique is misplaced: Bartol'd defends Rashid al-Din's authorship of the dynastic history that Ghazan had commissioned in 1302. The parallel texts that Blochet cites as evidence for Qashani's authorship are drawn from Qashani and Rashid al-Din's respective world histories.

Despite the truth of Blochet's assessment, later scholars have tended to follow Bartol'd, continuing to credit Rashid al-Din as the authorial voice behind the *World History*. At most, a scholarly consensus has emerged, in the absence of access to the few extant manuscripts of Qashani's work, that

Rashid al-Din employed a group of 'research assistants' to aid in the assembly of information.[40] In fact, his entire *World History* was conceptually based on that of 'Abd Allah Qashani, with many sections demonstrating major textual dependence and a major portion lifted full cloth from Qashani's *Cream of Histories*. Rashid al-Din certainly would not have had time to write the *World History* in the three years following his presentation of the *Blessed History*. During that time, he continued to manage the work of the state and, as discussed below, he composed three collections of treatises on theological topics.

In the introduction to his *Collected Histories*, Qashani claims that the work was a product of his own design. Rashid al-Din never acknowledges Qashani's involvement in the process of writing the *World History*, but he also refrains from naming himself as the work's author. Instead, he credits the project to his patron, Oljeitu. In the general introduction to his own later *Collected Histories*, immediately after describing the presentation of the *Blessed History*, Rashid al-Din writes that,

> Since the Padishah of Islam has a constant interest in various sciences and the arts of history and storytelling and spends most of his felicitous time acquiring various accomplishments, after reading and correcting this [*Blessed*] *History* he said, 'until now no one at any time has made a history that contains the stories and histories of all inhabitants of the climes of the world and the various classes and groups of humans, there is no book in this realm that informs about all countries and regions, and no one has delved into the history of the ancient kings. In these days, when, thank God, all corners of the earth are under our control and that of Chinggis Khan's illustrious family, and philosophers, astronomers, scholars, and historians of all religions and nations – Cathay, Machin, India, Kashmir, Tibet, Uyghur, and other nations of Turks, Arabs, and Franks – are gathered in droves at our glorious court, each and every one of them possesses copies of the histories, stories, and beliefs of their own people, and they are well informed of some of them. It is our considered opinion that of those detailed histories and stories a perfect compendium should be made in our royal name, and it should be written in two volumes along with an atlas and gazetteer and appended to the [*Blessed*] *History* so that the aggregate of that book would

be peerless and include all sorts of histories. Inasmuch as the opportunity is at hand, and the composition of such a memorial, the likes of which no kings have ever possessed, is possible, it must be completed without neglect or delay so that it may cause our name and fame to endure.'[41]

Oljeitu appears here as the genius behind the grand historical collection that we now know as the *Collected Histories*, even as he graciously allows the dynastic *Blessed History* to carry his deceased brother's name. However, when viewed alongside the theological works that Rashid al-Din was simultaneously preparing for Oljeitu, this image of the magnanimous and inspired sovereign takes on new light.

Buildings and Beliefs

While he was preparing the *World History*, Rashid al-Din embarked on a new scholarly project. This was the production of five collections of theological essays, including Qur'an commentaries and treatises on various questions, that occupied him from about 1306 until 1311.[42] During this period, a new shrine city rose on Oljeitu's bequest on the fields of Qongqur-Oleng, west of Qazvin.[43] As was the case with Shamb, Arghun had first developed this site in 1290 as a summer residence. Oljeitu monumentalised it as a purpose-built capital city beginning as early as 1305; it was completed in 1313/14 to great fanfare.[44] The citadel walls of the new capital can still be traced, though most of its buildings have fallen into ruin. The most prominent structure on it by far is one of the few that have survived: a monumental dome, 25 metres across and 50 metres high, intended as Oljeitu's tomb.[45] The complex surrounding the tomb included a constellation of pious and charitable foundations which, again like Shamb, were supported by properties that Oljeitu had endowed for that purpose.[46] Unlike the shrine-city that Ghazan had built, or the one that Rashid al-Din was simultaneously having constructed (discussed below), Oljeitu did not name his new capital after himself, but rather after his office, calling it Sultaniya, 'the imperial'.

Such a building programme was possible in part because Oljeitu's reign was relatively peaceful, other than his disastrous military effort to subdue the province of Gilan.[47] The event that has attracted the most historical attention from the reign of Oljeitu was his decision early in 1310 to adopt

Shi'ism as the formal creed of the state by including the names of the twelve imams on his coinage (*sikka*) and in the Friday sermon (*khutba*). Oljeitu had already taken a famously itinerant route through the major religions of the Mongol world – born Buddhist, he had been baptised Christian before his conversion to Islam – and his son and successor Abu Sa'id reinstated standard Sunni institutions and practices after he came to the throne in 1316.[48] For these reasons, Oljeitu's embrace of Shi'ism is often dismissed as a failed conversion. This is true despite the fact that one local history names it as the most important moment in Ilkhanid history while failing even to mention Ghazan's conversion in 1295.[49]

Oljeitu's embrace of Shi'ism occurred as Rashid al-Din neared the end of his main phase of theological writing and as the city of Sultaniya and its great dome rose above the fields of Qongqur-Oleng. Like those projects, the conversion was not a spontaneous event, but the culmination of a long process. The general chronology of this conversion can be traced through a long narrative digression in Qashani's history of Oljeitu's reign.[50] As part of his account of the *hijri* year 709 (11 June 1309–30 May 1310), Qashani writes about Oljeitu's visit to the shrine of 'Ali in Najaf, a site that had also helped to inspire Ghazan's decision to build his own shrine at Shamb. This was the first year that Oljeitu wintered in the vicinity of Baghdad; previously, the season had been spent closer to Tabriz, and Oljeitu had made annual visits to his brother's tomb at Shamb.[51] It was after his visit to Najaf, Qashani writes, that Oljeitu decided to adopt Shi'i markers of state. Having thus set the goal for the subsequent narrative, he shifts his narrative back seven years to 1302, when sectarian conflict during Friday prayers in Baghdad had resulted in the death of a *sayyid*, a biological descendant of Muhammad. As discussed in Chapter 3, Ghazan had at that time responded with a call for religious freedom, claiming both Muhammad and Chinggis Khan as his inspiration. Qashani, whose work elsewhere suggests Shi'i sympathies, claims that Ghazan himself even considered converting to Shi'ism after learning about the story of 'Ali, Fatima and their descendants.[52]

Having established a philosophical affinity between the Ilkhanid family and Shi'ism, Qashani tells of a religious debate between jurists of the Hanafi and Shafi'i schools that occurred at Oljeitu's court in 1306. The dispute over finer points of Islamic legal thought is interrupted by the Mongol Amir

Qutlughshah, who laments the move away from Mongol custom and towards Islam. 'What have we done,' Qutlughshah asks,

> that we have set aside the new law (*yasa*) and custom (*yosun*) of Chinggis Khan and taken up the ancient religion of the Arabs that is divided into seventy-odd sects? And the choice of either of these schools is a disgrace and an infamy, in that one of them allows marriage to one's daughter, and the other to one's mother and sister-in-law, God forbid either! We ought to return to the *yasa* and *yosun* of Chinggis Khan.[53]

Qutlughshah here presents the opposite position to that taken by Ghazan after the death of the ʿAlid in Baghdad in 1302. In contrast to Ghazan, who saw Muhammad and Chinggis Khan as co-equal precedents for a policy of religious tolerance, Qutlughshah insists that Islamic and Mongol traditions are irreconcilably opposed.

In Qashani's narrative, Qutlughshah's outburst initiated a period of religious doubt at court, which carried into the Gilan campaign of 1307. During that campaign, several members of the royal household were killed by a lightning strike. Buddhist monks or shamans (the word *bakshi* is regularly used for both) pointed to this as the result of Oljeitu's embrace of Islam, but it was the Muslim Mongol Amir Taramtaz who reminded Oljeitu of the solution which Qashani has already primed his reader to hear: that Shiʿism, with its particular reverence for genealogical succession, was aligned with the *yasa* of Chinggis Khan, even if it was not accepted by all Muslims. Shiʿism offered Oljeitu a negotiated position that could satisfy both Mongol and Muslim custom and affirm him as the leader of both communities. Qashani dutifully wraps up his narrative by recapping the visit to Najaf and the adoption of Shiʿi markers of state, as if Amir Taramtaz's observation had catalysed the decision.

Three years passed between the Gilan campaign and Oljeitu's first winter in Baghdad, when he finally embraced Shiʿism. During that time, Rashid al-Din continued to produce his theological writings. These demonstrate a steady escalation in their ideological tone, which casts further light on the new role that Oljeitu was beginning to assume as a ruler for all communities, sanctioned by both his Mongol heritage and by the full array of Islamic sects.[54] Rashid al-Din's theological writings show the conversion to be neither rash nor reactive, but part of an effort to present a unified theory of sovereignty in the post-caliphal Islamic world.

Rashid al-Din's first three collections of theological writings were completed by March 1307, though it is not entirely clear when he had begun working on them. In the first of these three collections, the *Book of Clarifications* (*Kitab al-Taudihat*), he reports that Oljeitu asked him to begin writing a commentary on the Qur'an after he had presented the *Collected Histories*.[55] In the second collection, the *Key to Commentaries* (*Miftah al-Tafasir*), he states even more generically that he had long been interested in the topic and had been trying his hand at it for a while.[56] As theology goes, these first two collections contain little of merit, presenting fairly standard interpretations of Qur'anic passages. They do, however, provide at least one interesting point of contrast with his later writings, throwing into sharp relief the ideological developments that took place at Oljeitu's court between his accession in 1304 and his embrace of Shi'i markers of state in 1310. That contrast appears in Rashid al-Din's description of his inspiration for embarking on theological writings.

In the *Book of Clarifications*, Rashid al-Din defends himself against an accusation that his conversion to Islam was insincere.[57] Over the course of this passage, we learn that the unnamed accuser was attempting to impugn Rashid al-Din based on his Jewish heritage after Rashid al-Din had not granted his accuser any windfall from Ghazan's estate. Such detractors, Rashid al-Din reports telling Oljeitu, were bound to arise because of his prominence at court, and he draws a comparison between himself and the earlier theologians Abu Hamid Ghazali (d. 1111) and Fakhr al-Din Razi (d. 1209), who suffered similar attacks in previous centuries.[58] Later in the collection, he solidifies this comparison by offering a commentary and addendum to Ghazali's self-defence against his own critics.[59]

To counter these accusations against the sincerity of his faith and the orthodoxy of his writings, Rashid al-Din describes the beginning of his career as a theologian, according to which he presented his earliest efforts in the genre to the scholar Taj al-Din al-Mu'mini, who encouraged him to continue his work. Other scholars in Tabriz eventually accepted Rashid al-Din's theology as orthodox, proof of which is found in a series of their endorsements preserved in manuscript copies of the *Book of Clarifications*.[60] Rashid al-Din's earliest theological collection is thus deeply concerned with justifying his own position as a theologian. Several of the endorsements he collected are dated to the *hijri* year 706 (13 July 1306–2 July 1307), a year that saw Qutlughshah's harangue against Islam and the difficult campaign in Gilan and when questions of the role of Islam in Mongol life were very much alive at court. Here we see Rashid al-Din stretching his legs as a theologian during a period when the court was realising a need for a new interpretation of Islam.

In his second collection, Rashid al-Din suggests that a synthesis might be negotiated among the various sects of Islam, just as Ghazali had proposed two centuries earlier.[61] Criticising authors from various schools for their narrow sectarianism, he promotes the scholarship of the tenth-century synthesist Abu'l Hasan al-Ash'ari (d. 936) alongside that of Hasan b. Yusuf al-Hilli (d. 1325), known as 'Allama al-Hilli, the leading advocate of Shi'ism at Oljeitu's court.[62] Rashid al-Din's promotion of these two is exemplified by his characterisation of Ash'ari as 'the greatest authority for Sunnis and the collective'.[63] This last concept – the collective (*jamā'a*) – introduces into Rashid al-Din's theological writing in 1307 the concept of universal integration of previously diverse ideas. This same sentiment characterises his *World History* and the same semantic marker is found in the title of the *Collected Histories* (*Jami' al-Tawarikh*).[64] As discussed below, this was just the beginning of a long engagement with the idea of collection that marks Rashid al-Din's late projects.

With his third theological work, the *Imperial Book* (*Kitab al-Sultaniya*), Rashid al-Din turns his focus away from himself and onto Oljeitu.[65] This work was inspired by a court audience on 14 March 1307, the first year that Oljeitu spent the summer at his new capital.[66] At this audience, Oljeitu instigated a debate over the nature of prophecy. Rashid al-Din here relates the story of the sultan's birth and the rain that accompanied it to show that Oljeitu himself served as the proof of prophecy.[67]

Rashid al-Din's ideas about Oljeitu developed significantly between spring 1307 and the end of 1310 – the same three years in which religious ambivalence and sectarian discord pushed Oljeitu towards a formal adoption of Shi'ism. In his last collection of theological works, the *Account of Truths* (*Bayan al-Haqa'iq*), Rashid al-Din repeatedly presents an image of his patron as a theological savant, spontaneously arriving at solutions to questions of revealed truth that surpassed the capacity of the scholars at his court to comprehend.⁶⁸ Oljeitu enjoys this special knowledge in spite of his inability to read, or perhaps more precisely because of that inability, a characteristic he shared with the Prophet Muhammad.

Rashid al-Din invokes various Qur'anic verses that help to substantiate such a presentation of his patron. In comparing Oljeitu's access to divine knowledge to that of the Prophet, he reminds his reader of Gabriel's injunction to Muhammad: 'God has taught you that which you did not know, and ever has the favour of God upon you been great' (Q. 4:113). This is paired with the 'authority verse', used to grant Oljeitu's secular kingship a degree of sacred authority: 'obey God and obey the Messenger and those in authority among you' (Q. 4:59).

Rashid al-Din's use of the throne verse was yet another nod to Ghazali, who had used it to justify obedience to the Saljuq sultans two centuries earlier. Late in his life, Ghazali had written a work in the genre of advice literature, the *Kingly Advice* (*Nasihat al-Muluk*), in which he draws on earlier theoretical works about caliphs and imams in order to propose a model of a secular ruler, or *sultan*, as distinct from the caliph.⁶⁹ In his work, Ghazali equates the sultan to 'the shadow of God on earth', deserving of obedience by virtue of God's periodic selection of certain rulers, administrators and scholars to make the world prosper.⁷⁰ While Ghazali's patrons had to negotiate sultanic authority with the parallel institution of the caliphate, Oljeitu was not similarly constrained and could assume a totalising authority in the world. By the time Rashid al-Din completed the *Account of Truths*, the last sections of which are dated to September 1310, Oljeitu had adopted the Shi'i markers of state on his coinage and in the weekly sermon. This was not a traditional conversion to Shi'ism, but rather a declaration to sceptical courtiers that Oljeitu, like the descendants of 'Ali, came from a storied genealogical tradition and enjoyed a privileged position of authority with special access to divine knowledge.

While Rashid al-Din revives Ghazali's model of the sultanate as an office, rooted in secular power but sanctioned by divine selection, he reserves for himself a unique and novel position at Oljeitu's side. When he describes the sultan answering theological questions beyond the ken of his court theologians, Rashid al-Din is there, either recording Oljeitu's words or else explaining to the scholars that their own ignorance is more remarkable than the sultan's knowledge.⁷¹ Rashid al-Din's last two collections of theological writings, the *Account of Truths* and, before it, the *Subtle Truths* (*Lata'if al-Haqa'iq*) of 1308, are both structured in question-and-answer format, in which Rashid al-Din responds to questions put to him by courtiers and theologians. His ability to resolve the most trenchant theological conundrums sets Rashid al-Din foremost among the religious authorities at Oljeitu's court. It places him in league with Fakhr al-Din Razi, whose own *Controversies* (*Munazarat*) of a century earlier had been framed to show their author's ability to answer questions posed from various philosophical and sectarian positions.⁷²

As he arrived at this new understanding of his personal role in the evolving relationship between secular power and religious knowledge, Rashid al-Din changed his story about how and why he began writing theology. He revisits this question in the *Subtle Truths*. In place of the earlier narrative, in which he relied on the encouragement of Taj al-Din al-Mu'mini and other scholars to justify his position as a theologian, Rashid al-Din now tells of a dream he witnessed on 11 April 1306, in which the early caliphs encouraged him to take up theology.⁷³ Emboldened by this, he tells his reader, he embarked on a feverish bout of writing, producing three works, the *Clarifications*, *Key* and *Imperial Book* in just eleven months. Rashid al-Din's theology, like Oljeitu's birth, is couched in the language of miracle, as a dream visitation propels him into his work.

Collecting a Legacy

When he completed the *Account of Truths* in late 1310 or early 1311, Rashid al-Din was without doubt the most influential figure at the court of Oljeitu. He still shared top administrative duties with Sa'd al-Din Sawaji, but by leveraging those responsibilities against his newly constructed image of himself as the indispensable companion to the sultan, he had assumed unmatched authority over the financial, cultural and intellectual resources of the realm. At the same time, he took steps to establish his image in society and for posterity. His most visible effort in this regard was a series of building projects, culminating in a massive new complex on the eastern edge of Tabriz, opposite his former patron's suburb of Ghazaniya. Both Ghazaniya and Oljeitu's new capital at Sultaniya were major urbanisation campaigns, backed by the absolute power of the ruler to direct state funds towards such civic and commercial projects. At the heart of each, however, was a core of charitable, scientific and memorial foundations.

Such foundations were established and maintained under the legal practice of endowment (*waqf*). This institution allowed an individual to protect his or her wealth from taxation and from posthumous dissolution by allocating it in perpetuity to support specific charitable foundations.[74] The legal deed of endowment (Ar. *waqfiya*, Pr. *vaqfnāmeh*) for such a foundation should name the endowed property and stipulate the use of its revenue, and should name an administrator of the endowment and a process for selecting future administrators to ensure the perpetual maintenance of the foundation.[75] Rashid al-Din served as administrator for the endowments of both Ghazan and his queen Bulughan Khatun, managing the finances of the royal couple's foundations at Shamb and at Baghdad.[76] In turn, Oljeitu named him as administrator of the endowment that supported his new construction at Sultaniya. This meant managing resources valued at a million dinars annually, if one instructor supported by the endowment is to be believed.[77]

From these appointments, and from the property he had already amassed and the rewards he received for his various scholarly projects, Rashid al-Din began establishing his own endowments to support foundations across the Ilkhanate, including in the new capital Sultaniya, his hometown of Hamadan, Yazd where he had studied medicine, and Bastam, where the shrine of Beyazid had so strongly influenced both Ghazan and Oljeitu.[78] By far his largest endowment supported the massive collection of charitable and scholarly institutions he created outside Tabriz, collectively called the Rashidi Quarter (*rabʿ-i rashīdī*).[79]

Remarkably, the original deed of endowment for the Rashidi Quarter has survived, part of it written in Rashid al-Din's own hand.[80] This document lists the various components of the Rashidi Quarter and specifies the number and type of employees who were to be maintained in its operation. Part of the endowment deed is missing, so we cannot fully reconstruct the properties that supported the foundation, but one estimate based on the description of operations at the Quarter has placed the annual revenue in the neighbourhood of 100,000 dinars, about one-tenth that of Sultaniya.[81] If Qashani is to be believed, Rashid al-Din could have secured this level of income by endowing to the Rashidi Quarter just half of the property he received as part of his reward for the *Collected Histories*. Thus, while it was a massive endowment, it paled alongside those of the *ilkhan*s, and it represented a relatively small portion of Rashid al-Din's overall fortune.

Since its rediscovery in 1970, the endowment deed has fuelled a body of scholarship on Rashid al-Din as a patron of charitable institutions, including several attempts to reconstruct the structure and function of the Rashidi Quarter.[82] It is clear that the Rashidi Quarter performed an important social function, providing medical care, accommodations and education to a society still rebuilding from a chaotic century. It also broadcast a very public image of Rashid al-Din as the provider of social welfare. The beginnings of the Rashidi Quarter project are not known for certain, though Qashani reports that Oljeitu encouraged haste in its construction as early as July 1305, just as the new construction at Sultaniya was getting underway.[83] The sultan's new city and his adviser's new district rose in tandem, twin projects of the duumvirate that ran the state. Such a date for the initial construction of the Rashidi Quarter corresponds with information found in Mamluk sources that Rashid al-Din purchased the land for the Rashidi Quarter using the payment he received for the *Blessed History* in 1304.[84] Subsequent additions to the original foundation can be recovered through the various additions and amendments that Rashid al-Din made to his endowment deed between 1309 and 1316. During that period, Rashid al-Din's position as Oljeitu's primary adviser and the recipient of the greatest royal patronage attracted increasing competition and resentment, as seen in Chapter 6. Rashid al-Din's responses to those developments are imbedded in the text of the endowment deed, which evolved over several years.

The oldest portion of the surviving endowment deed is dated to 1309, but it is already a copy of an earlier document, updated to include an expanded list of endowed properties.[85] This expansion was probably at least in part motivated by the proceeds Rashid al-Din received for the *Collected Histories* after he presented it in 1307. Rashid al-Din made the expansion of 1309 just as he was formulating his theological arguments for Oljeitu's special spiritual knowledge and his own essential role as the mouthpiece for the sultan. An initial addendum to this expanded original deed, added by early 1311, specifically mentions the *Account of Truths*, where this image of Oljeitu and Rashid al-Din is most fully articulated.[86] The early growth of Rashid al-Din's massive endowment was a manifestation of his power and of the cycle of patronage in which he and Oljeitu were bound.

Later additions to the Rashidi Quarter endowment deed reflect the emerging challenges to Rashid al-Din's position at court. When Sa'd al-Din attempted to confiscate funds from members of Oljeitu's court in 1311, he also targeted endowments, including the Rashidi Quarter. Almost immediately after this, Rashid al-Din assisted in the events that initiated Sa'd al-Din's fall from grace and execution, described in Chapter 6. In a new addendum made to the endowment deed in 1313/14, Rashid al-Din strikes a markedly humbled tone, assigning himself only the title of cook while crediting Oljeitu as the real patron of the Rashidi Quarter.[87] Of course, this sentiment is technically true, as Oljeitu was the ultimate source of Rashid al-Din's wealth and position, but it marks a departure from the supreme confidence of his earlier writing. By 1313, Rashid al-Din had become more guarded than he had been just a few years earlier. As described in Chapter 6, this corresponds to intrigues at court that damaged his reputation and invited challenges from his political opponents.

As Rashid al-Din's wealth and influence increased, so too did the most well-known of the many activities supported at the Rashidi Quarter. This was the book-making operation at the Quarter's scriptorium and Rashid al-Din's instructions, modified over the various addenda to the endowment deed, to produce a quota of deluxe manuscripts.[88] In the earliest portion of the endowment deed from 1309, Rashid al-Din specifies that the staff of the scriptorium were to produce one copy annually of the Qur'an and another of Ibn al-Athir's collection of *hadith*. By that time, Rashid al-Din had already gathered his first four theological collections into a compendium, just as he had previously gathered his two historical works into the *Collected Histories*. Rashid al-Din calls this compilation of four works the *Rashidi Collection* (*Majmuʻa Rashidiya*), using the same semantic marker of integration and collectivity under which his historical works had already been compiled and with which he had praised the synthesising theology of Ashʻari. He instructed, as he would later do for all of his works, that it be copied in both its original Persian form and in Arabic translation, making it available to the greatest possible audience.

Remarkably, the original exemplar copy of the *Rashidi Collection* has survived, as has the exemplar of the Arabic translation that Rashid al-Din had prepared.[89] The Persian original is dated 5 May 1309, though it was not until 1311 that the Arabic translation was complete. That later Arabic translation contains a description of an even larger collection, which was to incorporate all of Rashid al-Din's work under a single title, the *Collected Writings of Rashid* (*Jami' al-Tasanif al-Rashidi*). According to this description, the *Collected Writings* were to include fourteen titles in two main divisions: one division on theology and natural philosophy; the other on history, narratives and geography (see Table 4.1).

Rashid al-Din's description of his *Collected Writings* has given modern scholars a convenient starting point from which to catalogue and appraise the relative merits of the extant manuscripts of his various works.[90] However, we must remember that it was a prescription for a collection, conceived as Rashid al-Din was beginning to depict Oljeitu as a divinely inspired sovereign and

Table 4.1 *The* Collected Writings of Rashid. *As described by Rashid al-Din, preserved in Istanbul Aya Sofya MS. 3833 44a–76b and Bibliothèque nationale de France MS. arabe 2324 248b–288a.*

Division One on theological and natural philosophy, composed of two parts
   Part One: Four books comprising the *Rashidi Collection*
     a. *Book of Clarifications*, of an introduction and nineteen treatises
     b. *Key to Commentaries*, of eight treatises in two parts
     c. *Imperial Book*, of a main text and its continuation
     d. *Subtle Truths*, of an introduction and fourteen treatises
   Part Two: Two books not in the *Collection*
     e. *Account of Truths*, of seventeen treatises
     f. *Works and Beings*, of twenty-four chapters
Division Two on history, narratives and geography, composed of two parts
   Part One: the *Collected Histories* in four volumes
     a. *The Blessed History of Ghazan*
     b. *World History*
     c. *Genealogies of Prophets and Kings and Caliphs*
     d. *Depiction of the Regions*
   Part Two: Translations from Chinese
     e. *Scientific and Folk Medicine of the Chinese*
     f. *Simple Chinese Medicines*
     g. *Simple Mongol Medicines*
     h. *On Chinese Government and the Management of the Chinese State*

himself at the sultan's side as the great transmitter of the world's knowledge. Also, the fact that this description of the *Collected Writings* does not appear in the 1309 Persian original of the *Rashidi Collection* indicates that the idea for the comprehensive collection came to Rashid al-Din relatively late. Writing even later, Wassaf also mentions this final, grand collection, and he assigns to it a somewhat expanded list of titles.[91] Wassaf specifies that the *Collected Writings* was to be written in ten volumes, reaching a total of 3,000 sheets of large paper and costing over 60,000 dinars. As described in Chapter 6, however, Wassaf's description of Rashid al-Din's intellectual legacy is to be read as part of a rejoinder to Qashani's account of events at court in 1312.

Alongside the assembly of these deluxe collections of his own writings, Rashid al-Din instructed the academic staff of the Rashidi Quarter to distribute and teach the students there an increasingly large share of those writings.[92] In his first appendix to the endowment deed, which was probably penned around the time that Rashid al-Din completed the *Account of Truths*, he alters his instructions for manuscript production, adding that the legal scholars employed at the Rashidi Quarter should produce copies of several of his works, including his historical and theological collections, the *Account of Truths* (which had not been included in the *Rashidi Collection*), and another collection of scientific topics called *Works and Beings* (*Athar wa Ahya'*). These were to be written in Persian and Arabic and distributed to the cities of the Ilkhanate. Furthermore, all of these except the histories were to be taught in the schools of the Quarter.

These initial instructions were issued in time to include them in the Arabic translation of the *Rashidi Collection* when it was copied in 1310/11. The later addendum to the endowment deed, which was added in 1313/14, adds two additional titles to those that are to be copied and distributed.[93] These titles correspond to ones found in Wassaf's list of the *Collected Writings*. Rashid al-Din here instructs those employed by his endowment to make regular copies of his entire *Collected Writings* and to distribute and teach all these texts, establishing a comprehensive curriculum for the students and an immense work obligation for all involved. These efforts were also to be undertaken at his endowed foundations in other cities, creating a schedule by which three copies of the entire *Collected Writings* could be produced each year.[94] The ambition of the project seems to have outstripped the capacity of

Rashid al-Din's foundations, as no known copies of the *Collected Writings* were ever prepared.

Rashid al-Din's efforts to propagate an image of himself and his patron as the guiding lights of secular and religious authority were not unique to the Ilkhanate. This model of the universal sovereign supported by a uniquely qualified non-royal adviser emerged elsewhere, as Mongol khans across Asia worked to integrate their sense of a privileged dynastic origin into the indigenous traditions of their subjects. In Central Asia, this took the form of a partnership between the rulers of the Chaghadai Khanate and the heads of regional Sufi groups.[95] In China, Qubilai Qa'an benefited from the guidance of the Tibetan monk Phags-pa, who recast his patron as a cakravartin king.[96] The Mongols may have converted to the religions of their subjects, but their exercise of power left lasting impressions on the expression of those religions in the political realm.

Despite Rashid al-Din's efforts, there is no evidence that the full *Collected Writings* were ever produced. After 1312, competing political pressures at court made Rashid al-Din an increasingly polarising figure, and some of his more elaborate efforts to commemorate his own works seem to have fallen by the wayside. Manuscripts of several individual works from the Rashidi Quarter scriptorium have survived, however. These include the Persian and Arabic *Rashidi Collections*, which demonstrate the scale and elaborate quality of the books that Rashid al-Din instructed to have copied. While no copies of the *Blessed History* can be said with certainty to survive from the Rashidi Quarter, enough early copies have survived to demonstrate that Rashid al-Din's early instructions to distribute and copy individual works had at least begun before the end of his life. Those early copies also reveal, however, that the *Blessed History* changed shape over the first decade of its existence. It is to those changes that we now turn.

Notes

1. For an overview of his patronage activity, see Blair, 'Patterns of Patronage'; van Ess, *Der Wesir*, offers an overview of the theological writings. For other scientific works, see Rashid al-Din, *Tangsuqnameh*; Berlekamp, 'The Limits of Artistic Exchange'; Lambton, 'The *Āthār wa aḥyā*'. For bibliography on his historical writings, see Appendix A.

2. Rashid al-Din, *Jamiʿ al-Tawarikh*, pp. 1317, 1430–41. For an elaboration of Rashid al-Din's representation of the Alafireng affair as an argument for Arghunid legitimacy, see Brack, 'Mediating Sacred Kingship', pp. 60–4.
3. A detailed description of this complex is offered by Wassaf, *Ketab-e Mostatab*, pp. 382–4. See also Wilber, *The Architecture of Islamic Iran*, pp. 124–6.
4. Rashid al-Din, *Jamiʿ al-Tawarikh*, p. 1384. This passage comes immediately after a portion of the endowment deed for the complex that Rashid al-Din preserves in his text: *Jamiʿ al-Tawarikh*, pp. 1377–84.
5. Rashid al-Din, *Jamiʿ al-Tawarikh*, p. 1376.
6. Rashid al-Din, *Jamiʿ al-Tawarikh*, p. 1282.
7. Suhrawardi al-Maqtul, *The Philosophy of Illumination*, pp. 77–8.
8. Rashid al-Din, *Majmuʿa*, p. 341; Brack, 'Mediating Sacred Kingship', pp. 195–217, discusses the significance of this anecdote.
9. Shabankaraʾi, *Majmaʿ al-Ansab*, p. 270.
10. This cycle is described by Hoffmann, *Waqf*, pp. 87–9.
11. Rashid al-Din, *Jamiʿ al-Tawarikh*, p. 8.
12. See Appendix A for brief descriptions of these sections and a discussion of their sources and manuscript reception.
13. This began with Jahn, 'Rašīd al-Dīn as a World Historian', and has been echoed by many others since.
14. Earlier examples of world histories produced in the Islamic world have been catalogued and discussed by Radtke, *Weltgeschichte und Weltbeschreibung*.
15. Khalidi, *Arabic Historical Thought*, pp. 132–6.
16. Radtke, *Weltgeschichte und Weltbeschreibung*, pp. 11–15.
17. Khalidi, *Arabic Historical Thought*, pp. 114–17; Duri, *The Rise of Historical Writing*, pp. 64–7.
18. Khalidi, *Arabic Historical Thought*, pp. 176–81.
19. For religious, commercial and art-historical perspectives on this, see Preiser-Kapeller, '*Civitas Thauris*'; Wing, '"Rich in Goods and Abounding in Wealth"'; and Blair, 'Tabriz: International Entrepôt', all published in Judith Pfeiffer's volume on Tabriz, *Politics, Patronage and the Transmission of Knowledge*.
20. Rashid al-Din, *Jamiʿ al-Tawarikh*, p. 1374.
21. Qashani's use of this title has already been noted by Morton, *The Saljūqnāma*, p. 24; Kamola, 'Rashīd al-Dīn', p. 248; Brack, 'Mediating Sacred Kingship', pp. 324–5.
22. Qashani, *Zubdat al-Tawarikh*, pp. 3–4, reproduced from Tehran University Faculty of Literature MS. 9076 190a.

23. Tehran University Faculty of Literature MS. 9076.
24. Brack, 'Mediating Sacred Kingship', p. 325, draws attention to the fact that the history of the Isma'ilis, in which this list of sections is found, was a later addition to the *Collection*.
25. Tehran University Faculty of Literature MS. 9076 329a.
26. Tehran University Faculty of Literature MS. 9076 370a.
27. Berlin Staatsbibliothek MS. Pertsch 368.
28. Berlin Staatsbibliothek MS. Pertsch 368 2a.
29. Berlin Staatsbibliothek MS. Pertsch 368 2a, reproduced by Blochet, *Introduction*, p. 141.
30. All three manuscripts of Qashani's historical writing discussed in this section have previously been catalogued as the *Cream of Histories*, even though two of them are reflections of the larger *Collected Histories*.
31. Tehran University Faculty of Literature MS. 9076 66b. Berlin Staatsbibliothek MS. Pertsch 368 lacks all headers, including this one, which would be expected on folio 102b.
32. Tehran University Faculty of Literature MS. 5715. Unfortunately, the first couple of folios are missing. Ashtiani, 'Noskhah-ha-ye masur', p. 40, no. 7, calls this a manuscript of Rashid al-Din's *Collected Histories*.
33. The date, ironically, is preserved by Qashani, *Tarikh-e Uljaytu*, pp. 54–5. Because Qashani lists several dates in the sentence containing this information, the presentation of the *World History* is often misdated to 9 April.
34. See, for example, manuscript P_2 51b, compared with Tehran University Faculty of Literature MS. 5715 93a.
35. Noted also by Brack, 'Mediating Sacred Kingship', p. 325.
36. Qashani, *Tarikh-e Uljaytu*, pp. 54–5, 240–1. Mamluk sources put the reward at a lump sum payment of a million dinars: Amitai-Preiss, 'New Material', pp. 24–5.
37. Qashani, *Tarikh-e Uljaytu*, pp. 54–5, 240–1.
38. Blochet, *Introduction*, pp. 132–57.
39. Bartol'd 'E. Blochet, *Introduction*'.
40. See, for example, Petrushevsky, 'Rashid-ad-dina i ego istoricheskiy trud', p. 26; Morgan, 'Rašīd al-dīn and Ġazan Khan', p. 184.
41. Translation modified from Thackston, *Rashiduddin Fazlullah's Jami'u't-Tawarikh*, p. 6, according to Rashid al-Din, *Jamiʿ al-Tawarikh*, pp. 8–9.
42. Many of these works await publication and systematic study. A valuable overview is offered by van Ess, *Der Wesir*.
43. On the new capital, see Blair, 'The Mongol Capital'; Wilber, *The Architecture*

of Islamic Iran, p. 139; Minorsky, Bosworth and Blair, 'Sulṭāniyya'; Little, 'The Founding of Sulṭāniyya'.

44. Wassaf, *Ketab-e Mostatab*, p. 477, gives 1304/5 as a foundation date, but see sources listed by Spuler, *Die Mongolen*, p. 374 n. 22, which date the foundation between 1306 and 1308.

45. On the tomb and its influence on later architecture in Iran and the West, see Blair, 'Monumentality'. For more on the tomb, see Godard, 'The Mausoleum'; Blair, 'The Epigraphic Program'; Sims, 'The "Iconography"'.

46. Blair, 'The Mongol Capital', pp. 144–5.

47. On this campaign, and the historiographical efforts to whitewash the Mongol failure to subdue the region, see Melville, 'The Īlkhān Öljeitü's Conquest of Gīlān'.

48. Ibn Battuta suggests that Oljeitu converted from infidelity directly to Shiʿism, but later rejected that sect in favour of Sunni Islam when the dogs he sent to devour a group of Sunnis refused to harm a prominent *qadi*: Gibb, *The Travels of Ibn Baṭṭūṭa*, vol. 2, pp. 302–4. This account is sometimes cited as possible evidence that Oljeitu converted back to Sunnism before his death, but is better read as a miracle tale in support of Ibn Battuta's own sectarian position.

49. Miller, 'Local History', p. 78. For recent discussions of Oljeitu's religious experience and conversion, see Pfeiffer, 'Conversion Versions'; Kamola, 'Beyond History'.

50. Qashani, *Tarikh-e Uljaytu*, pp. 90–100.

51. For a discussion of the patterns of Oljeitu's itinerant court, see Melville, 'The Itineraries of Sultan Öljeitü'.

52. Qashani, *Tarikh-e Uljaytu*, pp. 90–5. On Qashani's Shiʿi sympathies, see Brack, 'Mediating Sacred Kingship', pp. 28, 335–6.

53. Qashani, *Tarikh-e Uljaytu*, p. 98. My thanks to David Morgan for pointing out the presence of the word 'new' in the sole manuscript of the work, a word that has been omitted from the edition and which further emphasises the difference between Mongol and Muslim traditions.

54. The following discussion is elaborated in greater detail in Kamola, 'Beyond History'.

55. van Ess, *Der Wesir*, p. 13.

56. van Ess, *Der Wesir*, p. 16.

57. This passage is translated by Quatremère, *Histoire*, pp. cxx–cxxx.

58. van Ess, *Der Wesir*, pp. 9, 15; Klein-Franke, 'Rashīd ad-Dīn's Self-defence', pp. 201–2.

59. Klein-Franke, 'Rashīd ad-Dīn's Self-defence'.
60. van Ess, *Der Wesir*, pp. 22–38, discusses various versions of the lists of these endorsements and identifies many of the individuals who wrote them.
61. For Ghazali's original proposal in this regard, see Campanini, 'Al-Ghazzālī', esp. pp. 264–71.
62. Klein-Franke, 'Rashīd al-Dīn's Treatise'. On 'Allama al-Hilli at Oljeitu's court, see Schmidtke, *The Theology of al-'Allāma al-Ḥillī*, pp. 23–32.
63. Klein-Franke, 'Rashīd al-Dīn's Treatise', pp. 540, with English summary at p. 535.
64. Klein-Franke, 'Rashīd al-Dīn's Treatise', p. 532.
65. van Ess, *Der Wesir*, pp. 17–19.
66. Qashani, *Tarikh-e Uljaytu*, p. 72.
67. Brack, 'Mediating Sacred Kingship', pp. 195–217, discusses the *Imperial Book* in depth, including the implications of the episode of Oljeitu's birth.
68. Rashid al-Din, *Bayan al-Haqa'iq*, pp. 81–6, 393–9.
69. Lambton, *State and Government*, pp. 107–26.
70. Lambton, *State and Government*, pp. 117–18.
71. Rashid al-Din, *Bayan al-Haqa'iq*, pp. 85–6, 395.
72. Kholeif, *A Study of Fakhr al-Dīn al-Rāzī* offers a translation and commentary of the *Controversies*.
73. Rashid al-Din, *Lata'if al-Haqa'iq*, vol. 1, pp. 44–5.
74. For an overview of the institution of *waqf*, see Peters et al., 'Waḵf'. For its role in medieval Islamic society, see Lambton, 'Awqāf'; Lev, *Charity, Endowments, and Charitable Institutions*, particularly pp. 53–67.
75. For a case study in how such an endowment could function over several centuries, see McChesney, *Waqf in Central Asia*.
76. Hoffmann, 'The Gates', p. 194.
77. Blair, 'Monuments', in Minorsky, Boswell and Blair, 'Sulṭāniyya'.
78. Blair, 'Writing and Illustrating History', p. 58.
79. On the site of the Rashidi Quarter, which is now in ruins, see Wilber, *The Architecture of Islamic Iran*, pp. 129–31.
80. Rashid al-Din, *al-Waqfiya al-Rashidiya*, ed. Minovi and Afshar in facsimile (1971) and ed. Minovi, Afshar and Karang in print (1977). On the manuscript's discovery, see also Irej [sic] Afshar, 'The Autograph Copy'.
81. Hoffmann, 'The Gates', pp. 192–3.
82. In addition to Afshar's initial announcement of the discovery, there were three papers dedicated to the endowment deed at the dedicatory conference on

Rashid al-Din held in Iran, 1–6 November 1969: Rahnama, 'Rashid al-Din'; Salim, 'Taʿlim va tarbiyat'; Mashkur, 'Rabʿ-e rashidi'. Other studies followed: Sotudeh, 'The Income and Expenditure'; Fragner, 'Zu einem Autograph'; Salim, 'Rashid ed-Din Fazlollah's Contribution'; Blair, 'A Medieval Persian Builder'; Hoffmann, 'Rašīduddīn Faḍlallāh'; Hoffmann, *Waqf*; Aryan et al., 'Investigating the Architectural Heritage'. For reconstructions, see Blair, 'Ilkhanid Architecture and Society'; Khafipour, 'A Hospital in Ilkhānid Iran'.

83. Qashani, *Tarikh-i Uljaytu*, p. 44.
84. Amitai-Preiss, 'New Material', pp. 24–5.
85. Hoffmann, 'The Gates', p. 191.
86. Rashid al-Din, *al-Waqfiya al-Rashidiya* (ed. Minovi and Afshar), pp. 293–6. Ben Azzouna, 'Rashīd al-Dīn Faḍl Allāh', p. 191, has shown that this is an earlier, and separate, addendum from the one dated to 1313/14.
87. Rashid al-Din, *al-Waqfiya al-Rashidiya* (ed. Minovi, Afshar and Karang), p. 245, discussed also by Hoffmann, 'Speaking about Oneself', p. 12.
88. Ben Azzouna, 'Rashīd al-Dīn Faḍl Allāh', proposes a new understanding of the manuscript operation based on the phases of the endowment deed, which parallels my own earlier attempt to explain Rashid al-Din's efforts to collect his various works: Kamola, 'Rashīd al-Dīn', pp. 237–44. The following paragraphs rely heavily on both of these studies.
89. The Persian original is Tehran Golestan MS. 2235, published in facsimile: Rashid al-Din, *Majmuʿa* and described by Bayani, 'Rasaʾel-e farsi'. The Arabic translation is Paris BnF MS. arabe 2324. Ben Azzouna and Roger-Puyo, 'The Question of the Formation', provides the results of a thorough material analysis of the Arabic manuscript, with further bibliography.
90. See, for example, Jahn, 'The Still Missing Works'; Rajabzadeh, *Khwaja Rashid al-Din*, pp. 302–25.
91. The relationship between Wassaf's list and Rashid al-Din's is discussed by Kamola, 'Rashīd al-Dīn', pp. 241–3 and fig. 5; Ben Azzouna, Rashīd al-Dīn Faḍl Allāh', pp. 193–4.
92. Ben Azzouna, 'Rashīd al-Dīn Faḍl Allāh', pp. 192–3.
93. Ben Azzouna, 'Rashīd al-Dīn Faḍl Allāh', pp. 193–8.
94. Ben Azzouna, 'Rashīd al-Dīn Faḍl Allāh', pp. 195–6, offers a reconstruction of this schedule.
95. Paul, 'Sheiche und Herrscher'; Schwarz, 'Ohne Scheich kein Reich'.
96. Franke, 'From Tribal Chieftain'.

5

Remaking Mongol History, 1307–1313

As Rashid al-Din compiled his *Collected Histories*, the Ilkhanid state was as strong as it had ever been, newly invigorated with the broad legitimacy lent by the conversion to Islam of the brothers Ghazan and Oljeitu. The capital city, Tabriz, was increasingly marked by the signs of Ghazan's patronage, particularly in the district of Shamb, now monumentalised and renamed Ghazaniya after himself. Among the merchants and envoys who came to the new commercial and political hub in northern Iran were those from the eastern reaches of the Mongol world, bringing with them information about their lands of origin and the other branches of the fractured ruling clan. The store of knowledge available to Rashid al-Din about the early Mongol Empire and its various regions and people thus grew with the flow of people visiting the cosmopolitan city of Tabriz.

Such newcomers – especially those members of the Mongol military elite who retained personal memories or records of the empire's history – could in a moment enrich or change Rashid al-Din's understanding of the Mongol past. From his contact with these travellers, Rashid al-Din knew that anything he wrote down might quickly become obsolete. To counter this, he built into the *Blessed History* a series of opportunities to update the text as new information came to light. Hodong Kim and Christopher Atwood have each demonstrated how Rashid al-Din's knowledge of Mongol history changed while he was first writing the *Blessed History*.[1] The surviving manuscripts of the work reveal that he continued to update it even after presenting it to Oljeitu. What is more, the experience of assembling the *World History* exposed Rashid al-Din to new ideas about how to present the past, ideas that he retroactively applied to his earlier dynastic history.

This chapter returns to Rashid al-Din's first completed work, the *Blessed*

History of Ghazan, to see how it changed in its content and form in the years after 1304. By the time he instructed the staff of his scriptorium to include the *Collected Histories* among the works reproduced in the deluxe editions described in the last chapter, Rashid al-Din had turned the *Blessed History* into a much more polished and visually impressive work than the one he originally presented to Oljeitu. Even as he disseminated this final, 'official' version, however, other individuals were already modifying his work, introducing new portions of text or else restructuring the *Collected Histories* to meet different historical concerns than those of the Ilkhanid court. This chapter discusses the relationship of these various versions of the *Blessed History* to one another and to the historical context in which they appeared in the last decade of Rashid al-Din's life. Reference to the different recensions of the work, and to individual manuscripts within those recensions, corresponds to the sigla assigned in the catalogue of manuscripts found in Appendix B.

Genealogical Trees

The entire *Collected Histories* demonstrates a strong concern for genealogy. The *Blessed History* is a dynastic history of the Mongols, and the various sections of the *World History* trace the lineage of kingly and prophetic families across Eurasia. Besides these individual genealogies, the *Collected Histories* ties the Mongols into larger genealogical structures that serve to embed them in established Judeo-Islamic historical traditions. As discussed in Chapter 3, Rashid al-Din opens the *Blessed History* by fitting the Mongols into a broader Turkic genealogy and nesting the Turks among the descendants of Noah.[2] The effect, right from the beginning of the work, is a conceptual genealogy that inserts the Mongols into a human taxonomy familiar to the Muslim, Jewish and Christian populations of the region.

One of the essential tools for making this genealogical case is the genealogical tree.[3] In describing the Mongol sources of his history, Rashid al-Din singles out the 'histories of origin and lineage' (*tevārīkh-e aṣl va nesb*) of the Turkic people.[4] Out of these records, in addition to his narrative history, he produced a series of diagrams showing the relationship among members of Chinggis Khan's family, beginning with Dobun Bayan and Alan Qo'a, the legendary ancestress of all Mongols. Beginning with the story (*dastan*) of Chinggis Khan, large spaces – sometimes covering several pages – are dedicated to these family trees. Changes in how these diagrams are presented provide some of the most immediately evident diagnostics for establishing the order in which different versions of the work appeared. Specifically, different recensions of the *Blessed History* describe these trees differently in the headers that accompany them. The manuscripts of the ε recension say that the trees show the arrangement (*waż*) of the descendants of the ruler in question. In copies of the β, γ, δ and ζ recension, by contrast, the headers to the genealogical trees specify the presence of images (*ṣūrat*). (See Figure 5.5 below for the relationship between these recensions.)

Unfortunately, few surviving copies of the *Blessed History* preserve the family trees themselves. Most of those that do are examples of Rashid al-Din's last version of the work (see manuscripts Z_1, Z_2 and Z_{12}, as well as K_2). These late trees were intended to include portraits of the individual rulers whose families they depict, alongside their spouses or royal consorts. The additions of such portraits presumably inspired the change in section headers to mention images. Only three such images have survived *in situ* in a manuscript of the *Blessed History* that may have been produced at Rashid al-Din's scriptorium in Tabriz. These are the portraits of Ogedei, Qubilai and Hulegu that appear in the early fourteenth-century copy now in Tashkent.[5] Other portraits have been cut out of this manuscript, some of which have been replaced with coarse copies patched in on separate sheets of paper.[6] Similar portraits cut from the genealogical trees of another copy or copies of the *Blessed History* were included in a series of albums collected by Heinrich Friedrich von Diez in Istanbul.[7] In the exemplar copy of the δ recension (manuscript D_1), the space for the large genealogical trees of Chinggis Khan's descendants has been repurposed for Mughal-period illustrations. Several of the trees, however, were at least partially completed before being repurposed. The small portraits of several khans and their queens have survived, being integrated into the texture of the new images.[8]

The genealogical trees of the ζ recension are comfortably familiar in their format. Stemming from the image of the ruler and his wife is an array of branched lines connecting his children and, occasionally, their descendants as well (see Figure 5.1). The manuscripts of the ζ recension further distinguish the gender of children by placing daughters in circles and sons in squares. However, there is evidence that this was not the original form of

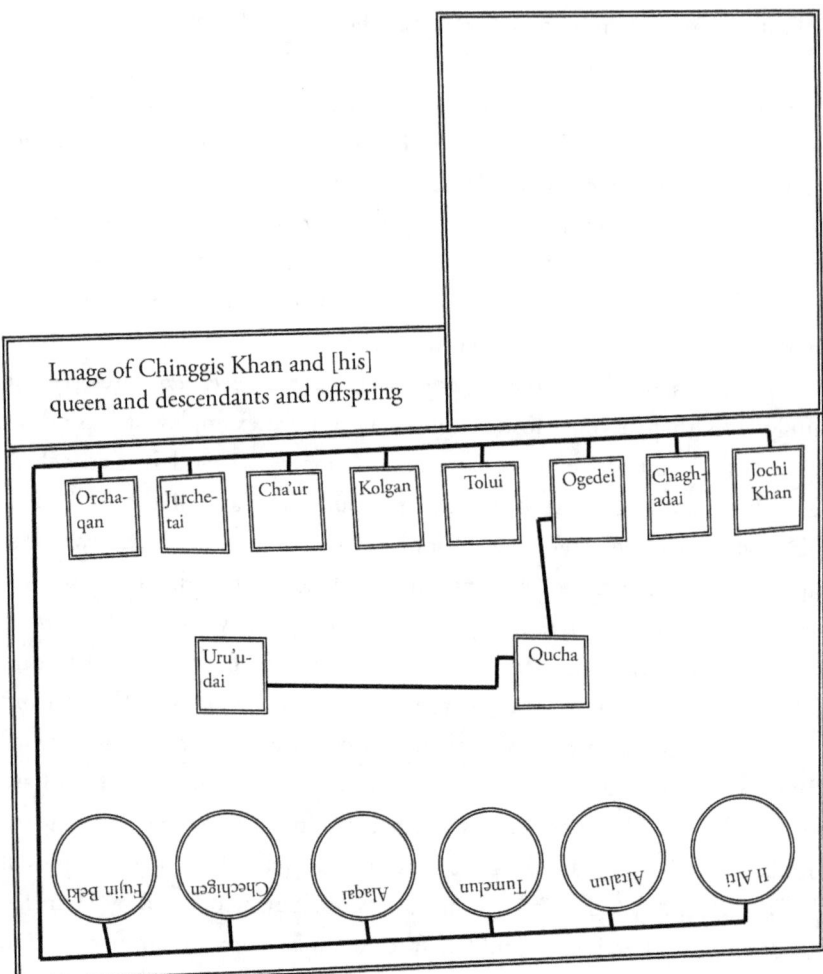

Figure 5.1 The genealogical tree of Chinggis Khan, from manuscript K₂ 64a. The large space in the upper right is left blank for a portrait of Chinggis and Borte. The line of descent to Qucha should come from Kolgan not Ogedei.

the genealogical trees in the *Blessed History*. As mentioned above, headers in the ε recension describe the trees as showing the arrangement (*waż'*) of the family in question, without an image, which was probably the original form that the family trees took. One manuscript of that recension (E₁₁) contains genealogical trees that contravene some of the conventions apparent in the later ζ recension. For example, in the tree of Chinggis Khan (the last in this

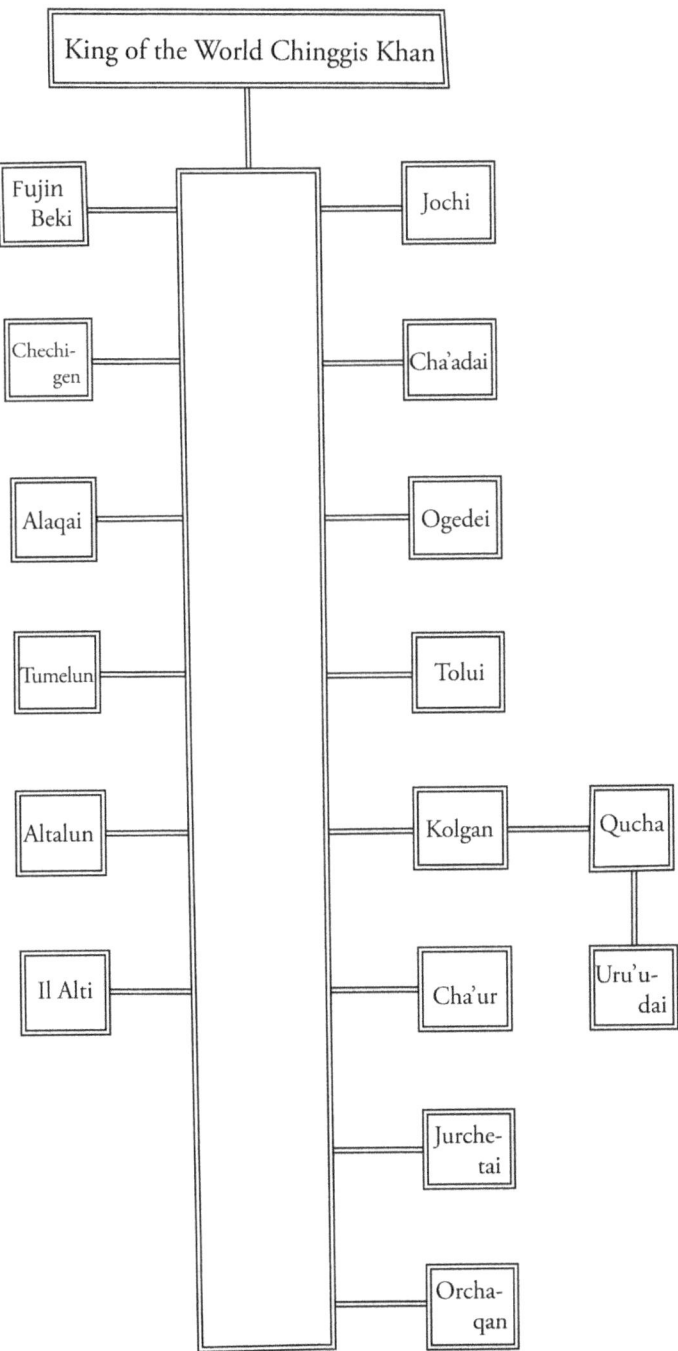

Figure 5.2 The genealogical tree of Chinggis Khan, from manuscript E_{11} 60a.

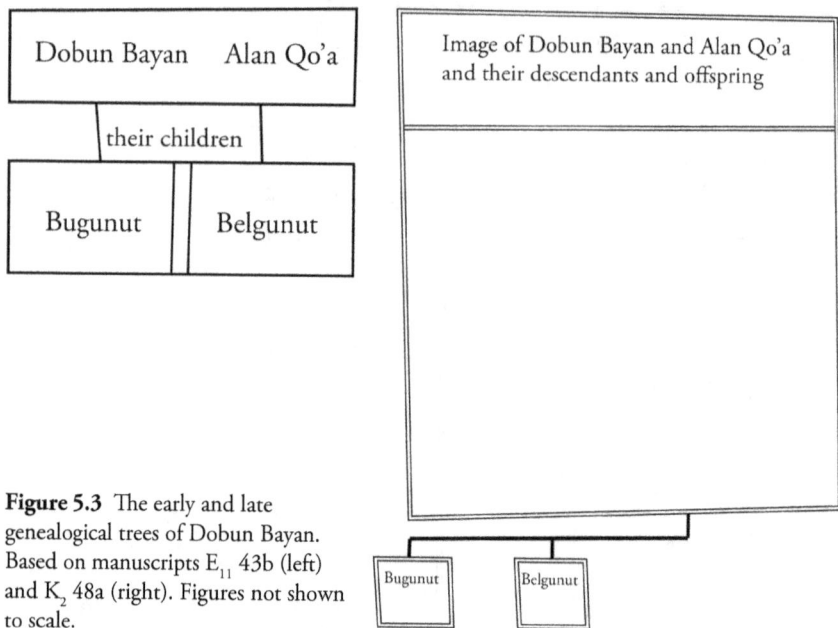

Figure 5.3 The early and late genealogical trees of Dobun Bayan. Based on manuscripts E$_{11}$ 43b (left) and K$_2$ 48a (right). Figures not shown to scale.

fragmentary manuscript), both sons and daughters are indicated in squares, and the generation of siblings are shown attached to a looped line, rather than a branching one (see Figure 5.2)[9]. More peculiar is the first genealogical tree in the work, that of Dobun Bayan. Whereas the manuscripts of the ζ recension show Dobun Bayan's sons Belgunut and Bugunut on the two arms of a branched line descending from Dobun Bayan and Alan Qo'a, manuscript E$_{11}$ shows a tabular box divided into several fields containing the names of family members and another field containing the phrase 'their children', explaining the relationship through words, rather than design (see Figure 5.3).

Similar tabular figures have been added to the margins of manuscript B$_1$. The headers for the genealogical trees in this manuscript indicate the presence of images, and yet the original copyist has not provided any of the actual trees. However, the manuscript was evidently later corrected by reference to a copy of the ε recension. In addition to the figure for Dobun Bayan also seen in manuscript E$_{11}$, manuscript B$_1$ shows similar tabular figures for the families of Alan Qo'a and Bartan Bahador.[10] Since the β and ε recensions are most closely related to the original *Blessed History*, it may well be that these simpler, tabular diagrams reproduce the Mongol 'histories of origin and lineage' that Rashid al-Din mentions. If so, Rashid al-Din must have encountered some other influence that inspired him to change the format of his genealogical diagrams. Such an influence can be deduced by looking at the other places where Rashid al-Din uses genealogical trees.

In the years between 1304, when Rashid al-Din first presented the *Blessed History* to Oljeitu, and 1307, when he finished the *World History*, he conceived of the idea of preparing a universal genealogical tree that would draw all the people of the world together into a single graphic display. He mentions this idea in his first collection of theological treatises, the *Book of Clarifications*, as early as 1306.[11] A slightly later theological treatise, the *Imperial Book*, written between 1307 and 1308, contains the earliest example of this form of universal genealogical tree.[12] A significant portion of the *Imperial Book* is dedicated to a series of lists of the companions of the Prophet, their followers, and the Umayyad, 'Abbasid and Fatimid caliphs. Immediately following these lists is a large genealogical tree that aggregates the various lines of Judeo-Islamic prophets and caliphs into a single graphic display. This display is oriented sideways to the book, so that it carries over across page breaks: flipping through the book presents the reader with an uninterrupted scrolling family tree (see Figure 5.4). In formatting this tree, Rashid al-Din placed the Fatimids along the central line of the branching tree of caliphal dynasties, reflecting the particular respect that Ghazan and Oljeitu both showed to the descendants of Muhammad's daughter, Fatima.[13]

In 1310, two years after the composition of the *Imperial Book* and three years after the *Collected Histories* were first presented to Oljeitu, Rashid al-Din wrote the prescription for his *Collected Writings*, where he lists a fourth volume as part of the historical compendium (see Table 4.1). He titles this volume the *Genealogies of Prophets and Kings and Caliphs* (*Shu'ab-e Anbiya va Muluk va Khulafa*). While no work has survived under that title, a single manuscript of a work fitting this description and written in the voice of Rashid al-Din has come down to us as the *Five Genealogies* (*Shu'ab-e Panjganeh*).[14]

The *Five Genealogies* is, in effect, a biological map of the various peoples treated in the *Collected Histories*. In its first section (folios 9a–63a), it traces forty-nine generations of descent from Adam to Muhammad. After this, it backs up chronologically to follow the lineage of Judeo-Islamic prophets from Adam, with contemporary kings alongside them (folios 66b–95b).

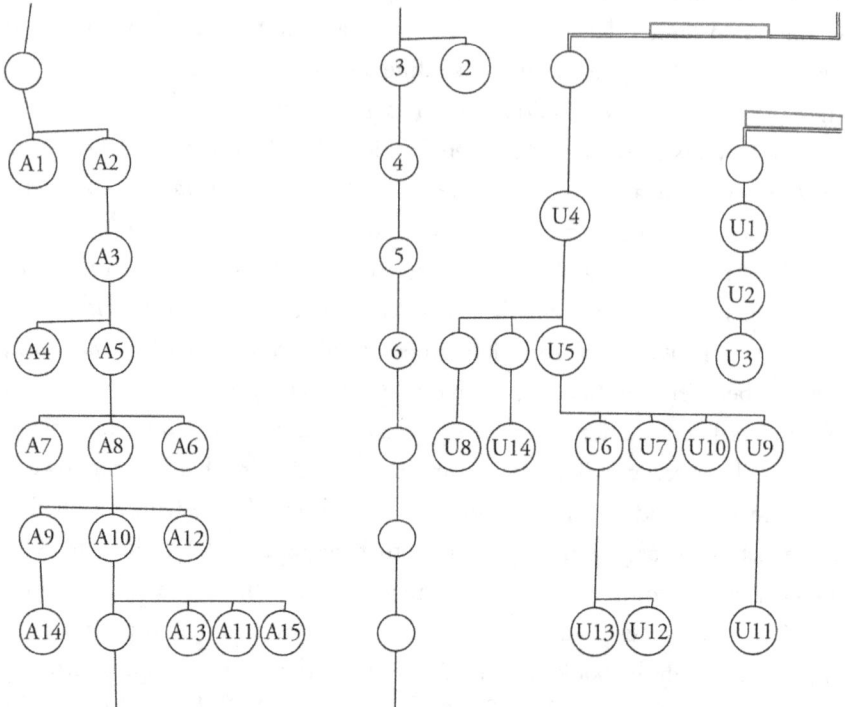

Figure 5.4 Part of the genealogy of caliphs from the *Imperial Book*. Caliphs are here numbered by dynasty: the Umayyads (U1–U14) on the right, early Abbasids (A1–A15) on the left. Al-Musta'im (A12) appears here as the brother, rather than the nephew, of al-Wathik (A9) and al-Mutawakkil (A10). In the centre, the Isma'ili imams, with Isma'il and Muhammad following Ja'far al-Sadiq (6). Numbers for imams have been supplied later; they follow the numbering of Twelver Shi'ism. Based on Tehran Golestan MS. 2235 p. 365, with numbering of imams supplied from St Petersburg IOM MS. C375 155a.

Next, it shifts to Chinggis Khan's own family, beginning with Dobun Bayan and ending with Ghazan Khan (96a–148b). These trees match those found in later versions of the *Blessed History*. Here they are stitched together into a single tree, formatted like the tree of Muhammad's ancestors and successors found in the *Imperial Book*. The effect of the *Five Genealogies*, like the rest of the *Collected Histories*, is to legitimise the Mongol dynasty of the *ilkhans* by situating them among other great secular and sacred dynasties. Rashid al-Din here does visually what he elsewhere does in text, placing his patrons at the centre of a larger historical tradition based on the idea of biological lineage.

In the same theological work where he assumes the grand titles quoted at the start of Chapter 4, Rashid al-Din claims to have invented the format of the genealogical tree.[15] His are indeed the earliest such trees in Islamic scholarship, though a proximate model can be found in late twelfth-century Christian historiography. In particular, a precedent for the genealogy of the Prophet and side-by-side presentation of Jewish prophets and contemporary kings is found in one of the most popular medieval European renditions of biblical history. This is the *Genealogy of Christ* (*Genealogia Christi*) of Peter of Poitiers (d. 1205). Peter was appointed chair of theology at the new University of Paris in 1169 and later served as the school's chancellor.[16] He created his *Genealogy*, which traces the lineage of Christ from Adam, with parallel histories of Jewish priests and gentile kings mentioned in the Bible, as a companion work for Peter Comestor's *Educational History* (*Historia Scholastica*). Originally displayed on classroom walls for the benefit students studying biblical history, Peter's *Genealogy* was soon copied into a portable format, either as a scroll or in the scrolling book format that is also employed in Rashid al-Din's *Imperial Book* and *Five Genealogies*. At least fifty copies of the *Genealogy* survive from the three centuries after its creation, and it became a primary source for four separate world chronicles written in Latin between the thirteenth and fifteenth centuries.[17]

In the *Genealogy*, Peter traces the descendants of Adam through Noah and Jacob, focusing on the lines that produced Israelite kings and priests, to the time of the unified monarchy of Saul, David and Solomon.[18] Beginning at this point, several lineages run parallel to the Jewish tradition, listing Assyrian, Chaldean, Medean and Persian kings, and a little later on, Alexander the Great and his successors leading up to the time of the birth of Christ. These same dynasties feature in Bar Hebraeus' list of secular and sacred dynasties, which was itself a main source for the first chapter of Rashid al-Din's history of the Franks (section II.K in Appendix A).

In short, Rashid al-Din began incorporating unified genealogical trees into his theological and historical works in the years immediately after he had compiled the histories of various peoples of Eurasia using their own sources. This suggests a debt to European works such as the *Genealogy* for the graphic representation of genealogies. Such an influence was ready at hand through the Italian merchants, ambassadors and mendicants who visited or lived in Tabriz during the Ilkhanid period. Rashid al-Din's decision to adopt this format for universal genealogical trees shows that he did not just accept European historical sources for their native historiographical sensitivity, but was also willing to incorporate useful elements of their representation of the past into his own work.

Illustrating the Past

The impact of Rashid al-Din's experience with foreign historical traditions on the presentation of the *Blessed History* is most evident in the illustrations that came to decorate the text in the years after it was first presented to Oljeitu. Prior to the Ilkhanate, Islamic historical texts had not been illustrated, but during the Mongol period manuscripts of the *Shahnameh* and other historical texts began to gain illustration as a way to educate readers and edify patrons.[19] Most notably, a copy of Abu ʿAli Balʿami's Persian translation of Tabari's *History of Prophets and Kings* was prepared in Baghdad around the year 1300, with thirty-seven illustrations that offer lessons in the Muslim faith for the newly converted Mongols.[20] Just a few years later, artists in northern Mesopotamia or Iran supplemented a copy of al-Biruni's *Chronology of Ancient Nations* (*Athar al-Baqiya*) with twenty-four illustrations of historical events associated with the creation of calendars in different traditions.[21] These include five images of the Prophet Muhammad, but also several of non-Muslim religious figures, which together demonstrate the *ilkhans*' devotion to Islam while acknowledging the significance of other faith communities in the early decades of the dynasty's history.[22]

The original *Blessed History* was written in the years between when these illustrated copies of Balʾami and al-Biruni were made. In its earliest form, Rashid al-Din's work does not seem to have been illustrated. Very soon, however, Rashid al-Din began adding images to his text, creating a cycle of illustrations for Mongol history. In addition to the broader appearance of illustrated histories, this choice was probably influenced by exposure to works from other historical traditions. Rashid al-Din's second volume of history was heavily illustrated in its original form, and in the process of assembling it, Rashid al-Din came into contact with examples of illustrated histories from across Eurasia. In particular, the historical traditions of China and Europe came to bear on the illustrations for which the *Collected Histories* is famous.

One vector of influence on the illustrations of the *Collected Histories* was Chinese block-printing technology. As discussed below, Rashid al-Din admired this technology as a means of accurately reproducing text. In China, block-printing was also used to illustrate books, as images could be engraved and reproduced alongside text. The precise reproduction of these images led, between the tenth and thirteenth centuries, to a stable iconography for illustrating Buddhist texts.[23] Many of the illustrations of the *Collected Histories* are in a broad horizontal format that imitates that of Chinese scrolls and butterfly-bound books. This format came to distinguish the images of early copies of the *Collected Histories*.[24] The effort to precisely reproduce these images according to Rashid al-Din's instructions for copying his works outstripped the capacity of the scriptorium at Tabriz. No complete illustrated copy of the *Collected Histories* has survived from the Rashidi Quarter, and it may be that few if any were ever produced.

A second, closer model for the atelier-based reproduction of a deluxe illustrated universal history can be found in the Crusader state of Acre, which fell to the Mamluks in 1291, little more than a decade before Ghazan's original commission for the *Blessed History*. As in the Islamic world, Latin Christian writers had wrestled for centuries with the task of correlating scripture with works of secular history. The earliest effort to do so in a vernacular language was the French *Universal History* (*Histoire Universelle*), written by Wauchier de Denain in the 1220s for Roger IV, châtelain de Lille.[25] Like Rashid al-Din, Wauchier stitched together various sources to create a new historical space justifying a nascent political and cultural entity, in his case positing a Trojan origin for the Franks. As with Rashid al-Din's *Collected Histories*, extant illustrated copies of the *Universal History* contain numerous scenes of combat and of enthroned royal figures. The consistency of scenes included in multiple manuscripts indicates an effort to reproduce not only the text of Wauchier's work, but the illustrative programme accompanying it.

Among the many extant witnesses to the *Universal History* is a heavily illustrated copy now in London.[26] Based on the style of its images, this manuscript has been linked to the scriptorium at Acre, and was possibly commissioned by the elite of that city as a welcome gift to their new King Henry II de Lusignan in 1286.[27] In the illustrations of the Genesis story in the Acre copy of the *Universal History*, the Hebrew patriarchs are depicted with significant detail and depth, in contrast to the rather flat figures that surround them. This suggests that painters of differing skill levels and specialisations worked according to a clear division of labour to produce an illustrative programme that was consistent overall, even if individual images are unevenly executed.[28] The size of the images in the Acre copy are also uniquely large, sometimes covering entire pages.

There is no direct evidence that Rashid al-Din drew from, or was even aware of, the Acre copy of the *Universal History*, and given the appearance of illustrated copies of the works of Firdausi, Bal'ami and Biruni during this period, it is safe to say that the illustration of historical works was a broad trend across the Near and Middle East in the Ilkhanid period. However, given the proximity in time and space between Crusader Acre and Ilkhanid Tabriz and the general mobility of artists in the medieval Islamic world, it is entirely possible that the Rashidi Quarter in Tabriz benefited from a diaspora of people, books and ideas from the Acre atelier after the fall of that city in 1291. Thus, while images of narrow rectangular format seem to look to Chinese block-printing, the large full-page compositions of city sieges that occur in the *Blessed History* find their closest comparanda in the art of Acre, a city well versed in siege warfare.

In the years after 1314, the scriptorium that Rashid al-Din had endowed struggled to keep up with his instructions to produce multiple copies annually of his historical and theological works. As a result, several copies of the *Collected Histories* were left unfinished by the time of his death.[29] Rashid al-Din's ambitious plans for reproducing his own work, including the consistent reproduction of large and ornate illustrations for his historical writings, may well have been the enthusiastic wishes of a wealthy patron attempting to integrate the artistic and technological innovations of foreign lands, whether that be Chinese block-printing or the atelier mode of reproduction seen at Acre. It is to be remembered, though, that the deluxe *Universal History* produced at Acre was always intended as a unique product, and the artists there likely would have similarly struggled to continue producing such manuscripts under the pressure of a schedule like the one that Rashid al-Din prescribed for his own atelier.

Enough partially illustrated copies have survived to demonstrate that two illustrative programmes were developed for the *Blessed History* during the years between 1307 and 1313. The δ recension, the first version to be illustrated, originally contained approximately seventy-five images, while the later ζ recension contained perhaps twenty fewer, a testament to the decreased ambitions of the atelier at the Rashidi Quarter over the last years of Rashid al-Din's life. Further details on these and other illustrative programmes of other versions of the work are elaborated in Appendix A.

Modifying the Text

As described in Chapter 3, Rashid al-Din assembled his *Blessed History* from various Persian and Mongol sources, including the first-hand accounts of members of the Mongol elite. As a result of this process of gathering information, Rashid al-Din's knowledge of the Mongol past expanded even as he composed the original work between 1302 and 1304. This is evident already in the *Blessed History*'s earliest chapters, describing the various Turkic tribes of Chinggis Khan's confederacy and the career of Chinggis himself. As part of his description of Turkic tribes, Rashid al-Din includes short notices about the notable members of each tribe, including those who served as commanders in Chinggis Khan's army. By the time he came to write his history of Chinggis Khan, Rashid al-Din had apparently learned more about the make-up of the Mongol army, so that the catalogue of military commanders at the end of the *dastan* of Chinggis Khan contains significantly more names than can be derived from the earlier section of text.[30] In the *Five Genealogies*, the volume of genealogical trees added to the *Collected Histories* at a later date (and discussed above), there are even more names on this list, indicating that the process of learning about Chinggis Khan's forces was ongoing.[31]

As if to acknowledge the fact that new sources of information were continually coming to light, Rashid al-Din regularly interrupts his chronicle with invitations to add such information as it became known. To return to the previous example, Rashid al-Din ends his catalogue of Chinggis Khan's commanders with a note recognising the need for continuous updating: 'What has been written here is the condition of the Mongol armies as has been ascertained so far. There is much that, because of the passage of time and the extent of the distance, has not appeared here. Subsequently, when it becomes known, it should also be related.'[32] Rashid al-Din builds similar opportunities for amendment into the end of the various chapters dealing with Chinggis Khan's descendants. As described in Chapter 3, the third section of each of these chapters offers an opportunity to present an essential portrait of each ruler's reign and character based on the information gathered from various books and individuals. The earliest known version of the *Blessed History* includes text in these third sections only for the chapters on Chinggis Khan, Ogedei and Ghazan, while the corresponding sections in the chapters on all other Mongol rulers seems to have been left blank.[33] Rashid al-Din's choice to include these headers even when no content was available for them shows that he did not consider his Mongol history complete in 1304.

Rashid al-Din was not the first Islamic historian to leave space in his work for new information to be added. As noted in Chapter 3, Wassaf had followed a similar strategy by regularly including headers that provide space for miscellaneous anecdotes. An example of how Wassaf made additions to such sections to respond to events at the Ilkhanid court is discussed in Chapter 6. The historiographical strategy of leaving space for new material looked even further back, however. In his *Perfect History*, Ibn al-Athir regularly included spaces at the end of the narrative of rulers' reigns for new information to be included as it became available.

In his introduction to the full *Collected Histories*, Rashid al-Din relates how Oljeitu proposed changes to the original *Blessed History* when presented with the work in 1304.[34] Whether this comment reflects reality or simple court flattery, it suggests that the shape of the work was already open for revision between 1304 and 1307. Since all known copies of the *Blessed History* include the general prologue of the *Collected Histories*, which was only completed in 1307, the extent of changes made before 1307 may never be known.[35] Tracking the progressive additions made to the *Blessed History* after that date, however, allows us to establish a relative chronology between the various recensions of the work, which is illustrated in Figure 5.5 and described below.

Absolute chronology is somewhat more difficult to determine. The original text of the *Blessed History* contains a brief mention of a battle that occurred in 1301 between the forces of Qaidu and Du'a, on the one hand, and the Great Khan Temur (Yuan Chengzong, 1294–1307), on the other.[36]

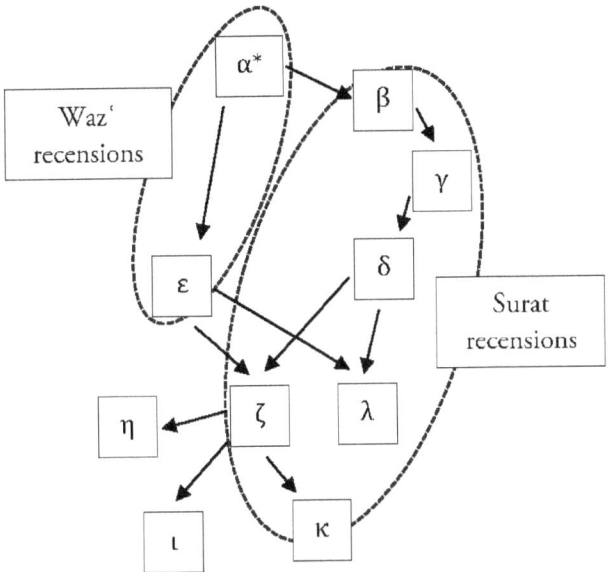

Figure 5.5 The relationships between recensions of the *Blessed History*.

Both Qaidu and Du'a were wounded at this battle, and while Qaidu died shortly thereafter, Du'a was still suffering from his wound at the time that the *Blessed History* was written. In the *Blessed History*, the battle is said to have happened 'last year', a reflection of the fact that the text was originally prepared in 1302. However, in Rashid al-Din's last version of the work, the ζ recension, a scribe has qualified the phrase 'last year' with the phrase 'which was the year 710,' making May 1311 the earliest that the ζ recension could have been prepared.[37] At the latest, the ζ recension was probably completed by 1313, as it was the version of the work intended to be reproduced at the scriptorium in Tabriz. Thus, between 1307 and 1313, Rashid al-Din regularly updated the text of his dynastic history with new passages of text and programmes of illustration. As a result, no fewer than five distinct recensions of the text – as well as several sub-recensions – have survived in the extant manuscripts of the work, all of which can be attributed to Rashid al-Din's own efforts to update the *Blessed History*. Meanwhile, other authors made their own changes to the text, a process that probably continued even after Rashid al-Din's scriptorium began producing the famous deluxe copies of the ζ recension.

Early Additions to the Ṣūrat *Recensions*

The earliest recoverable changes to the *Blessed History* are found in three groups of manuscripts catalogued in Appendix B as the β, γ and δ recensions. In contrast to the parallel ε recension, these all include headers to the genealogical trees of Mongol rulers that mention the presence of an image (*ṣūrat*). Since the ε recension genealogical trees probably preserve Rashid al-Din's first attempt to reproduce Mongol genealogical diagrams, these *ṣūrat* recensions are the first evidence of illustrations being included in the work. Other than the mention of these images, the single manuscript of the β recension contains none of the additional passages of text that began to accrete in later versions, making it possibly the closest witness to the 1307 form of the *Blessed History* in every way except the inclusion of the small portrait images.[38] In turn, the γ recension contains a few new passages that do not appear in the β or ε recensions.[39] For example, a long digression on the early relationship between Chinggis Khan and the young Tatar Shigi Qutuqu, who grew into one of his closest advisers, appears for the first time in the γ recension.[40] The same is true for a shorter passage relating how the Naiman prince Gushlug ingratiated himself to Gurbasu, wife of the Qarakhitai Gur Khan, and married her daughter.[41]

Similarly, the manuscripts of the γ recension begin to introduce new text to the third section of the *dastan*s of Mongke and Guyug, sections that had initially been left blank. These additions respond directly to Rashid al-Din's invitations to add material as it became known. One known manuscript of this recension includes the added passage on Mongke.[42] It opens with a reminder that Mongke's good qualities had already received mention, but that one story deserves special attention. This story tells of how certain promises that Guyug and his family made to merchants had driven the court into debt. After Mongke's accession, and against the advice of his ministers, the new Great Khan insisted on honouring those debts, to the cost of 500,000 bars of silver. Guyug's largess, in short, becomes an opportunity for Mongke to demonstrate his magnanimity. A different manuscript of the same recension contains an added passage in the third *qism* on Guyug that compliments this idea by establishing the image of Mongke's predecessor as sickly, autocratic and debauched, 'possessed of the arrogance of grandeur and conceit of pride'.⁴³ The excesses of Guyug's alcoholism in this account is only made worse by his support for Christians and his efforts to outdo his father Ogedei in largess. These two additions support the same effort to elevate Mongke's historical memory at the expense of Guyug. Until more manuscripts come to light, the reason for their inconsistent inclusion in the γ recension remains unexplained.

More significant textual additions begin to appear with the δ recension, in addition to the those already found in the γ recension. In addition to the passages on Shigi Qutuqu and Gushlug, the manuscripts of this group contain further short passages about various Turkic tribes.⁴⁴ Several of these passages begin with the phrase 'they say', suggesting that they originate in oral sources that Rashid al-Din had encountered after having completed his preliminary version. A section created for unusual events occurring during the reign of Qubilai has been left blank in most versions of the *Blessed History*.⁴⁵ In the δ recension, several short anecdotes appear in this space, including the deaths of Badr al-Din Lu'lu', Mu'ayid al-Daula Urzi, Nasir al-Din Tusi and Arghun Aqa, and two earthquakes: one in Nishapur in 1270, and another in Tabriz in the winter of 1262/3.⁴⁶

Manuscripts of the δ recension also reveal the first extensive programme of illustrations added to the text, as discussed above. It is also here that we see the first changes made to the family tree of Chaghadai.⁴⁷ The new family tree lists several descendants of Chaghadai that do not appear in earlier versions. Most of these were probably added as new information became available about the family of Chaghadai, or as new princes were born into it. However, there may be some political motivation behind some of the changes. In the revised description, Chaghadai's eldest son, Mochi Yebe, is not said to be born of Chaghadai's chief wife Yesulun Khatun, as the earlier version makes clear. Instead, it tells of how a drunken Chaghadai dragged a servant woman away from her work in Yesulun's camp and raped her, from which Mochi Yebe was born. This has the effect of diluting Mochi Yebe's legitimacy, and that of his descendants. Given that two of Mochi Yebe's sons, Teguder and Ahmad, had actively fought against Ilkhanid forces during the reign of Abaqa, this change may be an effort to delegitimise one particularly antagonistic branch of the Mongol royal clan.

Preparing the Final Version

The textual changes just described, along with the introduction of a major illustrative programme, make the δ recension a landmark in the evolving shape of the *Blessed History*. It was not, however, the work's final form. For that, Rashid al-Din made a new series of emendations. In doing this, he seems to have started from an earlier version than the modified γ or δ recensions. One group of manuscripts (the ε recension) omits the various textual additions added to the γ and δ recensions, and it gives no indication that it was ever intended to be illustrated. This suggests that it is very close to the original unillustrated version in many respects. The ε recension does, however, update the list of Chaghadai's descendants beyond the state already present in the δ recension, which must thus predate it. In ε, Chaghadai is said to have six sons, instead of eight. The two other sons of Chaghadai, Baiju and Qadaqai, are reassigned as a grandson and a great-grandson, respectively. Several other descendants are reorganised in this later version, which also adds even more names to the roster of Chaghadai's growing family tree.[48]

The ε recension also introduces new text into the *Blessed History*. This includes a folk etymology of 'Kereyid' from the Turkic *qara et* (meaning 'black-fleshed') and the genealogical division of the Kereyid nation, a discussion of different accounts of the sons of Qaidu Khan, and a short note about the number of years that Chinggis Khan lived.[49] One manuscript copied at the end of the fourteenth century contains three of the short additions about Turkic tribes from the δ recension in its margins, suggesting that it had been at least partially compared with a manuscript of that parallel line.[50] This manuscript provided the source text for at least five others (manuscripts E_{12}–E_{16}), some of which preserve these marginal corrections.

The version of the *Blessed History* that Rashid al-Din had reproduced in deluxe copies at his scriptorium in Tabriz combines changes and additions made to the γ, δ and ε recensions. This is perhaps the 'collation of the *Collected Histories*' that Ibn al-Fuwati mentions taking place in 1314/15.[51] This new recension, catalogued as ζ in Appendix B, includes some of the textual additions of the γ and δ recensions, though curiously not the added third *qism* texts on Mongke and Guyug. It also demonstrates the new style of genealogical trees and spaces for illustrations, although the programme of illustration here is less ambitious than that in the δ recension. From the ε recension it adopts the third version of the family tree of Chaghadai and a couple of short passages of text first found there.

This latest version also introduced two lengthy textual additions on the political dynamics of the Mongol steppe before the rise of Chinggis Khan. The first of these is a story about Quryaquz (Cyriacus) Buyuruq Khan, the father of the Kereyid Ong Khan who had been one of Temujin's early allies in his rise to become Chinggis Khan.[52] As with several of the notes first added to the δ recension, this episode opens by mentioning – but not naming – its source: 'it has been found in another book in Mongolian that ...' It then offers a narrative of internecine struggle within the Kereyid royal family and the decision of Temujin's father Yessugei to ally himself with Ong Khan as the latter fled his adversaries in his struggle to take the Kereyid throne. The story shows many parallels with the traditional narrative of Temujin's early career, as it stresses the importance of personal loyalty in the face of intra-clan conflict and intersperses short wisdom sayings into the telling of history.

The ζ recension also introduces a second narrative about inter-tribal relations on the steppe before Temujin's lifetime. This is the story of Hambaqa'i Qa'an, a member of the Tayichi'ud lineage of Mongols, the first cousin once removed and chosen successor of Qabol Qa'an two generations before Chinggis. According to the *Secret History*, after delivering his daughter to the Ayiri'ud Buiru'ud branch of the Tatars, he was abducted by another branch of Tatars, the Juyin, who sent him to the Altan Qa'an, emperor of the Jin Dynasty of northern China. In China, he was nailed to a wooden frame and executed. However, while in captivity, he managed to send a message back to his relatives explaining what has happened and establishing his succession.[53]

Rashid al-Din refers to the abduction and execution of Hambaqa'i several times in the early versions of the *Blessed History*, and each time he promises to tell the story of the abduction in its proper place.[54] Despite these promises, the episode only enters the text with the ζ recension.[55] The story of Hambaqa'i Qa'an found in the *Blessed History* is significantly different from and more elaborate than that of the *Secret History*. Here, it is Hambaqa'i who insists on a marriage alliance between the Tatars and his son. On his way to find a Tatar princess bride, he disregards inauspicious omens and is eventually seized. While Hambaqa'i is depicted as brash and rude, his brother and travelling companion Tudan Otchigin exhibits wisdom in the face of the ill omens and modesty in the households where they stay as guests on their way to the Tatars. Tudan escapes capture, and the Tatars punish the Bayan Duqlad for assisting him in his escape. Compared with the version of the story found in the *Secret History*, this story has a highly literary and moralising quality, relying on tropes of hubris and its punishment in contrast to the beneficial results of observing appropriate guest–host relations.

The ζ recension makes a number of smaller textual changes, as well. So, for example, it is only here that we read about the burial sites of Chinggis and Ogedei in two parallel passages that describe the mountain setting of the tombs and the rivers that flow from them.[56] Also, in the interim between the initial writing of the *Blessed History* and the preparation of its final version, Najib al-Din Farrash of Juvayn must have died, as a passage referring to his ongoing prosperity has been replaced by a memorial emphasising his descendants' inheritance of his position as superintendent of a lodge that Ghazan built at Buzinjird.[57] Similarly minor alterations may be accidental, or they may be the result of trimming information determined to be duplicative.

The Challenge of Reproduction

This rather complex early history of the *Blessed History* demonstrates just how open the text was, as Rashid al-Din continued to gather and insert information about his patrons' family and their subjects. Such a flexible attitude towards the text runs at cross purposes to Rashid al-Din's later decision to include the *Collected History* among the works reproduced at his scriptorium in Tabriz. The idea of reproducing books according to a set schedule and certifying them as exact copies of their exemplars was one of several ideas that Rashid al-Din probably gained from his experience assembling the histories of other parts of Eurasia. To implement it, he had to set aside his original ideas about a living, changing *Blessed History*.

Rashid al-Din owed his idea for a programme of book reproduction to a new knowledge of the technology of block-printing in China. Rashid al-Din describes this technology in two places in his writing: once in the introduction to the history of China included in the *World History*, and again in his translated collection of Chinese medical texts, the *Treasurebook of the Ilkhans on the Branches of Chinese Sciences* (*Tangsuqnameh-ye Ilkhan dar Funun-e ʿolum-e Khataʾi*). In the history of China, immediately after mentioning the source material for his text (section II.I in Appendix A), Rashid al-Din describes the Chinese technology of block-printing, by which a clean copy of a finished work, written in a good hand, was engraved into a series of wooden blocks, which were then deposited under official seal. These blocks could, for a fee, be impressed on paper, producing an exact copy of the original in relatively little time.[58] Such block-printing projects had become increasingly common in China during the Tang Dynasty (618–907), fuelled by a demand for copies of large Buddhist and Taoist religious texts. Major state-sponsored projects in the early Song period (late tenth to early eleventh century) led to the creation of massive uniform canons of Buddhist and Taoist texts, together requiring more than 200,000 page blocks.[59]

Rashid al-Din was clearly impressed with the possibilities that printing represented, comparing it favourably to the process of manuscript transmission by which his own works were copied: 'the people of China are known for the elegance of their printing and a delicacy of image. How can it be imagined that they would exchange something so concise, useful, and simple with something prolonged, ungainly, and difficult?'[60] Similarly, in the introduction to the *Treasurebook*, Rashid al-Din describes how engraved printing blocks allow a single printer to produce in one day what would take a year to accomplish in manuscript.[61]

Rashid al-Din's own theological treatises, along with the Qurʾan, which was among the first books reproduced on Rashid al-Din's instructions, function much like the canons of Chinese scripture for which block-printing had been developed: they admit no emendment or interpolation and thus are perfectly suited to the kind of stable reproduction programme that Rashid al-Din sought to create. The self-consciously changeable *Blessed History* defies such a project, though by the time Rashid al-Din proposed his programme of manuscript reproduction, he was more concerned with projecting an image of himself and his patron as the culmination of political and intellectual authority than he was with updating his history of the Mongols.

Rashid al-Din's enthusiasm aside, Chinese printing technology never caught on in the Ilkhanate. (A similar enthusiasm for Chinese medicine also never gained traction, as the *Treasurebook* remained an anomalous text in a medical tradition dominated by Galen and Avicenna.[62]) In his instructions for reproducing texts, however, Rashid al-Din attempts to create for his own works a level of copy control comparable with that which existed for the great scriptural canons of China. This effort to replicate in manuscript what the Chinese were doing with block-printing placed extraordinary demands on the workers of his scriptorium. It is perhaps no surprise, then, that no complete copy of the *Collected Histories*, let alone his much larger *Collected Writings*, survives from the Rashidi Quarter. Rashid al-Din's ideas about the precise reproduction of books dovetailed nicely with the grand ideological programme of Olejitu's reign, which presented the sultan and his vizier as the uniquely enlightened minds of their age. It ran into trouble, however, against the realities of manuscript book production and the ever-changing text of Rashid al-Din's *Blessed History*.

Later Variants

The variants outlined above all seem to have been introduced on Rashid al-Din's initiative. In the years after he completed his *Collected Histories* and instructed that it be reproduced in his scriptorium alongside his other works, other individuals continued the process of modifying the work. The clearest example of this is the abridgement that Abu Sulayman Banakati (d. 1329/30) completed in 1317.[63] Ghazan had granted Banakati the title 'Prince of Poets' (*Malik al-shuʿarā*) in 1302, the same year that he undertook his major patronage of historical narratives in preparation for what proved to be his last invasion of Mamluk Syria. Banakati's abridgement of the *Collected Histories* amplifies the image of Ghazan as a salvific figure through the addition of his own verses and those of his brother in the section dedicated to Ghazan's conversion.[64] This amplification of the sacred nature of Ilkhanid legitimacy, appearing as it does at the end of Oljeitu's reign, further demonstrates the ongoing blending of traditional Mongol notions of Chinggisid lineage with Islamic notions of authority that marked Oljeitu's reign.

Less comprehensive changes than Banakati's were made to manuscripts of the *Blessed History* by at least three individuals even before Rashid al-Din had died. These scribes were in part responding to Rashid al-Din's invitation to add information to the work as it became known. They were also, however, repurposing the work for new intellectual and ideological ends. The first of these was an individual well known to Rashid al-Din, namely, Nizam al-Din ibn al-Raʾis of Yazd, also known as Nizam Yazdi, who had been involved in implementing Ghazan's administrative reforms and who inserts mention of this into a copy he made of the work.[65] Other members of Nizam Yazdi's family, both older and younger than he, were closely involved with Rashid al-Din and his various projects. Members of the family testified to the orthodoxy of Rashid al-Din's theological writings, assembled his uncollected theological and scientific works, and imitated his practice of charitable endowment with a series of institutions in Yazd.[66] Two other individuals intervened with the manuscript reception of the *Blessed History* more substantially than Nizam Yazdi. Their modifications have enriched and complicated the modern study of Mongol history through the *Blessed History*.

The Other Rashid

One distinct group of additions to the *Blessed History* can be confidently attributed to a scribe named Rashid Khwafi.[67] These additions shed a sliver of light into an otherwise undocumented corner of the Ilkhanid administration, as Rashid Khwafi was not just a scribe, but a scholar personally invested in the rise and fall of the bureaucratic apparatus of the Juvayni brothers. As his name suggests, he was a native of the region of Khwaf, southeast of Nishapur, and thus an eastern Iranian compatriot of the Juvaynis.[68] He may have joined the migration of eastern scholars and administrators who populated the Ilkhanid bureaucratic apparatus in its first generation. From his additions to the *Blessed History*, we can tell that he was certainly at the Ilkhanid court by the end of the reign of Abaqa in 1282. We also know that he was in the Juvaynis' orbit after their move to the west, as he is responsible for copying out the earliest dated manuscript of ʿAlaʾ al-Din Juvyani's *History of the World Conqueror*, a copy he completed in December 1290.[69]

We do not have a date for the additions that Rashid Khwafi made to the *Blessed History*. However, it must have been relatively late, since he worked with a copy of Rashid al-Din's ζ recension, which was only completed between 1311 and 1313. One copy of his modified text (manuscript K_2) preserves aspects of the work's final formatting and mentions the presence of illustrations, both features of Rashid al-Din's last phase of modifications to the text. The spaces left for images largely, though not entirely, match the three main exemplars of Rashid al-Din's last version of the work (manuscripts Z_1, Z_2 and Z_{12}).

Some of Rashid Khwafi's smaller additions comment on the fact that Rashid al-Din had left space for such amendments, and they justify Rashid Khwafi's initiative in making his additions. For example, in a list of the administrative districts of China under Qubilai Qa'an, Rashid al-Din had left the entry for the capital city of Khanbaligh unsatisfyingly blank. In this space, Rashid Khwafi comments that 'a chancellor (*chingsang*) is here', and notes that 'in the original manuscript this was blank'.[70] A little later on, in the empty third section of the chapter on Timur (1294–1307), successor to Qubilai as Great Khan, Rashid Khwafi reiterates the idea that 'readers should write what they know', encouraging later scribes to make further emendations to the text or at least justifying his own additions to Rashid al-Din's work.[71]

Two of Rashid Khwafi's additions fill out third sections of the *dastan*s of early *ilkhan*s that are left blank in other recensions. The purpose of these additions diverges from the passages on Mongke and Guyug that appear in the γ and δ recensions. Instead of producing essentialised portraits of their subjects, these additions reveal more about Rashid Khwafi himself and his connection to the eastern reaches of the Ilkhanate. In one of them, in the third section of the chapter on Abaqa, Rashid Khwafi mentions an earthquake in the city of Nishapur.[72] The date of the earthquake is here omitted, but it is to be remembered that one of the anecdotes added at the end of the chapter on Qubilai in the δ recension mentions an earthquake in Nishapur in the year 1270.[73]

Perhaps the most famous, and most misunderstood, of Rashid Khwafi's additions comes in the third section of the chapter on Ahmed Teguder, where the scribe identifies himself as 'the writer of this blessed book'.[74] In that anecdote, Rashid Khwafi tells of how a slave of his was stolen during the reign of Abaqa, but he waited until the reign of the Muslim Ahmed before seeking reparation for the loss. When he is frustrated in his plaint, his narrative casts doubt on Ahmed Teguder's sincerity of faith. Some scholars, taking as a cue the first-person voice of this anecdote, have ascribed it to Rashid al-Din.[75] However, Rashid al-Din is all but silent about himself in his historical writing, and there is some question as to whether, as a Jew during the reign of

Abaqa, he would have been allowed to own a slave at all. Thankfully, Rashid Khwafi elsewhere uses the same phrase to identify himself as 'the writer of this blessed book', allowing us to identify the added passages as his and him as the aggrieved owner of the stolen slave.

Rashid Khwafi's additions are not limited to the third sections of the various chapters on Mongol rulers or other places where Rashid al-Din leaves blank space for emendation. Into the main narrative of the *Blessed History*, Khwafi also inserts a chronogram for the death of Shams al-Din Kart of Ghur, who died in Abaqa's custody in 1278, and another for Abaqa himself.[76] The chronogram for Shams al-Din Kart is credited to Nur al-Din al-Rasadi, perhaps the same scholar of that name whom Ibn al-Fuwati tells us worked for Baha' al-Din and 'Ala' al-Din Juvayni, and whose name implies a connection to Nasir al-Din Tusi's astronomical observatory (*raṣad*).[77]

Furthermore, Rashid Khwafi supplements Rashid al-Din's narrative of the attacks by Majd al-Mulk against the Juvayni brothers with a dramatic climactic scene. In it 'Ala' al-Din Juvayni interrogates his accuser and Majd al-Mulk suffers a grisly execution 'in Ajighi's tent behind Ahmed's camp':

> While they stuffed his head with straw to send it to Baghdad, just then the writer of this document, Rashid Khwafi, gave voice to these words: 'That head, which was ripe with much desire, full of ambition for the vizierate, we saw full of straw, to the delight of his enemy's heart. Each tender limb was in a different person's hand.'[78]

Not only does Rashid Khwafi here identify himself by name, he also reveals his relationship to some of the major figures at the court of the early Ilkhanate. His inclusion of two chronograms and one verse of poetry (the last of which he credits to himself) composed on the death of significant individuals situates the author of these passages within the Islamic intellectual milieu of the Juvayni administration, where ornately stylised writing and a facility with spontaneous versification were highly valued skills. His report on the earthquake at Nishapur, meanwhile, reveals his continued concern for that region, as his home district of Khwaf must have been affected by the tremor.

Modifying other peoples' historical texts was not a new exercise for Rashid Khwafi. Already in his 1290 copy of Juvayni's history, he took the liberty of making his own contribution to the text. To Juvayni's work, he adds a verse on the vagaries of fate and converts at least one sum into an alpha-numeric cipher, again showing his engagement with the elite literary culture of scholar-bureaucrats that prevailed in the Juvayni administration.[79] A quarter-century later, and still evidently close to the centre of Ilkhanid court life, Rashid Khwafi made his copy of the *Blessed History*. Responding to what he perceived as an invitation by Rashid al-Din to add anecdotes to an imperfect and expanding work, he took the opportunity to contribute his perspective on the lives of his fellow natives of Khurasan, the Juvaynis, and the court culture that they had cultivated. The result is a unique and intimate glimpse into the outer circles of the educated elite with whom the Juvaynis had taken some of the first steps towards building the Mongol state.

The λ Recension

A second late alteration to the *Blessed History* that was not sanctioned by Rashid al-Din is found in the manuscripts of the λ recension. This new variant was evidently created by referencing several extant versions. The λ recension lacks most of the short textual additions of the δ recension, but it does include the new text added to the third sections of the chapter on Mongke that is first found there. The creator of this new version also evidently had access to a manuscript of the ε recension, in which the Chaghadaid family had been updated for a second time. Confronted with two versions of the family of Chaghadai, the compiler of the λ recension simply consolidated the two into one maximal family tree, with the result that several individuals who had been reassigned to different lines of the family in the ε recension appear in two locations in the new hybrid list.[80]

To these known versions, the λ recension adds new text to the previously empty third *qism* of the *dastan* of Arghun. This new addition tells of the building projects of Arghun Khan, including the first phase of the monumentalisation of Shamb, as well as a new city on the pasture of Qongqur-Oleng.[81] These two sites, in time, became the major shrine cities of Arghun's two sons, Ghazan and Oljeitu. This added anecdote ends with an apology for Arghun's obsession with alchemy and his support of alchemists. After mentioning Arghun's ongoing support of the science that probably led to his death, the author of this passage puts a short speech in the *ilkhan*'s voice addressing Qutb al-Din Shirazi, in which Arghun explains that he continued to support alchemists in order to retain the trust of other scholars. Arghun, who had opposed the administration of the Juvaynis and alienated his Mongol *amirs* by empowering Saʿd al-Daula to the vizierate, emerges from this anecdote as a patron of building and of learning, two of the main pillars of Ghazan and Oljeitu's ideological programmes a decade and a half after their father's death. For the most part, this addition attributes Arghun with those characteristics that fit the ideological programme of the court at the time that Rashid al-Din was assembling his *Collected Histories* and other works. On the other hand, the passage ends with a reproving note that 'nothing had been achieved' from Arghun's support for alchemy 'other than financial loss and ruin'.[82]

The most notable addition to the λ recension, however, is Qashani's celebratory history of Ghazan's conversion. As discussed in Chapter 3, Qashani, who is better known for writing the only contemporary history of Oljeitu's reign and for claiming authorship of the *Collected Histories*, probably wrote a history of Ghazan's early life and reign that cast Ghazan in an even greater eschatological role than the one originally proposed by Rashid al-Din. This version of Ghazan's life up to the time of his accession as *ilkhan* has been included in the *Blessed History* of the λ recension. In turn, Banakati used the version containing Qashani's narrative to prepare his abridgement of the *Collected Histories*.

Assigning a precise date to the λ recension presents some difficulty. Given Banakati's use of the alternate narrative of Ghazan in 1317, at least part of this recension must have been prepared already during Rashid al-Din's lifetime. On the other hand, the composite family tree of Chaghadai, containing as it does multiple entries for certain members of the family, suggests that the compiler was not closely familiar with affairs in the Mongol world in the early fourteenth century. If the entire λ recension was assembled during Rashid al-Din's lifetime, it was done by someone outside the circle of court scholar-bureaucrats who would have had access to information about the Chaghadaid family.

It is possible that the λ recension was assembled in two stages. In this scenario, Qashani's celebratory history of Ghazan Khan would have been added before 1317, when Banakati evidently used it for his abridgement. The second phase could have happened at any point before the early fifteenth century, when our earliest copies of the λ recension (manuscripts L_{11} and

L_{12}) were made. If this were the case, then no examples of the first phase have survived. However, they may have been lost or destroyed in the process of assembling the second phase of this recension. The most likely milieu for this second phase, given the date and provenance of the manuscripts involved, is the court of Shahrokh at Herat. There, as discussed more fully in the Epilogue, the court historian Hafez-e Abru accommodated his patron's interest in the Mongol past by producing several copies of Rashid al-Din's work and completing at least two manuscripts of the *World History* that had survived in only fragmentary form from the Tabriz scriptorium (manuscripts S_1 and S_{11}). The most famous copy of the λ recension, a heavily illustrated but lacunose book now in Paris (manuscript L_{11}), was produced as part of this effort, and may in fact have been copied by Hafez-e Abru himself. A second manuscript, more finely copied but unillustrated (manuscript L_{12}), was also produced under Shahrokh and is also now in Paris. It contains the full λ recension, as well as a series of additional marginal notes with even further additions to the text, suggesting that the effort to update the *Blessed History* continued more than a century after it was completed.

Because of their early accession into Parisian collections and their relatively deluxe quality, these two manuscripts were important sources for early Western studies of Rashid al-Din's work. Edgard Blochet's partial edition of the *Blessed History*, which contains material unique to the λ recension, including the hybrid version of the Chaghadaid family, was for much of the twentieth century the standard edition of the portion of the work dealing with the Mongol rulers from Ogedei to Timur Qa'an, and so this version of the work informed generations of scholarship on this period of Mongol history. Karl Jahn's edition of the history of Ghazan Khan, meanwhile, made use of the illustrated Paris manuscript, which contains part of Qashani's alternate text but suffers a significant lacuna for most of it.[83] Jahn meticulously documented the difference between the two versions of the early life of Ghazan, but his careful notes were stripped away from the text when it was reproduced in Bahman Karimi's effort to produce a unified edition of the *Blessed History*.[84] As a result, Qashani's version of the history of Ghazan has gotten mixed up in the main text and footnotes of Wheeler Thackston's translation of the *Blessed History*.[85]

The second, unillustrated, Paris manuscript also includes a 'continuation' (*dhayl*) to the *Blessed History* that tells of the reigns of Oljeitu and Abu Sa'id (1316–35). This continuation is clearly based on Qashani's *History of Oljeitu*, reformatted to match the three-part structure of other chapters of the *Blessed History*. It appears to be an initial step in Hafez-e Abru's effort to extend the narrative of the *Blessed History*. The ultimate shape of Hafez-e Abru's continuation drew on other works (such as Hamd Allah Mustaufi's *Book of Victory*, discussed in Chapter 6) and extended the narrative down to 1395. Manuscript L_{12} thus integrates much of Qashani's historical *oeuvre* into the *Blessed History*, as it contains both his celebratory history of Ghazan's rise and conversion and a rendition of his *History of Oljeitu*, reshaped to fit the format established by Rashid al-Din. The fact that this effort to rectify the works of Rashid al-Din and Qashani appears only in manuscripts of the λ recension further implicates Hafez-e Abru as that recension's author. Several of the other manuscripts in this recension are copied from manuscript L_{12} and similarly contain Hafez-e Abru's preliminary continuation. The last version of the *Blessed History* may have only taken shape a century after its author's death.

Notes

1. Kim, 'A Re-examination'; Atwood, 'Six pre-Chinggisid Genealogies'.
2. Kamola, 'History and Legend', pp. 565–7.
3. Binbaş, 'Structure and Function', pp. 485–99, gives an overview discussion of Rashid al-Din's genealogical trees.
4. Rashid al-Din, *Jami' al-Tawarikh*, p. 35.
5. Manuscript Z_1 108b, 167a and 190b.
6. Manuscript Z_2 was evidently copied from this manuscript after the excisions were made.
7. On the images from family trees of the *Blessed History* in the Diez Albums, see Kadoi, 'The Mongols Enthroned', pp. 269–75.
8. For examples, see Rice, 'Mughal Interventions', pp. 154, fig. 5, 159, fig. 8.
9. E_{11} 60a.
10. B_1 126a, 126b, 134b.
11. van Ess, *Der Wesir*, p. 14.
12. St Petersburg, IOM MS. C375, 147a–156a; Tehran Golestan MS. 2235 184b–196b; discussed in Binbaş, 'Structure and Function', pp. 494–9.
13. Binbaş, 'Structure and Function', pp. 498–9; Kamola, 'Rashīd al-Dīn', pp. 213–14.

14. Istanbul TSM MS. AIII 2937.
15. Rashid al-Din, *Lata'if al-Haqa'iq*, vol. 2, pp. 8, 14; Binbaş, 'Structure and Function', pp. 486–7.
16. On Peter's life and the early history of the *Genealogia*, see Vivancos, 'Pedro de Poitiers'.
17. Metropolitan Museum of Art Cloisters Collection, 2002.433 is a very early British copy of *c*. 1230. A copy from just after the time of Rashid al-Din and demonstrating influences of the Franciscans of Tuscany is now in the Vatican and has been published in facsimile: Peter of Poitiers, *Genealogia Christi*.
18. For a translation of the text found on the *Genealogia*, see Vivancos, 'Comienza la genealogía'.
19. For an overview of this, see Blair, 'The Development of the Illustrated Book'.
20. Fitzherbert, '"Bal'ami's Tabari"'.
21. Soucek, 'An Illustrated Manuscript'; Hillenbrand, 'The Arts of the Book', pp. 143–5.
22. Hillenbrand, 'The Arts of the Book', pp. 144–5.
23. Huang, 'Early Buddhist Illustrated Prints'.
24. Blair, 'Illustrating History', pp. 9–10. See also Yuan and Ming era examples demonstrating significant similarities to paintings in the *Collected Histories*: Luo, *A Concise Illustrated History*, pp. 79 fig. 5.18, 94–5 fig. 5.44.
25. On the *Histoire Universelle*, see Buchtal, *Miniature Painting*, pp. 68–87. The work has recently been partially edited in two volumes: Wauchier, *L'Histoire Ancienne* (ed. Rouchebouet on Persian history and Gaulier-Bougassas on the Macedonians).
26. London BL MS. Add. 15268, available in digital facsimile with further bibliography online at: http://www.bl.uk/manuscripts/FullDisplay.aspx?ref=Add_MS_15268&index=0.
27. This argument was first put forward by Buchtal, *Miniature Painting*, pp. 86–7, and elaborated by Folda, *Crusader Art*, pp. 419–24.
28. Folda, *Crusader Art*, pp. 422–3.
29. Blair, 'Writing and Illustrating History', pp. 62–3.
30. Kim, 'A Re-examination'.
31. Kim, 'A Re-examination', pp. 91–6.
32. Rashid al-Din, *Jami' al-Tawarikh*, p. 617.
33. This is the hypothesised α recension, reflected in this regard in the β, γ and ε recensions.
34. Rashid al-Din, *Jami' al-Tawarikh*, p. 8.

35. Shiraiwa has argued that the marginal notes found in manuscript E_{11} may be the alterations that Oljeitu proposed in 1304, copied into the margins of Rashid al-Din's working draft: Shiraiwa, 'Rashīd al-Dīn's Primary Sources'. Even that manuscript, however, includes the general preface, and as argued in Appendix B, probably is a copy from a slightly later working copy that was then used to prepare the ζ recension.
36. Rashid al-Din, *Jamiʿ al-Tawarikh*, p. 627.
37. Manuscript D_1 fol. 541a leaves a small gap in place of this passage, perhaps recognising how dated it had become even before the changes of the ζ recension.
38. Several of the passages that were added later, as well as several genealogical trees, have been provided in the margins of manuscript B_1, but they seem to be taken from a manuscript of the ε recension.
39. Here and below, the discussion of textual additions is meant to be representative not comprehensive.
40. This passage is found at Rashid al-Din, *Jamiʿ al-Tawarikh*, pp. 84–6: G_{13} 426b–427a; but see B_1 96b, E_{11} 18b.
41. Rashid al-Din, *Jamiʿ al-Tawarikh*, p. 461: G_{13} 500a; but see B_1 179b, E_{11} 92a.
42. Manuscript G_{12} 214a. This passage has been included in the edition of Rashid al-Din, *Jamiʿ al-Tawarikh*, pp. 861–2, where it is supplied from Blochet, *Djami el-Tévarikh*, pp. 348–9, based on the λ recension.
43. Manuscript G_{14}, pp. 228–9. This translation is Thackston, *Rashiduddin Fazlullah's Jamiʿuʾt-Tawarikh*, p. 395, but is too good to improve on. Raushan and Musavi take the text from Blochet, *Djami el-Tévarikh*, pp. 252–3. For a discussion of Guyug's reign that pushes back against this image, see Kim, 'A Reappraisal'.
44. Shiraiwa has identified several of the additions made to the *Blessed History* between its earliest and last phase: Shiraiwa, 'Rashīd al-Dīn's Primary Sources', pp. 48–52. Of the twenty-one items on Shiraiwa's list, number 3 is the passage on Shigi Qutuqu that first appears in the γ recension, number 18 was added to the later ε recension, and numbers 2 and 7 to the even later ζ recension. The rest first appear in the δ recension.
45. Rashid al-Din, *Jamiʿ al-Tawarikh*, pp. 937–8.
46. See MS. D_1 p. 150.
47. The variations in the lists of descendants of Chaghadai are further elaborated in Kamola, 'Untangling the Chaghadaids'.
48. Kamola, 'Untangling the Chaghadaids'.

49. These passages fall at Rashid al-Din, *Jamiʿ al-Tawarikh*, pp. 113–14, 238–41 and 309: E_3 425b, 447b–448a and 460b.
50. This is manuscript E_{11}. The added marginal notes are numbers 1, 2 and 4 on Shiraiwa's list.
51. Ibn al-Fuwati, *Majmaʿ al-Adab*, vol. 4, pp 263–4, no. 3814.
52. The added episode appears at Rashid al-Din, *Jamiʿ al-Tawarikh*, pp. 116–17. It is number 7 on Shiraiwa's list of additions.
53. de Rachewiltz, *The Secret History of the Mongols*, pp. 10–11.
54. Rashid al-Din, *Jamiʿ al-Tawarikh*, pp. 80, 236, 240, 261, 587.
55. Despite the fact that manuscript Z_{12} provides the base text for Raushan and Musavi's 1994 edition of the *Blessed History*, this story has been omitted from that edition, perhaps because it seems so anomalous. The story should be inserted at Rashid al-Din, *Jamiʿ al-Tawarikh*, p. 236, line 15.
56. Rashid al-Din, *Jamiʿ al-Tawarikh*, pp. 541, 674, the latter discussed by Boyle, 'The Burial Place'.
57. Rashid al-Din, *Jamiʿ al-Tawarikh*, p. 1221–2. This substitution may have already appeared in the ε recension, but all known manuscripts of it break off before this point.
58. Rashid al-Din, *Tarikh-e Chin*, pp. 87–8.
59. Twitchett, *Printing and Publishing*, pp. 35–8.
60. Rashid al-Din, *Tarikh-e Chin*, p. 88.
61. Rashid al-Din, *Tangsuqnameh*, pp. 36–7.
62. Berlekamp, 'The Limits of Artistic Exchange'.
63. On Banakati, see Jackson, 'Banākatī'. For the date of the work, see Banakati, *Rawzat*, p. 2.
64. Brack, 'Mediating Sacred Kingship', pp. 171–6.
65. These additions were first identified and discussed by Aubin, 'Le patronage culturel', pp. 111–12. They are found in manuscripts of the γ recension, suggesting that a copy of that recension was in Yazd for Nizam Yazdi to copy and modify.
66. For the involvement of the family of Nizam Yazdi with the work and legacy of Rashid al-Din, see Aubin, 'Le patronage culturel'.
67. These additions are found in the κ recension.
68. The region of Khwaf was already a main source of administrative staff under the Khwarazmshahs: Manz, *Power, Politics and Religion*, pp. 95–100; Bosworth, 'Khwaf'.
69. Paris BnF MS. Suppl. persan 205, 176b.
70. K_2 177b.

71. K_2 189a.
72. K_2 226b.
73. Rashid al-Din, *Jamiʿ al-Tawarikh*, p. 937, taken from Blochet, *Djami el-Tévarikh*, p. 558. Evidence for these earthquakes is gathered by Ambraseys and Melville, *A History of Persian Earthquakes*, p. 43. For the difficulty of establishing the date of the 1270 quake, see Melville, 'Earthquakes', pp. 110–11.
74. K_2 233b.
75. See, for example, Melville, 'Jameʿ ol-Tawārik͟h'; Pfeiffer, 'Reflections', p. 383.
76. K_2 224a, 226b.
77. Ibn al-Fuwati, *Majmaʿ al-Adab*, vol. 4, p. 299, no. 3879.
78. K_2 229a. Jahn, *Taʾrīḫ-i-Mubārak-i-Ġāzānī*, p. 59. Hammer-Purgstall, *Geschichte der Ilchane*, vol. I, pp. 327–8, identifies the author of this episode and verse as Rashid al-Din.
79. Paris BnF MS. Suppl. persan 205 63b, 77b.
80. Kamola, 'Untangling the Chaghadaids'.
81. L_2 241b–242a.
82. Rashid al-Din, *Jamiʿ al-Tawarikh*, p. 1185, trans. Thackston, *Rashiduddin Fazlullah's Jamiʿuʾt-Tawarikh*, p. 577.
83. Jahn, *Geschichte Ġāzān-Ḫānʾs*.
84. Karimi, *Jamiʿ al-Tawarikh*, pp. 839–95.
85. Thackston, *Rashiduddin Fazlullah's Jamiʿuʾt-Tawarikh*, pp. 606–10, 621–2, 626–7.

6

Creating the Image of Rashid al-Din, 1312–1335

At the start of 1311, Rashid al-Din was completing the *Account of Truths*, which includes the fullest articulation of his new vision of sultanic power, and he was beginning to issue instructions for the reproduction of his collected works in increasingly deluxe editions. Even though he still shared the reins of administrative authority with Saʿd al-Din Sawaji, Rashid al-Din was at the height of his influence at court. His command over the wealth of the state, both through his administrative work and his personal wealth made him the gatekeeper of patronage. With such a monopoly on cultural production, his rival ʿAbd Allah Qashani's claim to be the real author of the *Collected Histories* was a dead letter. However, Qashani remained active as a writer at court, and in that capacity he describes Rashid al-Din as an agent in the unfolding history of the Ilkhanate. It should come as no surprise that Qashani casts Rashid al-Din in unflattering light. By contrast, Wassaf and other contemporary chroniclers of the Ilkhanate owed their positions to Rashid al-Din and present a glowing encomium of their patron.

This chapter traces the image of Rashid al-Din as it formed in the writings of other scholars at the Ilkhanid court and in the broader Islamic world in the decades immediately following his death. Because of Rashid al-Din's involvement in both the politics of court and the dispensation of patronage, even the earliest accounts of his life reveal their authors' personal and political positions with regard to their subject. Qashani and Wassaf in particular are responsible for an enduring dichotomy in the historical memory of Rashid al-Din as simultaneously a brilliant scholar and a guileless thief, a diligent state servant and a ruthless political operator. Beyond his appearance in court chronicles, Rashid al-Din was a subject for authors in the genre of biography, which was experiencing a golden period particularly in Mamluk territories in the fourteenth century. Here again, our earliest sources are touched in one way or another by their authors' personal experience with Rashid al-Din's activity and reputation.

The writer who engaged most fully with Rashid al-Din's life and legacy was undoubtedly his political protégé, Hamd Allah Mustaufi of Qazvin, who created a compelling historical portrait of the senior statesman. Hamd Allah accomplished this in the same way that Nasir al-Din Tusi and the Juvayni brothers had integrated the early *ilkhan*s into Iranian society: by drawing on Iranian heroic and historical traditions, including the *Shahnameh* of Firdausi. Mustaufi uses these sources to depict his subject as an essential pillar of society despite lingering concerns about Rashid al-Din's political and religious allegiance. Hamd Allah Mustaufi's portrait of his late patron, together with the biographical material and the polemic views on Rashid al-Din found in the writing of Qashani and Wassaf, provide the raw material for any attempt to reconstruct the life of Rashid al-Din. By analysing and contextualising these early sources on the life and legacy of Rashid al-Din, this chapter seeks to explain why he has remained an enigmatic figure in later attempts to evaluate his life.

The Two Faces of Rashid al-Din in Ilkhanid Court Chronicles

In the winter of 1311/12, relations between the two viziers Rashid al-Din and Saʿd al-Din soured, ending ultimately in the latter's execution. The fact that Rashid al-Din survived this conflict suggests that he enjoyed Oljeitu's special favour. However, the accounts of Qashani and Wassaf paint starkly different pictures of the events of that winter, establishing the contours of the two faces that Rashid al-Din wears in subsequent historiography.

In his *History of Oljeitu*, Qashani dedicates significant space to the political intrigues and executions that occurred during the *hijri* year 711 (20 May 1311–8 May 1312).[1] As is true for his telling of Oljeitu's embrace of Shiʿism and for his attack against Rashid al-Din for having stolen his *Collected Histories*, Qashani here crafts an elaborate narrative charged with a particular moral judgement. The primary plot of Qashani's account concerns the deteriorating relations between Rashid al-Din and Saʿd al-Din, ending with the latter's torture and execution on 29 February 1312. Across this account, Qashani weaves the story of a second political execution, that of Taj al-Din Awaji, on 9 April of the same year. Ever the stylist, Qashani capitalises on natural rhymes between the names of the two victims to state that there were really only two events of note to occur that year: 'one event was the affair of *sahib* Sa'd al-Din Sawaji, the second event was that of the *sayyid* Taj al-Din Awaji'.[2]

Qashani's narrative can be summarised as follows: a Baghdadi jeweller, Taj al-Din 'Alishah (not to be confused with Taj al-Din Awaji), had gained the good favours of Oljeitu through an extensive programme of building, including elaborate palaces at the new capital of Sultaniya. Sa'd al-Din attempted to rein in 'Alishah's ambitions by auditing his accounts, but fortune smiled on the jeweller and he continued to rise in prominence while the vizier fell out of favour. Rashid al-Din encouraged the rise of 'Alishah, creating conflict between himself and Sa'd al-Din. The latter's clientele abandoned him, and affairs devolved to the extent that, in the exasperated view of Qashani, it became common to see the royal entourage entirely populated by Jews. 'Alishah further undermined Sa'd al-Din's position by creating a farcical presentation for Oljeitu Sultan to demonstrate just how much the vizier's corrupt practices had drained state coffers. Faced with this new challenge, Sa'd al-Din resorted to a series of increasingly desperate measures, trying to restore the state funds by confiscating the wealth of courtiers. In the end, Sa'd al-Din was forced to seek refuge with Rashid al-Din, who made an empty promise of protection. Finally, in February 1312, Sa'd al-Din was arrested, tortured and executed.

At this point in the narrative, Qashani switches to a parallel episode concerning a Jewish doctor who had ostensibly converted to Islam.[3] This doctor, Najib al-Daula, conspired with certain rivals of Rashid al-Din to have letters written in Hebrew implicating Rashid al-Din in a scheme to assassinate Oljeitu. Faced with the trap set by a converted Jewish doctor, Rashid al-Din managed to deflect the charge, pinning the false letters on a deputy of Sa'd al-Din.

Only now does Qashani transition to the second narrative, that of Taj al-Din Awaji. He explains that the *sayyid* had been entrusted with the management of a number of tombs and shrines. When he built a mosque at the tomb of Ezekiel, between Najaf and Hilla, he appropriated this holy site away from the Jewish community of the region. In Qashani's telling, this roused the anger of Rashid al-Din, who harboured a lasting affinity to the Jewish faith of his birth. Rashid al-Din brought his grievance to Oljeitu. The sultan, who had recently converted to Shi'ism, asked how he might justify killing a biological descendant of the Prophet. In response, Rashid al-Din doctored the document on which Taj al-Din preserved his genealogy, making it appear as if another name had been erased and Taj al-Din's name written in its place. Oljeitu declared the *sayyid*'s genealogical charter void and gave permission to execute Taj al-Din.

This account strikes a notably literary tone in several regards, beginning with its structure. Individual scenes are set apart from one another by verse passages and wise sayings, many of them put in the voice of 'the learned' (*'ulama*). These function like the choral interludes of Greek tragedy, alternately exonerating Sa'd al-Din as the victim of a cruel fate and censoring Rashid al-Din for improper behaviour, such as his empty promise to protect his colleague. Furthermore, the accounts run parallel to one another through their shared use of narrative elements: the political manoeuvrings that brought about the executions and Rashid al-Din's devious use of documents to implicate his detractors in crimes of which they were in fact innocent.

Another similarity between the two stories of intrigue and execution is, of course, the repeated suggestion that Rashid al-Din's true loyalty lay with the Jewish community, and not with the Ilkhanid court or the Islamic faith. Although Taj al-Din's death is justified on the grounds of a fabricated *sayyid* lineage, his troubles begin when Rashid al-Din champions the grievance of the Jews of Najaf and Hilla. In the affair of Najib al-Daula and the forged Hebrew letters, Qashani reminds us once again of both Rashid al-Din's Jewish background and his medical profession. Najib al-Daula stands in as a doppelganger for the Rashid al-Din that Qashani wants his reader to see: an insincere convert given to mendacity and treason. To remind us of this association, Qashani everywhere refers to Rashid al-Din as Rashid al-Daula, marking his subject as a Jew despite his conversion to Islam.

A very different vision of Rashid al-Din emerges from Wassaf's account of the executions of 1312. This is included in the fourth book of his chronicle, the first book that Wassaf wrote after Ghazan had taken him under royal patronage. Completed in 1312, it includes the end of the life and reign of Ghazan Khan and the early reign of Oljeitu, followed by a summary of Juvayni's *History of the World Conqueror*. Remarkably, Wassaf's autograph copy of this fourth book has survived.[4] From it, we can tell that at some point – or at several points – after completing the original fourth book, Wassaf made additions to the text, inserting new episodes into the course of the narrative. One such addition consists of eight folios relating the events of spring and summer 1312 that Wassaf interfoliated into his holograph manuscript.[5] The first of these eight folios contains a section heading titled 'space for discrete accounts', just one of many similarly titled sections appearing throughout Wassaf's chronicle that offer opportunities for the author to add parenthetical material to his historical record without disrupting the integrity of the main text. In this instance, Wassaf uses the added space to offer his own vision of Rashid al-Din as a man and as an administrator.

In his added text, Wassaf presents the executions of Sa'd al-Din and Taj al-Din alongside one another, just as Qashani does.[6] He also draws the two executions together through certain literary devices, but instead of the dramatic narrative structure of Qashani's account, Wassaf glosses these events as normal judicial actions and their outcomes as the appropriate punishment for Sa'd al-Din and Taj al-Din's corrupt practices. Whereas Qashani heightens the accusatory tone of his account by inserting the story of Najib al-Daula and the forged Hebrew letters, Wassaf breaks up his narrative of the executions with a description of Rashid al-Din's scholarly work. This tempers the narrative with a strong reminder of his patron's contributions in areas of scholarship and patronage. The original text of the added passage gives only a bare mention of the execution of Sa'd al-Din before moving on to the description of Rashid al-Din's scholarship. To this, Wassaf later added a further series of marginal notes. One of these clarifies the date of Sa'd al-Din's execution and the names of those executed alongside him, while another mentions the execution of Taj al-Din.

We gain insight into Wassaf's writing process from the fact that he added these notes on the events of 1312 only after his initial completion of Book Four. He updated his history both to add information and to engage in a polemic unfolding at the Ilkhanid court. In particular, the addition of the marginalia embellishing an otherwise spare account of Sa'd al-Din's death make this narrative a mirror image response to Qashani's accusations. Wassaf's first marginal note simply repeats information found in Qashani's account, and the choice to add the affair of Taj al-Din to this portion of the history marks Wassaf's text as a structural copy of Qashani's. However, here Rashid al-Din's Jewish origins are omitted, replaced by a description of his scholarly achievements. According to Wassaf, the judicial duty of prosecuting and punishing the vizier and the *sayyid* are mere side-notes to Rashid al-Din's larger project of recording and disseminating religious and scientific scholarship. For Wassaf, Rashid al-Din continued to be a loyal servant of the state.

The Fall of Rashid al-Din

In the aftermath of Sa'd al-Din's execution, Rashid al-Din sponsored 'Alishah's promotion to the position of vizier, but this new administrative alliance did not last long. As early as 1315, the two had grown apart. According to Hamd Allah Mustaufi, this was due to 'Alishah's disrespectful behaviour, which invited the resentment of the elder vizier.[7] Rashid al-Din asked Oljeitu to pick one or the other to administer the state, perhaps hoping that his own deep personal ties to the family of the young sultan – and his recent efforts to portray Oljeitu and himself as a cosmically unique political duumvirate – would settle the matter in his favour as they had during earlier conflicts with Sadr al-Din Zanjani and Sa'd al-Din Sawaji. However, Oljeitu refused to do away with either the aging and reliable adviser or the young, capable and ambitious manager. Instead, the sultan divided the administrative jurisdiction of the state into geographic regions, putting Rashid al-Din in charge of the eastern and southern provinces, while 'Alishah managed the central lands of Iraq and Azerbaijan along with Anatolia.

Unsatisfied with this arrangement, or perhaps to undermine his young colleague's position, Rashid al-Din withdrew from Oljeitu's capital at Sultaniya to Tabriz to nurse his rheumatic legs. This left Taj al-Din to bear the brunt of the resentment brewing among the Mongol military elite, who were once again jealous of the influence of Persian administrators over their khan. While in Tabriz, Rashid al-Din expanded the endowment of the Rashidi Quarter, an act which only fuelled accusations of his having wrongly consolidated state wealth in his own hands.[8]

The final struggle with ʿAlishah occurred early in the reign of Oljeitu's son and heir, Abu Saʿid (1316–35). It began, like the first disgrace of Sadr al-Din in 1294 and the fall of Saʿd al-Din in 1312, with a state fiscal crisis, as the two viziers tried to foist onto one another the responsibility for raising money to pay the army. According to Maqrizi, during a peace embassy to Cairo in 1316, Majd al-Sallami presented the Mamluk Sultan al-Malik al-Nasir with an unspecified gift from Rashid al-Din.[9] Among the Qurʾans surviving from the Mamluk period is one dated to April 1315 and produced in Rashid al-Din's system of scriptoria.[10] We do not know whether Rashid al-Din sent this specific Qurʾan to al-Nasir in 1316, or if Maqrizi, writing a century after these events, may have interpreted the presence of the 1315 Qurʾan as part of al-Sallami's embassy. Whether as a result of such a gift of this Qurʾan or something else, by September 1317 accusations of disloyalty, extortion and mismanagement swirled so densely around Rashid al-Din that he returned once more to Tabriz, where he lived through the last winter of his life.

During that winter of 1317/18, the Ilkhanid court languished in fiscal mismanagement, so that the prominent Mongol Amir Chupan, one of Rashid al-Din's political allies and the kingmaker of the late Ilkhanate, visited Tabriz and asked Rashid al-Din to resume his position.[11] Rashid al-Din's return to court motivated ʿAlishah to renew his attacks, leading ultimately to the accusation that the elder statesman and doctor had arranged to have Oljeitu poisoned. Chupan initially resisted the charge, but was ultimately unable to protect Rashid al-Din, just as a third of a century earlier Amir Buqa had forestalled but not prevented the execution of Shams al-Din Juvayni. On 17 July 1318, outside the village of Abhar in the district of Qazvin, Rashid al-Din was executed along with his son, who had been convicted of administering the poison his father had prepared.[12]

Early Biographical Material on Rashid al-Din

The genre of biography expanded greatly in the decades surrounding Rashid al-Din's death, with several major biographical encyclopaedias created across the eastern Islamic world. One of the greatest of these was composed under Hulegu and his descendants by Kamal al-Din ibn al-Fuwati (1244–1323), who worked alongside Nasir al-Din Tusi for a while as the librarian at the latter's observatory in Maragha.¹³ From his connections to the intellectual life of that city and of Baghdad, where he later lived and worked in the Mustansiriya library, Ibn al-Fuwati assembled historical information about the period of the Mongol conquest and about the noteworthy individuals living under Mongol rule.

In addition to an as-yet unidentified history of the seventh *hijri* century (thirteenth century AD), Ibn al-Fuwati composed a massive encyclopaedia of biographies, the *Literary Collection Alphabetised by Title* (*Majmaʿ al-Adab fi Muʿjam al-Alqab*). Unfortunately, given the extensive detail that this work included about the personalities and livelihoods of the subjects of the Ilkhanate, it has not survived. In its place we have only a partial copy of a summary that Ibn al-Fuwati prepared of his larger work. Even the known part of the *Summary* exists mostly in copies made by Ibn al-Fuwati himself that have survived for seven centuries. This most important of biographical collections for reconstructing Ilkhanid society has come down to us by the narrowest of transmissions.

In his capacity as librarian at Maragha, Ibn al-Fuwati knew Rashid al-Din's father and uncle, who had joined Hulegu's court as part of the migration of scholars from the patronage of the Ismaʿili imam to the Mongol prince in 1257. He refers to the brothers as 'highly respected physicians and philosophers', but makes no mention of ʿImad al-Daula's son, Rashid al-Din.¹⁴ Most frustratingly, the volume of the *Summary* that would have included a separate biographical entry for Rashid al-Din is not known to have survived. If it ever turns up, this and every other study of Rashid al-Din's life will have to be revised to account for what must have been the most immediate and insightful biography ever written of the man.

Across the Euphrates from the Ilkhanid capitals, the Mamluk territories of Egypt and Syria also produced important biographers in the fourteenth century, two of whom offer entries on Rashid al-Din.¹⁵ Ibn al-Suqaʿi (d. 1326) was a Christian administrator in Mamluk Damascus. Late in his life, he composed a continuation of the biographical dictionary of Ibn Khallikan (d. 1282), adding entries for prominent individuals who died between 1258 and 1324. In his entry on Rashid al-Din, we see the perspective of an elderly Christian living outside the Ilkhanate: the vizier's execution echoes here biblical themes of martyrdom and dismemberment.¹⁶ The prolific Mamluk writer

Salah al-Din al-Safadi (d. 1363) composed several collections of biographies. While his writing was separated from the life of Rashid al-Din in both time and space, his information on the Ilkhanid vizier was purportedly gleaned from an unnamed immigrant from Ilkhanid Isfahan, who would have had somewhat more direct experience of Rashid al-Din's impact on politics and society. Unfortunately, al-Safadi's account preserves little more than the spare outline of a life, including Rashid al-Din's medical training, his Jewish background and conversion to Islam, his immense wealth and influence, and his execution.

One final near-contemporary biography of Rashid al-Din was composed by Nasir al-Din Munshi Kirmani, who is best known as the author of the only surviving local history of his home town of Kirman, in the southern reaches of the Ilkhanate.[17] Like the Mamluk biographers, Kirmani focuses on the dramatic events of the last months of Rashid al-Din's life, including his fall from grace, conviction and execution. As a result of this preference in the earliest sources, Rashid al-Din's death became the single most frequently narrated part of his life in later Persian chronicles and biographies.

Late Ilkhanid Historiography

After the execution of Rashid al-Din, his endowed district east of Tabriz was ransacked and his property seized. Abu Sa'id subsequently either regretted the action or was able to see past Rashid al-Din's disgrace to appoint the latter's son, Ghiyath al-Din Muhammad, as vizier in 1327. Giyath al-Din rebuilt at least part of the Rashidi Quarter, and he resumed his father's work as patron and statesman.[18] As part of this, he sponsored historical writing, but was never responsible for anything nearly as ambitious as his father's *Collected Histories*. Muhammad ibn 'Ali Shabankara'i produced for Giyath al-Din a summary history of the independent dynasties of Iran since the Saffarids of the ninth century.[19] As a collection of dynastic histories, it fits securely into the pattern established by Baydawi and expanded by Rashid al-Din, but its limited scope, quality and distribution mark a sharp decline from the more popular historical works of the earlier Ilkhanate.

The decline of dynastic prose histories in the latter Ilkhanate was offset by a surge of interest in epic verse narratives. The great exemplar of this genre, Firdausi's *Shahnameh*, was more than two centuries older than the

Ilkhanate. As we have seen in Chapter 3, interest in the *Shahnameh* had been limited to the courts of eastern Iran and in Saljuq Anatolia, but it played a role in the earliest efforts by Persian scholar-bureaucrats such as Juvayni to integrate the Mongol conquerors into a familiar cultural framework. There is little evidence, however, that this interest in the *Shahnameh* carried on at the Ilkhanid court into the reigns of Ghazan and Oljeitu. Unlike Juvayni, the *Collected Histories* make very limited reference to the *Shahnameh*, citing it only a few times. Qashani's pre-Islamic history, which formed the basis for the *World History* that Rashid al-Din presented to Oljeitu, relied on Arabic prose histories, rather than Persian verse epic.[20]

Firdausi's epic enjoyed renewed popularity beginning in the last years of the Ilkhanate, as new illustrated manuscripts were produced under elite patronage. This occurred both at Tabriz and in the southern city of Shiraz, where the Injuid and Muzaffarid dynasties produced such books as part of an effort to assume the Ilkhanid mantle of political legitimacy after the death of Abu Saʿid in 1335.[21] Interest in the *Shahnameh* during the late Ilkhanate went beyond the production of new manuscripts, as several authors composed new works about Mongol history in the style and meter of Firdausi's poem.[22] In one of these, the *Shahnameh of Chinggis*, Shams al-Din Qashani explicitly states his intention to versify the *Collected Histories*.[23] Around the end of the Ilkhanate, then, historians accepted Rashid al-Din's account of Mongol history as an authoritative narrative of events, but they worked to reshape it in the poetic meter and epic form of the *Shahnameh*.

A Book-length Mirror

The fullest example of how Rashid al-Din's narrative was reshaped to align with Firdausi's epic treatment of the past is seen in the career of Hamd Allah Mustaufi, whom Rashid al-Din had appointed as revenue collector over his home district of Qazvin. During his career, Hamd Allah Mustaufi took after his patron not only in administrative affairs, but in his broad appetite for scholarly production. His known works demonstrate how, in the generation after Rashid al-Din's death, the *Collected Histories* were reimagined in a new form as a moralising epic.

Hamd Allah Mustaufi undertook several historical projects during his career. His earliest was an edition of the *Shahnameh*, which he completed around 1320. By his own account, Mustaufi spent six years preparing the text, and he consulted over fifty unique manuscripts to arrive at a definitive version.[24] He was not, however, a dispassionate editor. In preparing his text, Mustaufi added some 5,000 lines of verse, as well as new title headings and elements of Turkic and Mongol vocabulary that would not have been available to Firdausi three centuries earlier.[25] We can only speculate why Mustaufi made these additions to the text. One possible motivation, which Abolala Soudavar has explored extensively, is that they allowed him to turn the *Shahnameh* into a historical analogy by creating parallels between Firdausi's work and the events of Mongol imperial history. For example, Mustaufi invents a wife for the first Sasanian ruler, Ardeshir Papakan (224–42), possibly as a historical precedent for the wife of Abu Saʻid.[26] Already while editing the work of another author, then, we see that Mustaufi was comfortable altering the historical tradition through a process of analogistic thinking to make that tradition more relevant to contemporary events.

Hamd Allah Mustaufi also created two original historical works, each of which engaged the same kind of analogistic thinking as his edition of the *Shahnameh*. One of these was the *Select History* (*Tarikh-e Gozideh*), the bulk of which consists of a universal history in prose of the type revitalised by Baydawi's *Order of Histories*.[27] Mustaufi bookends this universal history with two catalogues of historical figures and their sayings, one on pre-Islamic prophets and sages and the other on religious dignitaries of the Islamic period. At the work's end, he added an additional local history of his home region of Qazvin.

The clear organisation and plain style of the *Select History* has made it a popular source for modern studies of the late Ilkhanate, for which it provides one of few surviving narratives. One feature that makes it particularly attractive to modern scholars is the list of sources that Mustaufi includes in his introduction, a list that includes the works of both Baydawi and Rashid al-Din.[28] As transparent as his prose can be, Mustaufi pursues a particular historiographical mission in the *Select History*, presenting the Mongol *ilkhans* in the light of Iranian tradition. This is conveyed through the figure of the great sage of the Sasanian court, Bozorgmehr, who appears in the text as the culmination of Iranian, Greek and Arabic wisdom traditions.[29]

The whole time that he was writing the *Select History*, Hamd Allah

Mustaufi was also engaged in a much larger project. This was the *Book of Victory* (*Zafarnama*), which brought together his work editing the *Shahnameh* and his composition of a new universal history. The *Book of Victory* is a 75,000-verse epic, written as a continuation of Firdausi's *Shahnameh* and extending the heroic narrative of that poem through the late Ilkhanate.[30] Late in the *Book of Victory*, Hamd Allah Mustaufi describes the process of composing it. Writing first about Rashid al-Din, he relates:

> When the record of the affairs of kings was complete, he gave it the name *Collected Histories*.
> I ordered that prose with great thoughtfulness and golden judgement.
> Each word revealed within it I checked with those who know.
> I passed off nothing contradictory and gave this account truthfully.
> When the material of this famous book was complete, it was beautiful as a bride in complexion and form,
> But the dress lacked beauty in one small way: a flaw in its clothing was its ruin.
> How can the face of the sun look good to the eye, when one has dressed it in muslin?
> I removed this garment from the body; I clothed this work in brilliant verse.
> With this fine form and content, its image became like the face of the sun.[31]

Mustaufi here lays out a two-step transformation of Rashid al-Din's historical collection. First, he reorganised the sections of the *Collected History*, putting the history of the Mongols from the *Blessed History* after the history of the various Islamic dynasties found in the *World History* and thus fitting the two volumes into one chronological sequence. This corrects the chronological incongruity of the *Collected Histories* that resulted from Rashid al-Din's two-stage commission, creating the good order mentioned in the second line quoted above. Once Rashid al-Din's massive and somewhat ungainly historical compendium had been brought into a consistent chronological form, it could be perfected through versification as the *Book of Victory*.

Hamd Allah Mustaufi was, of course, well qualified to render Islamic and Mongol history into epic verse. Having spent six years editing the

Shahnameh, he was intimately familiar with the content and style of that work. His ability to adapt the epic tone and literary tropes of Firdausi to the telling of Mongol history shows just how much the Iranian heroic tradition could provide a new model for understanding the Mongol past during the last years of the Ilkhanid dynasty. To be fair, the received historical tradition about the Iranian past presented certain natural parallels with recent events. Rashid al-Din and his contemporaries had recognised some of these and had already begun to refer to the Ilkhanate as the 'Land of Iran'. The idea of Iran as coterminous with the Ilkhanate is a major feature of Mustaufi's *Select History*.[32] In the *Book of Victory*, Mustaufi elaborates on these historical parallels and invents new ones in order to cast the Ilkhanate as the historical and aesthetic equivalent to the Sasanian state.

Bozorgmehr and the Wisdom of History

Hamd Allah Mustaufi makes an immediate nod to the Iranian heroic tradition in the title of the *Book of Victory*. *Zafarnama* is a New Persian calque on the Middle Persian *Piruzinamak*. That is the title assigned to a work of advice literature purportedly translated into New Persian by the great polymath Ibn Sina, a contemporary of Firdausi.[33] The *Piruzinamak* fits into a genre of Middle Persian works in the form of an audience between ruler and subject during which the latter responds to a request for a discourse on moral, ethical or courtly conduct.[34] The Sasanian ruler most often represented in this genre is Khosrau Anoshiravan (531–79), who is credited with directing that previously oral material be written down, including the historical traditions that provided the basis for the *Shahnameh*. More broadly, Anushirvan is associated with the Sasanian programme of knowledge production, gathering and developing sciences from across the ancient world in a series of royally sponsored academies that laid the precedent for later ʿAbbasid efforts in the same vein. At his side in these efforts is his semi-legendary vizier, Bozorgmehr, who in different places in the historical record interprets Khosrau's dreams, invents the game of backgammon, and solves problems posed to Khosrau by foreign rulers, despite going blind in captivity after falling under suspicion from the court.[35]

In the case of the *Piruzinamak* translated by Ibn Sina, Anoshiravan puts eighty questions to Bozorgmehr. By contrast, Firdausi dramatises

Bozorgmehr's wisdom discourse into a series of audiences with the king that contribute to an overall depiction of the vizier as the wisest and most just member of the king's court. In Firdausi's telling, the rise of Bozorgmehr to political prominence begins, like that of the biblical Joseph, when he is able to successfully interpret one of the king's dreams that had stymied the court oneiromancers.[36] This event establishes Bozorgmehr as a uniquely capable, though not formally trained, interlocutor at court – a handy analogy for Mustaufi to apply to his own patron, Rashid al-Din.

Once established in Anoshiravan's graces, according to Firdausi, Bozorgmehr attends a series of seven weekly audiences, at which Anoshiravan confronts his advisers with various moral questions, many of which correspond to questions found in the *Piruzinamak*.[37] Consistently, Anoshiravan's other advisers fail to respond to the questions, but Bozorgmehr answers them to the satisfaction of the ruler, who rewards him for his wisdom. Firdausi calls this chapter 'Bozorgmehr's discourse on wisdom' (*pandnāmeh-ye bozorgmehr*). Like the prose *Piruzinamak*, it celebrates the vizier's wisdom, but it adds the particular trope of Bozorgmehr's success in the face of other ministers' ignorance.

Hamd Allah Mustaufi engages with the story of Bozorgmehr's discourse on wisdom already in the *Select History*, which contains the earliest prose version of the *Piruzinamak* composed in New Persian.[38] Mustaufi places Bozorgmehr as the culminating figure in a catalogue of philosopher-sages that includes Judeo-Islamic, Greco-Hellenistic and Iranian individuals.[39] After a group of wise statements in the voice of Bozorgmehr, Mustaufi launches into a long catalogue of questions posed by Bozorgmehr to his own teacher, and his teacher's responses to them. In its question-and-answer format, this passage resembles the prose *Piruzinamak* attributed to Ibn Sina, rather than the 'discourse on wisdom' model employed by Firdausi. By contrast, since Mustaufi wrote the *Book of Victory* as a continuation of the *Shahnameh*, he there defers to Firdausi's representation of Bozorgmehr's 'discourse on wisdom' in seven weekly audiences. Of course, Mustaufi ultimately assigned his epic the name of the *Piruzinamak* – updated to the New Persian *Zafarnameh* – marking the entire *Book of Victory* as a discourse on good governance.

Hamd Allah Mustaufi was not the only fourteenth-century verse historians to appropriate the motif of the royal audience as a site for transmitting wisdom: in the *Book of Ghazan* (*Ghazannameh*) dedicated to the Jalayirid Shaykh Uvays (1356–74), Nur al-Din Azhdari frequently employs a dialogic structure for interactions between Ghazan Khan and various wise men.[40] In later centuries other writers followed this same approach, giving the title of *Book of Victory* to a series of historical chronicles.[41] For Hamd Allah Mustaufi and those after him, the didactic potential of historical narrative was exemplified by the figure of the wise vizier instructing his patron and king, for which Bozorgmehr serves as the essential prototype.

Hamd Allah Mustaufi's strategy for associating Rashid al-Din with Bozorgmehr may be evident in the very structure of his *Book of Victory*. The earliest and most important manuscript of the work creates a physical as well as a literary association between Rashid al-Din and Bozorgmehr. This is a manuscript copied in Timurid Shiraz in 1405.[42] In it, the text of the *Book of Victory* is found in the main text block of each page, surrounded by Hamd Allah's edited *Shahnameh* copied in the margins. While this manuscript dates to eighty years after the original work, the fact that it contains Mustaufi's unique edited version of the *Shahnameh* alongside his original *Book of Victory* suggests that it reflects his larger project to edit and extend Firdausi's work.

In this manuscript, an invented 'discourse on wisdom', in the voice of Rashid al-Din, appears in the main text block, immediately after pages whose margins are taken up with 'Bozorgmehr's discourse on wisdom'. They are then immediately followed by another episode demonstrating Bozorgmehr's great wisdom. This is the story of how he deciphered the Indian game of chess and in turn baffled the Indian embassy with his invention of backgammon. Like the seven audiences of Bozorgmehr's *pandnameh*, this episode shows the Sasanian vizier succeeding in a test of wits where other members of Anoshiravan's court had failed. Between the two discourses on wisdom and the invention of backgammon, more than sixty contiguous manuscript pages of this deluxe copy extol the wisdom of royal viziers, each of whom emerges as uniquely qualified at court to deliver wisdom to the ruler and untangle the ethical and diplomatic challenges facing the state.[43] Rashid al-Din makes this comparison himself in his late theological writing, where he points to Bozorgmehr as a precedent for his own unique qualifications to answer Oljeitu's religious questions.[44]

Just as Rashid al-Din and Bozorgmehr are drawn into one another's orbit, so too do their patrons become historical mirrors of one another. There was strong historical basis for comparing Ghazan Khan with Khosrau Anoshiravan: both kings advanced programmes of religious and administrative reform, defeated uprisings from among the ranks of their military establishment, and reached out to China in the face of nomadic threats from Inner Asia. Hamd Allah Mustaufi draws attention to these similarities by literally placing the two reigns next to each other on the pages of his *Book of Victory*.

This juxtaposition of Ghazan and Anoshiravan verifies an analogistic connection between the two rulers that 'Abd Allah Qashani acknowledges in his *History of Oljeitu*. Qashani explains that different *ilkhan*s were by tradition associated with different characteristics: Hulegu with conquest and scholarship; Abaqa with agriculture and building; and so on.[45] In this scheme, 'the time of Ghazan the Just Khan was characterised by ingenuity and governance and justice and equity and devotion', many of the same attributes associated with Anoshiravan in the *Shahnameh*. Mustaufi makes this similarity explicit in the *Book of Victory*. In his introductory remarks on the reign of Ghazan Khan, he compares Ghazan's qualities with those of Anoshiravan.[46] This association between Ghazan and Anoshiravan enhances the effort to cast Rashid al-Din in the form of Bozorgmehr.

Nizam al-Mulk and the Morality of History

Bozorgmehr was not the only vizier from Persian history to inform Hamd Allah Mustaufi's presentation of Rashid al-Din. He also draws on the historical memory and writings of Nizam al-Mulk (d. 1092), who served under the Saljuq rulers Alp Arslan (1063–73) and Malikshah (1073–92). Like Bozorgmehr, Nizam al-Mulk's position relative to his patrons provided a remarkably close analogy to the role Rashid al-Din played for the Mongols. As an educated member of the Persian bureaucratic class, he served the most acculturated members of a nomadic dynasty and mediated between their elite military culture and the indigenous traditions of the Islamic world. Like Rashid al-Din, he directed major programmes of administrative reform and intellectual and architectural patronage and he promoted particular forms of Islamic scholarship in order to consolidate the political authority he had built alongside the sovereigns he served. Each of the two advisers had fallen out of favour and died in disgrace, only to be succeeded as vizier by his son, who was also ultimately executed.

As with his use of the *Piruzinamak* tradition, Hamd Allah Mustaufi draws on the literary and historical tradition surrounding Nizam al-Mulk to cast him as an antetype for Rashid al-Din. In this case, Hamd Allah could use Nizam al-Mulk's own words, in the form of the Saljuq vizier's handbook on moral and effective governance, the *Lives of Kings* (*Siyar al-Muluk*), also known as the *Book of Government* (*Siyasatnameh*), which Mustaufi lists as one of his sources in the beginning of the *Select History*.[47] Nizam al-Mulk wrote this work in response to specific aspects of the Saljuq administration that he felt needed correction, but he presents his proposals in a general form as a didactic treatise for running an effective government. The *Lives of Kings* is a political work not a historical one, but it illustrates its various propositions through numerous historical anecdotes.[48] While it lacks an overall literary form, individual sections are presented in a consistently structured way, opening with a general moral exhortation, followed by one or more illustrative episodes, and ending with a restatement of the intended lesson.

Mustaufi adopts this pattern for many of the episodes in the *Book of Victory*, giving his history a double structure, both as a running historical narrative and as a series of discreet moralising tales. For example, Hamd Allah Mustaufi's account of the siege of Baghdad in 1258 largely agrees with the *Blessed History* in its basic sequence of events.[49] As Hulegu approaches Baghdad and engages the caliph in negotiations, the city administration is crippled by a power struggle between the vizier, Mu'ayyid al-Din ibn 'Alqami, and the 'lesser' Dawatdar, Mujahid al-Din Aybak. This conflict, and the caliph's unwillingness to pay his troops despite the desperation of his situation and the extent of his wealth, results in a breakdown in the city defences. Hulegu sacks Baghdad and kills the caliph, who realises no benefit from his amassed treasure. Where the *Book of Victory* diverges from Rashid al-Din's account is in framing the episode explicitly as a moral lesson. The story opens in the voice of the author, who exhorts his reader to heed how power transfers into the hands of those who deserve it and how the haughty late 'Abbasids earned the hatred of the people and the displeasure of God while Hulegu's fortune rose.

The narrative of the siege itself follows under its own header. In relating these events, Hamd Allah Mustaufi emphasises the deceit and avarice of the caliph, who repeatedly spurns Hulegu's call for submission as well as the counsel of his own vizier. At pivotal moments in the narrative, Mustaufi interjects moral lessons in the voice of the narrator. After writing about how the caliph refused to pay his army, for example, Hamd Allah Mustaufi addresses the reader directly to note that avarice is particularly contemptible in the case of rulers. He then returns to his narrative as an 'aged friend' advises the caliph in vain about the virtue of generosity. Such moral lessons, put in the voice of characters or of the author, continue through the story of the fall of Baghdad. Like Qashani's use of verse and wise sayings, they punctuate the narrative with moral reflections, lending the overall account a didactic purpose. Throughout the story, the caliph remains deaf to the lessons presented to or about him. In the end, he abandons his throne and his life, but only after giving the spurned vizier one more chance to lecture him on the errors of his ways.

Shortly after relating the siege of Baghdad, Hamd Allah Mustaufi shows that he is willing to depart from the historical events related in Rashid al-Din's *Blessed History* in order to advance the moralising programme of his work. When Hulegu withdrew from the Near East to Central Asia in 1260, he left his deputy Ked Buqa to maintain the Mongol military presence in Syria in the face of Mamluk and Crusader threats. Hearing of Hulegu's withdrawal, the Mamluk Sultan Sayf al-Din Quduz (1259–60), assembled an army and confronted Ked Buqa at 'Ayn Jalut, in northern Palestine.[50] Quduz defeated Ked Buqa, helped in part by the decision of the Ayyubid al-Ashraf Musa of Hims to abandon his support of the Mongols.[51] Ked Buqa was killed during the battle and his head sent to Cairo. Rashid al-Din offers a significantly different account of events from the more reliable Mamluk sources. According to Rashid al-Din, Quduz draws Ked Buqa into an ambush and annihilates his army. At the end of the battle, according to Rashid al-Din, Ked Buqa is captured, brought before Quduz, and executed after expressing his disdain for a ruler who had once been a slave.[52] This account accords more with Rashid al-Din's need to justify the Mongol loss at 'Ayn Jalut than with any eyewitness description of the battle.[53]

In his prose history, the *Select History*, Hamd Allah Mustaufi relates the battle of 'Ayn Jalut in the unadorned prose that distinguishes that work.

News of the death of Mongke Qa'an reached [Hulegu] in Damascus. He turned back and gave Amir Ked Buqa Noyan authority for the liberation of Egypt and Syria. From Egypt, Sultan Quduz came to war with him. Amir Ked Buqa was killed in that war and the Mongol army was routed.

By contrast, the account of the Battle of 'Ayn Jalut found in the *Book of Victory* recasts the fiction of Rashid al-Din's account as an object lesson about arrogance. As with the siege of Baghdad, Hamd Allah Mustaufi begins this story with an exhortation to the reader in the first-person voice of the author before beginning the narrative proper. In this version of events, Ked Buqa launches a hasty attack, which leaves him vulnerable to Quduz's ambush. The inclusion of the ambush betrays Rashid al-Din's narrative as the source for this account, but then Hamd Allah Mustaufi deviates from his source to drive home his lesson. The arrogant Ked Buqa is slain on the battlefield, but the other Mongol general, Baidar, escapes to Hulegu's court, only to be killed by his own son for having abandoned his commander. Here again, Mustaufi invokes a generic 'voice of wisdom' to tell the moral of the story and transition into the next episode, a council called by Hulegu to address the setback of 'Ayn Jalut.

The Image of the Great Vizier

Even as Hamd Allah's writing imitates the didactic structure of episodes found in the *Lives of Kings*, he also models his portrayal of Nizam al-Mulk after Bozorgmehr, creating a two-layer historical precedent for Rashid al-Din. He draws this connection in his *Book of Victory* by composing original discourses on wisdom (*pandnameh*) for both Nizam al-Mulk and Rashid al-Din. Hamd Allah Mustaufi's continuation of the *Shahnameh* includes a narrative of the dynasty of Saljuqs under whom Nizam al-Mulk had served.[54] Very few contemporary accounts of Saljuq history are known to have been produced. Of these, the *Saljuqnameh* of Zahir al-Din Nishapuri (d. 1187) served as the main source for all later Persian retellings of the period, including that of Rashid al-Din (section II.D in Appendix A).[55] Because of this limited source base, extant Persian versions of Saljuq history show only superficial variations from one another. Such continuity throws into sharp relief Hamd Allah Mustaufi's *Book of Victory*, which stands apart from the synoptic tradition of

Saljuq history for its wealth of invented material, including the discourse on wisdom in Nizam al-Mulk's voice.⁵⁶

Mustaufi presents Nizam al-Mulk's *pandnameh* as a series of discreet exhortations, more like the *Piruzinamak* tradition than Firdausi's 'discourse on wisdom' in the *Shahnameh*. This form of discourse seems to have been popular in the late Ilkhanid period: three other examples of this type of advice literature are included in a large collection of texts assembled by a certain Abu'l-Majd in Tabriz, and another is included in Shams al-Din Qashani's versification of Mongol history.⁵⁷ Within the *Book of Victory* of Hamd Allah Mustaufi, Nizam al-Mulk does not claim the various pieces of advice as his own. Instead, he presents them in the voices of a parade of historical figures. Beginning with Adam, Nizam al-Mulk catalogues the wise sayings of pre-Islamic prophets and then of the companions of the Prophet Muhammad. He continues with members of pre-Islamic Iranian dynasties from Hoshang through the late Sasanian period, pre-Islamic Arabian political leaders and Greek philosophers, and finally several caliphs and Shi'ite imams.

The actual content of the wisdom sayings attributed to these various figures only occasionally corresponds to the character or actions associated with them in the historical tradition. The benefit of creating such a catalogue of historical actors lies not in its content, but it the structure of the list, which turns Nizam al-Mulk's *pandnameh* into a type of universal history. Like Baydawi's *Order of Histories* Hamd Allah Mustaufi's *Select History*, or even Rashid al-Din's *World History*, this *pandnameh* begins with the Judeo-Islamic prophets and progresses through the various periods of pre-Islamic and Islamic history. In Mustaufi's treatment, Nizam al-Mulk becomes an antecedent to Rashid al-Din in his ability to muster the many dynasties of the past into a cohesive presentation of history.

By the time Hamd Allah's narrative arrives at the life and career of Rashid al-Din, his reader is prepared through the figures of Bozorgmehr and Nizam al-Mulk to see the Ilkhanid statesman as one more member in a lineage of great administrators and advisers. His portrait of his patron is resonant with Firdausi's depiction of Bozorgmehr. Hamd Allah Mustaufi borrows the vocabulary of the *Shahnameh* in referring to Rashid al-Din both as vizier and as chief priest (*sar-e mobadān*). The structure of Rashid al-Din's *pandnameh*, furthermore, takes its cue from Firdausi's account of Bozorgmehr.⁵⁸ Rashid al-Din meets with Ghazan once per month for twelve months and delivers twelve homilies on the virtues of a good ruler, whereas Bozorgmehr had delivered seven homilies in seven successive weeks. What is more, each of Rashid al-Din's homilies engages the same framing structure seen in other episodes of the *Book of Victory* and that stems ultimately from Nizam al-Mulk's *Lives of Kings*, beginning with an exhortation, which is then substantiated with an anecdote and restated with a final moral dictum. The historical tradition of both Sasanian and Saljuq viziers thus provides Hamd Allah Mustaufi's organisational strategies for Rashid al-Din's discourse on wisdom.

By associating Rashid al-Din with Nizam al-Mulk and Bozorgmehr, Hamd Allah Mustaufi suggests a potential rehabilitation for his recently disgraced patron. Each of the historical viziers suffered ignominy at the hands of his patron but was ultimately vindicated. Mustaufi thus establishes Rashid al-Din as a paradigmatic Persian vizier: a man of state and a wise counsellor, whose historical memory would outlast the suffering brought by political machinations. This image dismisses Rashid al-Din's active participation in the mercilessly partisan politics of the Ilkhanid court or his unscrupulous use of Qashani's material to enrich himself, instead robing the doctor from Hamadan with an image 'like the face of the sun' that has survived for seven centuries.

Notes

1. Qashani, *Tarikh-e Uljaytu*, pp. 121–34, on which the following summary is based.
2. Qashani, *Tarikh-e Uljaytu*, p. 121.
3. The conversion is related at Qashani, *Tarikh-e Uljaytu*, p. 49.
4. This holograph manuscript, Istanbul Nuruosmaniye MS. 3207, has been published in facsimile: Wassaf, *Tajziyat*, ed. Afshar.
5. Wassaf, *Tajziyat*, ed. Afshar, pp. 483–98, reproducing folios 242–9 of the manuscript.
6. Wassaf, *Tajziyat*, ed. Afshar, p. 483, reproducing folio 242a.
7. Hamd Allah Mustaufi, *Tarikh-e Gozideh*, pp. 608–9.
8. Hoffmann, *Waqf*, p. 86.
9. Maqrizi, *Kitab al-Suluk*, vol. 2, p. 175.
10. James, *Qurʾāns of the Mamlūks*, pp. 127–31 and figs. 83–7.

11. On Chupan's role in the late Ilkahnate, see Melville, 'Abu Saʿid'; Melville, *The Fall of Amir Chupan*, pp. 12–26.
12. Hamd Allah Mustaufi, *Ẓafarnāma*, p. 1451, where the stability of the meter and rhyme has preserved the name of the exact place, *Khasakdar*, a name that has become corrupted in all copies of the *Select History*.
13. On Ibn al-Fuwati and his work as a historical source, see DeWeese, 'Cultural Transmission'.
14. Ibn al-Fuwati, *Majmaʿ al-Adab*, vol. 4.2, pp. 719–20, no. 1043.
15. On the Mamluk biographical dictionaries as sources on Rashid al-Din's life, see Amitai-Preiss, 'New Material'.
16. Ibn al-Suqaʿi, *Tali*, entry 312 (Arabic text pp. 183–4, French translation pp. 211–12).
17. Kirmani, *Nasaʾim al-Ashar*, pp. 112–14. For the history of Kirman, see Kirmani, *Simt al-ʿUla*.
18. Blair, 'Patterns of Patronage', p. 56.
19. This work has been edited as Shabankaraʾi, *Majmaʿ al-Ansab*. For information on Shabankaraʾi, see Storey, *Persian Literature*, pt. 1.2, pp. 84–5.
20. See Appendix A, section II.A.
21. Sims, 'Thoughts on a *Shāhnāma* Legacy'.
22. For a discussion of these verse histories, see Melville, 'Between Firdausi and Rashīd al-Dīn'; Melville, 'The Mongol and Timurid Periods', pp. 192–7.
23. Melville, 'Between Firdausi and Rashīd al-Dīn', pp. 52–3.
24. Hamd Allah Mustaufi, *Ẓafarnāma*, p. 7.
25. Soudavar, 'Zafarnama', p. 754.
26. Soudavar, 'Zafarnama', p. 754.
27. Published in edition as Hamd Allah Mustaufi, *Tarikh-e Gozideh*.
28. Hamd Allah Mustaufi, *Tarikh-e Gozideh*, pp. 6–7.
29. Marlow, 'The Wisdom of Buzurgmihr'.
30. Four manuscript copies of this work survive, of which by far the most important is in London, BL MS. Or. 2833, on which see the facsimile edition, Hamd Allah Mustaufi, *Ẓafarnāma*, as well as Rieu, *Supplement to the Catalogue*, pp. 172–4 no. 263. This manuscript also forms the basis for Leonard Ward's unpublished dissertation, 'The Zafar-Nāmah', which includes a study on the author and work and a partial translation. Two other manuscripts are in Istanbul: Turkish and Islamic Arts Museum MSS. Evkaf 2401 and 2402. A fourth, Cambridge University Library MS. 19.1–2, was copied from BL MS. Or. 2833 for Edward G. Browne and is of little interest.

31. Hamd Allah Mustaufi, *Zafarnāma*, p. 1415.
32. On earlier Ilkhanid uses of the term Iran, see Chapter 3. On its appearance in the *Select History*, see Marlow, 'The Wisdom of Buzurgmihr'.
33. On this work, see Sadiqi, *Zafarnama*.
34. Louise Marlow has published extensively on this genre. Her article on 'Advice and advice literature' in the third edition of the *Encyclopaedia of Islam* provides the phrase 'book-length mirror' borrowed here as a section header.
35. On the *vita* of Bozorgmehr, see Marlow, 'The Wisdom of Buzurgmihr'.
36. Firdausi, *Shahnameh*, vol. vii, pp. 167–77.
37. Sadiqi, *Zafarnama*, pp. 23–5.
38. Hamd Allah Mustaufi, *Tarikh-e Gozideh*, pp. 68–70.
39. Discussed by Marlow, 'The Wisdom of Buzurgmihr'.
40. Azhdari, *Ghazannama*, pp. 168–74, 246–56, 307–10 and 318–21.
41. For a list of works with this title, see Sadiqi, *Zafarnama*, pp. 11–15.
42. London BL MS. Or. 2833, reproduced in facsimile in Hamd Allah Mustaufi, *Zafarnāma*.
43. Hamd Allah Mustaufi, *Zafarnāma*, pp. 1344–409.
44. Brack, 'Mediating Sacred Kingship', p. 274 and n. 660.
45. Qashani, *Tarikh-e Uljaytu*, pp. 106–7.
46. Hamd Allah Mustaufi, *Zafarnāma*, p. 1351.
47. On this work, see Yavari, 'Mirrors for Princes'.
48. For an example of how this work can inform the study of history, see Paul, 'Alptegin'.
49. Hamd Allah Mustaufi, *Zafarnāma*, pp. 1192–221. Compare with Rashid al-Din, *Jamiʿ al-Tawarikh*, pp. 994–1021.
50. Amitai, '"Ayn Jālūt Revisited' provides a reconstruction and discussion of the battle that corrects various earlier misrepresentations through a careful consideration of the available sources.
51. Amitai, '"Ayn Jālūt Revisited', pp. 139–40, discusses various interpretations of al-Ashraf's change of allegiance, which range from battlefield defection to a request for asylum from the Mamluks well after the battle.
52. Rashid al-Din, *Jamiʿ al-Tawarikh*, pp. 1031–3.
53. Amitai, 'Rashīd al-Dīn as a Historian of the Mamluks', pp. 74–9; Amitai, '"Ayn Jālūt Revisited', pp. 138–9 and 141. Amitai, '"Ayn Jālūt Revisited', p. 139, also shows how Wassaf's account of the battle is to be discounted on similar grounds.
54. Hamd Allah Mustaufi, *Zafarnāma*, pp. 639–759.

55. The reliance of later accounts of Saljuq history on the *Saljuqnameh* has been demonstrated by A. H. Morton's reconstruction of that text, based on a single corrupt manuscript with reference to various later derivative works. See Nishapuri, *Saljuqnameh*.
56. The *pandnama* of Nizam al-Mulk is found at Hamd Allah Mustaufi, *Ẓafarnāma*, pp. 662–77.
57. van den Berg, 'Wisdom Literature'; Melville, 'Between Firdausi and Rashīd al-Dīn', pp. 60–1.
58. Hamd Allah Mustaufi, *Ẓafarnāma*, pp. 1369–86.

Epilogue
Rashid al-Din at the Court of Shahrokh

The most intensive engagement with Rashid al-Din's historical writing occurred a century after his death at the court of Shahrokh (1405–47). There the historian 'Abd Allah b. Lutf Allah Bihdadini, better known as Hafez-e Abru (d. 1430) undertook a series of historiographical projects that drew the *Collected Histories*, along with other prominent historical texts, into a new framework for understanding the past.[1] Two of his earliest works deal with the history of the early Timurid period with which Hafez-e Abru was personally familiar. These are a continuation of Nizam al-Din Shami's biography of Timur that Hafez-e Abru wrote in 1412, taking the narrative from the point where Shami left off in 1404 up to the death of Timur the following year, and an original history of Shahrokh up to AH 816/1413–14 CE.[2] Just as these works advanced the emerging Timurid prose historiographical tradition, Hafez-e Abru also extended the narrative of Rashid al-Din's *Blessed History*. This was a two-stage process. First, Hafez-e Abru reformatted 'Abd Allah Qashani's *History of Oljeitu* into the three-*qism* format of Rashid al-Din's dynastic history, drawing on other works including Hamd Allah Mustaufi's *Book of Victory* to elaborate the narrative and extend it through the fall of the Ilkhanid dynasty in 1335. This first version of the continuation is found appended to several manuscripts of the *Blessed History* (see the λ recension in Appendix B, also discussed in Chapter 5). In the second phase of composing his continuation, Hafez-e Abru drew more extensively from Hamd Allah Mustaufi and he abandoned the three-*qism* format for a more straightforward running historical narrative, which he now extended through much of the fourteenth century.

This continuation of Rashid al-Din's narrative spans the gap in coverage between the fall of the Chinggisid *ilkhan*s and the rise of Amir Timur. It thus provides a bridge between what had originally been the *Blessed History* of a specific family and Shami's work celebrating the rise of a new non-Chinggisid Mongol conqueror. This instinct to draw various historical traditions together into a cohesive narrative is fully on display in one of Hafez-e Abru's greatest historical collections, his *Collection* or *Totality of History* (*Majmuʿa-ye Hafez-e Abru* or *Kulliyat-e Tarikhi*). This collection, which Shahrokh commissioned in 1417/18, is built around Balʿami's translation of Tabari's *History of Prophets and Kings*, Rashid al-Din's *Collected Histories* and Shami's history of Timur. To these three great sources, Hafez-e Abru adds a series of small continuations and supplements in order to create an expanded history of the world from its creation to the time of his own patron. The resulting *Collection* redeploys Rashid al-Din's *Collected Histories* as part of a grand narrative culminating in the rise of the Timurid dynasty.

At the same time that he was assembling this new universal history, Hafez-e Abru was working on another history with universal scope, the *History* or *Geography of Hafez-e Abru* (*Tarikh-e Hafez-e Abru* or *Joghrafiya-ye Hafez-e Abru*).[3] Hafez-e Abru's description of the commission of this work mentions Shahrokh's desire to see a new historical compendium based on the works of Balʿami and Rashid al-Din, and so it seems to have been a twin project with the *Collection*.[4] Much work remains to be done on all of Hafez-e Abru's *oeuvre*, but a general impression emerges of a new effort to do much of what Rashid al-Din had done a century earlier, namely, compile histories and geographical knowledge in order to demonstrate a dynasty's unique and universal command. Rashid al-Din and others at the Ilkhanid court presented the royal Mongols as universal sovereigns, combining the Chinggisid tradition of the steppe with Judeo-Islamic ideas of genealogy and prophecy and a virtuosic display of the many regions of Eurasia with which they had contact. For Timurid historians, in turn, Timur and Shahrokh represent a new pinnacle of history, pregnant with its own unique significance and symbolism that go beyond the scope of this study.[5]

Hafez-e Abru's engagement with Rashid al-Din's historical writing did not stop when he resituated the *Collected Histories* within a new and expanded historical narrative. He was also actively involved with reproducing Rashid al-Din's work on its own and refurbishing copies that had survived the turbulent intervening century in poor condition. Several such manuscripts of the *Blessed History* can be dated to the court of Shahrokh, representing two different recensions of the work (see manuscripts G_{12}, G_{13}, L_{11} and L_{12} in Appendix B). Two of these are sibling copies based on a rather disordered source manuscript of the recension created by Nizam Yazdi (the γ recension), one of which includes a calligraphic *bismallah* in the hand of Shahrokh's son Baysonghor (d. 1433). The others are the earliest copies of the λ recension described in Chapter 5. One of them also contains the earliest copy of Hafez-e Abru's initial continuation of the *Blessed History*, and so it may be that some of the changes introduced to the λ recension are his work as well.

Hafez-e Abru refurbished two fragmentary manuscripts of the *World History* that had originally been produced in Rashid al-Din's lifetime. The most famous of these is a heavily illustrated copy of the *World History* now in Istanbul (manuscript S_1). Just over half of this manuscript's 435 folios were produced at Rashid al-Din's scriptorium in Tabriz. The rest Hafez-e Abru copied out himself in 1425/6 in order to restore the complete *World History*. In doing this, Hafez-e Abru was not entirely faithful to Rashid al-Din's original work. He offers a highly abbreviated history of India and omits the history of the Jews entirely, perhaps reflecting decreased interest and/or tolerance for these alternate historical visions. Most notably, he replaces the history of pre-Islamic Iran with a new composition of his own. While Rashid al-Din's history of Iran (which, it will be remembered, was originally the work of Qashani) combines information from Arabic and Persian prose sources, Hafez-e Abru presents a version of events rooted in Iranian heroic tradition, including extensive citations from Firdausi's *Shahnameh*. Just as Hamd Allah Mustaufi's *Book of Victory* provided an important source for Hafez-e Abru's final continuation of the *Blessed History*, here too we see the tradition of Persian epic verse, revived during the late Ilkhanate, provide his basic model for the ancient past.

At least eight copies of Hafez-e Abru's autograph refurbishment of the *World History* survive (see manuscripts S_2–S_9 in Appendix B). A ninth, closely related manuscript (manuscript S_{11}) has long been considered another copy of the same. After coming to the attention of the West at the exhibition of Iranian art at the Pennsylvania Museum in 1926, this manuscript was dismembered, its painted folios being sold off in a series of brokered sales and public auctions. For this reason, it has escaped systematic study until recently.[6] An examination of the pages of the remnant manuscript and many of the dispersed folios reveals that this book could not have been copied from the famous refurbished volume just described. Like that copy, it had at its heart a gathering of pages that were originally produced at Rashid al-Din's scriptorium in Tabriz.[7] It was, therefore, a separate effort to refurbish a second fragmentary manuscript of the *World History* that had suffered through the previous century. Unlike the more famous manuscript S_1 or its many copies, the now dispersed manuscript S_{11} contained Rashid al-Din's history of India in its entirety, though it also seems to have omitted the history of the Jews. Surprisingly, while approximately 144 folios of this manuscript contain Hafez-e Abru's version of pre-Islamic history based in Iranian heroic epic, the last twelve folios of that section revert abruptly back to the version found in Rashid al-Din's *World History*. This manuscript awaits further reconstruction and study.

Some pages from the introduction of the dispersed manuscript's text were apparently removed before it was exhibited in Philadelphia. They have been replaced by two folios copied on mid-nineteenth-century Venetian paper. The text on these pages largely matches introductory material from the *History* or *Geography* of Hafez-e Abru, a work he completed well before beginning on the refurbished volume now in Istanbul. By all indications, this dispersed refurbished manuscript was an earlier effort, perhaps contemporaneous to the *History* and the *Collection*. A page in the Freer Study Collection catalogued simply as a 'folio from a Persian manuscript', was in fact once the title page for this dispersed book.[8] The centre of the page is dominated by a calligraphic passage that a later note in pencil identifies as the hand of Baysonghor. It reads simply 'a book of histories' (*kitab al-tawarikh*). By the second decade of the fifteenth century, as Hafez-e Abru produced several related historical collections for the Timurid Sultan Shahrokh and his bibliophile and artistic son Baysonghor, Rashid al-Din's historical writings had become both a source for universal history and the subject of antiquarian interest, to be reproduced, refurbished and revised according to new historical tastes.

Notes

1. On Hafez-e Abru, see Subtelny and Melville, 'Ḥāfeẓ-e Abrū'. Hafez-e Abru's engagement with Rashid al-Din's historical writing is properly the subject of a separate study. Its general contours are given here to show how it has impacted the manuscript reception of the *Collected Histories*.
2. Woods, 'The Rise of Tīmūrid Historiography', p. 96.
3. Hafez-e Abru, *Joghrafiya-ye Hafez-e Abru*.
4. Subtelny and Melville, 'Ḥāfeẓ-e Abrū'.
5. These have been explored by Moin, *The Millennial Sovereign*.
6. Ghiasian, 'The "Historical Style"'; Ghiasian, *Lives of the Prophets*, pp. 89–91.
7. Ghiasian, *Lives of the Prophets*, pp. 81–91, discussed this manuscript and the relationship between its original fourteenth-century pages and those of manuscript S_1. Ghiasian still considers this manuscript a copy of that one.
8. This is Freer, FSC-MS-11, digitised online at: http://archive.asia.si.edu/collections/edan/object.php?q=fsg_FSC-MS-11.

Appendix A
The *Collected Histories* and its Illustrations

The following pages briefly describe the sections of the *Collected Histories* as they have been preserved in the various recensions and manuscripts of the work. Each section is assigned a unique number–letter indicator (I.A, II.B, etc.) to assist with cross-referencing. Standard editions of each section are given in the notes. Page numbers for the Raushan and Musavi edition of the *Blessed History* (indicated as 'R+M') and for Thackston's translation of it are provided in the headers of the respective sections (I.A-G), while previous partial editions and translations are named in the notes. Also for the *Blessed History*, a brief summary is offered of the changes that were introduced with successive recensions of the text. These are described in more detail in Chapter 5. Where possible, the surviving illustrative programmes are compared with one another, though no effort is made at a formal art historical analysis. The heavily illustrated Paris manuscript (L_{11}) is not included in this comparison because it was a late elaboration based on multiple recensions with many new additions. It therefore does not represent the early modifications made or illustrations added to the *Blessed History* during Rashid al-Din's lifetime.

Volume 1: The *Blessed History*

I.A Introductory Material (R+M pp. 1–37, Thackston pp. 3–19)

The introductory material of the *Collected Histories* consists of two parts: a general introduction to the collection and a second introduction to the *Blessed History*.[1] No extant manuscript has the introductory material to the *Blessed History* without that of the *Collected Histories*, indicating that the very earliest version of the dynastic history – the hypothesised α recension of Appendix B that would have existed before the *World History* was added to it – has not survived.

Marginal notes in manuscript D$_{31}$ indicate the presence of two images during the introductory material of that variant.² One of these was probably a two-page scene of Oljeitu's coronation at Ujan, the other falls right at the end of the introduction to the *Blessed History*, perhaps to illustrate the composition or presentation of the book. The illustrated copy of the λ recension (manuscript L$_{11}$) is lacunose at the start but includes the latter of these two images, the only image of Rashid al-Din in a known manuscript. Along with section I.B, this is one of few portions of the *Blessed History* that is more heavily illustrated in the ζ recension than in earlier lines. Rashid al-Din's final version contained as many as four illustrations: one at the mention of Muhammad; then at the redemption of Ishmael from sacrifice; then of Ghazan, envy of all princes; and, finally, illustrating the presentation of the book.³

I.B The Tribes of Turks (R+M pp. 39–212, Thackston pp. 21–112)

In this section, Rashid al-Din catalogues the nomadic tribes gathered into Chinggis Khan's new military conquest state. It is organised into four parts, creating a historical scheme for understanding the relationships between the tribes of the Inner Asian steppe, culminating with the Mongols themselves.⁴ This section shows some of the most extensive modification between recensions, as anecdotes were added to it at various times, particularly concerning the Tayichi'ut clan of Mongols that played such a significant – and oppositional – role in the rise of Temujin. This section was of particular interest to Russian academicians during the period of intensified imperial involvement in Central Asia, and was among the earliest sections published.⁵

Copies of illustrated recensions contain space for three scenes in this section: illustrating Oghuz Khan's golden tent; the northern forest tribes; and the Uriangqad method of building sleds.⁶

I.C The Ancestors of Chinggis Khan (R+M pp. 213–86, Thackston pp. 113–40)

Rashid al-Din here narrates the lives of the ancestors of Chinggis Khan, beginning with the generation of the legendary ancestress Alan Qo'a.⁷ Changes between the γ and δ recensions to headers for the genealogical trees of these individuals suggest that the section did not originally contain any images but came to include small enthronement scenes as part of the trees. In the early fifteenth-century manuscript L₁₁, the spaces for genealogical trees have been repurposed for illustrations.

As in the previous section, the late ε and ζ recensions introduced significant new portions of text to this section, particularly dealing with the affairs of the aristocratic Tayichi'ut clan.

I.D Chinggis Khan (R+M pp. 287–616, Thackston pp. 141–301)

The sections of Chinggis Khan and Ghazan Khan (see below, section I.G) stand out as the longest in the entire *Blessed History*, creating an equivalency between the great conqueror and his fifth-generation descendant.[8] Given the length of this section, the additions that occur between recensions are relatively minor: added stories concern the Naiman prince Gushlug and the drowning of Khwarazmshah Jalal al-Din's family, with an additional brief note about the length of Chinggis Khan's life added to the ε recension. This indicates a very stable tradition concerning Chinggis Khan. The ζ recension also adds a passage about Chinggis Khan's selection of his own burial site, with a parallel passage also appearing there concerning the burial site of Ogedei.

Marginal notes in manuscript D₃₁ indicate the location of at least twenty-six illustrations in this section, many of which correspond to images found in manuscript L₁₁ and to images in the fragmentary manuscript D₂₁.[9] This suggests a very intensive programme of illustration in the δ recension, which was used in preparing the λ recension. Extant copies of the later, 'official' ζ recension show a significantly less ambitious cycle of sixteen illustrations.

I.E The Sons and Successors of Chinggis Khan through Timur (R+M pp. 617–960, Thackston pp. 303–470)

This section covers the reigns of Chinggis Khan's successors in eight chapters: on Ogedei, Jochi and his descendants, Chaghadai and his descendants, Tolui, Guyug, Mongke, Qubilai and Timur. It shows several significant variations between recensions.[10] Rashid al-Din updated his list of the descendants of Chaghadai on two occasions; the second and third of these were later conflated in the λ recension.[11] In addition, the δ recension introduces new material into third *qism* of the *dastan* of Mongke and to a section dedicated to miscellaneous events during the reign of Qubilai, and at least one manuscript (D_{31}) also adds new material to the third *qism* of the *dastan* of Guyug. These variants were carried into the late λ recension, and thence into modern scholarship through Blochet's edition of this section. Rashid al-Din's last version, the ζ recension, drops a few passages of redundant text relating to the descendants of Chaghadai, but adds a long passage about Qaidu's death and his daughters.[12]

This and the following section best demonstrate the decreasing illustrative cycle of the *Blessed History* between the δ and ζ recensions. The main exemplar of the δ recension picks up during this section, so that it can be compared with manuscripts of the ζ recension. Between the three manuscripts of the δ recension (none of them a complete witness to the text or its illustrations), we can conclude that this section included as many as thirty illustrations, while the manuscripts of the later ζ recension leave space for only half as many.

I.F Ilkhans from Hulegu to Geikhatu (R+M pp. 961–1203, Thackston pp. 471–587)

The variations in this section are primarily the work of Rashid Khwafi (on whom, see Chapter 5), who adds several additional notes and verses, particularly relating to the early Ilkhanid administration.[13] Otherwise, variations are limited to new material in the third *qism* of the *dastan* of Arghun added to the λ recension and a series of small lacunae in the ζ recension in the history of Hulegu.

The δ recension illustrative programme of this section is almost entirely preserved in manuscript D_1, which contains twenty illustrations (not counting seven added later in spaces originally not intended for illustration). Most of these are also indicated in the marginal notes of manuscript D_{31}. Fully half of the δ recension illustrations pertain to Hulegu's campaign of 1256–1258. The later ζ recension contains spaces for just eight illustrations, of which only the siege of Baghdad relates to Hulegu's campaign.[14] The other spaces are for images of the coronations of Abaqa, Teguder, Arghun and Geikhatu, and for three narrative scenes: Arghun Aqa's reception of Hulegu after crossing the

Oxus; the celebration of the new year of 1257; and Abaqa's defeat of Baraq in 1270.

I.G Ghazan Khan (R+M pp. 1205–530, Thackston pp. 589–762)

This is in many respects the most important and most stable section in the *Blessed History*, though the manuscript tradition contains a few major discrepancies.[15] Unlike other *dastan*s in the work, this one begins with Ghazan's youth, rather than his rise to the throne. This allows Rashid al-Din to tell us of his patron's formative years in his grandfather's camp and his inherent inclination towards Abrahamic monotheism. Many of the changes made in this section can be attributed to scribes and editors working outside Rashid al-Din's system of scriptoria, namely, Nizam Yazdi (whose amendments are found in the extant manuscripts of the γ recension) and whoever is responsible for introducing Qashani's celebratory history of Ghazan's conversion into the text of the λ recension. Otherwise, the section provides our best narrative of Ghazan's career, even if it is carefully crafted to serve Rashid al-Din's overall ideological aim of presenting his patron as a devout Muslim and legitimate Mongol khan.

As in the previous section, here the δ recension shows a significantly more ambitious illustrative programme than the later ζ recension. Marginalia in manuscript D_{31} indicate thirteen images, while surviving witnesses to the later recension give space for only seven or eight.

The *World History*

Four partial manuscripts of the *World History* have survived from Rashid al-Din's lifetime, as well as one of Qashani's *Cream of Histories*, which provided the first two sections (II.A and B) of Rashid al-Din's world history. These can be used to reconstruct the original shape of the work. The most famous of these manuscripts is also the earliest, a partial 1314 copy of the Arabic translation, surviving in two fragments divided between Edinburgh University and the Nasser Khalili collection (manuscript R_1 in Appendix B). Because of the uniquely high quality of its paintings and its importance in the development of Islamic book art, it has attracted significant attention from art historians.[16]

Only one copy of the Persian *World History* (manuscript P_2) has survived nearly complete from the time of Rashid al-Din. It is dated to 1317, and has been tied to Rashid al-Din's scriptorium in Tabriz, but, as discussed in Appendix B, it is more likely to be a regional copy of an original from Tabriz. Two further Persian copies of the *World History* can be tied to Rashid al-Din's scriptorium in Tabriz. These were both already fragmentary by the early fifteenth century, when the librarian and historian Hafez-e Abru, working for the Timurid ruler Shahrokh, attempted to restore them and apply Rashid al-Din's historical vision to his own patron's benefit. Hafez-e Abru included pieces of both fragments in one of his reconstructions (manuscript S_1).[17] Of its 435 folios, 239 are original to the time of Rashid al-Din, covering roughly from the end of Muhammad's life through the history of China (sections II.B–I).[18] Hafez-e Abru himself resupplied the remaining folios between 1425 and 1426. Of these reconstructed sections, the first and the last are significantly different from Rashid al-Din's original. In place of Rashid al-Din's pre-Islamic history, Hafez-e Abru supplied his own version of events, as described in the Epilogue. The history of India found in this reconstruction is also greatly abbreviated from Rashid al-Din's original.

The second of Hafez-e Abru's reconstructions of an original Rashidi Quarter manuscript (manuscript S_{11}) had its illustrated pages cut out and sold in a series of sales between the 1920s and 1980s, and so it has avoided systematic study until very recently.[19] This manuscript had at its core a section of perhaps fifty-four folios of a manuscript made at Rashid al-Din's scriptorium in Tabriz, covering from the very end of the history of the caliphate almost to the end of the section on the Saljuqs (sections II.B–D).[20] To this fragment, Hafez-e Abru attached new copies of missing sections, replacing the pre-Islamic portion with his own version of that period, as he also did for manuscript S_1. Here, however, he retains Rashid al-Din's original history of India. None of the illustrations in this dispersed manuscript can be dated to the Ilkhanid period. They were added later, probably at the time of its reconstruction.[21]

From these early manuscripts of the *World History*, we can determine the shape that Rashid al-Din gave to the work. The Arabic copy is both the earliest and most elaborate of the three, and probably represents Rashid al-Din's original intention for the deluxe copies of his own work. The Persian copy of 1317, and Hafez-e Abru's first reconstruction contain more limited illustrative programmes. Comparing the Persian copy of 1317 with the Arabic of

1314, Sheila Blair has suggested that the artists at Rashid al-Din's scriptorium could not maintain the intensity of illustration evident in the Arabic copy.[22] However, if as described in Appendix B the 1317 Persian manuscript was indeed prepared outside Tabriz, it only suggests that the regional scriptorium at which it was produced was less ambitious.

On the other hand, the 239 Ilkhanid folios from manuscript S_1, Hafez-e Abru's autograph reconstruction of the *World History*, match in their format with the Arabic copy and with other copies made at the Rashidi Quarter. They include sixty-eight illustrations original to the Ilkhanid period and are dated to 1314, just a few months after the Arabic copy was made.[23] Where the coverage of these manuscripts overlap, a direct comparison is therefore possible between the illustration of the Arabic and Persian versions made in Tabriz in 1314.

II.A History of pre-Islamic Iran

This is one of the longest sections of the *World History*, and the only one that still has not been properly edited. Muhammad Raushan's three-volume edition of 2013 purports to be the text of this and section II.B.[24] However, that text is based on manuscript S_1, which contains Hafez-e Abru's longer version of pre-Islamic history. Rashid al-Din's original Persian text of the pre-Islamic history is available in manuscripts of the o and π groups, as well as Qashani's *Cream of Histories*, while most of the Arabic translation is preserved in manuscript R_1b. Some comments are here offered concerning the sources and nature of Rashid al-Din's history of the pre-Islamic period, though these will undoubtedly need to be revisited once the text receives a full and dedicated edition.[25]

The closest we have to a direct explanation of the sources of this section is provided by Qashani, in his introduction to his modified *Collected Histories* that he prepared after Rashid al-Din submitted his own work of that title.[26] Immediately after his description of the decision to compose the *Cream of Histories* (described in Chapter 4), Qashani describes his process of composition in his typically elaborate style. Unfortunately, the only source that can be immediately identified from his description is the *Perfect History* (*Kamil fi'l-Ta'rikh*) of Ibn al-Athir (d. 1233), which clearly provided significant material for this and the following section of the *Collected Histories*. Charles

Melville has demonstrated that for the earliest portion of the text, treating the legendary first Pishdadiyan kings very briefly, the immediate source is evidently the *Order of Histories* of Baidawi (on which, see Chapter 3).[27] To identify other sources, particularly for the lengthy passages on Hellenistic and Roman history, is a project for another study.

As already mentioned, Hafez-e Abru significantly rewrote the pre-Islamic history in preparing his reconstructions of the *World History*. The original text relies on Arabic prose texts derived from the late-Sasanian *Book of Lords* (*Khwadaynamag*). By contrast, Hafez-e Abru's version frequently quotes the *Shahnameh*, and his narrative of the heroic Iranian past aligns closely with that of Firdausi's poem. Hafez-e Abru's text is also much longer than Rashid al-Din's. This is due in part to the added passages of verse, but Hafez-e Abru's basic prose narrative is also more elaborate than that of the *World History*. Since this is the only section of the work that Hafez-e Abru significantly modified, it is possible to quantify the net result of his modifications by comparing the relative length of this section with that of section II.B, which he did not modify. In Hafez-e Abru's reworked text, the pre-Islamic history is more than 20 per cent longer than the history of Islam (283 manuscript pages as compared with 236 in manuscript S_1). By contrast, Rashid al-Din's original pre-Islamic history is well under half the length of section II.B (94.5 manuscript pages as compared with 232.5 pages in manuscript P_2 or 105.5 pages as compared with 292 pages in manuscript O_{12}).

The fullest Persian manuscript from Rashid al-Din's lifetime, manuscript P_2, contains space for twenty-eight illustrations, though most of the images were added in the Timurid period.[28] Several of these illustrations resemble those of the Arabic copy of 1314 in their composition and were probably modelled after it.[29] The Arabic copy of this portion is somewhat corrupt. A folio seems to be missing on either side of the current folio 5. In the corresponding Persian version, these pages include two images from the story of Joseph and one of Job. Folios 6–11 of the Arabic copy are correctly ordered, but have each been inserted into the manuscript backwards after being re-margined. Between folios 11 and 12 there should be four folios. The second and fourth of these are currently folios 17 and 16. The other two are missing, roughly corresponding to folios 16 and 17b–18a of the Persian copy. If they matched the Persian copy, they would have contained one image of Hud and two of Solomon.

While the text of the Persian and Arabic copies corresponds quite closely, the illustrative programmes diverge from one another in some respects. The first four images in the Arabic copy (of Iram, Salih, Hushang and Tahmurasp) are not included in the Persian, nor are images of the discovery of Moses, Joshua, Samson, Jeremiah and George forced to worship idols.[30] Besides the five images of prophets that may have been lost to lacunae in the Arabic version, the complete Persian copy includes unique images of the Iranian rulers Humay Chaharezad, Ashk b. Ashkan and Shapur b. Ardashir, and one of the Abyssinian invasion of Mecca with elephants.[31] Under the header of Bahman b. Isfandiyar, the Persian version has a generic enthronement scene, while the Arabic copy shows the death of Rostam and Shaghad, the only image in any known copy of the work to illustrate a scene from Ferdowsi's *Shahnameh*.[32] Besides these differences, the Persian and Arabic versions share seventeen images in common, a number that could rise as high as twenty-two if we count the five images of prophets that may have appeared on folios missing from the Arabic copy. This is the majority of the twenty-eight images of the Persian copy and the twenty-seven (or up to thirty-two) of the Arabic. The differences between the two illustrative programmes show a slight preference for images of Iranian kings in the Persian version and for sacred history in the Arabic version, though exceptions are evident in the Arabic copy's paintings of Hushang and Tahmuras and the Persian copy's depiction of the siege of Mecca. Since manuscript P_2 may be a regional Ilkhanid copy of an original from the Rashidi Quarter, it is currently impossible to know if these differences reflect a decision on the part of Rashid al-Din's scriptorium or a modification to the Persian text at a regional studio.

II.B History of Muhammad and the Caliphate

This is the longest section of the *World History*. As with section II.A, the available edition is based on Hafez-e Abru's reconstructed manuscript. However, since Hafez-e Abru here preserves Rashid al-Din's text unaltered, this does not inhibit study of the section in the same way as it does for the history of Iran. As with section II.A, this section is lifted from Qashani's *Cream of Histories*, which draws most heavily on the works of Tabari and Ibn al-Athir. For the life of Muhammad and the early caliphal period, this section preserves a narrative structure, with fully forty folios (about one-third of the entire section) dedicated to the life and career of Muhammad. Beginning near the start of the history of the ʿAbbasids, the narrative switches to an annalistic structure, listing the events of each year under a header for that year, with additional headers marking the start of each caliph's reign. This is probably due to the nature of the source material, which offers ample narrative material for the earliest years of Islam from the biography (*sira*) tradition of Muhammad and his earliest followers, but relies on administrative chronicles for later periods of Islamic history.

The early copies of the history of Islam contain different numbers and selections of images, though all images in all copies pertain only to the life of the Prophet Muhammad and the years immediately after his death. The history of Islam from the 1314 Arabic copy (manuscript R_1) is divided between the two fragments held in different collections. Together, they contain thirteen images: the discovery of Zamzam (R_1b 41a); the birth of Muhammad (R_1b 42a); Muhammad recognised by Bahira (R_1b 43b); the placing of the black stone in the Kaʿba (R_1b 45a); Muhammad's call to prophecy (R_1b 45b); the persecution of early believers (R_1b 48b); Muslim refugees in Abyssinia (R_1b 52a); the meeting of the Quraysh (R_1b 54a); Muhammad's night journey (R_1b 55a); Abu Bakr and Muhammad in flight (R_1b 57a); the Battle of Badr (R_1a 7r); the victory over the Qaynuqaʿ (R_1a 8r); and the submission of the Banu al-Nadir (R_1a 3r).

By comparison, the 1317 Persian copy (manuscript P_2) includes spaces for twelve illustrations, all of which were filled during the Timurid period. Spaces were left for: the birth of Muhammad (55b); Muhammad recognised by Bahira (57a); the placing of the black stone in the Kaʿba (59a); the persecution of early believers (62a); Muslim refugees in Abyssinia (66a); the meeting of the Quraysh (68b); Muhammad's night journey (69a); Abu Bakr and Muhammad in flight (73b); the Battle of Badr (79a); the victory over the Qaynuqaʿ (80a); the Battle of Uhud (81b); and the submission of the Banu al-Nadir (83b).

In the autograph copy of Hafez-e Abru's reconstruction of the *Collected History* (manuscript S_1), the history of Islam covers 118 folios (folios

149–266). Twenty-two of these, folios 149–63 and 220–6, are in Hafez-e Abru's hand; the rest seem to originate in Rashid al-Din's own scriptorium. This copy contains only seven images, the first three are part of Hafez-e Abru's reconstruction, while the last four are original. The seven images are: Muhammad's call to prophecy (154a); Abu Bakr and Muhammad in flight (160b); the building of the Prophet's mosque (161b); the Battle of Badr (165b); the victory over the Qaynuqaʿ (167a); the Battle of Uhud (169a); and the punishment of the Banu al-Nadir (170b). The four original illustrations correspond to spaces left in manuscript P_2. By extension, we might assume that the portion of this section reconstructed by Hafez-e Abru probably originally contained the eight other images found in manuscript P_2.

II.C–D Histories of the Ghaznavids and Saljuqs

Having carried the history of the central Islamic political institution, the caliphate, to its demise at the hands of Hulegu, Rashid al-Din turns to tell the histories of various Islamic dynasties that existed alongside the ʿAbbasids. In doing this, he follows the pattern set by ʿAbd al-Hayy Gardizi and refreshed in the early Ilkhanate by Nasir al-Din Baydawi (on which, see Chapter 3). The immediate source for the first section of this part of the *World History* is ʿUtbi's *Kitab al-Yamini*, which Jarbadhqani had already translated into Persian under the Saljuqs. Following Jarbadhqani, Rashid al-Din focuses on the Samanid and Buyid families and how the Ghaznavids under Sebuktegin and Mahmud rose up to carve out their short-lived period of independence in eastern Iran and Afghanistan.[33] Of all the sections of the *World History*, this and the history of the Khwarazmshahs are the only ones that do not have corresponding sections in Qashani's *Collected Histories*.

The next section of the *Collected Histories* is the history of the Saljuqs, which overlaps significantly with the chronology of the Ghaznavid history.[34] Rashid al-Din makes no effort, however, to stitch these into a uniform or consistent narrative. Instead, he adheres to the presentation of material as found in his source texts. The primary source for the Saljuqs, as for almost all Persian-language histories of that dynasty, is the *Saljuqnameh* of Zahir al-Din Nishapuri (d. 1187).[35] Nishapuri's text breaks off during the reign of Sultan Tughril III (1174–94), who reigned past the end of Nishapuri's life. In 1202/3, Abu Hamid Muhammad b. Ibrahim added a short continuation summarising the end of the dynasty.[36] This is the version to which Rashid al-Din and ʿAbd Allah Qashani had access. Each of them ended up modifying this expanded *Saljuqnameh*, adding material from Qiwam al-Din al-Bundari's abridgement of a dynastic history of the Saljuqs written by Nishapuri's contemporary, ʿImad al-Din al-Isfahani (d. 1201), as well as otherwise unknown romantic and dramatic material concerning the Anatolian Saljuqs and the court of Masʿud (1135–52).[37] The two Ilkhanid authors, however, draw on this material in different ways, so that neither work can be said to derive from the other. Based on the similarities between the texts, Alexander Morton has hypothesised that Qashani composed a preliminary version of the *Collected Histories*, which provided Rashid al-Din with his basic narrative as well as his title, and then further modified the text to produce his own finished version.[38]

As described above and in Appendix B, manuscript S_1 contains a core section that dates to 1314, including sixty-eight original Ilkhanid images.[39] Also, manuscript S_{11} was reconstructed around a group of about fifty-four folios also originally from Rashid al-Din's scriptorium. Each of these partial original copies covers the histories of the Ghaznavids and Saljuqs. They, in addition to the full Persian copy (manuscript P_2), allow for a more robust comparison of the original illustrative programme of this section.

The Arabic copy (manuscript R_1b) contains twenty-seven images of the Ghaznavids and six of the Saljuqs. The Persian copy of 1317 (manuscript P_2) contains twenty-two images of the Ghaznavids and sixteen of the Saljuqs. Among the fragmentary Persian copies, S_1 contains twenty images of the Ghaznavids and fifteen of the Saljuqs, while the known folios of S_{11} contain sixteen images of the Ghaznavids (with three folios unaccounted for) and thirteen of the Saljuqs (with two folios unaccounted for). In all cases, most images are of battles and enthronements, with almost exclusively enthronement scenes for the Saljuqs. When the same scene is depicted in all three manuscripts, there is a high degree of consistency between them, but no two manuscripts contain identical illustrative programmes. The Persian copies each contain significantly more images of the Saljuqs than the Arabic copy does, while the Arabic copy has a slightly higher illustrative rate for the Ghaznavids. This suggests that the histories of these two dynasties resonated differently with different audiences. This is perhaps due to the original language of the two main source texts. 'Utbi's history of Mahmud of Ghazna was originally written in Arabic, while Nishapuri's *Saljuqnameh* was written in Persian, and so each text was likely to be more familiar to one linguistic community than the other.

II.E–G Histories of the Khwarazmshahs, Salghurids and Isma'ilis

These three short sections together make up only about 10 per cent of the *World History*.[40] They can be found in their entirety in manuscript S_1, with the colophon dated to 1314 falling at the end of the history of the Isma'ilis. Manuscript P_2 breaks off near the end of the history of the Khwarazmshahs and entirely lacks those of the Salghurids and Isma'ilis. As this was the ultimate source for at least five later copies (manuscripts P_{11}–P_{15}, and possibly P_{21}), this lacuna is common among witnesses to the *World History*. Of the forty-six folios that these three sections collectively fill in the best surviving copy (manuscript S_1), thirty-three make up the history of the Isma'ilis, while the Khwarazmshahs fill nine and one-half folios and the Salghurids just three. The Arabic copy breaks off three pages into the history of the Khwarazmshahs.

Qashani and Rashid al-Din's sources for these sections have been well established. The history of the Khwarazmshahs is extracted directly from Juvayni's *History of the World Conqueror*. Juvayni also provides much of the history of the Isma'ilis, though Qashani and Rashid al-Din also employ other sources that would have been available from the seizure of the Isma'ili libraries in 1256.[41] The history of the Salghurids is condensed from passages of Wassaf's *Allocation of Cities*.

The decision to include these three dynasties demonstrates the influence of early Ilkhanid historiography on the process of creating the *World History*. Juvayni's family had long experience working for the Khwarazmshahs, and Juvayni had immediate access to the library of the Isma'ili imam at Alamut. Wassaf and Baydawi had served in the Salghurid government, and each included sizeable passages about them in his history. Furthermore, the geographical extent of these states fell within the boundaries of the Ilkhanate, which may explain the exclusion of the histories of other late- and post-Saljuq regional dynasties, such as Ibn al-Athir's history of the Zangids of Mosul, or any of the local histories of Saljuq Rum or Syria, all of which would have been available to Rashid al-Din.[42]

The two early Persian copies (manuscripts P_2 and S_1) contain the same five illustrations for the history of the Khwarazmshahs: three battle scenes; one enthronement; and the scene of Jalal al-Din's escape from Chinggis Khan across the Indus River. In the sole early copy of the other sections (manuscript S_1 339–375), the history of the Salghurids is entirely unillustrated, while the Isma'ilis receive nineteen images in sixty-six manuscript pages.[43] These include enthronements and battle scenes, but also several narrative scenes, including the assassinations of Nizam al-Mulk and his son. That the Isma'ilis – early and avid opponents to the Mongol *ilkhan*s – should receive such rich visual treatment in the *World History* is perhaps surprising. However, the final image is of Rukn al-Din Khurshah surrendering his treasury to Hulegu. Like Juvayni's history discussed in Chapter 3, this section thus ends on a triumphal note, as the notoriously intransigent Isma'ilis succumb to the new Mongol rulers.

II.H History of the Oghuz Turks

This section offers an etiology for the Turkic dynasties of the steppes of western Asia, including the Saljuqs, Qarakhanids and Uyghurs.[44] Chronologically, it should fall before section II.C. Placed where it is, however, it expands the geography of the *World History* gradually outward from the lands of Iraq and Iran, where previous sections of the *World History* and earlier Islamic universal histories had focused. It also serves as a bit of a metonym for Ilkhanid history, as the itinerary of Oghuz across the Middle East resembles somewhat that of Hulegu in the 1250s.[45] It is thus the first of five sections that treat the history of non-Muslim peoples through the epistemological lens of their own traditions. In the case of the Oghuz Turks, this means a story framed in the narrative and cultural patterns of Inner Asian nomads.[46]

Rashid al-Din's history of the Turks amounts to the earliest witness to what later became a popular Turkic origin narrative for the Oghuz or Ghuzz Turks of western Asia, the so-called *Oghuznameh* tradition.[47] Just two centuries before Rashid al-Din, Mahmud al-Kashghari glossed the word *oghuz* in his dictionary of Turkic dialects simply as 'a tribe of the Turks'.[48] By the time of Rashid al-Din, a legend had emerged around an eponymous ancestor, Oghuz Khan. Rashid al-Din offers a short summary of the life of Oghuz in his *Blessed History*, and promises to append an extended version to that work.⁴⁹ Once Oljeitu commissioned the *World History*, this original appendix was folded into that second volume. Even there, however, it serves the overall ideological programme of the *Blessed History* by creating an Abrahamic pedigree for Ghazan that the Mamluks of Egypt could not match. It also emphasises the *ilkhans*' *de facto* command of the Middle East by virtue of conquest, despite the counterclaims of the Jochids on the basis of Chinggis Khan's dispensation of territory among his four sons.⁵⁰ After the story of Oghuz, Rashid al-Din traces the branches of his descendants, who become the ancestors of various contemporary tribes of Turks.

The two extant Persian copies of this portion of the *World History* from Rashid al-Din's lifetime are both minorly defective. Between folios 238 and 239 of manuscript P_2 there occurs a lacuna of probably two folios, which should include three images. In manuscript S_1, folios 377 and 384 have been transposed, probably as two sides of a bi-folio that has been inserted backwards into its gathering. These early manuscripts also include tabular lists of the branches of the tribes of Turks descended from Oghuz, which were intended to include the branding marks, or *tamgha*s, of each tribe. These have not survived in this section, but they are preserved in several manuscripts of the ε recension of the *Blessed History* as part of the brief account of Oghuz Khan at the beginning of that work. Rashid al-Din names twenty-four tribes of Oghuz Turks, the titular ancestors of which were the twenty-four grandsons of Oghuz Khan, four by each of his six sons, who are divided evenly among the Buzoq and Uchoq branches. This contrasts to the description of Oghuz tribes by Mahmud al-Kashghari, whose scheme was adopted by Mamluk writers, including 'Ayni.⁵¹

The illustrative programme of the history of the Turks is perfectly consistent between the two early Persian copies, notwithstanding the loss of three images in the lacuna of manuscript P_2 and the fact that one image has not been completed in S_1. The thirteen images of this section depict: Dib Yaqui enthroned with his four sons; a woman warning Oghuz of war with his uncle; a battle in that war; the building of wagons by the Turks; Oghuz's journeys to the Land of Darkness and India; his war against the tribes of Turkestan; the submission of Damascus; an embassy to Oghuz; the enthronement of Kun Khan; the dog Qara Buraq; the enthronement of Erki Khan; and the capture of Shahmalik.⁵² The first seven of these in S_1 are part of the portion originally prepared at Rashid al-Din's scriptorium.⁵³ Thirteen images in twenty-seven pages of manuscript text makes this one of the most heavily illustrated sections of the *World History*. Only the history of India (section II.L), with its numerous landscape scenes and the sections on China and the Franks (II.I and K) with their serial portraits of rulers contain more paintings per page of text.

II.I History of China

The history of China is the only place in the *World History* where we read an explicit description of the process of composition.⁵⁴ As discussed in Chapter 4, the introduction to this section mentions two Chinese scholars Kamsun and Litaji, who offered a summary history that had been composed by three Chinese monks. Neither Qashani nor Rashid al-Din name the source text. Francesco Calzolaio and Francesca Fiaschetti have recently demonstrated that the text must have been a Chan (Zen) Buddhist universal history from the early Yuan period.⁵⁵ Remarkably, such universal histories performed in the Chinese context much of the same function that the *World History* performed for Oljeitu, casting the Mongol rulers of China as universal *cakravartin* rulers.⁵⁶ Rashid al-Din was, therefore, using a very relevant text for telling the history of China in the Mongol world.

The material of Rashid al-Din's catalogue of Chinese emperors adds nothing to our understanding of Chinese history: it is little more than a series of king lists for the various Chinese imperial dynasties. It does, however, include a description of Chinese block-printing that offers some insight into Rashid al-Din's attitude towards reproducing and illustrating texts, as discussed in Chapter 5. The early Persian copies of this section each contain space for an illustration of the Chinese scholars' audience with Oljeitu. The 1317 copy (manuscript P_2) includes an image – painted, like most of the images in this manuscript, in the Timurid period – showing Oljeitu enthroned outdoors, with several groups of courtiers and one Chinese scholar in front of a book resting on a *rihal*, or book stand, while another narrow book and a round object (possibly an astrological device) lie on the ground nearby. Hafez-e Abru's reconstructed volume (manuscript S_1) contains space for this same image, but it has not been completed. Other than these single images in the early Persian copies, the illustrations in the history of China consist of over one hundred portraits of Chinese emperors, depicted without background or surroundings. These portraits are reminiscent of Chinese depictions, including the 'Thirteen Emperors' scroll' of Yan Liben, copies of which may have been available as models for the artists of Rashid al-Din's scriptorium.[57]

II.J History of the Jews

Rashid al-Din was born and raised Jewish, and this section represents a new approach to Jewish history in Islamic historiography. Earlier Muslim historians relied on Qur'anic material for Judeo-Islamic prophets, and incorporated Hebrew biblical material only in a form consistent with Islamic prophetic tradition.[58] As elsewhere in Rashid al-Din's world history, this section follows the historical epistemology of its subject, rather than that of previous Islamic histories, by closely following the Biblical and Rabbinic traditions.[59] The level of understanding of Hebrew and Aramaic biblical literature demonstrated by this section has been taken as evidence that Rashid al-Din received an extensive education in the Rabbinic circles of Hamadan.[60] However, a version of this section appears also in Qashani's *Collected Histories*, and so the Rabbinic learning lying behind it may well be that of another educated Jewish scholar. Only a dedicated comparison of Qashani and Rashid al-Din's texts alongside contemporary Jewish historical traditions can settle this question.

The paintings of the Jewish history in the 1314 Arabic copy of the *Collected Histories* have received some attention, especially with regard to the figure of Moses.[61] Of the seven images of Moses found in manuscript R_1, however, only two come from this section; the other five are part of the pre-Islamic history of kings and prophets (II.A). Of those five, four are also included in the Persian manuscript P_2, so the cycle of Mosaic images is not as unique to the Arabic version as has elsewhere been claimed.[62] Altogether, the history of the Jews in manuscript P_2 contains eight images, depicting Noah's ark (275a), Jacob wrestling with the Angel (278b), Joseph and his family (280b), the burning of the golden calf (283b), Moses' appointment of Joshua as his successor (286a), the suicide of Saul during the war against the Philistines (288a), the judgement of Solomon (289a), and Jonah and the whale (291b). By comparison, Arabic fragment R_1a includes images of Noah's ark (28a), Jacob and his family (29b), Joseph before Potiphar (30a), Joseph and his brothers (31a), Moses' punishment of apostates (32a), the death of Moses (33b), the suicide of Saul (34a), and Jonah and the whale (35a). Each has eight images, though only the first and the two last of these are the same in both Persian and Arabic versions.

II.K History of the Franks

Like the histories of China and India, Rashid al-Din's history of the people of Europe begins with a general discussion of culture and geography and then offers an illustrated list of its leaders.[63] It is divided into two chapters (*qism*), each with four sections (*fasl*). Most of these are largely unremarkable in their sources and presentations. Rashid al-Din's history of the Franks, however, is notable as the first serious treatment of Europe in Islamic historical writing. Prior to this, only Mas'udi had bothered to offer a list of kings for a region that was otherwise dismissed as uncivilised and uninteresting.[64] Rashid al-Din's encounter with European sources is perhaps also to be seen in his adoption of European models for the universal genealogical trees that begin to appear in his work in 1307 (on which, see Chapter 5). The chapter on Europe is entirely missing from manuscript R_1. Qashani's corresponding history is significantly different and invites further comparative study.[65]

The four sections of the first chapter, giving ten lists of kingly and prophetic dynasties and the generations of prophets and kings of the Jewish tradition from Adam to the birth of Jesus, rely on the work of Bar Hebraeus, but also probably reflect Rashid al-Din's own familiarity with Hebrew scripture. The first three sections of the second chapter offer brief treatments of the Christian faith, the land of Armenia and the geography of Europe. They do not reveal their immediate sources, but in the milieu of Mongol Tabriz, where Armenian clergy and Italian merchants rubbed shoulders, there is little surprise that Rashid al-Din had access to such information. As with the selection of post-Saljuq dynasties that Rashid al-Din chooses to include (sections II.E–G), the special treatment given to Armenia is undoubtedly a result of its relevance to the Ilkhanid state, as Armenians had been deeply involved in all stages and various aspects of Ilkhanid history.

The final section of the history of the Franks, in both Qashani and Rashid al-Din's rendering, consists of parallel lists of popes beginning with St Peter and of Roman, Byzantine, and Holy Roman Emperors since Augustus Caesar. The text is a Persian translation of one version of the *Chronicle of Popes and Emperors* (*Chronicon Pontificum et Imperatorum*) of Martinus Polonus (d. 1278), also known as Martinus Oppaviensis or Martin of Troppau.[66] Martinus' *Chronicle* has largely fallen out of view of scholars of the European Middle Ages, as it contains no unique historical information. In the centuries immediately after Martinus' death, however, his work enjoyed wide readership and influenced chronicles written across Europe.[67] As with the history of China, Rashid al-Din here drew on a current and popular source for his presentation of Europe.

The *Chronicle* is most remarkable for its layout, as it presents the histories of popes and emperors parallel to one another: popes on the verso of the page and contemporary emperors on the facing recto, with approximately one line of text for each year of a papal or imperial reign.[68] In this way, each two-page spread of the book covers exactly fifty years of history, and allows easy reference between holders of the two most powerful offices in Europe. Later copyists frequently disregarded this attention to formatting, conflating the histories of popes and emperors into a single running text.

In the Persian version of this text, Qashani and Rashid al-Din preserve Martinus' original layout with some modifications. They fit both popes and emperors on the same page, with text running in columns down the two sides of the page. The parallel histories are kept in synch, so that a series of popes might be listed across from one long-serving emperor or vice versa. The strict division of fifty years per page, however, is here abandoned. Such a layout is evident in the sole manuscript of Qashani's work, as well as in manuscript P_2. In the Timurid reconstructions S_1 and S_{11}, the histories of popes and emperors are condensed into a single text block, muddling the text in the same way that happened to Martinus' original *Chronicle*. There is no way of knowing whether this was Hafez-e Abru's choice, or whether he had access to a source manuscript where this condensation had already occurred.

Rashid al-Din's version of the list of popes and emperors deviates from Qashani's in its inclusion of illustrations. In its illustrations, as in the overall structure of the section, the history of the Franks resembles the preceding history of China. Here again we see isolated portraits of individual leaders, unframed and without any background or other visual context. Each pope is depicted seated on an open-frame seat, wearing a broad hat and a short pelerine. Comparable images of popes can be found in collections of Latin canon law, or Decretals, from the twelfth and thirteenth centuries, and particularly the *Decretum Gratiani*.⁶⁹ The kings are depicted sitting cross-legged before the popes, dressed in robe and crown. These are similar to many other sovereigns depicted in various sections of the *Collected Histories*, but might also be compared with an exactly contemporary Armenian gospel which shows the ancestors of Jesus as isolated seated figures with crowns similar to those in this section.⁷⁰

These portraits are largely interchangeable – they are institutional, rather than individual portraits, lacking any narrative quality or individuality. However, the iconography of the pope enjoyed some later life in Persian book painting. It is noteworthy that the only image included for the Franks in Hafez-e Abru's reconstructed manuscript (S_1, folio 416a) shows an outdoor scene with an enthroned ruler on the right facing a papal figure seated on a bench on the left, a composition that echoes the peculiar illustrative programme of Rashid al-Din's original version of this section by putting pope and emperor facing one another. Hafez-e Abru may well have worked from a fully illustrated copy of Rashid al-Din's original, but chose to remove the repetitive portraits in the interest of space or resources, replacing them with a single representative image before the catalogue of popes and emperors.

II.L History of India

The final section of the *World History* is an account of Indian land, history and religion in two parts.⁷¹ The first part begins with an overview of the geography of India based on Abu'l-Rayhan al-Biruni's *Description of India*, completed in 1030. This is followed by a description of the Indian system of measuring the ages of the world, or *yugas*, and then by a history of the sultans of Delhi taken from Wassaf's historical chronicle. The second chapter of the section on India consists of a biography of Gautama Shakyamuni, the historical Buddha, and accounts of his teachings. For the description of *yugas*, as well as the entire second part on Buddha's life and teaching, this section relies on information from a Kashmiri Buddhist monk named Kamalashri. Because of this, the description of Buddhist doctrines and history found here aligns most closely with that of Kashmiri Buddhism, rather than the Tibetan form that had captured the imagination of Qubilai and his family in China.⁷² Although direct routes of trade and travel run between Kashmir and Iran,

Kashmiri monks had also been present at Mongol courts in East Asia, and traces of East and Central Asian Buddhism appear in this largely Kashmiri rendering, so the transmission of Kamalashri's ideas probably came via this longer route.[73]

At the time of Hulegu's conquest of the Middle East, Buddhism was already a minority religion in Kashmir. The first *ilkhan* had been attracted to it, and he continued to support Buddhist communities in Kashmir.[74] In subsequent decades, both Tibetan and Kashmiri Buddhist monks were active in the Ilkhanate: Rashid al-Din lists both Kashmiri and Tibetan among the languages spoken at Ghazan's court.[75] While Buddhism fell out of favour – and was briefly persecuted – after Ghazan's conversion to Islam, it continued to exercise influence both politically and intellectually.[76] It has been argued that Rashid al-Din's ecumenism in assembling the *Collected Histories* reveals an overall Buddhist historical framework, which allows for divergent histories from different cultural epistemologies to co-exist.[77] Given the extensive involvement of the Mongol ruling family with Buddhism across Asia, there may indeed be some relation between Buddhist cosmology and the idea of world history, even if Rashid al-Din does not acknowledge it.

Rashid al-Din's history of India takes slightly different forms in surviving Persian and Arabic copies. This is a unique instance where the text of the *Collected Histories* differs between the two languages in which it was copied. The Persian manuscript P_2 contains a lacuna of probably two folios after folio 341, but copies made from it contain the complete Persian text, suggesting that this loss occurred after 1664, when manuscript P_{11} was made. Hafez-e Abru's reconstructed manuscript S_1 contains a severely abbreviated text for the second chapter of this section, dealing with the life and teachings of the Buddha, but the other Timurid reconstruction, S_{11}, contains the full text. The Arabic version largely corresponds to the full Persian text, but it contains a separate header not found in any Persian copy for a small section of text in the first part of the history concerning the beginning of the present *yuga*.[78] It also includes a list of Buddhist books in the second part on the life and teachings of the Buddha.[79]

In addition to these divergences between the Persian and Arabic histories of India, some manuscripts append to this section Rashid al-Din's refutation of the Indian philosophy of metempsychosis that is also found among his theological works. This appendix is found in P_2 and R_1, but not in the Timurid reconstructions. As a result of these variations, the exact length of the history of India in Rashid al-Din's final version of the *Collected Histories* is more difficult to pin down than others. In the Arabic copy, it covers forty-six pages of text, though there is a lacuna near the end of the work.[80] The Persian copy of 1317 covers sixty-four pages of text, while Hafez-e Abru's much abbreviated version covers only twenty-nine.

Notes

1. This section was translated by Khetagurov in 1952 and edited by Romaskevich, Khetagurov and Alizadeh in 1965.
2. D_{31} 4a, 10a.
3. Z_1 contains space for the first two at 3a and 2a; Z_{12} has space for the last at page 15 (folio 8b). Each of these is lacunose but manuscript K_2 of the κ recension (which originated from a copy of the ζ recension) contains space for the first three of these images at 6b, 7b and 8b.
4. This portion of the text was translated by Khetagurov in 1952 and edited by Romaskevich, Khetagurov and Alizadeh in 1965.
5. Erdmann, *Vollständige Übersicht*; Berezin, '"Sbornik" Letopisey', issue 5 (1858) with Russian translation and commentary, and issue 7 (1861) with Persian text.
6. Spaces for these images appear in Z_1 9a, 20a, 20b and Z_{12} pp. 22, 45, 46 (folios 12a, 23b, 24a), with marginal notes in D_{31} 12a, 21a and 28b indicating they appeared in that recension as well. L_{21} 8a and 22b gives images of the first and third of these. K_2 has space for the those same two, and for a unique image of the revenge of Quryaquz Buyruq's wife: 13a, 24b, 26a.
7. This section was translated by Smirnov in 1952.
8. This section was edited and translated by Berezin, '"Sbornik" Letopisey', issue 13 (1868), for the section up to Chinggis Khan's coronation after the defeat of Ong Khan Toghril, and issue 15 (1888) for the remainder of the section. It was translated by Smirnov in 1952.
9. These are items 1–8 in Gray, 'An Unknown Fragment'.
10. This section was edited by Blochet, *Djami el-Tévarikh*, based on manuscripts of the λ recension. Blochet's edition was then translated into English by Boyle, *The Successors*. The main version was translated by Verkhovsky in 1960 and edited by Alizada in 1980 (the latter including the reign of Ogedei only).
11. See Chapter 5 and Kamola, 'Untangling the Chaghadaids'.

12. This is found at Rashid al-Din, *Jamiʿ al-Tawarikh*, pp. 629–31.
13. The portion on Hulegu was the first part of the *Jamiʿ al-Tawarikh* to be published in the West: Quatremère, *Histoire*, with Persian text and French translation. The rest of this section was published in Persian and German translation by Jahn, *Taʾrīḫ-i-Mubārak-i-Ġāzānī*. It was translated into Russian by Arends in 1946, which translation was reproduced, along with a Persian edition by Alizada in 1957.
14. K$_2$ 204a also contains a space for an illustration of the surrender of the caliph.
15. It was translated into Russian by Arends in 1946, which translation was reproduced with a Persian edition by Alizada in 1957. The third *qism* was also edited by Jahan Biglu in 1957.
16. See most recently, Blair, 'Illustrating History'; Hillenbrand, 'Holy Figures'; and MS. R$_1$ in Appendix B for further bibliography.
17. Ghiasian, *Lives of the Prophets*, pp. 81–9, presents the 'divided manuscript' theory that advances the idea that portions of both fragmentary manuscripts were included in S$_1$.
18. Ghiasian, *Lives of the Prophets*, p. 81 n. 155, corrects the previous interpretation by Inal, 'The Fourteenth-Century Miniatures', p. 43, which considers the history of China as part of Hafez-e Abru's reconstruction.
19. Ghiasian, 'The "Historical Style"'; Ghiasian, *Lives of the Prophets*, pp. 89–91, though Ghiasian still considers this a copy of manuscript S$_1$.
20. Ghiasian, *Lives of the Prophets*, p. 85, estimates that the *rashidi* pages of this manuscript numbered around sixty-five, by comparison with manuscript S$_1$. However, comparison of the length of missing text to that of the known folios yields the smaller number.
21. Ghiasian, 'The "Historical Style"', offers one effort to reconstruct the order in which the paintings of this manuscript were made. A full material analysis of available images, and a reconstruction of the full manuscript, is still awaited.
22. Blair, 'Writing and Illustrating History', pp. 63–4.
23. These have been analysed by Inal, 'The Fourteenth-Century Miniatures', with a list of the sixty-eight Ilkhanid illustrations at pp. 45–50.
24. Rashid al-Din, *Tarikh-e Iran va Islam* (ed. Raushan)
25. Melville, 'Rashīd al-Dīn and the *Shāhnāmeh*', offers some preliminary remarks in this direction, though Melville did not have either of the Istanbul manuscripts in question available to him for his comparison. He is thus somewhat tentative in identifying TSM MS. H.1653 the base text of Rawshan's edition and

suggesting that 'we may question, indeed, whether Raushan's text can really be Rashīd al-Dīn's *Jāmi' al-tawārīkh* at all' (p. 207; see also his conclusion on p. 213 that it represents 'later reworkings and enlargements associated with the work of Ḥāfiẓ-i Abrū').

26. Berlin Staatsbibliothek MS. Pertsch 368 2a.
27. Melville, 'Rashīd al-Dīn and the *Shāhnāmeh*', p. 208, already identifies the similarity between the text of Rashid al-Din (found in manuscript O_{12}) and the work of Baydawi.
28. Inal, 'The Fourteenth-Century Miniatures', p. 34, has suggested that the first three illustrations in this manuscript (all on folio 5a and b) may date to the Ilkhanid period, 'but they are too damaged to give a clear idea of their style'.
29. Inal, 'Some Miniatures'.
30. These are on R_1b 1a, 1b, 2a, 2b, 7a, 10b, 11a, 13b and 24a.
31. These are on P_2 25a, 27b, 36b and 45a.
32. Unlike most of the history of pre-Islamic Iran, Rashid al-Din's description of the death of Shaghad echoes the *Shahnameh* quite closely.
33. Ateş, *Cāmi' al-Tavārih. II. Cild, 4. Cüz*, pp. 12–17, offers a comparison between Rashid al-Din's text and that of Jarbadhqani.
34. Ateş, *Cāmi' al-Tavārih. II. Cild, 5. Cüz*; translated by Luther and Bosworth, *The History of the Saljuq Turks*.
35. Morton, *The Saljūqnāma*, is a reconstruction of the work based on a unique though incomplete manuscript. Ateş, *Cāmi' al-Tavārih. II. Cild, 5. Cüz*, pp. 10–15, offers some comparison between Rashid al-Din's text and that of Rawandi, which is also based on Nishapuri's *Saljuqnameh*.
36. For information on Abu Hamid Muhammad b. Ibrahim, who also wrote a history of the Saljuqs of Kerman, see Ateş, *Cāmi' al-Tavārih. II. Cild, 5. Cüz*, pp. 16–19.
37. Morton, 'Qashani and Rashid al-Din', pp. 168–75.
38. Morton, *The Saljūqnāma*, pp. 23–5; Morton, 'Qashani and Rashid al-Din', p. 167.
39. These images are listed by Inal, 'The Fourteenth-Century Miniatures', pp. 45–50.
40. Rashid al-Din, *Tarikh-e Salatin-e Khwarazm*; Rashid al-Din, *Tarikh-e Salghuriyan*; Rashid al-Din, *Tarikh-e Isma'iliyan*; Daneshpazhuh and Mudarrisi (eds), *Qesmat-e Isma'iliyan*.
41. Daneshpazhuh and Mudarrisi (eds), *Qismat-e Isma'iliyan*, p. 14.
42. Kamola, 'A Sensational and Unique Novelty'.
43. Inal, 'The Fourteenth-Century Miniatures', p. 57, lists only sixteen of these,

omitting images on folios 357b, 362a and 370a, and listing the image on 360b as being on 360a.

44. Rashid al-Din, *Tarikh-e Oghuz*, translated by Jahn, *Die Geschichte der Oġuzen*. See also Jahn, 'Zu Rašīd al-Dīn's "Geschichte der Oġuzen und Türken"', where this section is considered to be the first attempt at a systematic history of Turkic tribes.
45. Kamola, 'History and Legend', pp. 567–8.
46. Jahn, 'Die ältesten schriftlich'.
47. For an overview of the *Oghuznameh* tradition, which only gained that name some decades after Rashid al-Din, see Binbaş, 'Oğuz Khan Narratives'.
48. Mahmud al-Kashghari, *Compendium of the Turkic Dialects*, pp. 101–2.
49. Rashid al-Din, *Jamiʿ al-Tawarikh*, pp. 48–52.
50. Kamola, 'History and Legend', pp. 565–74.
51. Çetin, 'Oghuz Turks'.
52. A number of these images are reproduced, along with two images from the dispersed Persian copy and one from Istanbul, Türk ve Islâm Eserleri Müzesi MS. 1593, in the plates of Jahn, *Die Geschichte der Oġuzen*.
53. These are listed by Inal, 'The Fourteenth-Century Miniatures', p. 50 nos 62–8.
54. This portion of the work has been edited in Rashid al-Din, *Tarikh-e Chin*; Rashid al-Din, *Tarikh-e Aqvam-e Padshahan-e Khitay*; and translated by Jahn, *Die Chinageschichte*.
55. Calzolaio and Fiaschetti, 'Prophets of the East', pp. 17–21. See also Franke, 'Some Sinological Remarks'.
56. Calzolaio and Fiaschetti, 'Prophets of the East', p. 22.
57. Blair, 'Illustrating History', p. 4.
58. Jahn, 'Die "Geschichte der Kinder Israels"', pp. 67–8.
59. The history of the Jews has been published in edition: Rashid al-Din, *Tarikh-e Bani-ye Israʾil*, and translated by Jahn, *Die Geschichte der Kinder Israels*.
60. Jahn, 'Die "Geschichte der Kinder Israels"', pp. 70–1.
61. Milstein, 'The iconography of Moses'; Natif, 'Rashīd al-Dīn's Alter Ego'; Hillenbrand, 'Holy Figures'.
62. For example, by Natif, 'Rashīd al-Dīn's Alter Ego', p. 23.
63. Rashid al-Din, *Tarikh-e Afranj, Papan, va Qayasira*; partially translated by Jahn, *Histoire Universelle de Rašīd al-Dīn*; Jahn, *Die Frankengeschichte*.
64. Morgan, 'Persian Perspectives', pp. 210–1; Jahn, 'Das christliche Abendland'; Jahn, 'Rashīd al-Dīn's Knowledge of Europe'.
65. Tehran University Faculty of Literature MS. 9076 308a–328b.

66. Martinus Oppaviensis, *Chronicon Pontificum*. On Martinus and his *Chronicle*, see von den Brincken, 'Zu Herkunft und Gestalt'; von den Brincken, 'Martin von Troppau'.
67. Ikas, 'Martinus Polonus' Chronicle'.
68. von den Brincken, '"In una pagina ponendo"'.
69. On the illustration of Decretals, see l'Engle and Gibbs, *Illuminating the Law*. For an example of this particular type of clerical portrait in the *Decretum Gratiani*, see Melnikas, *The Corpus of the Miniatures*, vol. 3, p. 1002 fig. 5.
70. See Mathews and Taylor, *The Armenian Gospels of Gladzor*, esp. pl. 10.
71. This portion of the work has been edited in Rashid al-Din, *Tarikh-e Hind*, and translated by Jahn, *Die Indiengeschichte*. However, these are based on defective manuscripts, as described below.
72. Jahn, *Rashīd al-Dīn's History of India*, pp. xxxi–lxxvii; Rohrborn, 'Die islamische Weltgeschichte'.
73. Rohrborn, 'Die islamische Weltgeschichte'.
74. Prazniak, 'Ilkhanid Buddhism', pp. 654–5.
75. Prazniak, 'Ilkhanid Buddhism', pp. 662–4; Rashid al-Din, *Jamiʿ al-Tawarikh*, p. 1356.
76. For a general discussion of Buddhism in the Ilkhanate, see Elverskog, *Buddhism and Islam on the Silk Road*, pp. 145–62.
77. Prazniak, 'Ilkhanid Buddhism', pp. 668–71.
78. Compare manuscript R_1a 29b (published in facsimile by Blair, *Compendium of Chronicles*, pl. 269b) to manuscript P_{12} 382a.
79. Manuscript R_1a 34b–35b (published in facsimile by Blair, *Compendium of Chronicles*, plates 274b–5b), discussed by Jahn, *Rashīd al-Dīn's History of India*, pp. lxx–lxxvii.
80. This lacuna falls between folios 274 and 275 in Blair's reconstruction of manuscript R_1: Blair, *A Compendium of Chronicles*, p. 117.

Appendix B
A Descriptive Catalogue of Manuscripts of the *Collected Histories*

The following is a list of the known manuscripts of Rashid al-Din's *Collected Histories*. Manuscripts containing the dynastic *Blessed History* are listed first and are divided into recensions according to the variations in text and illustration described in Chapter 5. Following the conventions of biblical textual studies, each recension is assigned a miniscule Greek letter. Each manuscript is assigned a unique siglum composed of a majuscule Roman letter corresponding to the Greek letter of its recension and a subscript number to identify it within the recension. Sub-recensions are identified in several cases by gaps in the numbering of sigla, and some sigla have been reserved for hypothesised source manuscripts. Illustrations were removed from at least one early copy of the *Blessed History* and included in the later Diez Albums.[1] These are not included in this catalogue, since they do not contain any portion of the text of the work. However, the specific images included in the albums correspond to images found only in the δ recension.

The differences between manuscripts of the *World History* typically have more to do with which portions of the text they contain, rather than variations in the text itself, and so the manuscripts of the *World History* are divided into less formal 'groups', rather than recensions. Most of these groups consist of manuscripts that are genetically related to one another, but the manuscripts of the υ group share in being products of the period of British colonialism in India. Manuscripts of the χ group cannot be allocated based on the information available for this study. The single copy of Qashani's stand-alone *Cream of Histories* is not included in this list, even though it provides the basic text for Rashid al-Din's Perso-Islamic history (sections II.A–B) and even though Iqbal Ashtiani has mentioned it as a copy of Rashid al-Din's work.[2]

The few manuscripts that contain both volumes of the *Collected Histories* are listed under the sigla μ and ν as 'combinations' rather than groups or recensions, since all of them are products of efforts to recombine the two volumes of the *Collected Histories* after Rashid al-Din's death. The manuscripts of μ are the result of Hafez-e Abru's efforts to preserve the work at the court of Shahrokh; the ν combinations stem from a latter reconstruction of the *Collected Histories* at the Safavid court. In both cases, the individual volumes are also catalogued separately, in order to indicate their relationship to other one-volume manuscripts (see the γ and ε recensions of the *Blessed History*, and the ο and π groups of *World History* manuscripts).

In all recensions, groups and combinations, an effort has been made to organise the extant manuscripts chronologically and to identify genetic relationships between them. As more manuscripts come to light, or as the manuscripts of the χ group are assigned to recensions or groups, this scheme will inevitably suffer. It is hoped that, for a few years at least, the following classifications can provide a shorthand for further comparison and analysis of the evidently quite varied manuscripts of Rashid al-Din's historical *oeuvre*.

This is not intended as a formal description of the manuscripts, as an inconsistent amount of codicological information has been available for this study. For these reasons, only basic codicological information is given here. Wherever possible, the standard catalogues for collections have been cited, to facilitate access for more formal analysis of the manuscripts. It is intended that a digital version of this catalogue maintained online will reflect more detailed and more extensive information, as it becomes available.

Two previous efforts have been made to list the known manuscripts of Rashid al-Din's historical writings: by Edward Browne in 1908 and Kazuhiko Shiraiwa in 1997.[3] These are listed before other catalogues in the entries for relevant manuscripts, as are two major supra-catalogues, Ahmad Monzavi's *Fehrest* and Mostafa Derayati's *Short Catalogue of Iranian* manuscripts (*Fehrestvare-ye Dastnevesht-ha-ye Iran*), abbreviated here as DENA.[4] The 'publications' section of each entry is reserved for print and digital facsimiles and for studies featuring the manuscript in question.

Recensions of the *Blessed History*

As discussed in Chapter 5, two main lines of manuscript recensions can be identified on the basis of added passages of text, including references to illustrations once they became part of the *Blessed History*. The general relationship among the following recensions is represented in Figure 5.5 on page 135. Their order here and in that figure accords with the hypothesised sequence of their production.

The α Recension

This is a hypothetical recension representing the earliest form of the *Blessed History*, as it might have appeared before the composition of the *World History*. No known manuscripts fall within it; if they did, we would expect them to lack the general preface to the *Collected Histories*. We would also expect them to match the manuscripts of the unillustrated ε recension in their presentation of family trees and the β recension in the way they list and organise the descendants of Chaghadai.

The β Recension: the Origin of the Ṣūrat *Lines*

The sole manuscript of this recension lacks the various additions made to the text in all later recensions. In it, the headers to the genealogical trees of the Mongol ruling family are regularly said to include images (*ṣūrat*) of the individual whose family is depicted. This distinguishes this recension, and the γ and δ recensions derived from it, from the recensions descended from the parallel ε recension, which makes no mention of illustrations.

Manuscript B_1: Munich BSB MS. Cod. Pers. 207 (also I_2)
Catalogues: Shiraiwa, 'Rashid al-Din', no. 7; Browne, 'Suggestions', no. 23; Aumer, *Die persischen Handschriften*, p. 69.
Publications: digitised online at: http://daten.digitale-sammlungen.de/~db/0009/bsb00093572/images.
Provenance: copied by ʿAli al-Katib al-Sharif al-Shirazi in 1545–6 (AH 952, folios 77–391) and ʿAli al-Qashani in 1606–7 (AH 1015, folios 1–68). Purchased by Joseph Marie Jouannin in January 1808; accessioned to the BSB in 1827.

Description: 391 folios of 34.5 × 24 cm, with a written surface of c. 24 × 15 cm and 19 lines of text per page. Folios 69–76 are blank.

This is a hybrid manuscript, in which the third *qism* of the *dastan* of Ghazan Khan appears before the rest of the *Blessed History*. Folios 77–391, containing the *Blessed History* through the second *qism* on Ghazan, were copied in the *hijri* year 952 (1545/6) from an exemplar of the β recension. The initial copying contained numerous lacunae, which have been supplied in the margins, apparently from a copy from the ε recension. During the copying, a note was added in the table of contents of the *dastan* of Ghazan Khan (folio 386b) stating that, since the forty anecdotes of the third *qism* were long and complicated and were already available in a separate booklet (*daftar*), a shortcut had been taken and that section omitted from the manuscript. This suggests that ʿAli al-Shirazi, the copyist of this portion of the manuscript, had available a stand-alone copy of the third *qism* of Ghazan, like those of the manuscripts of the ι recension. ʿAli al-Shirazi's shortcut was corrected in the *hijri* year 1015 (1606/7) by ʿAli al-Qashani, who supplied a new copy of the third *qism* of Ghazan Khan, with the header *Ketab-e Tarikh-e Qanunnameh-ye Sultan-e Sayyid Sultan Ghazan*, which is now bound at the beginning of the manuscript.

The γ Recension

The manuscripts of this recension are closely related to β, but they contain at least two passages of text – one on Chinggis Khan's adopted son Shigi Qutuqu and the other on the Naiman prince Gushlug – not found in β. At least three copies (G_{12}–G_{14}) descend from a copy that was further modified by Nizam Yazdi, as they contain three additions he made to the text, as discussed in Chapter 5. Here Yazdi's hypothesised original manuscript is assigned the siglum G_{11}. It is possible that an earlier sub-recension existed with the added passages of text on Shigi Qutuqu and Gushlug but without Yazdi's additions. Sigla G_1–G_{10} are reserved for this hypothetical sub-recension. The copies of the Yazdi sub-recension differ in their inclusion of text for the third *qism* of Mongke and Guyug, a reflection perhaps of the flexible nature of the text in its earliest recensions. Manuscripts G_{21} and G_{22} have not been consulted for this study, but they can be matched with this recension based on Tauer's description.

Manuscript G_{12}: St Petersburg NL MS. PNS 46 (manuscript M_1), gathering 2 (186 folios)
See manuscript M_1 for general information and description.
The 186 folios from the *Blessed History* that survive for this copy do not include the sections that would have contained Nizam Yazdi's additions. However, they do include the added text on Shigi Qutuqu and Gushlug, and the extant pages correspond on an almost page-for-page basis with folios in manuscript G_{13}, save for a few cases where that manuscript seems to correct errors in this one. This manuscript is thus probably to be identified with the γ recension, although it also includes the third *qism* of the *dastan* of Mongke, which elsewhere only appears in manuscripts of the δ recension. That text could either have been added when this copy was made, or omitted in the copying of manuscript G_{13}.

Manuscript G_{13}: London BL MS. Add. 7628 (manuscript M_2), folios 404–728
See manuscript M_2 for general information and description.
This manuscript contains no text for either the third *qism* of Mongke or for that of Guyug.

Manuscript G_{14}: Tehran Melli manuscript F-1569
Catalogue: Shiraiwa, 'Rashid al-Din', no. 11; DENA no. 74968; Anvar, *Fehrest-e Nosakh*, pp. 62–3.
Publication: digitised online at: http://dl.nlai.ir/UI/44ad11ad-018c-4a35-8c13-7ce9f5b86906/LRRView.aspx.
Provenance: Dated by Anvar to the seventeenth century, though possibly earlier.
Description: 216 folios of 40.5 × 27 cm, with a written surface of 35.5 × 23cm. and 31 lines of text per page.
This copy of the *Blessed History* matches manuscripts G_{12} and G_{13} in its format and in much of its content, including certain transpositions of text, and it therefore must be closely related to them. It does include, however, text for the third *qism* of Guyug that is not found in the other two. The script of this copy changes abruptly after the first twenty-nine folios from *naskh* to *nastaliq*, so it may have been copied at two different times, but diagnostic

markers in both sections link it to the γ recension. Anvar has dated it 'probably' to the seventeenth century. Its size and layout, as well as the leatherwork on the cover and the *naskh* of the early section of the manuscript, however, make a Timurid origin possible. It has only been examined in low-resolution facsimile, so no definitive statement in this regard can be made at this time.

Manuscript G_{21}: Istanbul Topkapı TSM MS. B.282 (manuscript M_{11}), folios 315–c. 464
See manuscript M_{11} for general information and description.
This and the following manuscript have not been consulted for this study. They can be grouped with the γ recension on several grounds. First, like the other manuscripts of this recension, they were produced in the context of Timurid efforts to recombine the entire *Collected Histories*. Second, there appears to have been no effort to illustrate these copies, which is only true of the early recensions β, γ and ε. Finally, the *explicit* given by Tauer in his description of manuscript M_{11} matches other manuscripts of the γ recension.

Manuscript G_{22}: Istanbul Süleimaniye MS. Damad Ibrahim 919 (manuscript M_{12}), folios 348–c. 505
See manuscript M_{12} for general information and description.

The δ Recension

This recension represents the first systematic updating of the *Blessed History*, made directly from the β recension. It includes several short textual additions, as well as a modified list of the descendants of Chaghadai that situates it chronologically between the γ and ε recensions.[5] This recension also contains the first large illustrative programme to be included in the *Blessed History*, as described in Chapter 5. This includes images of Mongol khans and their consorts within various family trees, two-page coronation scenes, and a selection of narrative images. D_1 appears to be the parent of manuscripts D_2, D_{21} and D_{22}.

The manuscripts of this recension incorporate the third *qism* of the *dastan* of Mongke first seen in manuscripts G_{12}, and they add new miscellaneous material for the reign of Qubilai. Of them, manuscript D_{31} also includes the text for the third *qism* of the chapter on Guyug first seen in manuscript G_{14}.

This passage has played an outsized role in the negative view of Guyug that prevails in modern scholarship. This is the result of the fact that this passage of text (like the other additions of this recension) is carried over into the influential λ recension. Manuscript D_{31} is otherwise very closely related to other manuscripts of this recension, and while it is not itself illustrated, internal evidence suggests that it was copied from an exemplar with an illustrative programme very close to that of D_1 and D_{21}. The only known candidate as its source is here catalogued as D_{11}, though it should be emphasised that the relation between D_{11} and D_{31} is here only hypothesised and can only be verified once D_{11} becomes available for study.

Manuscript D_1: Rampur Reza Library MS. P.1820
Catalogues: Shiraiwa, 'Rashid al-Din', no. 71; Monzavi, *Fehrest*, vol. 6, p. 4134 no. 42536; Schmitz and Desai, *Mughal and Persian Paintings*, pp. 171–9.
Publications: Rice, 'Mughal Interventions'.
Provenance: mid- to late fourteenth-century Iran.
Description: 135 folios of 45.5 × 32.5 cm, with a written surface of 39.5–41.5 × 27–28 cm and 25 lines of text per page.
This manuscript is defective at the beginning and end, picking up at the very end of the life of Chinggis Khan and breaking off again early in the section on Ghazan. It also suffers from several small internal lacunae. Many of the catchwords in the early part of this manuscript have been corrected, suggesting that it has been reordered from an earlier, disordered state. (See entry for manuscript D_2 for one possible scenario.) Despite these defects, it is a crucial witness to an intermediate phase in the evolution of the *Blessed History*.

The extant illustrations of this manuscript were added in several phases, beginning in Iran in the late fourteenth century and ending at the court of Akbar the Great in the 1590s.[6] The Mughal miniatures have been added to spaces left blank at the end of sections, which were not originally intended to contain images. In several instances, large court scenes have been painted into spaces that had originally been formatted for family trees. Initial sketches of enthroned Mongol rulers and their consorts had evidently been prepared for those family trees, as such sketches have been preserved and integrated into the later paintings.[7] While this manuscript is incomplete, it is possible to reconstruct much of the original illustrative programme, as discussed in Chapter 5 and Appendix A.

Manuscript D_2: London BL MS. IO Islamic 1784
Catalogues: Shiraiwa, 'Rashid al-Din', no. 21; Browne, 'Suggestions', no. 12; Ethé, *Catalogue of the Persian Manuscripts*, cols. 8–9 no. 17.
Provenance: On folio 394b, dated to 12 *Ramadan*, with no year given. W. Kirkpatrick presented the manuscript to the India Office library on 30 May 1804.
Description: 394 folios of 29.5 × 18 cm, with a written surface of 20.5 × 11.5 cm and 21 lines of text per page, plus additional blank pages at the beginning of the book.
This is a relatively late copy, probably made in India and almost certainly from manuscript D_1. A gap on folio 188b corresponds to the page break between folios 25 and 26 in manuscript D_1. The catchword in that manuscript has been corrected; the original catchword indicates that folio 25 was once followed by folio 24. Just before the gap on folio 188b of this manuscript, the scribe has written the original catchword (*aghāz-e dāstān-e Chaghadai*), though the text below the gap resumes correctly with the text now found on folio 26a of manuscript D_1 (*pesar-e sevvom*). It may be that the disorder of the opening pages of manuscript D_1 was recognised and corrected in the process of copying this manuscript, perhaps as the scribe arrived at this point in the copying.

Manuscript D_{11}: Tehran Golestan Palace Library MS. 2234
Catalogue: DENA 74988; Atabay, *Fihrist-e Tarikh*, pp. 81–3 no. 38.
Provenance: In the collection of Naser al-Din Shah Qajar by 1865.
Description: 425 folios of 47.5 × 33 cm, with 31 lines of text per page.
This manuscript has not been consulted for this study. From Atabay's description, it seems to be a very complete copy of the *Blessed History*, and possibly very early. It can be assigned to this recension based on the critical apparatus in Raushan and Musavi's edition, and may have provided the source material for manuscript D_{31}.

Manuscript D_{21}: Kolkata Asiatic Society MS. D31
Catalogues: Shiraiwa, 'Rashid al-Din', no. 22; Ivanow, *Concise Descriptive Catalogue*, p. 2 no. 4.
Publication: Gray, 'An Unknown Fragment'.
Provenance: Fifteenth or sixteenth century?
Description: 124 folios of 47 × 32 cm, with a written surface of 34 × 20 cm and 25 lines of text per page.
This and the following manuscript have not been directly consulted for this study. They are identified as part of the δ recension based on the evident relationship between the illustrative programmes of this manuscript and manuscript D_1.[8]

Manuscript D_{22}: Kolkata Asiatic Society MS. D32
Catalogues: Shiraiwa, 'Rashid al-Din', no. 13; Ivanow, *Concise Descriptive Catalogue*, p. 3 no. 5.
Provenance: India *c.* 1900.
Description: 204 pages of 29.5 × 20 cm, with a written surface of 22.5 × 12 cm and 19 lines of text per page.
This is a copy of manuscript D_2, probably prepared, according to Ivanow, to preserve the text of that deteriorating manuscript.

D_{31}: London BL MS. Or. 2927
Catalogues: Shiraiwa, 'Rashid al-Din', no. 23; Browne, 'Suggestions', no. 9; Rieu, *Supplement to the Catalogue*, p. 15 no. 25.
Provenance: Copied in India, dated 11 November 1586 (29 Aban in the thirty-first *ilahi* year of Akbar). Later owned by Maharaja Tikait Rai and Nathaniel Bland.
Description: 256 folios of 33 × 23 cm, with a written surface of 27.5 × 17 cm and 27 lines of text per page. Some spaces have been left for illustrations, with marginal notes indicating the location of additional illustrations in the source manuscript.
This copy was owned by Maharaja Tikait Rai, who was heavily involved in the financial administration of Awadh and who attempted to reassert the authority of that city over Rampur after Faizullah Khan's death in 1794.[9] It later came into the possession of the Persian scholar Nathaniel

Bland (1803–65) and, after his death, into the collection of the British Museum.

Frequent marginal notes mark the location of approximately seventy-five illustrations as well as the ten family trees of Chinggis Khan and his ancestors. These suggest that this manuscript was copied from a heavily illustrated exemplar. Such a manuscript has as yet not been identified, but it may have been the same manuscript used in assembling the λ recension, since the main exemplar of that recension (manuscript L_{11}) contains a programme of illustrations similar to the one described in the marginalia of this manuscript.

The ε Recension

This recension contains two sub-recensions. The first represents the Safavid recombination of the two-volume *Collected Histories* (manuscript N_1, here E_2). The original source copy for the *Blessed History* portion of these manuscripts is as yet unidentified. Siglum E_1 is here reserved for that manuscript, which should be an early (pre-1663) fragmentary copy of the *Blessed History*. These copies contain no mention of paintings, either in the genealogical trees or in the body of the text. In this respect, they probably adhere closely to the hypothesised α recension, the earliest version of the *Blessed History*. However, they contain a revised version of the family tree of Chaghadai that must have been developed later than the one found in the δ recension.[10] Unfortunately, all manuscripts of this group contain numerous short lacunae and disordered pages, making a full systematic comparison to other recensions difficult.

The second sub-recension contains a series of fragmentary manuscripts containing the beginning of the *Blessed History* through the early reign of Chinggis Khan. In their text, they are very similar to the first sub-recension, save for the inclusion of the brands (*tamgha*s) of the twenty-four branches of the Oghuz, as well as three short notices about Turkic tribes that first appear in the margins of manuscript E_{11}. The fact that all of the manuscripts of this sub-recension break off at nearly the same spot suggests that they originate from a single source manuscript, possibly the one here identified as E_{11}.

Manuscript E_2: Tehran Golestan Palace MS. Saltanat 2256 (manuscript N_1), folios c. 823–1225

See manuscript N_1 for general information and description.

Manuscript E_3: London BL MS. I.O. Islamic 3524 (manuscript N_2), folios 403–599
See manuscript N_2 for general information and description.

Manuscript E_4: Tehran Majlis MS. 8734 (manuscript N_3), folios 396–607
See manuscript N_3 for general information and description.

Manuscript E_5: St Petersburg National Library MS. Chanykov 62 (manuscript N_4), folios 322a–478a
See manuscript N_4 for general information and description.

Manuscript E_6: St Petersburg National Library MS. PNS 47 (manuscript N_5), folios 1–403
See manuscript N_5 for general information and description.

Manuscript E_7: Tehran Melli MS. F-1606 (manuscript N_6), folios 273–362
See manuscript N_6 for general information and description.

Manuscript E_{11}: Tehran Majlis MS. 2294
Catalogues: Shiraiwa, 'Rashid al-Din', no. 1; Monzavi, *Fehrest*, vol. 6, p. 4133 no. 42514; DENA, no. 74955; Nafisi, *Fehrest*, pp. 107–8.
Publications: Ashikaga et al., *Iran no Rekishi to Gengo* (facsimile); Shimo, 'Ghâzân Khan'; Shimo, 'Three Manuscripts'; Shiraiwa, 'Rashīd al-Dīn's Primary Sources'. Digitised online through the Majlis website (record number 494158), though no stable url can be determined. Download available at: http://dlib.ical.ir/multiMediaFile/1383765-4-1.pdf.
Provenance: Late fourteenth-century Shiraz?
Description: 98 folios of 29 × 19 cm, with 29 lines of text per page.
Shiraiwa has argued that this represents Rashid al-Din's original fair copy of the *Blessed History*, which he presented to Oljeitu in 1304, and that the marginal notes present here were the additions suggested by the sultan on that occasion.[11] However, it contains the general introduction to the full *Collected Histories*, and so it must originate from a manuscript prepared in or after 1307. Furthermore, the format, orthography and illumination all suggest a

later production, probably in the late fourteenth century, and quite possibly in Shiraz.[12] This manuscript should therefore be seen as part of the effort by the Muzaffarid dynasty to adopt the legacy of the Ilkhanate by emulating their patterns of patronage. The fact that the scribes worked from an early version of the text demonstrates the distance of the Muzaffarid court from the Ilkhanid capital region and centre of manuscript production in Tabriz. Rashid al-Din's many family connections in Yazd, where the Muzaffarids first came to power, provides one possible avenue of transmission of such a rare early copy. It is entirely possible that this manuscript was copied directly from a manuscript that had stayed within Rashid al-Din's extended family in Yazd and that preserved part of the process of revision. According to this scenario, Rashid al-Din would have noted a number of passages to be added to the text in the margins of this copy, marginalia that were subsequently integrated into the text of the ζ recension at Rashid al-Din's scriptorium in Tabriz but which were faithfully reproduced in the current copy.

In its current condition, the manuscript breaks off slightly earlier than manuscripts E_{13}, E_{14} and E_{15}.[13] It appears that one folio has been lost since those copies were made.

Manuscript E_{12}: Paris BnF MS. Supplément persan 1643
Catalogues: Shiraiwa, 'Rashid al-Din', no. 12; Blochet, *Catalogue des Manuscrits Persans*, vol. 4, pp. 225–7 no. 2280.
Provenance: Probably sixteenth century.
Description: 188 folios of 21 × 14.5 cm, with a written surface of 15 × 10 cm and 17 lines of text per page.
As Blochet notes, this copy was made by a scholar and not a professional scribe from an early source manuscript (probably E_{11}), as it preserves very correct vocalisation on Mongol names, though it does not include the brands of Turkic tribes found in other manuscripts of this sub-recension. The marginal notes of manuscript E_{11} were included in the copying, but have suffered from later trimming. The last folio is torn and badly patched, so that the exact end of the text is not clear, but it breaks off significantly earlier than the other manuscripts in this group. If it was indeed copied from an already fragmentary manuscript E_{11}, then the last few pages of this copy have been subsequently lost.

Manuscript E_{13}: Istanbul Süleimaniye Hekimoğlu 'Ali Paşa MS. 703
Catalogues: Shiraiwa, 'Rashid al-Din', no. 9; Tauer, 'Les manuscrits: Ire partie', p. 99 no. 35.
Provenance: Probably sixteenth century.
Description: 218 folios of 25 × 20 cm, with a written surface 12.5 cm wide and 18 lines of text per page.
Inexplicably, Tauer includes this manuscript among the copies of Hafez-e Abru's *Collection of Histories* (*Majmu'a al-Tawarikh*), though it only contains a portion of Rashid al-Din's dynastic history. It and manuscripts E_{14} and E_{15} all break off at exactly the same point, indicating that they were all copied from the same fragmentary source. This manuscript has not been available for the current study, so the height of its written surface and the presence or absence of the brands of Turkic tribes has not been determined.

Manuscript E_{14}: St Petersburg IOM MS. C376
Catalogues: Shiraiwa, 'Rashid al-Din', no. 14; Monzavi, *Fehrest*, vol. 6, p. 4134 no. 42532; Miklukho-Maklai, *Opisanie*, vol. 1, p. 137 no. 900; Miklukho-Maklai, *Persidskie i Tadzhikskie Rukopisi*, p. 50 no. 224.
Provenance: Possibly seventeenth century.
Description: 182 folios of 24.5 × 14.5 cm, with a written surface of 17 × 9.5 cm and 18 lines of text per page.
Like manuscript E_{11}, this manuscript contains the brands of the Turkic tribes (folios 17a–18a). It does not, however, include the additional passages of text found in the margins of that manuscript. It can be included among the descendants of manuscript E_{11} because it breaks off in the same place as manuscripts E_{13} and E_{15}.

Manuscript E_{15}: Mashhad Astan-e Qods MS. 4101, folios 1–168 (see also Z_3)
See manuscript Z_3 for general information and description.
This is the first part of a hybrid manuscript (see manuscript Z_3 for the remaining portion), the first 168 folios of which are related to manuscripts E_{13} and E_{14}, and which may be copied from manuscript E_{11}. (Manuscripts E_{13} and E_{14} were both outside of Iran by the time this copy was made.) It

preserves the brands of Turkic tribes (folios 23a–24a). Because it has only been consulted in facsimile, the dimensions of its written surface have not been determined.

Manuscript E_{16}: Tehran Majlis MS. 1108
Catalogue: DENA 74987.
Publication: Digitised online through the Majlis website (record number 1040235), though no stable url can be determined. Download available at: http://dlib.ical.ir/multiMediaFile/7421792-4-1.pdf.
Description: 207 folios of 26 × 16.5 cm with 17 lines of text per page.
This manuscript breaks off shortly before E_{11} does.[14] Its last lines deviate somewhat from the text of that manuscript.

The ζ Recension: Rashid al-Din's 'Official' Version

The manuscripts of this group probably represent Rashid al-Din's final vision for the *Collected History*, the version that he instructed in 1313 be copied and distributed as part of his *Collected Writings* (on which, see Chapter 4). Manuscripts Z_1 and Z_{12} are entirely consistent with one another in their size and format, though from internal inconsistencies it can be determined that neither of them is a copy of the other. They also have the same written surface area as manuscripts of the *World History* produced at the Rashidi Quarter in Tabriz in the last years of Rashid al-Din's life (see below, manuscripts N_1 and R_1), though they only have twenty-nine lines of text per page, while those copies of the *World History* have thirty-one. They are most likely copied from originals that had been distributed from the scriptorium in Tabriz. The other two manuscripts in this recension are copies of manuscript Z_1.

As with the ε recension, these manuscripts lack the text additions of recensions γ and δ in the third *qisms* of Mogke and Guyug, and the miscellaneous events catalogued for the reign of Qubilai. They introduce at least two new additions, the stories of Quryaquz Buyruq Khan and Hambaqa'i Qa'an discussed in Chapter 5. As also discussed in that chapter, this recension evidently contained a more limited illustrative programme than the δ recension.

Manuscript Z₁: Tashkent Abu Rayhon Beruni Institute MS. 1620
Catalogues: Shiraiwa, 'Rashid al-Din', no. 16; Semenov, *Majmu'a-ye Noskhah-ha*, p. 2 no. 8; Semenov, *Sobranie Vostochnykh Rukopisei*, vol. 1, pp. 21–2 no. 22.
Provenance: Early fourteenth century. This manuscript may have been relocated to Central Asia in the Timurid period, perhaps after the suppression of Iskandar Mirza's rebellion against Shahrokh in 1415.
Description: 263 folios of 40 × 28 cm, with a written surface of *c*. 34 × *c*. 23 cm and 29 lines of text per page.
This manuscript is probably to be dated to the lifetime of Rashid al-Din, and was possibly created at Rashid al-Din's scriptorium in Tabriz. It retains three original portraits of Ogedei with Boraqchin (108b), Qubilai with Chabi (167a), and Hulegu with Doquz (190b) at the head of their respective family trees, the only images to remain *in situ* in any Ilkhanid copy of the *Blessed History*.[15] They are different stylistically to the eleven comparable images found in Berlin Staatsbibliothek MS. Diez A folio 71, but are almost certainly contemporary with those. Folio 57a includes the preliminary sketch for an incomplete painting of Temujin's punishment of seditious enemies by boiling after the battle of Dalan Baljud. Other pages and partial pages that may have contained similar sketches have been excised from this manuscript, including pages that would have held two-page coronation scenes like those found in manuscript D_1 and in albums in Berlin and Istanbul.[16] These excisions have been repaired, and in some cases the missing text has been supplied in the margins.

Manuscript Z₂: Toronto Aga Khan Museum MS. AKM517
Provenance: Later fourteenth or early fifteenth century, probably at a Timurid provincial court (Herat or Shiraz?).
Description: 344 folios of 37 × 27 cm, with a written surface of 28 × 20 cm and 29 lines of text per page.
This is one of the finest extant copies of the *Blessed History*, but it has previously avoided study. Its text is very correct and almost complete, with only four folios missing, three of which would have contained genealogical trees. The extant folios are numbered by page (not folio), and are somewhat out of order. The correct order (using the extant page numbers) is: 1–27, 336–7,

(one folio missing), 338–9, 328–31, 340–3, 332–5, (one folio missing), 514–61, 344–513, 562–619, 632–5, (two folios missing), 636–43, 620–31, 644–89.[17]

That this remarkable manuscript has so far escaped notice inspires hope that additional copies of such quality are yet to come to light. In its layout, it matches manuscripts Z_1 and Z_{12} almost page for page, though it is of smaller dimensions than either of those. That it is a copy of manuscript Z_1 can be established in two ways. First, blank spaces have been left that exactly correspond to lacunae in Z_1 resulting from the excision of portraits of Mongol rulers and their consorts. Second, the text of the sons of Chaghadai breaks off after the fourth son of Mutugan, just where a page of manuscript Z_1 has been removed. Inconsistencies in short lacunae between this manuscript and manuscript Z_{12} make it impossible for that manuscript to be the source of this one. One peculiarity, however, is the fact that this manuscript contains Rashid Khwafi's postscript (see manuscript K_1), which seems to have been modified from manuscript Z_{12}, but it does not contain the unique episodes that Rashid Khwafi added to the text of the *Blessed History*.

This manuscript is undated, but its opening illumination can be compared with manuscripts of the late Ilkhanid period, or to those of Jalayirid Baghdad or of Shiraz during the Muzaffarid or early Timurid period.[18] It may be that manuscript Z_1 was sent from the Rashidi Quarter to Shiraz or another southern city and this copy was made there in subsequent decades. This manuscript was probably still in Iran in the early to mid-nineteenth century, as it has been rebound and covered with a goat-hair paisley tweed fabric likely produced in Kerman around 1840.[19]

Manuscript Z_3: Mashhad Imam Reza Library MS. 4101, folios 169–547 (see also E_{15})
Catalogues: Shiraiwa, 'Rashid al-Din', no. 15; Monzavi, *Fehrest*, vol. 6, p. 4134 no. 43531; DENA, no. 74990; Fikrat, *Fehrest*, p. 160; Astan-e Qods-e Rezavi, *Fehrest*, vol. 3, p. 82.
Provenance: copied by Muhammad 'Ali Rezavi and dated to May 1883 (*Rajab* 1300).
Description: 20 lines of text per page.

This is a hybrid manuscript (see above, manuscript E_{15}). Beginning on folio 169, it demonstrates the same lacunae as manuscript Z_2, suggesting that manuscript as a source.[20] Folios 548–649 of this manuscript contain the preliminary version of the *Continuation* also found in manuscripts L_{12}, L_{13} and L_{14}. Since this manuscript does not include the variant text of the λ recension found in those copies, this probably represents a scribal choice to include the *Continuation* from a separate source manuscript.

Manuscript Z_{12}: Istanbul TSM MS. R.1518
Catalogues: Monzavi, *Fehrest*, vol. 6, p. 4134 no. 43513; Karatay, *Topkapı Sarayı*, p. 53 no. 139; Tauer, 'Les manuscrits: Ire partie', p. 93 no. 19.
Provenance: Dated to October 1318 (*Sha'ban* 717) in Baghdad.
Description: 343 folios of 41 × 29.5 cm, with a written surface of 34 × 23.5 cm and 29 lines of text per page.
This is the earliest dated copy of the *Blessed History*. It was completed in Baghdad a few months after Rashid al-Din's death. In its format, however, it is almost identical to manuscripts Z_1, Z_2 and K_2, suggesting that they all look back to the standardised formatting of the Rashidi Quarter. This manuscript contains an endnote describing the scribe's decision to include the history of Oljeitu at the end of the *Blessed History* for the benefit of anyone who wants to copy it but does not have access to the second volume, where Oljeitu's history was originally to be found. There follows most of one folio of text about Oljeitu's rise to the throne. Rashid Khwafi evidently used this or a related manuscript when he made his additions to the text (on which, see Chapter 5 and the κ recension), as he also modifies this endnote and includes the added passage of text (see below, manuscript K_1).

The η Recension: the Arabic Version

As mentioned in Chapter 4, Rashid al-Din sponsored the translation of the *Collected Histories*, along with other of his works, from Persian into Arabic. Several partial copies of the Arabic *World History* exist (see the ρ recension, below). Only two partial Arabic copies of the *Blessed History* are known; their condition and location have prevented a comprehensive comparison between the work's Persian and Arabic versions for this study.

Manuscript H₁: Istanbul Süleimaniye MS. Aya Sofya 3034
Catalogues: Shiraiwa, 'Rashid al-Din', no. 20; Browne, 'Suggestions', no. 25.
Publications: Jahn, 'Study on Supplementary Persian Sources', p. 198.
Provenance: Dated 1383/4 (AH 785).
Description: 418 folios with 13 lines of text per page.
This manuscript is significantly disordered, and the later folios contain only a list of headers for the latter part of the *Blessed History*. The extant portions, however, match most closely with the ζ recension of the Persian original, suggesting that the Arabic translation of the *Blessed History* was prepared from the work's final Persian form.

Manuscript H₂: Tashkent Abu Rayhon Beruni Institute MS. 2
Catalogues: Shiraiwa, 'Rashid al-Din', no. 5; Semenov, *Sobranie Vostochnykh Rukopisei*, vol. 1, pp. 23–4 no. 25.
Provenance: Dated March–April 1526 (*Jumada II* 932).
Description: 511 folios of 36.5 × 24 cm, with 17 lines of text per page.
This manuscript has not been available for this study.

The ι Recension: the Book of Laws

These manuscripts suggest that the third *qism* of the *dastan* of Ghazan Khan circulated as an independent manual on kingship, either under the Persian title *Qanunnameh* or the Turkic *Tuzuk*.

Manuscript I₁: Paris BnF MS. Supplément persan 1561
Catalogues: Shiraiwa, 'Rashid al-Din', no. 19; Blochet, *Catalogue des Manuscrits Persans*, vol. 1, p. 281 no. 448; Blochet, *Catalogue de la Collection*, pp. 133–4.
Provenance: Late fourteenth-century Baghdad or western Iran. Later part of the Schefer collection acquired by the BnF in 1899.
Description: 125 folios of 28 × 25 cm with a written surface of 20.5 × 14 cm and 15 lines of text per page.
This is the earliest extant stand-alone copy of the *Qanunnameh*, though the exact location and date of its creation is unknown, as the end of the manuscript has been lost. The text breaks off mid-way through the thirty-eighth of forty anecdotes of this section of the *Blessed History*.[21]

This manuscript contains a more extensive illustrative programme for the third *qism* of the chapter on Ghazan Khan than any other known copy from the fourteenth century. Fourteen frames have been left for illustrations, of which eight have initial outlining of figures in red that are contemporary with the manuscript's production.[22] The other six frames contain later sketches and scrawls, as do the spaces surrounding Ghazan's decrees that are included in the text. Based on the intended illustrative programme, it appears that Hafez-e Abru consulted this manuscript or a closely related one in the preparation of manuscript L_{11}, the heavily illustrated manuscript of the λ recension now in Paris. Of the fourteen spaces initially intended for illustrations in this manuscript, eight correspond to images found in manuscript L_{11}, while four more would be found in lacunae of L_{11} and may at one time have been included in that manuscript. Only two of the fourteen images in this copy are definitively absent from manuscript L_{11}.

This manuscript, or another one like it, may also be the *daftar* mentioned in the note on folio 386b of manuscript B_1/I_2. No definite connection can be drawn between the two manuscripts, since neither of them can be precisely located at any point before their acquisition by European scholars in the nineteenth century.

Manuscript I_2: Munich BSB MS. Cod. Pers. 207 (manuscript B_1), folios 1–66
See manuscript B_1 for general information and description.
The first sixty-six folios of this hybrid manuscript are a replacement copy of an earlier *daftar* containing the *Qanunnameh*, which the original scribe used as a pretence for not recopying the long third *qism* of the *dastan* of Ghazan Khan.

Manuscript I_3: London BL MS. IO Islamic 4710
Catalogue: Sims-Williams, *Handlist*, p. 8.
Provenance: Copied in Kolkata, dated 15 February 1800 (20 *Ramadan* 1214).
Description: 189 folios of 20.5 × 12.5cm, interleaved with blank pages, with a written surface of 15 × 7 cm and 15 lines of text per page.
This is a clean copy of the third *qism* of the chapter on Ghazan Khan, though the opening omits the name of Ghazan Khan and replaces the singular

farmude with the plural *farmude-and*, reframing the work as a general manual on kingship.

The κ Recension: Rashid Khwafi's Variant

Rashid Khwafi is responsible for introducing a series of new passages into this variant of the *Blessed History*. As discussed in Chapter 5, the most interesting of these deal with the administrators of the early Ilkhanate, including the Juvayni brothers and Khwafi himself. Khwafi's source manuscript was evidently a copy of the ζ recension, as the text of this recension, and the formatting of manuscript K_2, reflect Rashid al-Din's last revision. Manuscript K_1 includes a postscript modified from one found in manuscript Z_{12}, which was copied in Baghdad in 1318. It may be that Khwafi produced the exemplar of this recension directly from manuscript Z_{12} or its source, which would have been produced in Rashid al-Din's scriptorium in Tabriz and sent to Baghdad to be copied. Given the importance of the city of Baghdad, this could well have been the first such copy distributed from the Rashidi Quarter. However, manuscript K_2 contains spaces for more images than any extant copy of the ζ recension, indicating that a different source manuscript may have been involved.

Manuscript K_1: London BL MS. Add. 16,688

Catalogues: Shiraiwa, 'Rashid al-Din', no. 3; Browne, 'Suggestions', no. 2; Monzavi, *Fehrest*, vol. 6, p. 4133 nos. 42511 and 42515; Rieu, *Catalogue of the Persian Manuscripts*, vol. 1, pp. 78–9.

Publication: Digitised online at: http://www.bl.uk/manuscripts/Viewer.aspx?ref=add_ms_16688_fs001r.

Provenance: Fourteenth century. The first two and last three folios are replacement folios dated 24 October 1524 by Muhammad ibn Abi Tahir Hassan. Later in the collection of William Yule and presented by his sons to the British Museum in 1847.

Description: 293 folios of 28 × 21 cm, with a written surface of 21.5 × 16 cm and 21 lines of text per page.

This is evidently an early manuscript, containing approximately the second half of the *Blessed History*, including many of Khwafi's most significant additions to the text. It contains the outlines of several family trees, though with the exception of the names of Abaqa, Arghun and Ghazan at the head of their respective trees, these have not been filled in. Unusually, these trees are formatted with circles for the male members of the families, rather than the squares used in other manuscripts. This is the only manuscript of this recension to include Khwafi's endnote, modified from the one found in manuscript Z_{12}, as well as the short passage of text telling of the accession of Oljeitu also found in that manuscript. As these pages are written in a later hand, however, their authenticity is uncertain.

Manuscript K_2: Vienna Österreichische Nationalbibliothek MS. mixt. 326
Catalogues: Shiraiwa, 'Rashid al-Din', no. 18; Browne, 'Suggestions', no. 21; Flügel, *Die arabischen, persischen, und türkischen Handschriften*, vol. 2, pp. 179–81 no. 957.
Publication: Digitised online at: http://digital.onb.ac.at/RepViewer/viewer.faces?doc=DTL_6649277&order=1&view=SINGLE.
Provenance: From the collection of Graf Wenzeslav Rzewuski, probably among those purchased by the ÖNB in 1831.[23]
Description: 333 folios of 32 × 23 cm, with a written surface of 25 × 12.5 cm and 27 lines of text per page.
This manuscript contains several short lacunae, as well as four of significant length. These longer lacunae are shared by manuscript K_3, suggesting a common source manuscript.[24] The largest of these shared lacunae, as well as another long lacuna unique to this manuscript at the end of the work, have been restored in a later hand from a manuscript of a different recension. This copy is bound together with a copy of Hafez-e Abru's *Continuation* (*dhayl*) of the *Blessed History*.

Manuscript K_3: Oxford Bodleian MS. Elliot 377, folios 332–567
Catalogues: Shiraiwa, 'Rashid al-Din', no. 6; Browne, 'Suggestions', no. 13; Sachau and Ethé, *Catalogue of the Persian, Turkish, Hindûstânî, and Pushtû Manuscripts*, no. 23.
Provenance: Copied by Ibn Sayyidi Ahmad al-Hafez Nasr Allah in 1537/8 (AH 944).
Description: 236 folios of 36 × 23.5 cm, with a written surface of 23 × 14 cm and 30 lines of text per page.

This copy of the *Blessed History* is part of a compilation of texts which, together, make up a universal history, including a Persian translation of Tabari, the current copy of the *Blessed History* and a copy of Hafez-e Abru's *Continuation* of the *Blessed History*. It might thus be considered a later attempt to assemble histories into a new universal narrative, similar to what Hafez-e Abru did in the early fifteenth century. This copy seems to be a more complete copy of the source it shares with manuscript K_2, though it does not preserve the formatting or spaces for illustrations seen in that manuscript.

The λ Recension

The version of the *Blessed History* found in these manuscripts has previously been called the P recension or variant, after the cities of Paris and St Petersburg, where the two most famous exemplars (here L_{11} and L_{12}) are held.[25] It is evidently a hybrid recension, copied from manuscripts of the δ and ε recensions. The resulting description of the family of Chaghadai includes several duplications, suggesting either a lack of concern for accuracy or a lack of immediate familiarity with the Chaghadaid family.[26]

This group has received increased attention in recent years for presenting an alternate version of Ghazan's early life and career prepared originally by ʿAbd Allah Qashani (see Chapters 3 and 5). This evidently was also the source for Banakati's abridgement of the *Collected Histories*, suggesting that the λ recension was assembled prior to 1317, when Banakati completed his work. All of the extant manuscripts, however, were either created at the court of Shahrokh or are copies of manuscripts that were. It remains possible, then, that Hafez-e Abru assembled the λ recension as part of his larger programme of gathering, collecting and collating versions of Rashid al-Din's historical writing. If that is the case, then we should not be surprised at some point to uncover an intermediate recension of the *Blessed History*, one that integrates Qashani's version of the early life of Ghazan but matches the δ recension in its presentation of the family of Chaghadai. For this reason, numbering here begins with L_{11}, to leave space for the hypothetical preliminary stage of this recension.

Manuscript L_{11}: Paris BnF MS. Supplément persan 1113
Catalogues: Shiraiwa, 'Rashid al-Din', no. 25; Browne, 'Suggestions', no. 19; Blochet, *Catalogue des Manuscrits Persans*, vol. 1, pp. 201–2 no. 254.

Publications: Richard, 'Un des peintres'; Shiraiwa, 'Sur la date'; Shimo, 'Three Manuscripts'.
Publication: digitised online at https://gallica.bnf.fr/ark:/12148/btv1b 8427170s
Provenance: Copied at the court of Shahrokh (whose effaced seal appears on folio 191a), possibly by Hafez-e Abru. Later in the Safavid shrine at Ardabil. Acquired by the Bibliothèque nationale de France in 1889 from Mahmud Qajar.[27]
Description: 285 folios of 32 × 23 cm, with 33 lines of text per page.
Long thought to be an original Ilkhanid copy, this manuscript is now a central example of the 'historical style' of illustration associated with Shahrokh's atelier.[28] As with other manuscripts painted in this style, the images demonstrate an attempt to imitate Ilkhanid painting, introducing a spatial flatness and compositional simplicity that had already been surpassed by more 'classical' Persian painting.[29] It was probably part of an early stage of Hafez-e Abru's efforts to restore, update and recirculate Rashid al-Din's historical works (see also the μ and σ groups). The folios are currently out of order.[30]

Manuscript L_{12}: Paris BnF MS. Supplément persan 209
Catalogues: Shiraiwa, 'Rashid al-Din', no. 4; Browne, 'Suggestions', no. 18; Blochet, *Catalogue des Manuscrits Persans*, vol. 1, pp. 202–3 no. 255; Richard, *Catalogue des Manuscrits Persans*, vol. 1, pp. 300–2.
Publication: digitised online at https://gallica.bnf.fr/ark:/12148/btv1b 52506438r
Provenance: Copied by Mas'ud b. 'Abd Allah at the court of Shahrokh on 4 February 1434 (4 *Rajab* 837). In Isfahan by 1621 (see manuscript L_{14}), where it was purchased in 1756 by Simon de Vierville. Later in the Arsenal Library.
Description: 534 folios of 35 × 26 cm, with a written surface of 23.5 × 17 cm and 23 lines of text per page.
Barthélemy d'Herbelot used this manuscript for information on the Mongols included in his *Bibliotheque Orientale*.[31] It contains the *Blessed History* (on folios 1b–442b), along with Hafez-e Abru's preliminary *Continuation* (folios 443a–530b). It is part of the same project as manuscript L_{11} to revive and reproduce Rashid al-Din's historical writings at the court of Shahrukh. The *Continuation* found in this and the following two manuscripts (which are

probably copies of it) has been catalogued as the *Continuation of the Collected Histories (Dhayl-e Jami ' al-Tawarikh)* of Hafez-e Abru. However, this version of the *Continuation* does not match the final edited version of that text. Instead, it is Hafez-e Abru's preliminary version, described in the Epilogue, adapting 'Abd Allah Qashani's *History of Oljeitu* to fit the format of the rest of the *Blessed History*, but missing significant additions that Hafez-e Abru later made to the text.

Manuscript L_{13}: St Petersburg IOM MS. D66
Catalogues: Shiraiwa, 'Rashid al-Din', no. 8; Monzavi, *Fehrest*, vol. 6, p. 4133 no. 42519; Miklukho-Maklai, *Persidskie i Tadzhikskie Rukopisi*, pp. 46–50 no. 223 (for the main text) and pp. 55–7 no. 228 (for the continuation); Miklukho-Maklai, *Opisanie* vol. 1, p. 137 no. 899.
Provenance: Dated 27 September 1576 (4 *Rajab* 984), signed as Mas'ud b. 'Abd Allah.
Description: 509 folios of 35.5 × 24 cm, with a written surface of 25.5 × 17 cm and 23 lines of text per page.
This is a lacunose copy of the *Blessed History*, bound together with Hafez-e Abru's preliminary *Continuation* (folios 425–509), with additional unrelated texts in the margins of some folios. The colophon is in the same name as manuscript L_{12}, from which it has likely been copied, with a later date supplied.

Manuscript L_{14}: London BL MS. Or. 2885
Catalogues: Shiraiwa, 'Rashid al-Din', no. 24; Browne, 'Suggestions', no. 10; Rieu, *Supplement to the Catalogue*, p. 16 no. 26.
Provenance: Copied 19 June 1621 (28 *Rajab* 1030) by 'Abd al-Aql Muhammad Sadiq b. Hussain in Khatunabad, in the 'kingdom of Isfahan'.
Description: 422 folios of 33.5 × 20 cm, with a written surface of 25.5 × 14 cm and 21 lines of text per page.
This copy dispenses with many of the original formatting features of the work, collapsing the text into a single block and leaving blank spaces in place of many of the genealogical trees. It was probably copied from manuscript L_{12}, which was purchased in Isfahan in 1756. Hafez-e Abru's preliminary *Continuation* begins on folio 363b.

Manuscript L_{15}: Rampur Reza Library MS. P. 1819
Catalogues: Shiraiwa, 'Rashid al-Din', no. 70; Monzavi, *Fehrest*, vol. 6, p. 4134 no. 42535.
Description: 356 folios of 31 × 19 cm, with a written surface of 22 × 13 cm and 25 lines of text per page.
This is a late, undated and disordered but mostly complete copy of the λ recension, though the first nineteen folios are lacunose and out of order. The first folio contains the beginning of Hafez-e Abru's preliminary *Continuation*, equivalent to folios 443a–444a of manuscript L_{12}. Folio 2 picks up abruptly with the *Blessed History* during the section of the Turkic tribes (section I.B in Appendix A), with continuous text on folios 4–13, 2–3 and 14–19. After a lacuna equivalent to about one folio of text, the text resumes on folio 20 and carries through the end of the *Blessed History*.

Manuscript L_{21}: St Petersburg National Library MS. Dorn 289
Catalogues: Shiraiwa, 'Rashid al-Din', no. 26; Dorn, *Catalogue des Manuscrits*, pp. 279–82 no. 289; Kostygova, *Fehrest* p. 45 no. 336; Kostygova, *Persidskie i Tadzhikskie Rukopisi*, vol. 1, p. 118 no. 336.
Provenance: dated 1528/9 (AH 935), later included in Shah 'Abbas's 1608 donation of manuscripts to the Safavid shrine at Ardabil.[32]
Description: 400 folios of 34.5 × 24.5 cm, with a written surface of 23.5 × 14.5 cm and 23 lines of text per page.
This manuscript is distinguished as a sub-recension because of the significant difference in its illustrative programme from other λ manuscripts. It contains only twenty-six images, significantly fewer than manuscript L_{11} or any other manuscript that contains images or spaces for images. Otherwise, it is largely indistinguishable from other copies of the λ recension.

Combinations of Both Volumes of the *Collected Histories*

At two points in its history, the *Collected Histories* was produced in two-volume editions. The first time this happened was at the court of Shahrokh, as Hafez-e Abru worked to recombine and reproduce Rashid al-Din's historical writings. The four extant two-volume witnesses to that process are here catalogued as the μ combinations. The ν combinations contains manuscripts descended from a second effort during the reign of Shah Abbas II (1642–66) to recombine the complete *Collected Histories* from dispersed manuscripts of its two volumes.

The μ Combinations: Timurid Versions of the Collected Histories

This group of manuscripts reflect Hafez-e Abru's work at the court of Shahrokh. The first subset includes two closely related manuscripts of the *Collected Histories*, in which Nizam Yazdi's rendition of the γ recension of the *Blessed History* is paired with a nearly complete copy of the *World History* from an unknown source manuscript. That source manuscript contained the rare histories of the Salghurids and Isma'ilis, which have been dropped from most extant copies of the *World History*. However, the Timurid copies omit Rashid al-Din's treatise on transubstantiation that came to be added to the end of his history of India. It may be that the Timurid copyists chose to omit this treatise, or it might be that this arrangement represents an early version of the *World History*, produced between 1307 and the time when Rashid al-Din added his treatise on transubstantiation. If the latter is the case, then it has important significance for the early life of the text, as it may also imply that Rashid al-Din intentionally dropped the Salghurids and Isma'ilis from later versions the *World History*. (No known manuscript contains all of these sections together.) For more on this possibility, see groups o and π.

The second subset contains two copies of the *Totality of History* (*Kulliyat-e Tarikhi*), also known as the *Collection of Hafez-e Abru* (*Majmu'a-ye Hafez-e Abru*), an early stage in Hafez-e Abru's effort to produce a new world history for his Timurid patron. This new collection, made for Shahrokh in 1417, was built around the histories of Tabari, Rashid al-Din and Shami, with continuations of each by Hafez-e Abru to create a unified history of the world, as described in the Epilogue. Neither of the two manuscripts in this subset has been available for this study, but enough diagnostic markers can be identified in previous descriptions of them to confirm a close relationship with the first subset.

Manuscript M_1: St Petersburg NL MS. PNS 46 (also G_{12}, O_{11})
Catalogues: Shiraiwa, 'Rashid al-Din', no. 57; Kostygova, *Fehrest*, p. 44 no. 333; Kostygova, *Persidskie i Tadzhikskie Rukopisi*, vol. 1, p. 117 no. 333.
Provenance: Copied by 'Abd Hajji Musafir al-'Attar, dated June 1407 (*Muharram* 810).

Description: 459 folios of 37.5 × 25.5 cm, with a written surface of 30 × 18.5 cm and 33 lines per page.

This is the earliest copy of Rashid al-Din's work that can be clearly attributed to Shahrokh's reign. It thus stands at the head of the Timurid resurgence of interest in the *Collected Histories*. It is unbound, kept in three cases of loose folios. Many of the folios have been split and mounted on card. The first and third gatherings together contain about two-thirds of the *World History*, while the second gathering contains somewhat more than half of the *Blessed History*. There is no indication of the order in which the volumes were originally bound, if indeed they were ever bound together.

This manuscript's current condition is much degraded. Many full and partial folios are missing, and many that remain are out of order. Even when corrected for this later degradation, it is evident that this manuscript contained several textual transpositions and omissions, which were corrected in manuscript M_2.

Manuscript M_2: London BL MS. Add. 7628 (also G_{13}, O_{12})
Catalogues: Shiraiwa, 'Rashid al-Din', no. 58; Browne, 'Suggestions', no. 1; Monzavi, *Fehrest*, vol. 6, p. 4133 no. 42517; Rieu, *Catalogue of the Persian Manuscripts*, vol. 1, pp. 74–8.
Publications: Browne, 'Suggestions'; De Nicola, 'The Travels'; digitised online at: http://www.bl.uk/manuscripts/Viewer.aspx?ref=add_ms_7628_fs001r.
Provenance: Court of Shahrokh, before 1433. Purchased by Claudius Rich in 1818.
Description: 728 folios of 46 × 28 cm, with a written surface of 32 × 19 cm and 33 lines per page.

This manuscript stands at the centre of two efforts to produce a complete and uniform edition of the *Collected Histories*. It can be directly tied to Hafez-e Abru's efforts at the court of Shahrokh, who is named as the book's owner in a note on folio 403b and whose ownership seal appears five times in the manuscript.[33] In addition, the *bismallah* at the start of the *Blessed History* is accompanied by a marginal note naming Shahrokh's son Baysonghor as the calligrapher.[34] The manuscript also contains seven impressions of Baysonghor's seal, two of them alongside the seal of his father.[35] Since Baysonghor died in 1433, the manuscript must have been copied before then. The second time this manuscript was involved with an effort to produce a complete edition of the *Collected Histories* was when Edward Browne featured it in his 1908 article that also includes the first attempt to catalogue all known copies of Rashid al-Din's historical writing.[36] Browne's argument that this manuscript contains a uniquely complete copy of the *Collected Histories* remains largely true, though it can now be shown that the version of the *Blessed History* found in it lacks several of the updates and additions that Rashid al-Din included in later versions of the text and includes at least three additions by Nizam Yazdi.[37] It is probably to be seen as an attempt by Hafez-e Abru to correct a corrupt manuscript line represented by manuscript G_{12}. Some of the most confused folios in that manuscript are here replaced by folios copied in a secretarial hand comparable to that of manuscript S_1, which is an autograph of Hafez-e Abru.[38]

Beyond the seals of Shahrokh and Baysonghor, additional seals and notes allow us to reconstruct the travels of this manuscript from Herat via the western Iranian world to the Ottoman Empire.[39] By the early nineteenth century it was back in Baghdad, where it was purchased by the British resident Claudius Rich.

Manuscript M_{11}: Istanbul TSM MS. B.282, folios 315–652 (also G_{21}, O_{21})
Catalogues: Shiraiwa, 'Rashid al-Din', no. 63; Tauer, 'Les manuscrits: Ire partie', pp. 97–8 no. 32; Karatay, *Topkapı Sarayı*, pp. 51–2 no. 138.
Publications: Togan, *On the Miniatures*, p. 42 and pll. 90–4; Sims and Stanley, 'The Illustrations of Baghdad 282'.
Provenance: Court of Shahrokh *c.* 1415.
Description: 342 folios of 42 × 32 cm, with a written surface of 29 × 21 cm and 31 lines of text per page.
This manuscript has not been consulted for this study. It is most famous for the twenty illustrations included within the translation of Tabari.

Manuscript M_{12}: Istanbul Süleimaniye MS. Damad Ibrahim 919, folios 348–700 (also G_{22}, O_{22})
Catalogues: Shiraiwa, 'Rashid al-Din', no. 59; Monzavi, *Fehrest*, vol. 6, p. 4133 no. 42518; Tauer, 'Les manuscrits: Ire partie', pp. 98–9 no. 33; Süleymaniye, *Defter-i Kutubkhane-ye Damad Ibrahim Paşa*, p. 65.

Provenance: Copied by Darwish Muhammad Taqani.
Description: 353 folios of 36 × 25.5 cm, with a written surface of 29 × 18 cm and 32 lines of text per page.
This manuscript has not been consulted for this study.

The ν Group: The Safavid Reconstruction

The manuscripts of this group stem from an effort under Shah Abbas II (1632–66) to recombine the two volumes of the *Collected Histories*. The result is here catalogued as manuscript N_1. As with the manuscripts of the μ group, these manuscripts contain both the *World History* and the *Blessed History*, in that order. They can be distinguished from manuscripts of the μ group in several ways. While those include the γ recension of the *Blessed History*, these manuscripts contain the ε recension. Also, these include the treatise on transubstantiation, but they lack the histories of the Salghurids and Isma'ilis. Based on these latter diagnostics, manuscript P_2 is here identified as the source manuscript for the *World History* portion of these copies.

Manuscript N_1: Tehran Golestan Palace MS. Saltanat 2256 (also E_2, P_{11})
Catalogues: Shiraiwa, 'Rashid al-Din', no. 67; DENA no. 75974; Monzavi, *Fehrest*, vol. 6, p. 4134 no. 42520; Atabay, *Fehrest*, pp. 84–7 no. 39, with three colour plates.
Provenance: Copied by Hossein b. Shaykh Mir 'Alem for Qilich Khan b. Sarvkhan between December 1663 and April 1664 (*Jumada* I to *Shawwal* 1074). Registered in the Safavid royal library between 1738 and 1749, and then in that of Fath 'Ali Shah in 1816/17.
Description: 1225 folios of 49 × 32 cm, with between 25 and 28 lines of text per page.
This is a hybrid manuscript, containing incomplete copies of the *World History* from manuscript P_2 and of the *Blessed History* from an unidentified copy of the ε recension, breaking off at the death of Abaqa.[40] The other manuscripts of this group all have near identical contents, suggesting they all descend from this manuscript. The fact that this manuscript was copied in the 1660s suggests that manuscript P_2 had not made its way to Istanbul during the reign of Osman II (1618–22) as Çağman and Tanındı have argued.[41]

Manuscript N₂: London BL MS. I.O. Islamic 3524 (also E₃, P₁₂)
Catalogues: Shiraiwa, 'Rashid al-Din', no. 62; Browne, 'Suggestions', no. 11; Ethé, *Catalogue of the Persian Manuscripts*, col. 1524–9 no. 2828.
Publications: Morley, 'A Letter'; Browne, 'Suggestions'.
Provenance: Copied by Tahir b. ʿAbd al-Baqi ʿAlaʾi between April and December 1671 (*Dhuʾl-Hijjah* 1081 and *Shaʿban* 1082) and included in the Safavid shrine endowment. Later acquired by Dr John Leyden.
Description: 599 folios of 36.5 × 23 cm, with a written surface of 26.5 × 16 cm and 25 lines of text per page.
This copy was identified among the manuscripts of the India House library by Professor Falconer and first described by William Morley as part of the flurry of excitement over Rashid al-Din's works that swept through European scholarship in the 1830s and 1840s. It was evidently copied from manuscript N₁ and then included in the Safavid dynastic shrine at Ardabil. John Leyden acquired it presumably between his arrival in Calcutta in 1806 and 1811, when he died on an expedition to Java. His literary estate was entrusted to a Mr Heber and Dr Hare of Calcutta.[42] It is presumably through these last that the manuscript came into the ownership of the India Office.

The manuscript is dated in several places, from which is it is evident that the *World History* was completed first. The *World History* is dated between April (*Dhuʾl-Hijjah* 1081) and August 1671 (25 *Rabiʿ I* 1081), and the *Blessed History* not until 8 December 1671 (6 *Shaʿban* 1082). Accordingly, the two volumes are bound in reverse order, as they appear in manuscript N₁ and manuscripts of the μ group. This manuscript contains spaces for the illustrations that are found in manuscript N₁, but none of these were executed.

Manuscript N₃: Tehran Majlis MS. 8734 (also E₄, P₁₃)
Publication: Digitised online through the Majlis website (record number 713501), though no stable url can be determined. Download available at: http://dlib.ical.ir//multiMediaFile/7395248-4-1.pdf.
Provenance: Dated July 1829 (*Muharram* 1245).
Description: 607 folios of 29.5 × 21 cm, with 24 lines of text per page.
The first folios of this copy have been lost: it begins during a section on the Caesars of Rome equivalent to folio 30a of manuscript N₂.

Manuscript N_4: St Petersburg National Library MS. Chanykov 62 (also E_5, P_{14})
Catalogues: Shiraiwa, 'Rashid al-Din', no. 69; Dorn, *Die Sammlung*, p. 25; Kostygova, *Fehrest* p. 44 no. 334; Kostygova, *Persidskie i Tadzhikskie Rukopisi*, vol. 1, pp. 117–18 no. 334.
Provenance: Dated 1840/1 (AH 1256)
Description: 477 folios of 43 × 25.5 cm, with a written surface of 32 × 16.5 cm and 33 lines of text per page.

This and manuscript N_5 were both copied from manuscript N_1 in the context of Qajar diplomatic relations with the Russian Empire. The text of the *Blessed History* found here is lacunose and disordered and breaks off at the same point as manuscript N_2. Most of the brands (*tamgha*s) of the Oghuz Turkic tribes have been reproduced on folios 330b–331b. A few spaces in this manuscript have been left for illustrations in the sections on the Ghaznavids and India, but the only images completed here, as in manuscript N_5, are the generic portraits of emperors in the history of China and of popes and emperors in the history of the Franks.

Manuscript N_5: St Petersburg National Library MS. PNS 47 (also E_6, P_{15})
Catalogues: Shiraiwa, 'Rashid al-Din', no. 61; Kostygova, *Fehrest*, pp. 44–5 no. 335; Kostygova, *Persidskie i Tadzhikskie Rukopisi*, vol. 1, p. 118 no. 335.
Provenance: Copied in the scriptorium of Fath 'Ali Shah and dated 1851 (AH 1268). Given to Prince Dmitri Ivanovich Dolgorukov (1797–1867).
Description: 607 folios of 47 × 30 cm, with a written surface of 34.5 × 20 cm and 28 lines of text per page.

This is a larger and more elaborately constructed copy than manuscript N_4, with significant use of gold borders and highly decorated *unvan*s. The two manuscripts are comparable copies of N_1, though the illustration programme here breaks off early in the history of Frankish popes and emperors, leaving most of that section formatted for illustrations that were never completed. Prince Dolgorukov, for whom this copy was prepared, served as the Russian ambassador to Iran from 1845 to 1854.

Manuscript N_6: Tehran Melli MS. F-1606 (also E_7, P_{16})
Catalogues: Shiraiwa: 'Rashid al-Din', no. 60 (listed as F-1656); DENA no. 74975; Anvar, *Fehrest-e Nosakh*, pp. 92–3.
Publications: Digitised online at: http://dl.nlai.ir/UI/b6f31fcb-9c39-4b53-84d5-fb23236a13fd/LRRView.aspx.
Provenance: Nineteenth century. From the collection of Naser al-Din Shah.
Description: 362 folios of 46.5 × 29 cm, with a written surface of 32.5 × 19 cm and 26 lines of text per page.
This manuscript has only been consulted through the online facsimile, which is too low resolution to allow close analysis. In its contents, it matches the previous three manuscripts, though it lacks any illustrations and the text of the *Blessed History* breaks off significantly earlier than in either of those copies, during the account of the reign of the Jochid Toqta.[43]

Manuscripts of the *World History*

The o Group: the First Persian Version of the World History

This and the following group represent manuscript lines of the *World History* in Persian. Manuscripts in this group include the histories of the Salghurids and Isma'ilis, but lack the treatise on transubstantiation. Manuscripts in the π group, by contrast, contain the treatise on transubstantiation, but not the sections on the Salghurids and Isma'ilis. All four manuscripts in the o group date to the reign of Shahrokh, and so it is unclear whether the absence of the treatise on transubstantiation was a Timurid modification (the Timurid reconstructions of the σ group similarly lack the treatise) or if they all originate from a lost *rashidi* original that did not include it.

Manuscript O_{11}: St Petersburg NL MS. PNS 46 (manuscript M_1), gatherings 1 (227 folios) and 3 (46 folios)
See manuscript M_1 for general information and description.

Manuscript O_{12}: London BL MS. Add. 7628 (manuscript M_2), folios 1–403
See manuscript M_2 for general information and description.

Manuscript O_{21}: Istanbul TSM MS. B.282 (manuscript M_{11}), folios c. 465–652
See manuscript M_{11} for general information and description.

Manuscript O_{22}: Istanbul Süleimaniye MS. Damad Ibrahim 919 (manuscript M_{12}), folios c. 506–700
See manuscript M_{12} for general information and description.

The π Group: the Second Persian Version of the World History

Manuscript P_2 is the parent of all other manuscripts in this group, with the possible exception of manuscript P_{21}. It is dated to 1317, the year before Rashid al-Din died. This fact has long been interpreted as the reason that few if any of the images in manuscript P_2 were completed in the Ilkhanid period: with the disgrace and death of Rashid al-Din and the sacking of the Rashidi Quarter, it is believed that this manuscript was left incomplete.[44] However, an alternate origin can be hypothesised for this group. Manuscript P_2, and all of the manuscripts descended from it, lack the end of the history of Khwarazm (section II.E) and the entire histories of the Salghurids and Isma'ilis (sections II.F–G). A note at the bottom of the colophon on folio 350a of manuscript P_2 mentions that a group of pages had been removed from the book, which probably refers to this lacuna. The angled colophon frame, however, is formatted to include this note, suggesting that the lacuna appeared already in the source from which manuscript P_2 was copied. It may be, then, that there is an original *rashidi* manuscript lying behind manuscript P_2, for which the siglum P_1 is reserved. P_2 itself would have then been copied outside Tabriz in 1317 after the group of folios had been removed. Seeing manuscript P_2 as the product of a regional scriptorium, rather than Rashid al-Din's main studio in Tabriz, would open the possibility that its images were left incomplete for lack of resources. It would also explain how this manuscript survived the looting of the Rashidi Quarter, and why it does not match the format of the other manuscripts that were copied there. This last point is perhaps most significant: manuscript R_1 and the original *rashidi* sections of manuscripts S_1 and S_{11} all have a written surface of 37 × 26 cm, with thirty-five lines of text per page. Manuscript P_2, by contrast, has a smaller written surface (34 × 24.5 cm) and fewer lines of text per page (thirty-one), closer in both respects to manuscript Z_{12}, which was copied in Baghdad in October 1318.

Manuscript P_2: Istanbul TSM MS. H.1654
Catalogues: Shiraiwa, 'Rashid al-Din', no. 50; Monzavi, *Fehrest*, vol. 6, p. 4133 no. 42516.
Publications: Togan, *On the Miniatures*, pp. 40–1 and pll. 69–81; Inal, 'Some Miniatures'.
Provenance: Copied in 1317, with paintings added during the reign of Shahrokh.
Description: 350 folios of 55 × 38 cm, with a written surface of 34 × 24.5 cm and 31 lines of text per page.
This is the most complete copy of the Persian version of the *World History* to survive from Rashid al-Din's lifetime. It was completed less than a year before his death. Most of the images were added during the Timurid period, possibly at the court of Shahrokh in Herat, though the manuscript does not bear his ownership seal. By the end of the sixteenth century, it was in the possession of Farhad Khan Qaramanlu (d. 1599), for whom illuminated headers were added and the whole book remounted in large margins of pink paper. It may have been Farhad Khan's brother, Zu'l-Faqar Khan (d. 1610) who presented the manuscript to the Safavid shrine in Ardabil during his term as governor of Azerbaijan over the first decade of the seventeenth century. The *waqf* seal of the shrine is evident on the manuscript.[45]

Manuscript P_{11}: Tehran Golestan Palace ms. Saltanat 2256 (manuscript N_1), folios 1–c. 822
See manuscript N_1 for general information and description.

Manuscript P_{12}: London BL MS. I.O. Islamic 3524 (manuscript N_2), folios 1–402
See manuscript N_2 for general information and description.

Manuscript P_{13}: Tehran Majlis MS. 8734 (manuscript N_3), folios 1–394
See manuscript N_3 for general information and description.

Manuscript P_{14}: St Petersburg National Library MS. Chanykov 62 (manuscript N_4), folios 2–321
See manuscript N_4 for general information and description.

Manuscript P_{15}: St Petersburg National Library ms. PNS 47 (manuscript N_5), folios 404–607
See manuscript N_5 for general information and description.

Manuscript P_{16}: Tehran Melli MS. F-1606 (manuscript N_6), folios 1–272
See manuscript N_6 for general information and description.

Manuscript P_{21}: Kolkata Asiatic Society MS. 14
Catalogues: Shiraiwa, 'Rashid al-Din', no. 55.
Publications: Elliot, *History of India*, vol. 3, pp. 18–21; Elliot, *Bibliographical Index*, pp. 19–22.
Provenance: Dated 1686/7 (AH 1098).
Description: 291 folios with 30 lines of text per page.
As with manuscript X_3, Elliot describes this manuscript at length, and his description makes it a clear desideratum for further study.[46] It evidently contains a large portion of the *World History* (sections II.C–E, H–L as described in Appendix A), though the history of the Ghaznavids has been transposed between those of Europe and India. It is tentatively included in the π group because, like the other manuscripts of this group and only of this group, it lacks the histories of the Salghurids and Isma'ilis.

The ρ Group: the Arabic Version

The earliest dated manuscript of the *World History* is the Arabic copy here catalogued as R_1, which was completed at Rashid al-Din's scriptorium in Tabriz in 1314. It is the most famous copy of Rashid al-Din's work, and was, along with Quatremère's partial edition of the *Blessed History*, responsible for the sharp increase in interest in the works of Rashid al-Din in England and France in the 1830s and 1840s. Two fragments of this manuscript survive in separate collections; they are catalogued here as R_1a and R_1b. Each of them entered British ownership in the second decade of the nineteenth century, but they were not identified as parts of the same manuscript until 1839. In a letter to William Morley dated 24 April of that year, Edwin Norris, Assistant Secretary of the Royal Asiatic Society, writes:

> A wonder!! The remainder of the fragment of Rashid eddin has been found!!! It is among the late Col. Baillie's m.s. and is entitled 'Tarikhi Tabari'. Professor [of Linguistics Duncan] Forbes of King's College has examined it, and found that it is not Tarikhi Tabari but Rashid eddin, and, what is <u>more</u> curious, that it is the portion of the volume of which we [the Royal Asiatic Society] have a fragment; and, what is <u>most</u> curious, that it is a portion of the same book, the same identical, physical, bodily book; that in fact the two fragments once formed one complete volume, but that some rascal with 'fatal scissors' has severed them, but not 'for ever and ever' we will hope.[47]

Morley had encountered manuscript R_1a in 1838 while preparing his catalogue of Royal Asiatic Society manuscripts and had prepared a description of it for publication in the Society's *Journal*. Norris offered quite literally to stop the presses in order to append a note about the almost simultaneous rediscovery of manuscript R_1b. In the end, it was not Morley but Professor Forbes who wrote the description of manuscript R_1b; his letter to the Royal Asiatic Society was published alongside Morley's in 1841.[48] In the course of his letter, Forbes acknowledges that it was actually Mir Afzal Ali, Vakil of the Maharaja of Satara who first made the connection between the two fragments.[49] Morley's letter dedicates more attention to describing Rashid al-Din's history of India than he does to any other portion of the text, providing a brief summary of each of its sections. The nineteenth-century British interest in the section on India is evident in the various manuscripts of the υ group that include that section. In particular, Morley used R_1a, among other manuscripts, in preparing manuscript U_2.

A note at the end of manuscript R_1b states that it once contained 303 folios, half of which had been stolen. Part of that missing portion is accounted for by manuscript R_1a, though an additional ninety or so folios have yet to come to light. The folios were numbered before this loss occurred, which allows a reconstruction of the 303-folio manuscript, which Sheila Blair has undertaken.[50] However, it is evident that the manuscript was already defective at the time the folios were numbered. Currently, the history of India follows immediately after the section on China in manuscript R_1a. However, the back of the last folio of the history of China exhibits a transferred ink pattern that matches the eight-lobed knotted pattern found at the beginning of the section on Jewish history.[51] The history of the Jews came immediately after the history of China in Rashid al-Din's original plan for the *World History*, and this ink transfer suggests that manuscript R_1 followed that original plan. It may have also included other sections that have since been lost, namely, those on the Salghurids, Isma'ilis, Oghuz Turks and Franks (sections II.F–H and K as described in Appendix A).

Despite these lacunae, manuscript R_1 is one of only four partial copies of the *World History* to survive from Rashid al-Din's lifetime (see also P_2, S_1 and S_{11}), and has been included in the effort (in Appendix A) to reconstruct the original illustrative programmes of the work. The other three manuscripts of this group are all descended from R_1.

Manuscript R_1a: Geneva, Nasser Khalili Collection MS. 727
Catalogues: Shiraiwa, 'Rashid al-Din', no. 48; Browne, 'Suggestions', no. 14; Morley, *A Descriptive Catalogue*, pp. 1–11 no. 1.
Publications: Blair, *A Compendium of Chronicles* (study and facsimile); Sotheby Parke Bernet & Co., *Catalogue of Rashid al-Din's 'World History'*; Robinson, 'Rashid al-Din's World History'.
Provenance: Copied at the Rashidi Quarter, completed in 1314. Later in the collections of Shahrokh, the Nawabs of Awadh, John Staples Harriot and Major-General Thomas Gordon. Bequeathed to the Royal Asiatic Society in 1841.
Description: 59 folios of 43.5 × 30 cm, with a written surface of 37 × 25.5 cm and 35 lines of text per page.
This fragment contains most of Rashid al-Din's history of China, the complete histories of the Jews and of India, and seven scattered folios from earlier in the *World History*. Captain John Staples Harriott acquired it in Danapur in 1813. He was able to identify it as part of the *World History* based on the description of the work given by Pétis de la Croix, which Harriott translates in a note on the manuscript's first page. Harriott also had copies of the histories of China and India made from this manuscript (see below, manuscripts R_2 and R_3). If a copy of the history of the Jews was also made, it is not currently

known. Major-General Thomas Gordon later acquired the manuscript in England and bequeathed it to the Royal Asiatic Society.

Manuscript R_1b: Edinburgh University Library MS. Or. 20
Catalogues: Shiraiwa, 'Rashid al-Din', no. 49; Hukk et al., *A Descriptive Catalogue*, pp. 15–17.
Publications: Rice and Gray, *The Illustrations*; digitised online at: https://images.is.ed.ac.uk/luna/servlet/media/book/showBook/UoEsha~4~4~647 42~103064.
Provenance: Copied at the Rashidi Quarter, completed in 1314. Later in the collection of Shahrokh, the Nawabs of Awadh, Farzada Kuli and John Baillie.
Description: 151 folios of 45 × 34 cm, with a written surface of 37 × 25.5 cm and 35 lines of text per page.
This fragment contains most of the pre-Islamic history and the history of Muhammad and the caliphate, and a lacunose copy of the history of the Ghaznavids, Saljuqs and Khwarazmshahs. It is incorrectly labelled as an autograph copy of the history of Tabari. Lieutenant-Colonel John Baillie of Leys, Scotland, acquired this portion of the manuscript in India, presumably while serving as resident at Lucknow between 1807 and 1815. (It is to be remembered that Harriott acquired manuscript R_1a during this period as well, and not far from Lucknow.) It is mentioned in the collection of an otherwise unknown Farzada Kuli, whom Duncan Forbes speculates was a member of the royal family of Awadh.[52]

Manuscript R_2: Oxford Bodleian MS. Arab b. 1
Catalogues: Shiraiwa, 'Rashid al-Din', no. 56.
Provenance: Copied from manuscript R_1a, probably in or near Lucknow in the 1820s. Entered the Bodleian Library in the mid-1880s.
Description: 10 folios of 38.5 × 27 cm, pasted onto larger sheets (43.5 × 29 cm), with a written surface of 37.5 × 26 cm and 35 lines of text per page. In the first volume of the catalogue of Persian manuscripts of the Chester Beatty Library, in an entry dedicated to four folios from the dispersed manuscript here catalogued as S_{11}, A. J. Arberry makes passing mention to this manuscript as 'some leaves of this work in the Bodleian'.[53] An unsigned note kept with these ten folios already identifies them as a near-exact copy

of the folios numbered 249–58 in manuscript R_1a, with few minor textual lacunae. That same note mentions manuscript R_3 as evidence that the owner of manuscript R_1a ordered copies of it to be made in the 1820s. As described above, John Staples Harriot owned manuscript R_1a at that time, and so it was probably he who commissioned or allowed this copy.

A letter in French dated 12 March 1885 from one H. Graf to an unidentified addressee is kept with this manuscript. It was sent from Paris to Britain along with the manuscript, which it offers for sale. Graf explains that the manuscript was sold to him under the title, *Vie et mort d'un comedien, manuscrit en persan avec animatures, complet*, but that he had taken the time to examine it and found that it was, in fact, written in Arabic, fragmentary and dedicated to the dynastic history of China. A note in pencil at the top of this letter indicates that it was 'bought from the writer for £2.2'.

Manuscript R_3: London Royal Asiatic Society MS. Arabic 27
Catalogues: Morley, *A Descriptive Catalogue*, p. 11 no. 2.
Provenance: Copied before May 1823, in or near Lucknow.
Description: 33 folios of 33 × 23.5 cm, with 20 lines of Arabic text per page, with interlinear Persian translation.
This is another partial copy of manuscript R_1a, containing the history of Shakyamuni from the history of India (section II.L in Appendix A) in its Arabic version. In 1823, Colonel William Francklin (d. 1839), regulating officer at Baghalpur, commissioned a Persian translation of this Arabic fragment. That translation was inserted between the lines of the Arabic text in May 1823. This manuscript has not been consulted for the current study, but a copy of the Persian translation is found in manuscript R_4, which also includes two notes, one of which seems to have been copied from this manuscript. Those notes identify the author of the translation as 'Abd al-Qadir. This, then, is perhaps an excerpt from the otherwise unknown re-translation into Persian of the Arabic *World History* that 'Abd al-Qadir Bada'uni claims to have prepared for Akbar the Great in the *hijri* year 1000 (1591/2 CE).[54] This manuscript was in the collection of the Royal Asiatic Society by 1854, when Morley included it in his catalogue of the historical manuscripts there.

Manuscript R_4: Manchester John Rylands Library MS. 364, folios 29b–65a

Catalogues: Shiraiwa, 'Rashid al-Din', no. 33; Browne, 'Suggestions', no. 15; Kerney, *Bibliotheca Lindesiana*, p. 166.

Provenance: Copied in India, presumably in or near Lucknow, between 1823 and 1836, when it was bound along with an 1817 copy of the *Jami'-e Jehan-numa* of Abu'l-Qasim b. 'Ali Simnani Sasani. Part of the collection of Nathaniel Bland (d. 1865) and later of James Ludovic Lindsay (d. 1913), 26th Earl of Crawford. Purchased for the John Rylands Library in 1901 by Enriqueta Rylands (d. 1908).

Description: 37 folios with 14 lines of text per page.

This is a copy of the Persian translation of the Arabic version of Rashid al-Din's history of India first found in manuscript R_3. A note on folio 27b largely restates the contents of a second note on folios 28b–29a, which seems to have been copied from manuscript R_3.

The s Group: Timurid Reconstructions of the World History

In the early fifteenth century, there were several efforts at Timurid courts to reproduce or reconstruct manuscripts of Rashid al-Din's historical writings. This group contains the results of three closely related projects. The first sub-group is frequently conflated with the *Collection of Histories* (*Majma' al-Tawarikh*), a massive four-volume universal history written by Hafez-e Abru for Shahrokh between 1423 and 1427.[55] It is also sometimes called the *Cream of Histories* (*Zubdat al-Tawarikh*), which is actually the title Hafez-e Abru gave to the fourth volume of the *Majma'*. In fact, they are the product of one of Hafez-e Abru's efforts to reconstruct a fragmentary copy of the *World History* during the same years that he was preparing the *Majma'*. Much of the resulting reconstruction is identical to Rashid al-Din's work, but it differs in its first and last section. For the history of pre-Islamic Iran (equivalent to section II.A in Appendix A), Hafez-e Abru provided his own version of events, which he had separately prepared for Shahrokh's son Baysonghor. The history of India (section II.L) found in these manuscripts is a significantly abbreviated form of Rashid al-Din's original.

The second sub-recension here consists of a single manuscript which is also the result of Hafez-e Abru's efforts to reconstruct fragments of Rashid al-Din's *World History*.⁵⁶ Its painted pages were dispersed in the early twentieth century, as a result of which it has escaped thorough study until recently. The final two manuscripts of this group are yet another closely related reworking of Rashid al-Din's *World History* that was completed at the court of Ulugh Beg (1447–9) in Samarqand.

Manuscript S_1: Istanbul TSM MS. H.1653
Catalogues: Shiraiwa, 'Rashid al-Din', no. 51; Karatay, *Topkapı Sarayı*, p. 38.
Publications: Ettinghausen, 'An Illuminated Manuscript'; Togan, *On the Miniatures*, p. 41 and pll. 82–9; Inal, 'The Fourteenth-Century Miniatures'.
Provenance: Fragments from Tabriz, one of them dated 1314, reconstructed with new sections by Hafez-e Abru in Herat, 1425/6.
Description: 435 folios of 54.5 × 38 cm, with a written surface of 37 × 26 cm and 31 lines of text per page (on folios 164–219, 227–341 and 343–410) or 31 × 23 cm and 35 lines of text per page (on folios 1–163, 342 and 411–35). This is Hafez-e Abru's autograph replacement volume for the *World History*. It is built around fragments of manuscripts of the *Collected Histories* prepared at Rashid al-Din's scriptorium in Tabriz. The book may have been brought to Herat by the late Ilkhanid general and kingmaker Choban (d. 1327), when he fled there towards the end of his life.⁵⁷

Manuscript S_2a: Paris BnF MS. Supplément persan 160
Catalogues: Blochet, *Catalogue des Manuscrits Persans*, vol. 1, pp. 209–10 no. 270; Richard, *Catalogue des Manuscrits Persans*, vol. 2, pp. 246–8.
Provenance: Probably copied by Muhammad b. Mulla Mir al-Katib in Herat in 1426/7 (based on comparison with manuscript S_2b). Sent from Isfahan by J. T. Simon de Vierville between 1754 and 1756 and, after passing through several ownerships, entered the royal French library in 1860.
Description: 227 folios of 33 × 20 cm, with a written surface of 23 × 11.5 cm and 25 lines of text per page, with six incomplete miniatures.
This and the following manuscript are two volumes of the same copy of manuscript S_1, though they have not previously been recognised as such. A note on the inside front cover identifying the work as Mirkhwand's *Rawzat al-Safa* has been crossed out, though Blochet and Richard each catalogue the work as Hafez-e Abru's *Cream of Histories*, by which they mean the *Collection*

of Histories. The manuscript contains a different version of pre-Islamic history than that found in the *Collected Histories*, matching instead the text that Hafez-e Abru had supplied in his autograph manuscript S_1. It also includes the introductory passage where Hafez-e Abru explains his negotiation with Shahrokh to make this substitution in what was otherwise meant to be a reconstruction of Rashid al-Din's *World History*.

This manuscript contains six incomplete images. Five of these are mirror-image matches to illustrations found in manuscript S_1, suggesting some image transfer technique was used in creating them. The sixth, on folio 134b, shows the Sasanian king Bahman in battle against the Sistanis. Manuscript S_{11} has a textual lacuna at this point (after folio 90), but provides a possible model for the image of Bahman. The fact that the image of Bahman has been included here suggests that a second manuscript besides S_1 was consulted in the preparation of this one, possibly manuscript S_{11}.

Manuscript S_2b: Paris BnF MS. Supplément persan 2004
Catalogues: Shiraiwa, 'Rashid al-Din', no. 52; Blochet, *Catalogue des Manuscrits Persans*, vol. 4, pp. 224–5 no. 2279.
Provenance: Copied by Muhammad b. Mulla Mir al-Katib in 1426/7 (AH 830), probably in Herat.
Description: 303 folios of 33 × 20 cm, with a written surface of 23 × 11.5 cm and 25 lines of text per page.
This volume contains the greater part of the replacement volume, from the history of Islam through to the history of India (sections II.B–L as described in Appendix A). Most of these sections are identical to copies of the *Blessed History*, except for Hafez-e Abru's abbreviated version of the history of India and the fact that the catalogue of popes and emperors in the history of the Franks has been condensed into a single block of running text. Both of these features match manuscript S_1, which can therefore be identified as the source for this manuscript. Other sections include a few illustrations, generally poorly executed. The identical *mise en page* of this volume with manuscript S_2a allow us to consider them two halves of one copy.

Manuscript S_3: Tehran Majlis MS. 9078
Catalogue: DENA 74971

Publication: Digitised online through the Majlis website (record number 515264), though no stable url can be determined. Download available at: http://dlib.ical.ir//multiMediaFile/1410389-4-1.pdf.
Provenance: Seventeenth century.
Description: 360 folios of 28 × 18 cm, with 25 lines of text per page.
This is a fragmentary copy of manuscript S_1, picking up near the top of folio 37a of that manuscript and breaking off during the history of the Isma'ilis.

Manuscript S_4: St Petersburg Institute of Oriental Manuscripts MS. C802
Catalogues: Miklukho-Maklai, *Persidskie i Tadzhikskie Rukopisi*, vol. 1, p. 504 no. 3821; Miklukho-Maklai, *Opisanie*, pp. 51–4 no. 226; Rosen, *Les Manuscrits Persans*, pp. 52–111 no. 7.
Provenance: Probably seventeenth century. A note on the flyleaf indicates that it was given to the Academy of Sciences by a Mr Pavloff in 1865.
Description: 489 folios of 29 × 20 cm, with a written surface of 20 × 13 cm and 25 lines of text per page.
Like other manuscripts in this group, this was originally identified as a copy of Hafez-e Abru's *Collection of Histories*, when in fact it is a copy from his replacement volume of the *Blessed History*, including his alternate version of pre-Islamic history. It also contains spaces for illustrations that match those found in manuscript S_1, though these have not been completed. This manuscript contains several significant lacunae. It was not dated at the time it was copied, but a note on folio 1a gives a date of AH 1120 (1708 CE), establishing a *terminus ante quam* for the copy.

Manuscript S_5: St Petersburg National Library MS. PNS 58
Catalogues: Shiraiwa, 'Rashid al-Din', no. 47; Kostygova, *Fehrest*, p. 163 no. 1133; Kostygova, *Persidskie i Tadzhikskie Rukopisi*, vol. 2, p. 169 no. 1133.
Provenance: Copied by 'Abd al-Javad Muhammad Tahir, dated 28 January 1820–15 March 1821 (12 *Rabi' II* 1235–10 *Jumada II* 1236).
Description: 579 folios of 33 × 23 cm, with a written surface of 26.5 × 13 cm and 24 lines of text per page.
Like other manuscripts in this group, this has incorrectly been catalogued as a copy of Hafez-e Abru's *Collection of Histories*, when in fact it is a copy from his replacement volume of the *Blessed History*, including his alternate version

of pre-Islamic history. This copy contains several marginal notes indicating the presence of images and lacunae in the source manuscript.

Manuscript S₆: St Petersburg Institute of Oriental Manuscripts MS. E5
Catalogues: Miklukho-Maklai, *Persidskie i Tadzhikskie Rukopisi*, vol. 1, p. 504 no. 3822; Miklukho-Maklai, *Opisanie*, p. 54 no. 226; Dorn, 'Über die aus dem Nachlasse des wirkl. Staatsrathes Graf', pp. 120–1 no. 17.
Provenance: Dated 23 May 1851 (22 *Rajab* 1267) by Mirza Rahim b. Mirza Muhammad Hassan Karim Isfahani, called 'state historian' (*muwarrikh al-daula*).
Description: 212 folios of 41.5 × 25.5 cm, with a written surface of 32 × 18 cm and 35 lines of text per page.
This manuscript was one of thirty-nine manuscripts acquired by the Asiatic Museum of the Imperial Academy of Sciences from the estate of State Councillor R. Graf (d. 1867).[58] Graf had been posted to Tbilisi as part of the Russian Foreign Ministry in 1860 and undoubtedly acquired this manuscript there during the last years of his life.

Manuscript S₇: St Petersburg National Library MS. PNS 57
Catalogues: Shiraiwa, 'Rashid al-Din', no. 54; Kostygova, *Fehrest*, p. 163 no. 1132; Kostygova, *Persidskie i Tadzhikskie Rukopisi*, vol. 2, p. 168 no. 1132.
Description: 332 folios of 38 × 24.5 cm, with a written surface of 30 × 19.5 cm and 30 lines of text per page.
As with other manuscripts of this group, this has incorrectly been catalogued as a copy of Hafez-e Abru's *Collection of Histories*, when in fact it is a copy from his replacement volume of the *Blessed History*, including his alternate version of pre-Islamic history. This copy is lacunose and incomplete.

Manuscript S₈: Lahore University of the Punjab Library MS. Pe I 55/2035
Catalogues: Shiraiwa, 'Rashid al-Din', no. 45; Monzavi, *Fehrest*, vol. 6, p. 4134 no. 42538; Abdullah, *A Descriptive Catalogue*, vol. 1, pp. 3–10 no. 4.
Description: 681 folios of 35.5 × 23 cm, with a written surface of 25.5 × 15.5 cm and 23 lines of text per page.
This manuscript has not been consulted for this study, but Abdullah's

description indicates quite clearly that it is a complete copy of Hafez-e Abru's replacement volume. There is no indication that it contains any illustrations.

Manuscript S_9: St Petersburg Institute of Oriental Manuscripts MS. C374
Catalogues: Shiraiwa, 'Rashid al-Din', no. 44; Mortezavi no. 42533; Miklukho-Maklai, *Persidskie i Tadzhikskie Rukopisi*, vol. 1, p. 137 no 901; Miklukho-Maklai, *Opisanie*, p. 51 no. 225; Salemann, 'Das Asiatische Museum', p. 76 no. 43.
Publications: *Mélanges asiatiques* 10, p. 276 no. 43.
Provenance: Undated. In Khiva in the nineteenth century.
Description: 240 folios of 24.5 × 16.5 cm, with a written surface of 19 × 10.5 cm and 25 lines of text per page.
This was one of 134 manuscripts purchased by the Asiatic Museum in 1890 from the estate of A. Kuhn (d. 1888), who had accompanied the Russian expedition to Khiva in 1873 that established a Russian protectorate over that khanate.[59] This may well have been one of the 300 or so manuscripts confiscated from Khiva at that time, some of which remained in Kuhn's personal collection.[60] It is missing the pre-Islamic history, but a set of Arabic ciphers starts with the number 280 on what is now folio 2. Comparing the lengths of Rashid al-Din and Hafez-e Abru's versions of pre-Islamic history with other sections in this manuscript suggests that this manuscript originally included the longer version by Hafez-e Abru, rather than Rashid al-Din's shorter original (see section II.A in Appendix A). This manuscript is thus tentatively catalogued here as a copy of S_1, though that attribution may change if the missing first half of the manuscript comes to light.

Manuscript S_{11}: Washington Freer-Sackler Gallery Art and History Trust MS. 22 and dispersed pages
Catalogues: Soudavar, *Art of the Persian Courts*, pp. 64–6 nos. 22–4.
Publications: Ghiasian, 'The "Historical Style"'.
Provenance: Prepared at the court of Shahrokh. Exhibited in Philadelphia in 1926 and then dispersed by Émile Tabbagh in the 1930s.
Description: Approximately 468 folios of 42.5 × 32 cm, with a written surface of 33 × 22.5 cm and 33 lines of text per page (approximately folios 1–296

and 351–69) or 37 × 25.5 cm and 35 lines of text per page (approximately folios 297–350).

This is a unicum manuscript, now largely dispersed, which has frequently been considered another early copy of manuscript S_1. Like that manuscript, it represents a stage in Hafez-e Abru's efforts to reconstruct incomplete copies of Rashid al-Din's work. Two main features distinguish it from the previous sub-group. The first is the fact that this manuscript has at its centre a group of approximately fifty-four folios original to Rashid al-Din's scriptorium in Tabriz. These are identical in size, layout and paper quality to those of the famous Arabic copy (manuscript R_1) and other *rashidi* manuscripts. The rest of the manuscript, made on a darker brown rag paper, is a Timurid reconstruction. This reconstruction, however, deviates from that of manuscript S_1 in several places. While much of the pre-Islamic history contains the text that Hafez-e Abru provided for manuscript S_1, the end of the history of the Sasanians in this manuscript switches abruptly back to Rashid al-Din's original text. The history of India in this manuscript also matches the original *World History*, rather than the abbreviated version of manuscript S_1.

The first two folios are replacement pages on Venetian paper, probably prepared in the 1860s.[61] The text on these replacement pages resemble the introduction to Hafez-e Abru's *Geography*. Lacking the original introductory pages, any authentic explanation of the creation of this replacement volume is therefore currently impossible.

Manuscript S_{21}: Istanbul TSM MS. AIII.2935
Catalogues: Shiraiwa, 'Rashid al-Din', no. 28; Monzavi, *Fehrest*, vol. 6, p. 4132 no. 42508; Karatay, *Topkapı Sarayı*, p. 43 no. 114.
Provenance: Made at the court of Ulugh Beg (1447–9) in Samarqand.
Description: 406 folios of 41 × 26 cm, with a written surface of 30.5 × 18 cm and 33 lines of text per page.
This and the following two manuscripts, which are copied from this one, contain the *Histories of the World* (*Tevarikh-e 'Alam*) prepared by Ahmad b. Muhammad b. Muhammad al-Bukhari for the Timurid sultan Ulugh Beg (1447–9). The text has not received much attention, though it has been erroneously conflated with Rashid al-Din's *World History*, and even provides the text for the first 297 pages of the edition of the pre-Islamic history that

Muhammad Raushan has published in Rashid al-Din's name.[62] It can perhaps best be seen as a Transoxanian response to the work that Hafez-e Abru had undertaken in Herat in previous decades. As had Hafez-e Abru before him, Bukhari reworked at least the pre-Islamic portion of Rashid al-Din's *World History*, adding significant amounts of verse and aligning the text more with the narrative of Ferdausi's *Shahnameh*.

Manuscript $S_{22}b$: Paris BnF MS. Supplément persan 1365
Catalogues: Shiraiwa, 'Rashid al-Din', no. 42; Browne, 'Suggestions', no. 20; Blochet, *Catalogue des Manuscrits Persans*, vol. 1, pp. 203–4 no. 258.
Provenance: Later nineteenth century copy made in Istanbul from manuscript S_{21}; acquired by the French National Library as part of the Schefer collection on 27 December 1899.
Description: 239 folios of 26 × 17 cm, with a written surface of 16.5 × 9 cm and 17 lines of text per page.
This and the following manuscript are two parts of a set copied in Istanbul from manuscript S_{21}. A hypothetical manuscript $S_{22}a$ may have contained the histories of the pre-Islamic period and of Muhammad and the caliphate (sections II.A–B in Appendix A), which are unaccounted for in the two known volumes of the set. Though this volume is catalogued after $S_{22}c$ in both the Schefer collection and the current BnF collection, it contains the intermediate portion of Bukhari's *Histories*, which reproduces Rashid al-Din's histories of the Ghaznavids, Saljuqs, Khwarazmshahs and the beginning of the history of the Salghurids (sections II.C–F in Appendix A). In addition to the abrupt end, this manuscript contains several internal lacunae.

Manuscript $S_{22}c$: Paris BnF MS. Supplément persan 1364
Catalogues: Shiraiwa, 'Rashid al-Din', no. 42; Browne, 'Suggestions', no. 20; Blochet, *Catalogue des Manuscrits Persans*, vol. 1, pp. 203–4 no. 257.
Provenance: Later nineteenth century copy made in Istanbul from manuscript S_1; acquired by the French National Library as part of the Schefer collection on 27 December 1899.
Description: 336 folios of 26 × 17 cm, with a written surface of 16.5 × 9 cm and 17 lines of text per page.
This volume of the copy of Bukhari's *Histories* contains Rashid al-Din's

history of the Fatimids, Oghuz Turks, China and India (sections II.G–I, L in Appendix A). Unlike Hafez-e Abru, Bukhari does not abbreviate the history of India, but reproduces Rashid al-Din's text in full.

The τ Group, Other Derivative World Histories

The manuscripts of this group represent two attempts to update Rashid al-Din's *World History* after the Timurid period. Neither can be exactly identified; they are separated by their sigla into two sub-groups. They are included here because they have been elsewhere mis-catalogued as manuscripts of Rashid al-Din. Other late texts that repurposed Rashid al-Din's historical writings could expand this catalogue greatly, but are omitted because they have not generally been confused with their source.

Manuscript T_1: Rampur Reza Library MS. P. 1821
Catalogues: Shiraiwa, 'Rashid al-Din', no. 72; Monzavi vol. 6, p. 4134 no. 42537.
Provenance: Copied by Muʿizz al-Din Husayn b. Muhammad Mirak al-Husayni al-Ustadi and dated January–February 1638 (*Ramadan* 1047).
Description: 203 folios of 31 × 19 cm, with a written surface of 24 × 12 cm and 25 lines of text per page (folios 1–24) or 22 × 12 cm and 23 lines of text per page (folios 25–203).
This manuscript is referred to as 'the Moradabad manuscript' in nineteenth-century British scholarship. It was the source for the following copies. It is clearly based on Rashid al-Din's *World History*, including the history of Islam, the Ghaznavids, China, Europe and India (sections II.B–C, I, K–L). However, the text of the history of Islam does not match that of Rashid al-Din. A later note, dated to 1776 or 1781 (AH 1190 or 1195) connects the work to the reign of Shah Jahan (1628–58), perhaps by reference to the colophon. It may thus represent an effort to update Rashid al-Din's world history for the Mughal ruler, just as Hafez-e Abru had earlier done for Shahrokh.

Manuscript T_2: University of Tehran Faculty of Literature MS. 76-b
Catalogues: Shiraiwa, 'Rashid al-Din', no. 30; DENA no. 74969; Monzavi, *Fehrest*, vol. 6, p. 4134 no. 42521; Daneshpazhuh, *Fehrest-e Noskhah-ha*, p. 146.

Provenance: Seventeenth century.
Description: 304 folios of 30.5 × 18 cm, with a written surface of 24 × 13 cm and 25 lines of text per page.
This copy includes most of the *World History*, from the history of the Prophet Muhammad through to the history of India. Its history of Islam matches the variant found in manuscript T_1.

Manuscript T_3: London BL MS. Add. 18,878
Catalogues: Shiraiwa, 'Rashid al-Din', no. 34; Browne, 'Suggestions', no. 3; Monzavi, *Fehrest*, vol. 6, p. 4134 no. 42524; Rieu, *Catalogue of the Persian Manuscripts*, vol. 1, p. 79.
Provenance: Dated 2 January 1819 (5 *Rabiʿ I* 1234).
Description: 164 folios of 24 × 15 cm, with a written surface of 15.5 × 9 cm and 11 lines of text per page.
This is a defective copy from manuscript T_1, including the histories of China, Europe and India, with spaces left for illustrations. Rieu dates it to September 1828, reading the colophon on 164a as 1244 instead of 1234.

Manuscript T_4: London BL MS. Or. 1786
Catalogues: Shiraiwa, 'Rashid al-Din', no. 41; Browne, 'Suggestions', no. 6; Monzavi, *Fehrest*, vol. 6, p. 4134 no. 42529; Rieu, *Catalogue of the Persian Manuscripts*, vol. 3, p. 883.
Provenance: Nineteenth century. Later in the collection of Henry Miers Elliot, and purchased from his son by the British Museum in 1878.
Description: 167 folios of 25.5 × 15.5 cm, with a written surface of 16 × 9.5 cm and 11 lines of text per page.
This is a defective copy from manuscript T_1, including the histories of China, Europe and India, with spaces left for illustrations.

Manuscript T_{11}: Manchester John Rylands Library MS. 406
Catalogues: Shiraiwa, 'Rashid al-Din', no. 32; Browne, 'Suggestions', no. 16; Kerney, *Bibliotheca Lindesiana*, p. 166.
Publications: Melville, 'Rashīd al-Dīn and the *Shāhnāmeh*'.
Description: 190 folios of 27.5 × 16 cm and 17 lines of text per page.
This seems to be a late abridged version of the *World History*, based on

a manuscript containing Hafez-e Abru's revised version of the pre-Islamic history as found in manuscripts S_1–S_9. As Charles Melville has documented, it shares several features with that text, which has recently been published as if it were Rashid al-Din's own.[63] However, this manuscript mentions Mirkhwand's *Rawzat al-Safa*, proving it could not have been assembled earlier than the fifteenth century.

The υ Group: Manuscript Produced in British India

These manuscripts are copied from various source manuscripts and, in some instances, multiple source manuscripts. For the most part, the source manuscripts, when known, have not been available for study and are therefore catalogued in the unallocated χ group. These manuscripts bear witness to the British interest in learning about the people of India and the broader Persianate world more than they suggest an interest in preserving or reproducing Rashid al-Din's work for its own sake. However, as the source manuscripts are often difficult to access or are lost, they can provide some evidence for the state of those earlier copies.

Manuscript U_1: London BL MS. Or. 2007
Catalogues: Shiraiwa, 'Rashid al-Din', no. 37; Browne, 'Suggestions', no. 5; Monzavi, *Fehrest*, vol. 6, p. 4134 no. 42527; Rieu, *Catalogue of the Persian Manuscripts*, vol. 3, pp. 822–3.
Provenance: Copied for Henry Miers Elliot before 1850. Later in the collections of William Morley and F. P. Buller. Sold to the British Museum by Revd Lettsom Henry Elliot in 1878.
Description: 122 folios of 27.5 × 21.5 cm, with a written surface of 21.5 × 13.5 cm and 15 lines of text per page.
This is a hybrid manuscript, containing passages from the history of India from the *World History* copied from the Lucknow and Kolkata manuscripts (manuscripts X_3 and P_{21}). As the former of these is lost and the latter has not been available for study, this manuscript can be an important textual witness for future editions, particularly of the history of India (section II.L in Appendix A). The portion copied from the Lucknow manuscript (folios 5–97) gives the Persian version of the history of India, including the refutation of metempsychosis. It contains space for twenty-six images, with a note

in pencil next to the first reading, 'in these and all other vacant spaces pictures are given in the original'. Additional marginalia note the difference between the Persian and Arabic versions of the history of India, almost certainly added by Morley (see also manuscript U_2). The portions copied from the Kolkata manuscript include a fragment of the history of India (folios 99–107) and excerpts on India taken from the history of the Ghaznavids and Isma'ilis (folios 111–22).

According to notes found in the manuscript in William Morley's hand, Henry Miers Elliot sent these two portions of the *World History* to Morley in 1850, while Morley was preparing an edition of Rashid al-Din's history of India. The resulting collated text (manuscript U_2) includes the sigla C and L for the Kolkata and Lucknow manuscripts, evidently based on the text conveyed in this manuscript. It was probably Morley who had the two fragments bound together, along with letters (folios 2–4, 108–9) pertaining to Elliot's time on the Jhelum River in 1851. The resulting book includes Elliot's bookplate, indicating that Morley considered it to be Elliot's property even while he was having it bound. Despite this, the book was purchased at the sale of Morley's estate by Williams and Norgate and later sold to Frederick Pole Buller, a pensioner of the Bengal Civil Service. Somehow it made its way back to the Elliot family, as it was among the manuscripts sold to the British Museum by Elliot's son, the Revd Lettsom Henry Elliot, in 1878.

Manuscript U_2: London BL MS. I.O. Islamic 3628
Catalogues: Shiraiwa, 'Rashid al-Din', no. 39; Ethé, *Catalogue of the Persian Manuscripts*, vol. 2, no. 3004.
Provenance: Created by William Morley after 1850.
Description: 322 folios of 33.5 × 21 cm, with a written surface of 27.5 × 14 cm and 15 lines of text per page, bound with 31 folios of notes and correspondences in various formats.
This is Morley's edited text of the history of India, assembled from four Persian manuscripts (those catalogued here as M_2, N_2, P_{21} and X_3, the latter two transmitted through U_1) and the Arabic of manuscript R_1a. The Persian text appears on the 'b' side of folios, with the corresponding Arabic on facing 'a' sides, plus numerous marginal and interlineal notes indicating manuscript

variants and the Sanskrit originals of technical terms transliterated into the Persian text.

Folios 323–41 of this manuscript contains a collection of notes and correspondences pertaining to Morley's work on the *World History*, including his autograph draft of the letter he sent to the Royal Asiatic Society identifying manuscripts R_1a and R_1b as two parts of one manuscript.[64] Folios 355–65 provide an English abstract of the *World History* in one column, with a second column left blank for the corresponding Persian or Arabic headers. The order of this abstract matches that of the Arabic copy R_1. The final folio (366) includes a fold-out sketch of Muhammad's night journey, copied from manuscript R_1b, folio 55a.

Manuscript U_3: London BL MS. Or. 1684
Catalogues: Shiraiwa, 'Rashid al-Din', no. 35; Browne, 'Suggestions', no. 4; Monzavi, *Fehrest*, vol. 6, p. 4134 no. 42526; Rieu, *Catalogue of the Persian Manuscripts*, vol. 3, p. 882.
Provenance: From the collection of Henry Miers Elliot. Sold to the British Museum by Revd Lettsom Henry Elliot in 1878.
Description: 249 folios of 31.5 × 19.5 cm, with a written surface of 22 × 12.5 cm and 17 lines of text per page.
This is a partial and disordered copy of the *World History*, probably copied for Henry Miers Elliot during his service in India. Its contents do not match any single known manuscript, but it more closely resembles the o group, rather than the π. It is one of few extant manuscripts that contain the complete histories of the Khwarazmshahs and Salghurids (sections II.E–F in Appendix A). Marginal notes in these sections (folios 163b and 183b) note lacunae in the text of manuscript M_2.

Folios 4–19a contain the beginning of the history of the Ghaznavids but then the manuscript transitions abruptly to the history of the Franks and of India, the last of which is incomplete. It then resumes the Ghaznavid history on folio 30a where it had broken off eleven folios earlier and carries the text into the history of the Isma'ilis, which is incomplete and disordered. All this suggests a source manuscript that was already highly defective.

Manuscript U₄: London BL MS. Or. 1958
Catalogues: Shiraiwa, 'Rashid al-Din', no. 36; Browne, 'Suggestions', no. 7; Monzavi, *Fehrest*, vol. 6, p. 4134 no. 42525; Rieu, *Catalogue of the Persian Manuscripts*, vol. 3, p. 883.
Provenance: Nineteenth-century copy, in the collection of Henry Miers Elliot. Sold to the British Museum by Revd Lettsom Henry Elliot in 1878.
Description: 137 folios of 22.5 × 14 cm, with a written surface of 17.5 × 9.5 cm and 11 lines of text per page.

This is an abstract of the *World History*, as indicated in a note on folio 1a. It contains a list of contents for sections of the work out of order.

Manuscript U₅: Cambridge University Library MS. Or. 1577
Catalogues: Shiraiwa, 'Rashid al-Din', no. 46; Browne, 'Suggestions', no. 26.
Provenance: From the library of Henry George Raverty. Bequeathed to Cambridge University Library by Reynold Alleyne Nicholson in 1945.
Description: 211 folios of 28 × 21.5 cm, with a written surface of 25 × 13.5 cm and 17 lines of text per page (folios 1–44) or 22.5 × 14 cm and 15 lines of text per page (folios 49–211).

This is referred to as 'the Raverty manuscript' in nineteenth-century British scholarship. It is another hybrid copy of the *World History*, evidently copied from two different sources. Folios 1–44 contain the history of the Turks and of China (sections II.H–I in Appendix A), with spaces left for illustrations of Chinese emperors. The source manuscript is not indicated. Folios 49–211 contain the history of the Ghaznavids, Saljuqs and Khwarazmshahs (sections II.C–E). A note on folio 49 indicates that the history of the Ghaznavids was copied from 'Ms. 14 of the A.S. Bengal', namely, manuscript P_{21}. The consistency of format throughout the latter sections of this manuscript suggests that the histories of the Saljuqs and Khwarazmshahs were also copied from the same source. These sections appear in the correct order here, even though in manuscript P_{21} the history of the Ghaznavids has been moved between those of Europe and India. Someone has compared the text to that of manuscript N_2, noting among other things where lacunae occur in that manuscript and providing a concordance correlating the folios of the two manuscripts.

According to a note by Edward G. Browne between the back flyleaves, Henry George Raverty donated this manuscript to the Trustees of the

E. J. W. Gibb Memorial Fund. In August 1945, R. A. Nicholson bequeathed the manuscript to Cambridge University Library. A copy of a letter dated 12 December 1949 from an unnamed librarian to Professor A. J. Arberry of Pembroke College has been inserted inside the last flyleaf suggesting that Nicholson's bequest was in error. According to the librarian, the book was still the property of the Gibb Memorial Trust, but that the Trust might be petitioned to allow the book to remain in the Library collection, as it had already been accessioned and stamped. The Trust evidently agreed to this, as indicated in a marginal note added later.

Manuscript U_6: London BL MS. Or. 2062, folios 24–59
Catalogues: Shiraiwa, 'Rashid al-Din', no. 40; Browne, 'Suggestions', no. 8; Rieu. *Catalogue of the Persian Manuscripts* vol. 3, p. 1057.
Provenance: From the collection of Henry Miers Elliot, and purchased by the British Library from his son.
Description: 36 folios of 22 × 14 cm, with a written surface of 17–18 × 8 cm and 11 lines of text per page.
This is a copy of various excerpts from the *World History*, mostly from the history of India. They are included among a compilation of excerpts assembled by Henry Miers Elliot.

Other Manuscripts of Rashid al-Din's Historical Writings

The χ Group: Uncategorised Manuscripts

Manuscript X_1: Paris BnF MS. Persan 68
Catalogues: Shiraiwa, 'Rashid al-Din', no. 2; Browne, 'Suggestions', no. 19; Blochet, *Catalogue des Manuscrits Persans*, vol. 1, p. 203 no. 256; Richard, *Catalogue des Manuscrits Persans*, vol. 1, pp. 97–8.
Provenance: First half of the fourteenth century. Inscribed in 1462 by ʿAla b. Husayn b. ʿAli, whose seal appears multiple times in the manuscript.
Description: 121 folios of 34 × 25.5 cm, with a written surface of 27 × 17 cm and 27 lines of text per page.
This is a very early manuscript, which played a uniquely important role in raising the awareness of European scholars to Rashid al-Din's work. It is fragmentary, breaking off near the beginning of the year-by-year account at the

end of the history of Chinggis Khan.⁶⁵ The last line of text has been squeezed to fit on the page, suggesting that the source manuscript may have already been fragmentary and the scribe worked to fit its final words onto the end of the last folio of this copy. Numerous headers are marked in large black lettering simply as *dastan* or *qism*, without the full text of the headers. The table of contents at the beginning of the work is similarly incomplete, containing only the skeleton of the contents of the *World History*. In this fragmentary state, all that can be said is that this is probably an idiosyncratic rendition of an early version of the *Blessed History*. It lacks textual additions that appear in the β, δ and ε recensions, while the headers that it gives for the family trees of the pre-Chinggisid Mongols do not conform to any known recension.

Antoine Galland sent this manuscript from Istanbul to Paris; it was received by the royal library in 1686 and subsequently translated into French by the younger François Pétis de la Croix, chair of Arabic at the Collège Royal from 1692. The latter's father prepared the first European study of Chinggis Khan before his own death in 1695, though that study was only published fifteen years later.⁶⁶ By 1722, the elder Pétis de la Croix's study had been translated into English, retaining the French transliteration of Chinggis as 'Genghis' and thereby initiating the use of that spelling in English scholarship.⁶⁷ In a letter of 21 March 1701, Galland mentions that 'the history of Chinggis Khan is in Paris in the hands of M. Le Grand, at the home of the Abbot of Estrées, rue Sainte-Anne'.⁶⁸ As part of the French royal collection, it bears the ownership seal of Napoleon I (1804–14).

Manuscript X_2: Tehran Golestan Palace Library MS. 2254
Catalogues: Shiraiwa, 'Rashid al-Din', no. 27; DENA no. 74989; Atabay, *Fehrest-e Tarikh*, pp. 88–9 no. 40, with three colour plates.
Publications: Marek, Knížková and Forman, *Tschingis-Chan und sein Reich*.
Provenance: Produced at the court of Akbar the Great and dated 15 May 1596 (28 *Ramadan* 1004). Brought to Tehran in 1739 after Nader Shah looted the Mughal imperial library.
Description: Surviving manuscript contains 304 of an original 550 folios of 39 × 29 cm, with a written surface ranging between 31.5–35.5 × 21–24 cm and 25 lines of text per page.
This is almost certainly the illustrated copy of the *Blessed History* that Abu'l

Fadl lists among the great works illustrated for his patron Akbar the Great.[69] Large numbers of its painted pages have been dispersed into collections around the world. This manuscript invites further study.

Manuscript X₃: The Lost Lucknow Manuscript
Catalogue: Shiraiwa, 'Rashid al-Din', no. 53.
Publications: Elliot, *History of India*, vol. 3, pp. 16–17; Elliot, *Bibliographical Index*, pp. 18–19.
Description: 105 folios with 35 lines of text per page.
This manuscript was once part of the royal collection of the Nawabs of Awadh at Lucknow, but it was presumably lost in the great fire that consumed that collection during the rebellion of 1857. Elliot describes it as a lavishly illustrated fragment of the *World History*, containing the history of the Ghaznavids, Saljuqs, Khwarazmians and part of the history of the caliphate (sections II.C–E and part of B as described in Appendix A). Part of it has been reproduced in manuscript U₁.

Manuscript X₄: Tashkent Abu Rayhon Beruni Institute MS. 1643
Catalogues: Shiraiwa, 'Rashid al-Din', no. 10; Semenov, *Majmu'a-ye Noskhah-ha* p. 2 no. 9; Semenov *Sobranie Vostochnykh Rukopisei*, vol. 1, p. 22 no. 22.
Provenance: Sixteenth century.
Description: 39 folios of 27 × 20 cm.
This manuscript has not been consulted for this study.

Manuscript X₅: University of Tehran Faculty of Literature MS. 35-j
Catalogues: Shiraiwa, 'Rashid al-Din', no. 29; DENA no. 74970; Monzavi, *Fehrest*, vol. 6, p. 4134 no. 42522; Daneshpazhuh, *Fehrest-e Noskhah-ha*, p. 147.
Provenance: Seventeenth century.
Description: 36 folios of 24 × 18 cm, with a written surface of 18 × 14 cm and 19 lines of text per page.
This manuscript contains Rashid al-Din's history of the Ghaznavids (section II.C in Appendix A).

APPENDIX B | 265

Manuscript X_6: Tashkent Abu Rayhon Beruni Institute MS. 1
Catalogues: Shiraiwa, 'Rashid al-Din', no. 31; Semenov, *Majmu'a-ye Noskhah-ha* p. 2 no. 10; Semenov *Sobranie Vostochnykh Rukopisei*, vol. 1, pp. 22–4 no 24.
Provenance: Eighteenth century.
Description: 369 folios of 29.5 × 19 cm.
This manuscript has not been consulted for this study.

Manuscript X_7: Tehran Malek MS. 3768
Provenance: Nineteenth century. Acquired by the Malek Museum from a 'Farahani' in 2014.
Publication: Digitised online at: http://malekmuseum.org, but no stable url can be determined.
Description: 123 folios with 14 lines of text per page.
This manuscript is a series of six disordered fragments, five of which contain various portions of the *Blessed History*. (The sixth is a portion of the *Rashidi Collection*.) Selections of these portions have been digitised online, but this is not enough material with which to assign this manuscript to a recension.

Manuscript X_8: Tehran Malek 4164
Catalogue: DENA 74977.
Provenance: Copied by Aqa Baba Shahmirzadeh b. Muhammad Mahdi and dated 1854/5 (AH 1271).
Publication: digitised online at: http://malekmuseum.org, but no stable url can be determined.
Description: 324 folios of 42 × 26.5 cm and 43 lines of text per page.
Only a few pages of this manuscript are available for view on the website of the Malek Museum. It is apparently bound with Hafez-e Abru's continuation. It may therefore belong to the λ recension, or it may be related to the o group or to manuscript K_3.

Manuscript X_9: Tehran Farhad Motamed MS. 30
Catalogues: Shiraiwa, 'Rashid al-Din', no. 68; Monzavi, *Fehrest*, vol. 6, p. 4134 no. 42528; DENA no. 74976
Provenance: Nineteenth century.

This manuscript has not been consulted for this study.

Manuscript X_{10}: Munich Bayerische Staatsbibliothek ms. 208
Catalogues: Shiraiwa, 'Rashid al-Din', no. 64; Browne, 'Suggestions', no. 24; Aumer, *Die persischen Handschriften*, pp. 71–2.
Description: 298 folios of 24.5 × 18 cm and 22 lines of text per page.
This is a highly defective copy of the *Collected Histories*, containing fragments of the pre-Islamic and Isma'ili histories and the histories of China, Europe and India, and then, beginning on folio 185, a portion of the *Blessed History* from the beginning of the history of Turkic tribes to near the end of the chapter on Chinggis Khan. Illustrations have been started in the section on China (folios 124–43), but these have been left incomplete. A coarse later hand wielding a writing pen has drawn faces over some of these, as well as various images of animals and anthrozoomorphic figures.

Manuscript X_{11}: Qom Mar'ashi Najafi Library MS. 3586
Catalogue: DENA 74978.
Description: 290 folios.
This manuscript has not been consulted for this study.

Manuscripts of Rashid al-Din's Historical Works

Table B.1 *Concordance of manuscripts of Rashid al-Din's historical works, by collection*

City	Collection	Inventory number	Sigla
Cambridge	Cambridge University Library	Or. 1577	U_5
Edinburgh	Edinburgh University Library	Or. 20	$R_1 b$
Geneva	Nasser Khalili	727	$R_1 a$
Istanbul	Topkapı Saray Muzesi	AIII.2935	S_{21}
		B.282	G_{21}, M_{11}, O_{21}
		H.1653	S_1
		H.1654	P_2
		R.1518	Z_{12}
	Süleimaniye	Aya Sofya 3034	H_1
		Damad Ibrahim 919	G_{22}, M_{12}, O_{22}
		Hekimoğlu 'Ali Paşa 703	E_{13}

Kolkata	Asiatic Society	14	P_{21}
		D31	D_{21}
		D32	D_{22}
Lahore	University of the Punjab Library	Pe I 55/2035	S_8
London	British Library	Add. 7628	G_{13}, M_2, O_{12}
		Add. 16,688	K_1
		Add. 18,878	T_3
		IO Islamic 1784	D_2
		IO Islamic 3524	E_3, N_2, P_{12}
		IO Islamic 3628	U_2
		IO Islamic 4710	I_3
		Or. 1684	U_3
		Or. 1786	T4
		Or. 1958	U_4
		Or. 2007	U_1
		Or. 2062	U_6
		Or. 2885	L_{14}
		Or. 2927	D_{31}
	Royal Asiatic Society	Arabic 27	R_3
Lucknow	Royal Library	[Lost]	X_3
Manchester	John Rylands Library	364	R_4
		406	T_{11}
Mashhad	Astan-e Qods	4101	E_{15}, Z_3
Munich	Bayerische Staatsbibliothek	Cod. Pers. 207	B_1, I_2
		Cod. Pers. 208	X_{10}
Oxford	Bodleian Library	Arab b. 1	R_2
		Elliot 377	K_3
Paris	Bibliothèque nationale de France	Persan 68	X_1
		Supplément persan 160	S_2a
		Supplément persan 209	L_{12}
		Supplément persan 1113	L_{11}
		Supplément persan 1364	S_{22}c
		Supplément persan 1365	S_{22}b
		Supplément persan 1561	I_1
		Supplément persan 1643	E_{12}
		Supplément persan 2004	S_2b
Qom	Mar'ashi Najafi Library	3586	X_{11}
Rampur	Reza Library	P. 1819	L_{15}
		P. 1820	D_1
		P. 1821	T_1
St Petersburg	Institute of Oriental Manuscripts	C374	S_9
		C376	E_{14}
		C802	S_4
		D66	L_{13}
		E5	S_6

St Petersburg	National Library of Russia	Chanykov 62	E_5, N_4, P_{14}
		Dorn 289	L_{21}
		PNS 46	G_{12}, M_1, O_{11}
		PNS 47	E_6, N_5, P_{15}
		PNS 57	S_7
		PNS 58	S_5
Tashkent	Abu Rayhon Beruni Institute	1	X_6
		2	H_2
		1620	Z_1
		1643	X_4
Tehran	Farhad Motamed	30	X_9
	Golestan Palace	2234	D_{11}
		2254	X_2
		2256	E_2, N_1, P_{11}
	Majlis	1108	E_{16}
		2294	E_{11}
		8734	E_4, N_3, P_{13}
		9078	S_3
	Malek	3768	X_7
		4164	X_8
	Melli	F-1569	G_{14}
		F-1606	E_7, N_6, P_{16}
	University of Tehran Faculty of Literature	35-j	X_5
		76-b	T_2
Toronto	Aga Khan Museum	AKM517	Z_2
Vienna	Österreichische Nationalbibliothek	mixt. 326	K_2
Washington	Art and History Trust	22	S_{11}

Notes

1. Most recently on these, see Gonnella et al., *The Diez Albums*.
2. Ashtiani, 'Noskhah-ha-ye masur', p. 40 no. 7.
3. Browne, 'Suggestions'; Shiraiwa, 'Rashid al-Din'.
4. Most of the manuscripts catalogued here can be found in Monzavi, *Fehrest*, vol. 6, pp. 4132–5; Derayati, *Fehrestvare*, vol. 3, pp. 547–8.
5. Kamola, 'Untangling the Chaghadaids'.
6. Schmitz and Desai, *Mughal and Persian Paintings*, pp. 171–9; Rice, 'Mughal Interventions'.
7. See, for example, the enthronements of Temur Oljeitu and Jochi, reproduced in Rice, 'Mughal Interventions', p. 154 fig. 5 and p. 159 fig. 8.
8. Schmitz and Desai, *Mughal and Persian Paintings*, p. 174.
9. Basu, *Oudh*, pp. 16–21, 68–70.

10. Kamola, 'Untangling the Chaghadaids', under section, 'The Second Revision'.
11. Shiraiwa, 'Rashīd al-Dīn's Primary Sources', p. 39.
12. My thanks to Sheila Blair and Elaine Wright for discussing this matter with me. Blair, 'Illustrating History', p. 3 and n. 16, with reference to Wright, *The Look of the Book*, ch. 2, also corrects Shiraiwa's assertion.
13. This manuscript breaks off after Rashid al-Din, *Jamiʻ al-Tawarikh*, p. 493 line 1, while the other three break off after *ḥāzr kard*, found at Rashid al-Din, *Jamiʻ al-Tawarikh*, p. 495 line 10.
14. This manuscript ends at the equivalent of Rashid al-Din, *Jamiʻ al-Tawarikh*, p. 490.
15. The image of Ogedei and, presumably, Boraqchin or Toregene, has been reproduced by Semenov, *Sobranie Vostochnykh Rukopisei*, pl. XIVb. The images of Ogedei and Hulegu have been reproduced by Poliakova and Rakhimova, *Miniatura i Literatura Vostoka*, pll. 6 and 7.
16. These are Berlin Staatsbibliothek MS. Diez A folio 70, pages 5, 10, 11, 20, 21 and 23; Istanbul TSM MS. H.2153 folios 23b, 53b, 148b and 166a.
17. This should correspond to folios 1–164, 169, (one missing folio), 170, 165–6, 176–7, 167–8, (one folio missing), 258–81, 173–257, 282–310, 317–18, (two folios missing), 319–22, 311–16, 323–46.
18. Elaine Wright, personal communication. See also Wright, *The Look of the Book*, figs. 33, 35 for images from a comparable manuscript dated 1365.
19. Jeff Spurr, personal correspondence.
20. Folio 254b is blank, like Z_2 page 327; folio 264a on the sons of Chaghadai matches Z_2 page 335; folio 493b line 3 shows a lacuna equivalent to two folios, matching the lacuna after page 635 of Z_2.
21. The text breaks off after *sārbānān* at Rashid al-Din, *Jamiʻ al-Tawarikh*, p. 1538 line 7.
22. For an example, see Richard, *Splendeurs Persanes*, p. 70 no. 32.
23. Flügel, *Die arabischen, persischen, und türkischen Handschriften*, p. xii. My thanks to Katharina Kaska for drawing this to my attention.
24. These lacunae correspond to Rashid al-Din, *Jamiʻ al-Tawarikh*, pp. 285–93, 378–95, 538–863 and 1085–8.
25. Kamola, 'Rashīd al-Dīn', pp. 89–92; Brack, 'Mediating Sacred Kingship', pp. 137–46; Kamola, 'Beyond History'.
26. See Kamola, 'Untangling the Chaghadaids'.
27. Francis Richard, personal communication.

28. So designated by Ettinghausen, 'An Illuminated Manuscript', p. 42. For an example from this manuscript, see Richard, *Splendeurs Persanes*, p. 76.
29. For a re-evaluation of this style as a 'neo-classical' revival in line with Shahrukh's religio-political ideologies, see Gruber, 'Questioning the "Classical"', pp. 9–11.
30. Shiraiwa, 'Sur la date', p. 39, establishes the correct order of folios.
31. Francis Richard, personal communication.
32. On the Shah 'Abbas donation, see Canby, *Shah 'Abbas*, pp. 120–3.
33. Folios 157a, 340a, 524a, 623a and 728a.
34. Folio 410b. A second note has been effaced next to the *bismallah* at the beginning of the general preface on folio 404b. It is illegible, but enough remains to suggest that it named someone other than Bayshonghor.
35. Baysonghor's seals appear on folios 237a, 272b, 307b, 404b, 410b, 524a and 623a, the last two beside the seal of Shahrokh.
36. Browne, 'Suggestions'.
37. Found on folios 672a, 678a and 700b; cf. Rashid al-Din, *Jami' al-Tawarikh*, pp. 1306, 1311 and 1421.
38. See, for example, folios 487, 492, 497 and 538, compared with G_{12}, folios 130, 133, 125.
39. See De Nicola, 'The Travels'.
40. The text breaks off at the equivalent of Rashid al-Din, *Jami' al-Tawarikh*, p. 1118.
41. Çağman and Tanındı, 'Remarks on Some Manuscripts', p. 140.
42. Brewster, *The Edinburgh Encyclopaedia*, pp. 719-720.
43. The text breaks off at the equivalent of Rashid al-Din, *Jami' al-Tawarikh*, p. 745.
44. For example, by Inal, 'The Fourteenth-Century Miniatures', p. 34.
45. Çağman and Tanındı, 'Remarks on Some Manuscripts', p. 140.
46. My thanks to Deborah Schlein for attempting to gain access to this manuscript during her research visit to Kolkata. The manuscript was on exhibit at the time and thus unavailable for study.
47. London BL MS. IO Islamic 3628 fol. 354a.
48. Morley and Forbes, 'Letters'. In 1841, Morley was hopeful of helping Quatremère prepare a full edition and translation of the *Collected Histories*, a project that was never completed: Wynn, 'Proceedings', p. viii; Morley, 'A Letter', p. 272.
49. Morley and Forbes, 'Letters', p. 34 and n. 1.
50. Blair, *A Compendium of Chronicles*.
51. Compare Blair, *A Compendium of Chronicles*, pll. 258b and 282a.
52. Morley and Forbes, 'Letters', p. 40.

53. Arberry, *The Library of A. Chester Beatty*, p. 17. My special thanks go to Alasdair Watson of the Bodleian Library for tracking down these folios among the yet unpublished collections there.
54. Bada'uni, *Muntakhab al-Tawarikh*, vol. 2 p. 269; Bada'uni, *The Muntakhab-ut-Tawārīkh*, p. 384.
55. The difference between the *Majma' al-Tawarikh* and this recension of Rashid al-Din's *Jami' al-Tawarikh* has been demonstrated by Rosen, *Les Manuscrits Persans*, pp. 52–111 no. 7.
56. In fact, the original *rashidi* fragment around which this second reconstruction was made may be from the same manuscript that provided some of the original folios of manuscript S_1: Ghiasian, *Lives of the Prophets*, pp. 81–4.
57. Çağman and Tanındı, 'Remarks on Some Manuscripts', pp. 136–9. A note on folio 410a refers to Choban posthumously, suggesting that the book was still owned by one of his descendants.
58. Dorn, 'Über die aus dem Nachlasse des wirkl. Staatsrathes Graf'.
59. Salemann, 'Das Asiatische Museum'; Yastrebova and Azad, 'Reflections on an Orientalist'.
60. For this and more information on Kuhn, see Munis Khorezmiĭ, *Firdaws al-Iqbāl*, pp. li–lii, with additional bibliography in Russian.
61. The watermark on these pages is identical to that found on Princeton Library MS. Garrett 3382Y, which is dated to 1864.
62. Rashid al-Din [sic], *Tarikh-e Iran va Islam*.
63. Melville, 'Rashīd al-Dīn and the *Shāhnāmeh*'.
64. Later published in Morley and Forbes, 'Letters'.
65. The text ends at the equivalent of Rashid al-Din, *Jami' al-Tawarikh*, p. 563 line 5.
66. Pétis de la Croix, *Histoire*. The younger Pétis de la Croix's original translation has never been published, nor is its location known.
67. Pétis de la Croix, *The History*.
68. Ormont, *Missions*, vol. 1, p. 202.
69. Abu'l-Fadl, *'Ain-i Ākbari*, p. 115.

Bibliography

Persian and Arabic names have been alphabetised according to the element most commonly in use, though this inevitably creates some inconsistency. Thus, 'Rashid al-Din Fadl Allah al-Hamadani' and 'Hamd Allah Mustaufi', but 'Wassaf, Sharaf al-Din 'Abd Allah'. When multiple editions of a work are cited, they are here distinguished between editions used for reference to the text (which are listed under the name of the author) and those that are cited primarily in discussions on reception (which are listed under the editor or translator's name). The only abbreviations used in this bibliography are those standard for *the Encyclopaedia of Islam* (*EI²*, *EI³*) and the *Encyclopedia Iranica* (*EIr*).

Abdullaeva, Firuza, 'The *Shahnameh* in Persian Literary History', in Barbara Brend and Charles Melville (eds), *Epic of the Persian Kings: the Art of Ferdowsi's Shahnameh* (London: I. B. Tauris, 2010), pp. 16–22.

Abdullah, Sayyid, *A Descriptive Catalogue of the Persian, Urdu, and Arabic Manuscripts in the Punjab University Library, Volume 1: Persian Manuscripts. Fasciculus 1: History.* (Lahore: Punjab University Library, 1942).

Abka'i-Khavari, Manijeh, 'Schach im Iran', *Iranica Antiqua* 35(4) (2002): 329–59.

Abu'l-Fadl, *'Ain-i Akbari: Volume 1*, trans. H. Blochmann (Calcutta: Baptist Mission Press, 1873).

Adler, Marcus Nathan, *The Itinerary of Benjamin of Tudela: Critical Text, Translation and Commentary* (New York: Philipp Feldheim, 1907).

Afshar, Iraj, 'Rashid al-Din Fazl Allah va Yazd', in Seyyed Hossein Nasr, Mojtaba Minovi, Manochehr Mortezavi and Iraj Afshar (eds), *Majmu'a-ye Khatabe-ha-ye Tahqiqi dar Bare-ye Rashid al-Din Fazl Allah Hamadani* (Tehran: Daneshgah-ye Tehran, 1971), pp. 25–32.

Afshar, Iraj, *Akhbar-e Moghulan (650–683) dar anbaneh-ye Mulla-ye Qotb* (Qom: Mar'ashi, 2010).

Afshar, Irej [sic], 'The Autograph Copy of Rashīd-al-dīn's vaqfnāmeh', *Central Asiatic Journal* 14(1/3) (1970): 5–13.

Aigle, Denise (ed.), *L'Iran Face à la Domination Mongole* (Tehran: Institut Français de Recherche en Iran, 1997).

Aigle, Denise, 'Le grand jasaq de Gengis-khan, l'empire, la culture mongole et la sharī'a', *Journal of the Economic and Social History of the Orient* 47(1) (2004): 30–79.

Aigle, Denise, *The Mongol Empire Between Myth and Reality: Studies in Anthropological History* (Leiden: Brill, 2015).

Akasoy, Anna, Charles Burnett, and Ronit Yoeli-Tlalim (eds), *Rashīd al-Dīn: Agent and Mediator of Cultural Exchanges in Ilkhanid Iran* (London: Warburg Institute, 2013).

Alizada, Abdulkerim Ali Oğlu (ed.), *Jami' al-Tawarikh: Volume 2, Part 1* (Moscow: Izdatel'stvo Nauka, 1980).

Alizada, Abdulkerim Ali Oğlu (ed.), *Jami' al-Tawarikh: Volume 3* (Baku: Azerbayjan SSR Elmler Akademiyasy Neshriyyaty, 1957).

Allsen, Thomas T., *Mongol Imperialism: the Policies of the Grand Qan Möngke in China, Russia and the Islamic Lands, 1251–1259* (Berkeley: University of California Press, 1987).

Allsen, Thomas T., 'Biography of a Cultural Broker: Bolad Ch'eng-Hsiang in China and Iran', in Julian Raby and Teresa Fitzherbert (eds), *The Court of the Il-Khans, 1290–1340* (Oxford: Oxford University Press, 1996), pp. 7–22.

Allsen, Thomas T., *Culture and Conquest in Mongol Eurasia* (Cambridge: Cambridge University Press, 2001).

Allsen, Thomas T., 'Sharing Out the Empire: Apportioned Lands under the Mongols', in Anatoly M. Khazanov and André Wink (eds), *Nomads in the Sedentary World* (Richmond: Curzon, 2001).

Ambraseys, N. N. and Charles Melville, *A History of Persian Earthquakes* (Cambridge: Cambridge University Press, 1982).

Amitai, Reuven, 'Wādī 'l-Khaznadār', *EI²*.

Amitai, Reuven, "'Ayn Jālūt revisited', *Tārīḫ* 2 (1992): 119–50.

Amitai, Reuven, 'The Logistics of the Mongol–Mamlūk War, with Special Reference to the Battle of Wādī 'l-Khaznadār', in John H. Pryor (ed.), *Logistics of Warfare in the Age of the Crusades* (Aldershot: Ashgate, 2006), pp. 25–42.

Amitai, Reuven, *Holy War and Rapprochement: Studies in the Relations Between the Mamluk Sultanate and the Mongol Ilkhanate (1260–1335)* (Turnhout: Brepols, 2013).

Amitai, Reuven, 'Rashīd al-Dīn as a Historian of the Mamluks', in Anna Akasoy, Charles Burnett and Ronit Yoeli-Tlalim (eds), *Rashīd al-Dīn: Agent and Mediator of Cultural Exchanges in Ilkhanid Iran* (London: Warburg Institute, 2013), pp. 71–88.

Amitai, Reuven and Michal Biran (eds), *Mongols, Turks and Others: Eurasian Nomads and the Sedentary World* (Leiden: Brill, 2005).

Amitai-Preiss, Reuven, *Mongols and Mamluks: the Mamluk–Ilkhānid War, 1260–81* (Cambridge: Cambridge University Press, 1968).

Amitai-Preiss, Reuven, 'New Material from the Mamluk Sources for the Biography of Rashīd al-Dīn', in Julian Raby and Teresa Fitzherbert (eds), *The Court of the Il-khans, 1290–1340* (Oxford: Oxford University Press, 1996), pp. 23–37.

Anvar, 'Abd Allah, *Fehrest-e Nosakh-e Khatti-ye Ketabhaneh-ye Melli: Volume 4* (Tehran: Vezarat-e Farhang va Hunar, 1973).

'Aqili, Hajji ibn Nizam, *Athar al-Wuzara': az Kutub-e Mu'allifah dar Nimah-ye Dovvom-e Qarn-e Nohom-e Hijri*, ed. Mir Jalal al-Din Husayni Urmavi Muhaddis (Tehran: Entesharat-e Ittila'at, 1985).

Arberry, A. J., *The Library of A. Chester Beatty: a Catalogue of the Persian Manuscripts and Miniatures: Volume 1* (Dublin: Hodges Figgis, 1959).

Arends, A. K. (trans.), *Rashid-ad-Din: Sbornik Letopisey: Volume 2* (Moscow: Akademii Nauk SSSR, 1946).

Aryan, Amirkhani et al., 'Investigating the Architectural Heritage of Ilkhanid Reign (with Particular Reference to Rabe Rashidi)', *International Journal of Academic Research* 2(5) (2010): 268–77.

Ashikaga, Atsuuji, Jitsuzo Tamura and Toshiyuki Etani, *Iran no Rekishi to Gengo* (Kyoto: Kyoto Daigaku, 1968).

Ashtiani, Iqbal, 'Noskhah-ha-ye masur-e *Jami' al-Tawarikh*-e Rashidi', *Yadgar* 2(3) (1945): 33–42.

Astan-e Qods-e Rezavi, *Fehrest-e Kotob-e Ketabkhaneh-ye Astan-e Qods-e Razavi* (Mashhad: Matba'ah-e Nau Behar, 1987).

Atabay, Badri, *Fehrest-e Tarikh, Safarnameh, Seyahatnameh, Ruznameh, va Jugrafiya-ye Khatti-ye Kitabkhanah-ye Saltanati* (Tehran: Ziba, 1977).

Ateş, Ahmed (ed.), *Cāmi' al-Tavārih. II. Cild, 4. Cüz: Tarikh-e Sultan Yamin al-Daula Mahmud ibn Sabuktagin va Aslaf va Akhlaf-e U* (Ankara: Türk Tarih Basımevı, 1957).

Ateş, Ahmed (ed.), *Cāmi' al-Tavārih. II. Cild, 5. Cüz: Dhikr-e Tarikh-e Al-e Salchuq* (Ankara: Türk Tarih Basımevı, 1960).

Atwood, Christopher, 'Six pre-Chinggisid Genealogies in the Mongol Empire', *Archivum Eurasiae Medii Aevi* 19 (2012): 5–58.
Atwood, Christopher, 'Chikü *Küregen* and the Origins of the Xiningzhou Qonggirads', *Archivum Eurasiae Medii Aevi* 21 (2014/15): 7–26.
Atwood, Christopher, 'Alexander Ja'a Gambo and the Origins of the Image of Jamugha in the Secret History of the Mongols', in Teligeng and Li Jinxiu (eds), *Neilu Ouya Lishi Wenhua Guoji Xueshi Yantaohui Lunwenji* (Höhhot: Inner Mongolia People's Press, 2015).
Atwood, Christopher, 'Pu'a's Boast and Doqolqu's Death: Historiography of a Hidden Scandal in the Mongol Conquest of the Jin', *Journal of Song-Yuan Studies* 45 (2015): 239–78.
Atwood, Christopher, 'The Indictment of Ong Qa'an: the Earliest Reconstructable Mongolian Source on the Rise of Chinggis Khan', *Historical and Philological Studies of China's Western Regions* 9 (2017): 267–302.
Atwood, Christopher, 'Rashīd al-Dīn's *Ghazanid Chronicle* and its Mongolian Sources', in Dashdondog Bayarsaikhan, Timothy May and Christopher Atwood (eds), *New Approaches to Ilkhanid History*, forthcoming.
Aubin, J., 'Le patronage culturel en Iran sous les Ilkhans. Une grande famille de Yazd', *Le Monde Iranien et l'Islam* 3 (1975): 107–18.
Aubin, Jean, *Emirs Mongols et Vizirs Persans dans les Remous de l'Acculturation* (Paris: Association pour l'Avancement des Études Iraniennes, 1995).
Aumer, Joseph, *Die persischen Handschriften der K. Hof- und Staatsbibliothek in München* (Munich: Staatsbibliothek, 1866).
Azhdari, Nur al-Din ibn Muhammad Nuri, *Ghazannameh-ye Manzum*, ed. Mahmud Mudabbiri (Tehran: Afshar, 1991).
Bada'uni, 'Abd al-Qadir b. Mulukshah, *The Muntakhab-ut-Tawārīkh: Volume 2*, trans. W. H. Lowe (Calcutta: Baptist Mission Press, 1898).
Bada'uni, 'Abd al-Qadir b. Muluk Shah, *Muntakhab al-Tawarikh*, ed. Ahmad 'Ali Saheb and Tawfiq Subhani (Tehran: Anjoman-e Asar va Mafakhir-e Farhangi, 2000/1).
Ball, Warwick and Leonard Harrow (eds), *Cairo to Kabul: Afghan and Islamic Studies Presented to Ralph Pindar-Wilson* (London: Melisende, 2002).
Banakati, Abu Sulayman Da'ud, *Rawzat Ula al-Albab fi Ma'rifat al-Tawarikh wa'l-Ansab*, ed. Ja'far Shi'ar (Tehran: Silsila Entesharat-e Anjoman Asar Melli, 1969).
Bar Hebraeus, *The Chronography of Gregory Abû'l Faraj*, trans. E. S. Wallis Budge (London: Oxford University Press, 1932).

Barthold, Vasilii, *An Historical Geography of Iran* (Princeton, NJ: Princeton University Press, 1984).

Bartol'd, Vasilii, *Turkestan Down to the Mongol Invasion* (London: Luzac, 1968).

Bartol'd, Vasilii, 'E. Blochet, *Introduction à l'histoire des Mongols de Fadl Allah Rashid ed-Din*', *Mir Islama* 1.1 (1912), republished in *Sochineniya, Vol. VIII: Raboty po Istochnikobedeniyu* (Moscow: Nauka, 1973), pp. 270–310.

Basu, Pernendu, *Oudh and the East India Company, 1785–1801* (Lucknow: Maxwell, 1943).

Bayani, Chirine, 'L'historie secrète des Mongols: une des sources de *Jāme-al-tawārīkh* de Rachīd ad-Dīn', *Acta Orientalia* 37 (1976): 201–12.

Bayani, Mahdi, 'Rasaʾel-e farsi-ye Rashid al-Din Fadl Allah', *Mehr* 8 (1952): 549–52.

Bayarsaikhan, Dashdondog, Timothy May and Christopher Atwood (eds), *New Approaches to Ilkhanid History*, forthcoming.

Baydawi, Nasir al-Din ʿAbd Allah, *Nizam al-Tawarikh*, ed. Mir Hashem Muhaddis (Tehran: Afshar, 2003).

Ben Azzouna, Nourane, 'Rashīd al-Dīn Faḍl Allāh al-Hamadhānī's Manuscript Production Project in Tabriz Reconsidered', in Judith Pfeiffer (ed.), *Politics, Patronage and the Transmission of Knowledge in 13th–15th-Century Tabriz* (Leiden: Brill, 2014), pp. 187–200.

Ben Azzouna, Nourane and Patricia Roger-Puyo, 'The Question of the Formation of Manuscript Production Workshops in Iran According to Rashīd al-Dīn Faḍl Allah al-Hamadhānī's *Majmūʿa Rashīdiyya* in the Bibliothèque nationale de France', *Journal of Islamic Manuscripts* 7 (2016): 152–94.

Berezin, Il'ya Nikolaevich, '"Sbornik" Letopisey: istoriya Mongolov', *Trudy Vostochnago Otdeleniya Imperatorskago Arkheologicheskago Obshchestva* 5 (1858), 7 (1861), 13 (1868), 15 (1888).

Berlekamp, Persis, 'The Limits of Artistic Exchange in Fourteenth-century Tabriz: the Paradox of Rashid al-Din's Book on Chinese Medicine, Part I', *Muqarnas* 27 (2010): 209–50.

Binbaş, İlker Evrim, 'Oğuz Khan Narratives', *EIr*.

Binbaş, İlker Evrim, 'Structure and Function of the Genealogical Tree in Islamic Historiography', in İlker Evrim Binbaş and Nurten Kılıç-Schubel (eds), *Horizons of the World: Festschrift for İsenbike Togan* (Istanbul: Ithaki, 2011), pp. 465–544.

Binbaş, İlker Evrim and Nurten Kılıç-Schubel (eds), *Horizons of the World: Festschrift for İsenbike Togan* (Istanbul: Ithaki, 2011).

Biran, Michal, *Qaidu and the Rise of the Independent Mongol State in Central Asia* (Richmond: Curzon, 1997).

Blair, Sheila, 'Ilkhanid Architecture and Society: an Analysis of the Endowment Deed of the Rabʿ-i Rashīdī', *Iran* 22 (1984): 67–90.

Blair, Sheila, 'A Medieval Persian Builder', *Journal of the Society of Architectural Historians* 45 (1986): 389–95.

Blair, Sheila, 'The Mongol Capital of Sulṭāniyya, "The Imperial"', *Iran* 24 (1986): 139–51.

Blair, Sheila, 'The Epigraphic Program of the Tomb of Uljaytu at Sultaniyya: Meaning in Mongol Architecture', *Islamic Art* 2 (1987): 43–96.

Blair, Sheila, 'The Development of the Illustrated Book in Iran', *Muqarnas* 10 (1993): 266–74.

Blair, Sheila, *A Compendium of Chronicles: Rashid al-Din's Illustrated History of the World* (Oxford: Oxford University Press, 1995).

Blair, Sheila, 'Patterns of Patronage and Production in Ilkhanid Iran', in Julian Raby and Teresa Fitzherbert (eds), *The Court of the Il-Khans, 1290–1340* (Oxford: Oxford University Press, 1996), pp. 39–62.

Blair, Sheila, 'Writing and Illustrating History: Rashīd al-Dīn's *Jāmiʿ al-Tavārīkh*', in Judith Pfeiffer and Manfred Kropp (eds), *Theoretical Approaches to the Transmission and Edition of Oriental Manuscripts* (Beirut: Orient-Institut, 2007), pp. 57–65.

Blair, Sheila, 'Tabriz: International Entrepôt under the Mongols', in Judith Pfeiffer (ed.), *Politics, Patronage and the Transmission of Knowledge in 13th–15th-Century Tabriz* (Leiden: Brill, 2014), pp. 321–56.

Blair, Sheila, *Text and Image in Medieval Persian Art* (Edinburgh: Edinburgh University Press, 2014).

Blair, Sheila, 'Illustrating History: Rashid al-Din and his *Compendium of Chronicles*', *Iranian Studies* 50(6) (2017): 819–42.

Blochet, Edgard, *Catalogue de la Collection de Manuscrits Orientaux – Arabes, Persans et Turcs – Formé par M. Charles Schefer* (Paris: Ernest Leroux, 1900).

Blochet, Edgard, *Catalogue des Manuscrits Persans de la Bibliotheque Nationale* (Paris: Imprimerie Nationale, 1905).

Blochet, Edgard, *Introduction à l'Histoire des Mongols de Fadl Allah Rashid ed-Din* (Leiden: Brill, 1910).

Blochet, Edgard, *Djami el-Tévarikh: Histoire Générale du Monde* (Leiden: Brill, 1911).

Bosworth, C. E., 'Salghurids', *EI²*.

Bosworth, C. E., 'Khwaf', *EI²*.

Boyle, J. A., 'Ibn al-Ṭiqṭaqā and the *Taʾrīkh-i-Jahān-Gushāy* of Juvaynī', *Bulletin of the School of Oriental and African Studies* 14 (1952): 175–7.

Boyle, J. A., 'The Longer Introduction to the "Zij-i ilkhani" of Nasir-ad-din Tusi', *Journal of Semitic Studies* 8(2) (1963): 244–54.

Boyle, J. A. (ed.), *The Cambridge History of Iran, Volume 5: the Saljuq and Mongol Periods* (Cambridge: Cambridge University Press, 1968).

Boyle, J. A., 'Dynastic and Political History of the Il-Khāns', in J. A. Boyle (ed.), *The Cambridge History of Iran, Volume 5: the Saljuq and Mongol Periods* (Cambridge: Cambridge University Press, 1968), pp. 303–421.

Boyle, J. A., 'The Burial Place of the Great Khan Ögedei', *Acta Orientalia* 32 (1970): 45–50.

Boyle, J. A., 'Ghazan's Letter to Boniface VIII: Where Was it Written?' in Denis Sinor (ed.), *Proceedings of the Twenty-seventh International Congress of Orientalists, Ann Arbor, Michigan, 13th–19th August, 1967* (Weisbaden: Harrassowitz, 1971), pp. 601–2.

Boyle, J. A., *The Successors of Genghis Khan* (New York: Columbia University Press, 1971).

Brack, Jonathan, 'Mediating Sacred Kingship: Conversion and Sovereignty in Mongol Iran', PhD dissertation: University of Michigan, 2016.

Brack, Jonathan, 'Theologies of Auspicious Kingship: the Islamization of Chinggisid Sacral Kingship in the Islamic World', *Comparative Studies in Society and History* 60(4) (2018): 1143–71.

Brandes, Wolfram and Felicitas Schmieder (eds), *Endzeiten: Eschatologie in den Monotheistischen Weltreligionen* (Berlin: Walter de Gruyter, 2008).

Brend, Barbara and Charles Melville (eds), *Epic of the Persian Kings: the Art of Ferdowsi's Shahnameh* (London: I. B. Tauris, 2010).

Brewster, David, *The Edinburgh Encyclopaedia* (Edinburgh: Blackwood,1830).

Broadbridge, Anne F., *Kingship and Ideology in the Islamic and Mongol Worlds* (Cambridge: Cambridge University Press, 1995).

Broadbridge, Anne F., 'Marriage, Family and Politics: the Ilkhanid–Oirat Connection', *Journal of the Royal Asiatic Society* 26(1/2) (2016): 121–35.

Browne, Edward G., 'Suggestions for a Complete Edition of the Jami'u't-Tawarikh of Rashidu'd-Din Fadlu'llah', *Journal of the Royal Asiatic Society of Great Britain and Ireland* (1908): 17–37.

Brunner, C. J., 'The Middle Persian Explanation of Chess and Invention of Backgammon', *Journal of the Ancient Near East Society of Columbia University* 10 (1978): 45–53.

Buchtal, Hugo, *Miniature Painting in the Latin Kingdom of Jerusalem* (Oxford: Clarendon, 1957).

Buell, Paul, 'Sino-Khitan Administration in Mongol Bukhara', *Journal of Asian History* 13 (1979): 121–51.

Büntgen, Ulf and Nicola Di Cosmo, 'Climatic and Environmental Aspects of the Mongol Withdrawal from Hungary in 1242 CE', *Scientific Reports* 6 (2016): No. 25606.

Çağman, Filiz and Zeren Tanındı, *The Topkapı Saray Museum: The Albums and Illustrated Manuscripts* (Boston, MA: Little, Brown, 1986).

Çağman, Filiz and Zeren Tanındı, 'Remarks on Some Manuscripts from the Topkapı Palace Treasury in the Context of Ottoman–Safavid Relations', *Muqarnas* 13 (1996): 132–48.

Calzolaio, Francesco and Francesca Fiaschetti, 'Prophets of the East: the Ilkhanid Historian Rashīd al-Dīn on the Buddha, Laozi and Confucius and the Question of his Chinese Sources', *Iran and the Caucasus* 23(1) (2019): 17–34.

Campanini, Massimo, 'Al-Ghazzālī', in Seyyed Hossein Nasr and Oliver Leaman (eds), *History of Islamic Philosophy: Part I* (London: Routledge, 1996), pp. 258–74.

Canby, Sheila R., *Shah 'Abbas: the Remaking of Iran* (London: British Museum Press, 2009).

Canby, Sheila, Deniz Beyazit, Martina Rugiadi and A. C. S. Peacock, *Court and Cosmos: the Great Age of the Seljuqs* (New York: Metropolitan Museum of Art, 2016).

Carey, Moya, 'The Gold and Silver Lining: Shams al-Dīn Muḥammad b. Mu'ayyad al-'Urḍī's Inlaid Celestial Globe (c. AD 1288) from the Ilkhanid Observatory at Marāgha', *Iran* 47 (2009): 97–108.

Çetin, Altan, 'Oghuz Turks in the Account of a Mamluk Historian', *Journal of Islamic Studies* 20(3) (2009): 376–82.

Chipman, Leigh, 'A Tale of Two Doctors: Rashīd al-Din and Quṭb al-Dīn al-Shīrāzī', in Anna Akasoy, Charles Burnett and Ronit Yoeli-Tlalim (eds), *Rashīd al-Dīn: Agent and Mediator of Cultural Exchanges in Ilkhanid Iran* (London: Warburg Institute, 2013), pp. 115–26.

Chittick, William C., 'Ibn 'Arabī', in Seyyid Hossein Nasr and Oliver Leaman (eds), *History of Islamic Philosophy: Part I* (London: Routledge, 1996), pp. 497–509.

Cook, David, 'Apocalyptic Incidents during the Mongol Invasions', in Wolfram Brandes and Felicitas Schmieder (eds), *Endzeiten: Eschatologie in den Monotheistischen Weltreligionen* (Berlin: Walter de Gruyter, 2008), pp. 293–312.

Dabashi, Hamid, 'The Philosopher/Vizier: Khwāja Naṣīr al-Dīn al-Ṭūsī and the Ismaîlis', in Farhad Daftary (ed.) *Medieval Isma'ili History and Thought* (Cambridge: Cambridge University Press, 1996), pp. 231–45.

Dabiri, Ghazzal, 'The Shahnama: between the Samanids and the Ghaznavids', *Iranian Studies* 43(1) (2010): 13–28.

Daftary, Farhad, *The Ismā'īlis: Their History and Doctrines* (Cambridge: Cambridge University Press, 1990).

Daftary, Farhad (ed.), *Medieval Isma'ili History and Thought* (Cambridge: Cambridge University Press, 1996).

Daneshpazhuh, Muhammad Taqi, *Fehrest-e Noskhaha-ye Khatti-ye Ketabkhaneh-ye Danishkadeh-ye Adabiyat* (Tehran: Majalla Danishkadeh-ye Adabiyat, 1963).

Daneshpazhuh, Muhammad Taqi and Muhammad Mudarrisi (eds), *Jami' al-Tawarikh: Qesmat-e Isma'iliyan va Fatimiyan va Nizariyan va Da'iyan va Rafiqan* (Tehran: Bungah-e Tarjama va Nashri Ketab, 1960).

Dawlatshah Samarqandi, *Tazkirat al-Shu'ara*, ed. Fatima 'Alaqa (Tehran: 'Olum-e Ensani va Mutala'at-e Farhangi, 2007).

Dawson, Christopher, *Mission to Asia* (Toronto: University of Toronto Press, 1980).

De Nicola, Bruno, 'The Travels of a Manuscript: Rashid al-Din's Compendium of Chronicles (Add. 7628)', *Asian and African Studies* (blog), British Library, 18 August 2015, available at: http://blogs.bl.uk/asian-and-african/2015/08/the-travels-of-a-manuscript-add-7628.html.

De Nicola, Bruno, 'The Queen of the Chaghatayids: Orghīna Khātūn and the Rule of Central Asia', *Journal of the Royal Asiatic Society* 26(1/2) (2016): 107–20.

de Rachewiltz, Igor, *The Secret History of the Mongols: a Mongolian Epic Chronicle of the Thirteenth Century* (Leiden: Brill, 2006).

de Rachewiltz, Igor, Hok-lam Chan, Hsiao Ch'i-ch'ing and Peter W. Geier (eds), *In the Service of the Khan: Eminent Personalities of the Early Mongol–Yuan Period (1200–1300)* (Wiesbaden: Harrassowitz, 1993).

Derayati, Mostafa, *Fehrestvare-ye Dastnevesht-ha-ye Iran* (Tehran: Majlis, 2010).

DeWeese, Devin, *Islamization and Native Religion in the Golden Horde: Baba Tükles and Conversion to Islam in Historical and Epic Tradition* (University Park, PA: Pennsylvania State University Press, 1994).

DeWeese, Devin, 'Cultural Transmission and Exchange in the Mongol Empire: Notes from the Biographical Dictionary of Ibn al-Fuwaṭī', in Linda Komaroff (ed.), *Beyond the Legacy of Genghis Khan* (Leiden: Brill, 2006), pp. 11–29.

Dorn, Boris Andreevich, *Catalogue des Manuscrits et Xylographes Orientaux de la Bibliothèque Impériale Publique de St. Pétersbourg* (St Petersburg: Imperial Academy of Sciences, 1852).

Dorn, Boris Andreevich, *Die Sammlung von morgenländische Handschriften, welche die kaiserliche öffentliche Bibliothek zu St. Petersburg im Jahre 1864 von Hrn. v. Chanykov* (St Petersburg: Imperial Academy of Sciences, 1865).

Durand-Guédy, David, *Iranian Elites and Turkish Rulers: a History of Isfahān in the Saljūq Period* (London: Routledge, 2010).

Duri, A. A., *The Rise of Historical Writing Among the Arabs* (Princeton, NJ: Princeton University Press, 1983).

Eilers, Wilhelm (ed.), *Festgabe deutscher Iranisten zur 2500 Jahrfeier Irans* (Stuttgart: Hochwacht, 1971).

Elliot, H. Miers, *Bibliographical Index to the Historians of Muhammedan India* (Kolkata: Baptist Mission Press, 1849).

Elliot, H. Miers, *The History of India as Told by its Own Historians: the Muhammadan Period* (London: Trübner, 1867).

Elverskog, Johan, *Buddhism and Islam on the Silk Road* (Philadelphia, PA: University of Pennsylvania Press, 2010).

Erdmann, Franz von, *Vollständige Übersicht der ältesten türkischen, tatarischen und mogholischen Völkerstämme nach Raschid-ud-Din's Vorgange* (Kazan: Kazan Imperial University Press, 1841).

Ethé, Hermann, *Catalogue of the Persian Manuscripts in the Library of the India Office* (Oxford: India Office, 1903).

Ettinghausen, Richard, 'An Illuminated Manuscript of Ḥāfiẓ-i Abrū in Istanbul: Part I', *Kunst des Orients* 2 (1955): 30–44.

Ettinghausen, Richard, 'Bahram Gur's Hunting Feats or the Problem of Identification', *Iran* 17 (1979): 25–31.

Fikrat, Muhammad Asif, *Fehrest-e Alfeba'i-ye Kutub-e Khatti-ye Ketabkhaneh-ye Markazi-ye Astan-e Qods-e Razavi/An Alphabetical Hand-List of the Manuscripts in the Astan Quds Razavi Central Library* (Mashhad: Astan-e Qods-e Razavi, 1990).

Firdausi, Abu'l-Qasim, *Shahnameh*, ed. Djalal Khalighi-Motlagh and Abolfazl Khatibi (New York: Persica, 2007).

Fischel, Walter J., 'Azarbaijan in Jewish History', *Proceedings of the American Academy for Jewish Research* 22 (1953): 1–21.

Fischel, Walter J., *Jews in the Economic and Political Life of Medieval Islam* (New York: Ktav, 1969).

Fitzherbert, Teresa, 'Portrait of a Lost Leader: 'Jalal al-Din Khwarazmshah and Juvaini', in Julian Raby and Teresa Fitzherbert (eds), *The Court of the Il-Khans, 1290–1340* (Oxford: Oxford University Press, 1996), pp. 63–77.

Fitzherbert, Teresa, '"Balʿami's Tabari": an Illustrated Manuscript of Balʿami's *Tarjama-yi Tārīkh-i Ṭabarī* in the Freer Gallery of Art, Washington (F59.16, 47.19 and 30.21)', PhD dissertation: University of Edinburgh, 2001.

Flügel, Gustav, *Die arabischen, persischen und türkischen Handschriften der Kaiserlich-Königlichen Hofbibliothek zu Wien* (Vienna: Nationalbibliothek, 1802–1870).

Folda, Jaroslav, *Crusader Art in the Holy Land: From the Third Crusade to the Fall of Acre* (Cambridge: Cambridge University Press, 2005).

Fragner, Bert, 'Zu einem Autograph des Mongolenwesirs Rašīd ad-Dīn Fazlallāh, der Stiftungsurgunde für das Tabrīzer Gelehrtenciertel Rabʿi Rašīdī', in Wilhelm Eilers (ed.), *Festgabe deutscher Iranisten zur 2500 Jahrfeier Irans* (Stuttgart: Hochwacht, 1971), pp. 35–46.

Fragner, Bert, *Geschichte der Stadt Hamadān und ihrer Umgebung in den ersten sechs Jahrhunderten nach der Hiğra* (Vienna: Notring, 1972).

Fragner, Bert (ed.), *Proceedings of the Second European Conference of Iranian Studies held in Bamburg, 30th September to 4th October 1991 by the Societas Iranologica Europaea* (Rome: Instituto Italiano per il Medio ed Estremo Oriente, 1995).

Franke, Herbert, 'Some Sinological Remarks on Rašīd ad-Dīn's history of China', *Oriens* 4(1) (1951): 21–6.

Franke, Herbert, 'From Tribal Chieftain to Universal Emperor and God: the Legitimation of the Yüan Dynasty', *Bayerische Akademie der Wissenschaften, Philosophisch-Historische Klasse* 2 (1978): 3–85.

Gardizi, Abu Saʿid ʿAbd al-Hayy, *The Ornament of Histories: a History of the Eastern Islamic Lands AD 650–1041*, trans. C. Edmund Bosworth (London: I. B. Tauris, 2011).

Ghiasian, Mohamad Reza, 'The "Historical Style" of Painting for Shahrukh and its Revival in the Dispersed Manuscript of *Majmaʿ al-Tawarikh*', *Iranian Studies* 48(6) (2015): 871–903.

Ghiasian, Mohamad Reza, *Lives of the Prophets: the Illustrations to Hafiz-i Abru's "Assembly of Chronicles"* (Leiden: Brill, 2018).

Gibb, H. A. R., *The Travels of Ibn Baṭṭūṭa, A.D. 1325–1354* (Cambridge: Haklyut Society, 1958).

Gil, Moshe, *Jews in Islamic Countries in the Middle Ages* (Leiden: Brill, 2004).

Gilli-Elewy, Hind, *Bagdad nach dem Sturz des Kalifats: die Geschichte einer Provinz unter ilhanischer Herrschaft (656–735/1258–1335)* (Berlin: Schwarz, 2000).

Godard, André, 'The Mausoleum of Öljeitü at Sultaniya', in Arthur Upham Pope and Phyllis Ackerman (eds), *A Survey of Persian Art from Prehistoric Times to the Present, vol. 3: Architecture, its Ornament, City Plans, Gardens*, 3rd edn (Tehran: Soroush Press, 1977), pp. 1103–18.

Gonnella, Julia, Friederike Weis and Christoph Rauch (eds), *The Diez Albums: Contexts and Contents* (Leiden: Brill, 2017).

Gray, Basil, 'An Unknown Fragment of the "Jāmiʿ al-tawārīkh" in the Asiatic Society of Bengal', *Ars Orientalis* 1 (1954): 65–75.

Gruber, Christiane, 'Questioning the "Classical" in Persian Painting: Models and Problems of Definition', *Journal of Art Historiography* 6 (2012): 1–25.

Gruendler, Beatrice and Louise Marlow (eds), *Writers and Rulers: Perspectives on their Relationship from Abbasid to Safavid Times* (Wiesbaden: Reichert, 2004).

Gutas, Dimitri, *Greek Thought, Arabic Culture: the Graeco-Arabic Translation Movement in Baghdad and Early Abbāsid Society (2nd–4th/8th–10th Centuries)* (New York: Routledge, 1998).

Hafez-e Abru, *Joghrafiya-ye Hafez-e Abru: Moshtamel bar Joghrafiya-ye Tarikhi-ye Diyar-e ʿArab, Maghrib, Andalus, Misr va Sham*, ed. Sadiq Sajjadi (Tehran: Miras-e Maktub, 1997).

Hamd Allah Mustaufi Qazvini, *Tarikh-e Gozideh*, ed. ʿAbd al-Husayn Navaʾi (Tehran: Amir Kabir, 1983).

Hamd Allah Mustaufi Qazvini, *Zafarnāma von Hamdallāh Mustaufī und Šāhnāma von Abuʾl-Qāsim Firdausī* (Tehran/Vienna: Daneshgah-ye Iran/Österreichischen Akademie der Wissenschaften, 1999).

Hammer-Purgstall, Joseph, *Geschichte der Ilchane* (Darmstadt: C. W. Leske, 1842).

Hermann, Gottfried, *Persische Urkunden der Mongolenzeit* (Wiesbaden: Harrassowitz, 2004).

Hillenbrand, Robert, 'The Arts of the Book in Ilkhanid Iran', in Linda Komaroff and Stefano Carboni (eds), *The Legacy of Genghis Khan: Courtly Art and Culture in Western Asia, 1256–1353* (New York: Metropolitan Museum of Art, 2002), pp. 135–67.

Hillenbrand, Robert, 'Holy Figures Portrayed in the Edinburgh Fragment of Rashid al-Din's *World History*', *Iranian Studies* 50(6) (2017): 843–71.

Hoffmann, Birgitt, 'Rašīduddīn Faḍlallāh as the Perfect Organizer: the Case of the Endowment Slaves and Gardens of the Rabʿ-i Rašīdī', in Bert G. Fragner (ed.), *Proceedings of the Second European Conference of Iranian Studies held in Bamburg, 30th September to 4th October 1991 by the Societas Iranologica Europaea* (Rome: Instituto Italiano per il Medio ed Estremo Oriente, 1995), pp. 287–96.

Hoffmann, Birgitt, 'The Gates of Piety and Charity: Rašīd al-dīn Faḍl Allāh as a Founder of Pious Endowments', in Denise Aigle (ed.), *L'Iran Face à la Domination Mongol* (Tehran: Institut Français de Recherche en Iran, 1997), pp. 189–201.

Hoffmann, Birgitt, *Waqf im mongolischen Iran: Rašīduddīns Sorge um Nachruhm und Seelenheil* (Stuttgart: Franz Steiner, 2000).

Hoffmann, Birgitt, 'Speaking about Oneself: Autobiographical Statements in the Works of Rashīd al-Dīn', in Anna Akasoy, Charles Burnett and Ronit Yoeli-Tlalim (eds), *Rashīd al-Dīn: Agent and Mediator of Cultural Exchanges in Ilkhanid Iran* (London: Warburg Institute, 2013), pp. 1–14.

Hope, Michael, 'Some Remarks About the Use of the Term "*īlkhān*" in the Historical Sources and Modern Historiography', *Central Asiatic Journal* 60 (2017): 273–99.

Huang, Shih-shan Susan, 'Early Buddhist Illustrated Prints in Hangzhou', in Lucille Chia and Hilde De Weerdt (eds), *Knowledge and Text Production in an Age of Print: China, 900–1400* (Leiden: Brill, 2011), pp. 135–65.

Huff, Dietrich, 'The Ilkhanid Palace at Takht-i Suleiman: Excavation Results', in Linda Komaroff (ed.), *Beyond the Legacy of Genghis Khan* (Leiden: Brill 2006), pp. 94–110.

Hukk, Mohammed Ashraful, Hermann Ethé and Edward Robertson, *A Descriptive Catalogue of the Arabic and Persian Manuscripts in Edinburgh University Library* (Hertford: Stephen Austin, 1925).

Ibn al-Fuwati, ʿAbd al-Razzaq ibn Ahmad, *Majmaʿ al-Adab fi Muʿjab al-Alqab* (Tehran: Muʾassassat al-Tibaʾah waʾl-Nashr, 1995).

Ibn al-Suqaʿi, Fadl Allah ibn Abi al-Fakhr, *Tali Kitab Wafayat al-Aʿyan: un Fonctionnaire Chrétien dans l'Administration Mamelouke*, trans. Jacqueline Sublet (Damascus: Institut Français de Damas, 1974).

Ibn al-Tiqtaqa, Safi al-Din Muhammad, *Al-Fakhri*, trans. C. E. J. Whitting (London: Luzac, 1947).

Ibn al-Tiqtaqa, Safi al-Din Muhammad, *Al-Fakhri*, ed. Ahmad ʿAbd Allah Farhud and ʿAbd al-Qadir Muhammad Mayu (Aleppo: Dar al-Qalam al-ʿArabi, 1997).

Ibn ʿInaba, Ahmad ibn ʿAli, *ʿUmdat al-Talib fi Ansab Al Abi Talib*, ed. Muhammad Hasan Taliqani (Najaf: al-Matbaʿa al-Haydariya, 1961).

Ikas, Wolfgang-Valentin, 'Martinus Polonus' Chronicle of the Popes and Emperors: a Medieval Best-seller and its Neglected Influence on Medieval English Chroniclers', *English Historical Review* 116(466) (2001): 327–41.

Ikas, Wolfgang-Valentin, *Martin von Troppau (Martinus Polonus), O.P. (†1278) in England* (Wiesbaden: Ludwig Reichert, 2002).

Ikas, Wolfgang-Valentin, *Fortsetzungen sur Papst- und Kaiserchronik Martins von Troppau aus England* (Hannover: Hahnsche Buchhandlung, 2004).

Inal, Sara Güner, 'Some Miniatures of the "Jamiʿ al-Tavārīkh" in Istanbul, Topkapi Museum, Hazine Library No. 1654', *Ars Orientalis* 5 (1963): 163–75.

Inal, Sara Güner, 'The Fourteenth-Century Miniatures of the *Jāmiʿ al-Tavārīkh* in the Topkapi Museum in Istanbul, Hazine Library No. 1653', PhD dissertation, University of Michigan, 1965.

Ivanow, Wladimir, *Concise Descriptive Catalogue of the Persian Manuscripts in the Collection of the Asiatic Society of Bengal* (Calcutta: Baptist Mission Press, 1924).

Jackson, Peter, 'Banākatī, Abū Solaymān', *EIr*.

Jackson, Peter, 'Chaghatayid Dynasty', *EIr*.

Jackson, Peter, 'Waṣṣāf', *EI*².

Jackson, Peter, 'The Dissolution of the Mongol Empire', *Central Asiatic Journal* 22(2/3) (1978): 186–244.

Jackson, Peter, *The Mongols and the West, 1221–1410* (Harlow: Pearson, 2005).

Jackson, Peter, 'Mongol Khans and Religious Allegiance: the Problems Confronting a Minister-Historian in Ilkhanid Iran', *Iran* 47 (2009): 109–22.

Jackson, Peter, *The Mongols and the Islamic World: from Conquest to Conversion* (New Haven, CT: Yale University Press, 2017).

Jahan-Biglu, Amir Hossein (ed.), *Tarikh-e Ejtemaʿi-ye Dure-ye Moghul* (Isfahan: Taʾid, 1957).

Jahn, Karl, *Geschichte Ġāzān-Ḫān's aus dem Taʾrīḫ-i-Mubārak-i-Ġāzānī* (London: Luzac, 1940).

Jahn, Karl (ed.), *Histoire Universelle de Rašīd al-Dīn Faḍl Allāh Abul-Khair, 1: Histoire des Francs* (Leiden: Brill, 1951).

Jahn, Karl, *Taʾrīḫ-i-Mubārak-i-Ġāzānī des Rašīd al-Dīn Faḍl Allāh Abī-l-Ḫair: Geschichte der Ilḫāne Abāġā bis Gaiḫātū* (The Hague: Mouton, 1957).

Jahn, Karl, 'Study on Supplementary Persian Sources for the Mongol History of Iran', in Denis Sinor (ed.), *Aspects of Altaic Civilization* (Bloomington: Indiana University Press, 1963), pp. 197–204.

Jahn, Karl, 'The Still Missing Works of Rashīd al-Dīn', *Central Asiatic Journal* 9(1) (1964): 113–22.

Jahn, Karl, *Rashīd al-Dīn's History of India: Collected Essays with Facsimiles and Indices* (The Hague: Mouton, 1965).

Jahn, Karl, 'Rašīd al-Dīn as a World Historian', in *Yádnáme-ye Jan Rypka* (Prague: Academia, 1967), pp. 79–87.

Jahn, Karl, 'Zu Rašīd al-Dīn's "Geschichte der Oġuzen und Türken"', *Journal of Asian History* 1(1) (1967): 45–63.

Jahn, Karl, 'Die ältesten schriftlich überlieferten türkischen Märchen', *Central Asiatic Journal* 12(1) (1968): 31–5.

Jahn, Karl, *Die Geschichte der Oġuzen des Rašīd ad-Dīn* (Vienna: Verlag der Österreichischen Akademie der Wissenschaften, 1969).

Jahn, Karl, *Die Chinageschichte des Rašīd ad-Dīn* (Vienna: Verlag der Österreichischen Akademie der Wissenschaften, 1971).

Jahn, Karl, 'Rashīd al-Dīn's Knowledge of Europe', in Seyyed Hossein Nasr, Mojtaba Minovi, Manochehr Mortezavi and Iraj Afshar (eds), *Majmu'a-ye Khatabe-ha-ye Tahqiqi dar Bare-ye Rashid al-Din Fazl Allah Hamadani* (Tehran: Daneshgah-ye Tehran, 1971), pp. 9–25.

Jahn, Karl, 'Die "Geschichte der Kinder Israels" in der islamischen Historiographie', *Anzeiger der phil.-hist. Klasse der Österreichischen Akademie der Wissenschaften* 109 (1972): 67–76.

Jahn, Karl, *Die Geschichte der Kinder Israels des Rašīd ad-Dīn* (Vienna: Verlag der Österreichischen Akademie der Wissenschaften, 1973).

Jahn, Karl, 'Das christliche Abendland in der islamischen Geschichtsschreibung des Mittelalters', *Anzeiger der phil.-hist. Klasse der Österreichischen Akademie der Wissenschaften* 113(1) (1976).

Jahn, Karl. *Die Frankengeschichte des Rašīd ad-Dīn* (Vienna: Verlag der Österreichischen Akademie der Wissenschaften, 1977).

Jahn, Karl, *Die Indiengeschichte des Rašīd ad-Dīn* (Vienna: Verlag der Österreichischen Akademie der Wissenschaften, 1980).

James, David, *Qur'āns of the Mamlūks* (New York: Thames & Hudson, 1988).

Jarbadhqani, Abu'l-Sharaf Nasih b. Zafar, *Tarjome-ye Tarikh-e Yamini* (Tehran: Bongah-e Tarjome va Nashr-e Ketab, 1966).

Ja'fari, Ja'far ibn Muhammad ibn Hasan, *Tarikh-e Yazd* (Tehran: Bongah-ye Tarjome va Nashr-e Ketab, 1959).

Juvayni, 'Ala' al-Din 'Ata-Malik, *Ta'ríkh-i-Jahán-Gushá of 'Alá'u 'd-Dín 'Atâ-Malik-i-Juwayní*, ed. Mirza Muhammad Qazwini (London: Gibb Memorial Trust, 1912).

Juvayni, 'Ala' al-Din 'Ata-Malik, *The History of the World-Conqueror*, trans. J. A. Boyle (Manchester: Manchester University Press, 1958).

Juzjani, Minhaj-e Siraj, *Tabaqat-e Nasiri*, trans. H. G. Raverty (Calcutta: Asiatic Society of Bengal, 1873).

Juzjani, Minhaj-i Siraj, *Tabaqat-e Nasiri, ya Tarikh-e Iran va Islam*, ed. 'Abd al-Hayy Habibi (Tehran: Dunya-ye Ketab, 1984).

Kadoi, Yuka, 'The Mongols Enthroned', in Julia Gonnella, Friederike Weis and Christoph Rauch (eds), *The Diez Albums: Contexts and Contents* (Leiden: Brill, 2017), pp. 243–75.

Kamola, Stefan, 'Rashīd al-Dīn and the Making of History in Mongol Iran', PhD dissertation: University of Washington, 2013.

Kamola, Stefan, 'History and Legend in the *Jāmiʿ al-Tawārikh*: Abraham, Alexander, and Oghuz Khan', *Journal of the Royal Asiatic Society* 25(4) (2015): 555–77.

Kamola, Stefan, 'A Sensational and Unique Novelty: the Reception of Rashid al-Din's *Jamiʿ al-Tawarikh*', *Iran: Journal of the British Institute for Persian Studies*, published online 13 November 2018.

Kamola, Stefan, 'Untangling the Chaghadaids: Why We Should and Should Not Trust Rashīd al-Dīn', *Central Asiatic Journal* (forthcoming).

Kamola, Stefan, 'Beyond History: Rashid al-Din and Iranian Kingship', in Sussan Babaie (ed.), *Iran After the Mongols. The Idea of Iran, Volume VIII* (London: I. B. Tauris, 2019), pp. 55–74.

Karatay, Fehmi Edhem, *Topkapı Sarayı Müzesi Kütüphanesi Farsça Yazmalar Kataloğu, no. 1–940* (Istanbul: Topkapı Sarayı Müzesi, 1961).

Karimi, Bahman (ed.), *Ketab-e Jamiʿ al-Tawarikh* (Tehran: Ketabkhaned-e Markazi, 1935).

Karimi, Bahman (ed.), *Jamiʿ al-Tawarikh* (Tehran: Iqbal, 1988).

Kateb, Ahmed ibn Hossein ibn ʿAli, *Tarikh-e Jadid-e Yazd* (Tehran: Amir Kabir, 1967).

Kennedy, E. S., 'The Exact Sciences in Iran under the Saljuq and Mongols', in J. A. Boyle (ed.), *The Cambridge History of Iran, Volume 5: the Saljuq and Mongol Periods* (Cambridge: Cambridge University Press, 1968), pp. 659–79.

Kerney, Michael P., *Bibliotheca Lindesiana: Handlist of Oriental Manuscripts* (Privately printed, 1898).

Khafipour, Hani, 'A Hospital in Ilkhānid Iran: Toward a Socio-Economic Reconstruction of the Rabʿ-i Rashīdī', *Iranian Studies* 45(1) (2012): 97–117.

Khalidi, Tarif, *Arabic Historical Thought in the Classical Period* (Cambridge: Cambridge University Press, 1994).

Khazanov, Anatoly M. and André Wink (eds), *Nomads in the Sedentary World* (Richmond: Curzon, 2001).

Khetagurov, L. A. (trans.), *Rashid-ad-Din: Sbornik Letopisey: Volume 1 Book 1* (Moscow: Akademii Nauk SSSR, 1952).

Kholeif, Fathalla, *A Study on Fakhr al-Dīn al-Rāzī and his Controversies in Transoxania* (Beirut: Dar el-Machreq, 1966).

Khwandamir, Ghiyas al-Din ibn Humam al-Din, *Dastur al-Wuzara*, ed. Saʿid Nafisi (Tehran: Iqbal, 1938).

Kim, Hodong, 'A Reappraisal of Güyüg Khan', in Reuven Amitai and Michal Biran (eds), *Mongols, Turks and Others: Eurasian Nomads and the Sedentary World* (Leiden: Brill, 2005), pp. 309–38.

Kim, Hodong, 'A Re-examination of the "Register of Thousands (*hazāra*)" in the *Jāmiʿ al-Tawārīkh*', in Anna Akasoy, Charles Burnett and Ronit Yoeli-Tlalim (eds), *Rashīd al-Dīn: Agent and Mediator of Cultural Exchanges in Ilkhanid Iran* (London: Warburg Institute, 2013), pp. 89–114.

Kirmani, Nasir al-Din Munshi, *Simt al-ʿUla lil-Hazrat al-ʿUlya*, ed. ʿAbbas Iqbal (Tehran: Asatir, 1983).

Kirmani, Nasir al-Din Munshi, *Nasaʾim al-Ashar min Lataʾim al-Akhbar: dar Tarikh-e Vuzara*, ed. Jalal al-Din Hosseini Muhaddis (Tehran: Entesharat-e Ettelaʿat, 1985).

Klein-Franke, Felix, 'Rashid al-Din's Self-defence through his Commenting on al-Ghazzālī's "Reply to the Opponents of the 'Proof of Islam'". A Philosophical Interpretation of the Koranic Expression of "al-amāna"', *Le Muséon* 115(1/2) (2002): 197–214.

Klein-Franke, Felix, 'Rashid al-Din's Treatise "On Free Will and Predestination". An Attempt to Overcome Inner-Islamic Differences', *Le Muséon* 117(3/4) (2004): 527–45.

Kolbas, Judith, *The Mongols in Iran: Chingiz Khan to Uljaytu* (London: Routledge, 2006).

Komaroff, Linda and Stefano Carboni (eds), *The Legacy of Genghis Khan: Courtly Art and Culture in Western Asia, 1256–1353* (New York: Metropolitan Museum of Art, 2002).

Komaroff, Linda, *Beyond the Legacy of Genghis Khan* (Leiden: Brill 2006).

Kostygova, G. I., *Persidskie i Tadzhikskie Rukopisi 'Novoi Serii' Gosudarstvennoi Publichnoi Biblioteki Imeni M. E. Saltykova Shchedrina: Alfavitnyi Katalog* (Leningrad: Gosudarstvennoi Publichnaia Bibliotheca Imeni M. E. Saltkova-Shchedrina, 1973).

Kostygova, G. I., *Fehrest-e Noskhah-ha-ye Farsi Maujud dar Ketabkhaneh-ye ʿOmumi-ye Daulati-ye Saltikuf-Shidrin*, trans. ʿArif Ramadan (Tehran: Sazman-e Madarik-e Farhangi-ye Enqelab-e Islami, 1996).

Krawulsky, Dorothea, *Īrān - das Reich der Īlḫāne: eine topographisch-historische Studie* (Weisbaden: Reichert, 1978).

Krawulsky, Dorothea, *The Mongol Īlkhāns and Their Vizier Rashīd al-Dīn* (Frankfurt: Peter Lang, 2011).
l'Engle, Susan and Robert Gibbs, *Illuminating the Law: Legal Manuscripts in Cambridge Collections* (London: Harvey Miller, 2001).
Lambton, A. K. S., *State and Government in Medieval Islam. An Introduction to the Study of Islamic Political Theory: the Jurists* (Oxford: Oxford University Press, 1981).
Lambton, A. K. S., *Continuity and Change in Medieval Persia: Aspects of Administrative, Economic and Social History, 11th–14th Century* (Albany: State University of New York, 1988).
Lambton, A. K. S., '*Awqāf* in Persia: 6th–8th/12th–14th Centuries', *Islamic Law and Society* 4(3) (1997): 298–318.
Lambton, A. K. S., 'The *Āthār wa aḥyā*' of Rashīd al-Dīn Faḍl Allāh Hamadānī and his Contribution as an Agronomist, Arboriculturalist, and Horticulturalist', in Reuven Amitai-Preiss and David O. Morgan (eds), *The Mongol Empire and its Legacy* (Leiden: Brill, 1998), pp. 126–54.
Lane, George, 'Arghun Aqa: Mongol Bureaucrat', *Iranian Studies* 32(4) (1999): 459–82.
Lane, George, *Early Mongol Rule in Thirteenth-Century Iran: a Persian Renaissance* (London: RoutledgeCurzon, 2003).
Lane, George, 'Mongol News: the *Akhbār-i Moghulān dar Anbāneh Qutb* by Quṭb al-Dīn Maḥmūd ibn Masʿūd Shīrāzī', *Journal of the Royal Asiatic Society* 22(3/4) (2012): 541–59.
Lee, Joo-Yup, 'The Historical Meaning of the Term *Turk* and the Nature of the Turkic Identity of the Chinggisid and Timurid Elites in Post-Mongol Central Asia', *Central Asiatic Journal* 59(1/2) (2016): 101–32.
Lev, Yaacov, *Charity, Endowments, and Charitable Institutions in Medieval Islam* (Gainesville: University Press of Florida, 2005).
Levy, Reuven, 'The letters of Rashīd al-Dīn Faḍl-Allāh', *Journal of the Royal Asiatic Society* 78 (1946): 74–8.
Little, David, 'The Founding of Sulṭāniyya: a Mamlūk Version', *Iran* 16 (1978): 170–5.
Luisetto, Frédéric, *Arméniens & Autres Chrétiens d'Orient sous la Domination Mongole: l'Ilkhanat de Ghâzân, 1295–1304* (Paris: Geuthner, 2007).
Luo, Shubao, *A Concise Illustrated History of Chinese Printing* (Paramus, NJ: Homa & Sekey, 2011).
Luther, Kenneth A. and Clifford Edmund Bosworth, *The History of the Seljuq Turks*

from the Jāmi' al-Tawārīkh: an Ilkhanid Adaptation of the Saljūq-nāma of Ẓahīr al-Dīn Nīshāpūrī (Richmond: Curzon, 2001).

Mahmud al-Kashghari, *Compendium of the Turkic Dialects (Diwān Luγāt at-Turk)*, ed. Robert Dankoff (Cambridge, MA: Harvard University Press, 1982).

Mancini-Lander, Derek, 'Memory on the Boundaries of Empire: Narrating Place in the Early Modern Local Historiography of Yazd', PhD dissertation: University of Michigan, 2012.

Mancini-Lander, Derek, 'Subversive Skylines: Local History and the Rise of the Sayyids in Mongol Yazd', *Bulletin of the School of Oriental and African Studies*, forthcoming.

Manz, Beatrice Forbes, *Power, Politics and Religion in Timurid Iran* (Cambridge: Cambridge University Press, 2007).

Maqrizi, Ahmad ibn 'Ali, *Kitab al-Suluk li-Ma'rifat Duwal al-Muluk*, ed. Muhammad Mustafa Ziyadah (Cairo: Dar al-Kutub, 1934).

Marek, Jiří, Hana Knížková and Werner Forman, *Tschingis-Chan und sein Reich* (Prague: Artia, 1963).

Marlow, Louise, 'The Wisdom of Buzurgmihr in Mustawfī's *Tārīkh-i guzīdeh*', in Niloofar Fotouhi et al., 'Hollyfest.org: a digital Festschrift', available at: http://www.thehollyfest.org/ index.php/louise-marlow.

Martinus Oppaviensis, *Chronicon Pontificum et Imperatorum*, in L. Weiland (ed.), *Monumenta Germaniae Historica Scriptores: Volume 22* (Hannover: Impensis Bibliopolii Hahniani, 1862), pp. 397–475.

Mashkur, Mohammad Javad, 'Rab'-e Rashidi', in Seyyed Hossein Nasr, Mojtaba Minovi, Manochehr Mortezavi and Iraj Afshar (eds), *Majmu'a-ye Khatabe-ha-ye Tahqiqi dar Bare-ye Rashid al-Din Fazl Allah Hamadani* (Tehran: Daneshgah-ye Tehran, 1971), pp. 283–302.

Masuya, Tomoko, 'Ilkhanid Courtly Life', in Linda Komaroff and Stefano Carboni (eds), *The Legacy of Genghis Khan: Courtly Art and Culture in Western Asia, 1256–1353* (New York: Metropolitan Museum of Art, 2002), pp. 74–103.

Mathews, Thomas and Alice Taylor, *The Armenian Gospels of Gladzor: The Life of Christ Illuminated* (Los Angeles, CA: Getty Trust Publications, 2001).

May, Timothy, 'The Conquest and Rule of Transcaucasia: the Era of Chormaqun', in Jürgen Tubach, Sophia G. Vashalomidze and Manfred Zimmer (eds), *Caucasus during the Mongol Period – Der Kaukasus in der Mongolenzeit* (Wiesbaden: Reichert, 2012), pp. 129–51.

May, Timothy, 'The Mongols as the Scourge of God in the Islamic World', in Robert Gleave and István T. Kristó-Nagy (eds), *Violence in Islamic Thought from* the Mongols to European Imperialism (Edinburgh: Edinburgh University Press, 2018), pp. 32–57.

McChesney, Robert D., *Waqf in Central Asia: Four Hundred Years in the History of a Muslim Shrine, 1480–1889* (Princeton, NJ: Princeton University Press, 1991).

Meisami, Julie Scott, *Persian Historiography to the End of the Twelfth Century* (Edinburgh: Edinburgh University Press, 1999).

Meisami, Julie Scott, 'Rulers and the Writing of History', in Beatrice Gruendler and Louise Marlow (eds), *Writers and Rulers: Perspectives on their Relationship from Abbasid to Safavid Times* (Wiesbaden: Reichert, 2004), pp. 73–95.

Meisami, Julie Scott, 'History as Literature', in Charles Melville (ed.), *Persian Historiography* (London: I. B. Tauris, 2012), pp. 1–55.

Melikian-Chirvani, Assadullah Souren, 'Le Royaume de Salomon: Les Inscriptions Persanes de Sites Achéménides', in Jean Aubin (ed.), *Le Monde Iranien et l'Islam: Societes et Cultures* 1 (1971): 1–41.

Melikian-Chirvani, Assadullah Souren, 'Le Livre des Rois, Miroir du Destin', *Studia Iranica* 17 (1988): 7–46.

Melikian-Chirvani, Assadullah Souren, 'The Light of Heaven and Earth: from the Chāhār-ṭāq to the Miḥrāb', *Bulletin of the Asia Institute* 4 (1990): 95–131.

Melikian-Chirvani, Assadullah Souren, 'Le Livre des Rois, Miroir du Destin, II: Takht-e Soleymān et la Symbolique du Shāh-nāme', *Studia Iranica* 20 (1991): 33–148.

Melikian-Chirvani, Assadullah Souren, 'Conscience du Passé et Résistance Culturelle dans l'Iran Mongol', in Denise Aigle (ed.), *L'Iran Face à la Domination Mongole* (Tehran: Institut Français de Recherche en Iran, 1997), pp. 135–77.

Melnikas, Anthony, *The Corpus of the Miniatures in the Manuscripts of Decretum Gratiani* (Rome: Studia Gratiana, 1975).

Melville, Charles, 'Earthquakes in the History of Nishapur', *Iran* 18 (1980): 103–20.

Melville, Charles, '*Pādshāh-i Islām*: the Conversion of Sultan Maḥmūd Ghāzān Khān', in Charles Melville (ed.), *Persian and Islamic Studies in Honour of P. W. Avery* (Cambridge: Centre for Middle Eastern and Islamic Studies, 1990), pp. 159–77.

Melville, Charles (ed.), *Persian and Islamic Studies in Honour of P.W. Avery* (Cambridge: Centre for Middle Eastern and Islamic Studies, 1990).

Melville, Charles, 'The Itineraries of Sultan Öljeitü, 1304–16', *Iran* 28 (1990): 55–70.

Melville, Charles, 'Abu Saʿid and the Revolt of the Amirs in 1319', in Denise Aigle (ed.), *L'Iran Face à la Domination Mongole* (Tehran: Institut Français de Recherche en Iran, 1997), pp. 89–120.

Melville, Charles, *The Fall of Amir Chupan and the Decline of the Ilkhanate, 1327–1337: a Decade of Discord in Mongol Iran* (Bloomington: Indiana University Press, 1999).

Melville, Charles, 'The Īlkhān Öljeitü's Conquest of Gīlān (1307): Rumour and Reality', in R. Amitai-Preiss and D. O. Morgan (eds), *The Mongol Empire and Its Legacy* (Leiden: Brill, 1999), pp. 73–125.

Melville, Charles, 'From Adam to Abaqa: Qāḍī Bayḍāwī's Rearrangement of History', *Studia Iranica* 30 (2001): 67–86.

Melville, Charles, 'Between Firdausi and Rashīd al-Dīn: Persian Verse Chronicles of the Mongol Period', *Studia Islamica* 104/105 (2007): 45–65.

Melville, Charles, 'From Adam to Abaqa: Qāḍī Bayḍāwī's Rearrangement of History (Part II)', *Studia Iranica* 36 (2007): 7–64.

Melville, Charles, 'The *Shahnameh* in Historical Context', in Barbara Brend and Charles Melville (eds), *Epic of the Persian Kings: the Art of Ferdowsi's* Shahnameh (London: I. B. Tauris, 2010), pp. 3–15.

Melville, Charles (ed.), *Persian Historiography* (London: I.B. Tauris, 2012).

Melville, Charles, 'The Historian at Work', in Charles Melville (ed.), *Persian Historiography* (London: I. B. Tauris, 2012), pp. 56–100.

Melville, Charles, 'The Mongol and Timurid Periods, 1250–1500', in Charles Melville (ed.), *Persian Historiography* (London: I. B. Tauris, 2012), pp. 192–7.

Melville, Charles, 'Rashīd al-Dīn and the *Shāhnāmeh*', *Journal of the Royal Asiatic Society* 26(1/2) (2016): 201–14.

Melville, Charles, 'The Illustrations of the Turko-Mongol Era in the Berlin Diez Albums', in Julia Gonnella, Friederike Weis and Christoph Rauch (eds), *The Diez Albums: Contexts and Contents* (Leiden: Brill, 2017), pp. 221–42.

Merçil, Erdoğan, *Fars Atabegleri Salgurlular* (Ankara: Türk Tarih Kurumu Basımevi, 1975).

Miklukho-Maklai, N. D., *Opisanie Tadzhiskikh i Persidskikh Rukopisei Instituta Vostokovedeniia: Volume 3* (Moscow: Nauka, 1975).

Miklukho-Maklai, N. D., *Persidskie i Tadzhikskie Rukopisi Institute Vostokovedeniya Rossiyskoy Akademii Nauk* (New York: Norman Ross, 1998).

Miller, Isabel, 'Local History in Ninth/Fifteenth-Century Yazd: the *Tārīkh-i Jadīd-i Yazd*', *Iran* 27 (1989): 75–9.

Milstein, Rachel, 'The Iconography of Moses in Islamic Art', *Jewish Art* 12/13 (1987): 199–212.

Minorsky, Vladimir, 'Roman and Byzantine Campaigns in Atropatene', *Bulletin of the School of Oriental and African Studies* 11(2) (1944): 243–65.

Minorsky, Vladimir, C. Edmund Bosworth and Sheila Blair, 'Sulṭāniyya', EI².
Moin, A. Azfar, *The Millennial Sovereign: Sacred Kingship and Sainthood in Islam* (New York: Columbia University Press, 2012).
Monzavi, Ahmad, *Fehrest-e Noskhah-ha-ye Khatti-ye Farsi* (Tehran: Moʿassasa-ye Farhangi-ye Mintaqa'i, 1969).
Morgan, David, 'Rashīd al-Dīn Ṭabīb', EI².
Morgan, David, 'Persian Perspectives of Mongols and Europeans', in Stuart B. Schwartz (ed.), *Implicit Understandings: Observing, Reporting, and Reflecting on the Encounter Between Europeans and Other Peoples in the Early Modern Era* (Cambridge: Cambridge University Press, 1994), pp. 201–7.
Morgan, David, 'Rašīd al-dīn and Ġazan Khan', in Denise Aigle (ed.), *L'Iran Face à la Domination Mongole* (Tehran: Institut Français de Recherche en Iran, 1997), pp. 179–88.
Morley, William H., 'A Letter to Richard Clarke, Esq., &c., &c., &c., Honorary Secretary to the Royal Asiatic Society, on a MS. of the Jámi al Tawárikh of Rashíd al-Dín, Preserved in the Library of the Honourable East India Company', *Journal of the Royal Asiatic Society of Great Britain and Ireland* 7(2) (1843): 267–72.
Morley, William H., *A Descriptive Catalogue of the Historical Manuscripts in the Arabic and Persian Languages, Preserved in the Library of the Royal Asiatic Society of Great Britain and Ireland* (London: John W. Parker & Son, 1854).
Morley, William H. and Duncan Forbes, 'Letters to the Secretary of the Royal Asiatic Society', *Journal of the Royal Asiatic Society of Great Britain and Ireland* 6(1) (1841): 11–41.
Morton, A. H., 'The Letters of Rashīd al-Dīn: Īlkhānid Fact or Timurid Fiction?' in Reuven Amitai-Preiss and David O. Morgan (eds), *The Mongol Empire and its Legacy* (Leiden: Brill, 1998), pp. 155–99.
Morton, A. H. (ed.), *The Saljūqnāma of Ẓahīr al-Dīn Nīshāpūrī: a Critical Text Making Use of the Unique Manuscript in the Library of the Royal Asiatic Society* (London: Gibb Memorial Trust, 2004).
Morton, A. H., 'Qashani and Rashid al-Din on the Seljuqs of Iran', in Yasir Suleiman (ed.), *Living Islamic History: Studies in Honour of Professor Carole Hillenbrand* (Edinburgh: Edinburgh University Press, 2010), pp. 166–77.
Mostaert, Antoine and Francis Woodman Cleaves, 'Trois Documents Mongols des Archives Secrètes Vaticanes', *Harvard Journal of Asiatic Studies* 15(3/4) (1952): 467–78.
Munis Khorezmiĭ, *Firdaws al-Iqbāl: History of Khorezm*, ed. and trans. Yuri Bregel (Leiden: Brill, 1988).

Nafisi, Sa'id, *Fehrest-e Kitabkhaneh-ye Majles-e Shura-ye Melli: Volume 6* (Tehran: Majles-e Shura-ye Melli, 1965).

Nasr, Said Hossein, Mojtaba Minovi, Manochehr Mortezavi and Iraj Afshar (eds), *Majmu'a-ye Khatabe-ha-ye Tahqiqi dar Bare-ye Rashid al-Din Fazl Allah Hamadani* (Tehran: Daneshgah-ye Tehran, 1971).

Nasr, Seyyed Hossein, and Oliver Leaman (eds), *History of Islamic Philosophy: Part 1* (London: Routledge, 1996).

Natif, Mika, 'Rashīd al-Dīn's Alter Ego: the Seven Paintings of Moses in *Jāmi' al-tawārīkh*', in Anna Akasoy, Charles Burnett and Ronit Yoeli-Tlalim (eds), *Rashīd al-Dīn: Agent and Mediator of Cultural Exchanges in Ilkhanid Iran* (London: Warburg Institute, 2013), pp. 15–37.

Naumann, Rudolph, 'Die Ausgrabungen am Feuertempel', in Hans Henning von der Osten and Rudolf Naumann (eds), *Vorläufiger Bericht über die Ausgrabungen 1959* (Berlin: Verlag Gebr. Mann, 1961).

Netzner, Amnon, 'Rashīd al-Dīn and his Jewish Background', *Irano-Judaica* 3 (1994): 118–26.

Nishapuri, Zahir al-Din [sic], *Saljuqnameh*, ed. Isma'il Khan Afshar (Tehran: Golale-ye Khavar, 1953).

Ormont, Henri, *Missions Archéologiques Françaises en Orient aux XVIIe et XVIIIe Siècles* (Paris: Imprimerie Nationale, 1902).

Patze, Hans (ed.), *Geschichtsschreibung und Geschichtsbewußtsein in späten Mittelalter* (Sigmaringen: Thorbecke, 1987).

Paul, Jürgen, 'Scheiche und Herrscher im khanat Cagatay', *Der Islam* 67 (1990): 278–321.

Paul, Jürgen, 'Alptegin in the *Siyāsat-nāma*', *Afghanistan* 1(1) (2018): 122–40.

Peacock, Andrew, 'Court Historiography of the Seljuq Empire in Iran and Iraq: Reflections on Content, Authorship and Language', *Iranian Studies* 47(2) (2014): 327–45.

Peter of Poitiers, *Genealogia Christi*, ed. Maria del Carmen Catalán Algás and Mònica Miró Vinaixa (Barcelona: M. Moliero, 2000).

Peters, R., Doris Behrens Abouseif, D. S. Powers, A. Carmona and A. Layish, 'Waḳf', *EI²*.

Pétis de la Croix, François, *Histoire du Grand Genghizcan, Premier Empereur des Anciens Moguls et Tartares* (Paris: Claude Barbin, 1710).

Pétis de la Croix, François, *The History of Genghizcan the Great, First Emperor of the Antient Moguls and Tartars*, trans. P. Aubin (London: J. Darby et al., 1722).

Petrushevsky, 'Rashid-ad-dina i ego istoricheskiy trud', in L. A. Khetagurov (ed.),

Rashid-ad-Din: Sbornik Letopisey: Volume 1, Part 1 (Moscow: Akademii Nauk SSSR, 1952).

Pfeiffer, Judith, 'Conversion Versions: Sultan Öljeytü's Conversion to Shi'ism (709/1309) in Muslim Narrative Sources', *Mongolian Studies* 22 (1999): 35–67.

Pfeiffer, Judith, 'Reflections on a "Double Rapprochement": Conversion to Islam among the Mongol Elite during the Early Ilkhanate', in Linda Komaroff, (ed.), *Beyond the Legacy of Genghis Khan* (Leiden: Brill, 2006), pp. 369–89.

Pfeiffer, Judith, '"A Turgid History of the Mongol Empire in Persia": Epistemological Reflections Concerning a Critical Edition of Vaṣṣāf'a *Tajziyat al-Amṣār va Tazjiyat al-aʿṣar*', in Judith Pfeiffer and Manfred Kropp (eds), *Theoretical Approaches to the Transmission and Edition of Oriental Manuscripts* (Beirut: Orient-Institut, 2007), pp. 107–28.

Pfeiffer, Judith, '"Faces like Shields Covered with Leather": Keturah's Sons in the post-Mongol Islamicate Eschatological Traditions', in İlker Evrim Binbaş and Nurten Kılıç-Schubel (eds), *Horizons of the World: Festschrift for İsenbike Togan* (Istanbul: Ithaki, 2011), pp. 557–94.

Pfeiffer, Judith, 'The Canonization of Cultural Memory: Ghāzān Khan, Rashīd al-Dīn, and the Construction of the Mongol Past', in Anna Akasoy, Charles Burnett and Ronit Yoeli-Tlalim (eds), *Rashīd al-Dīn: Agent and Mediator of Cultural Exchanges in Ilkhanid Iran* (London: Warburg Institute, 2013), pp. 57–70.

Pfeiffer, Judith (ed.), *Politics, Patronage and the Transmission of Knowledge in 13th–15th Century Tabriz* (Leiden: Brill, 2014).

Pfeiffer, Judith and Manfred Kropp (eds), *Theoretical Approaches to the Transmission and Edition of Oriental Manuscripts* (Beirut: Orient-Institut, 2007).

Poliakova, Elena Artemovna and Z. I. Rakhimova, *Miniatura i Literatura Vostoka: Evolutsiia Obraza Cheloveka* (Tashkent: Izd-vo Literaturi i Iskusstva im. Gafura Gulama, 1987).

Pope, Arthur Upham and Phyllis Ackerman (eds), *A Survey of Persian Art from Prehistoric Times to the Present, Volume 3: Architecture, its Ornament, City Plans, Gardens*, 3rd edn (Tehran: Soroush Press, 1977).

Porman, Peter E. and Emilie Savage-Smith, *Medieval Islamic Medicine* (Edinburgh: Edinburgh University Press, 2007).

Pourjavady, Reza and Sabine Schmidtke, 'The Quṭb al-Dīn al-Shīrāzī (d. 710/1311) Codex (ms. Marʿashī)', *Studia Iranica* 36(2) (2007): 279–301.

Prazniak, Roxann, 'Ilkhanid Buddhism: Traces of a Passage in Eurasian History', *Comparative Studies in Society and History* 56(3) (2014): 650–80.

Preiser-Kapeller, Johannes, '*Civitas Thauris*: the Significance of Tabriz in the Spatial Frameworks of Christian Merchants and Ecclesiastics in the 13th and 14th Centuries', in Judith Pfeiffer (ed.), *Politics, Patronage and the Transmission of Knowledge in 13th–15th-Century Tabriz* (Leiden: Brill, 2014), pp. 251–300.

Qashani, 'Abd Allah, *Tarikh-e Uljaytu*, ed. Mahin Hambali (Tehran: Bongah-ye Tarjoma va Nashr-e Ketab, 1969).

Qashani, 'Abd Allah, *Zubdat al-Tawarikh: Baksh-e Fatimiyan va Nizariyan*, ed. Muhammad Taqi Danishpazhuh (Tehran: Mu'assasa-ye Mutala'at va Tahqiqat-e Farhangi, 1977).

Quatremère, Étienne, *Histoire des Mongols de la Perse* (Paris: Imprimerie Royale, 1836).

Raby, Julian, 'Contents and Contexts: Re-viewing the Diez Albums', in Julia Gonnella, Friederike Weis and Christoph Rauch (eds), *The Diez Albums: Contexts and Contents* (Leiden: Brill, 2017), pp. 15–51.

Raby, Julian and Teresa Fitzherbert (eds), *The Court of the Il-Khans, 1290–1340* (Oxford: Oxford University Press, 1996).

Radtke, Bernd, *Weltgeschichte und Weltbeschreibung im mittelalterlichen Islam* (Stuttgart: Franz Steiner, 1992).

Rahnama, Majid, 'Rashid al-Din va Rab'-e Rashidi', in Said Hossein Nasr, Mojtaba Minovi, Manochehr Mortezavi and Iraj Afshar (eds), *Majmu'a-ye Khatabe-ha-ye Tahqiqi dar Bare-ye Rashid al-Din Fazl Allah Hamadani* (Tehran: Daneshgah-ye Tehran, 1971), pp. 112–22.

Rajabzadeh, Hashem, *Khwaja Rashid al-Din Fazl Allah* (Tehran: Tarh-e Nau, 1998).

Rashid al-Din Fadl Allah al-Hamadani, *al-Waqfiya al-Rashidiya bi-Khatt al-Waqif fi Bayan Shara'it Umur al-Waqf wa al-Masarif*, ed. Mojtaba Minovi and Iraj Afshar (Tehran: Offset Press, 1971).

Rashid al-Din Fadl Allah al-Hamadani, *Tangsuqnameh, ya Tibb-e Ahl-e Khita*, ed. Mojtaba Minovi (Tehran: Entesharat-e Daneshkadeh-ye Adabiyat va 'Olum-e Ensani, 1971).

Rashid al-Din Fadl Allah al-Hamadani, *Lata'if al-Haqa'iq*, ed. Gholamreza Taher (Tehran: Daneshgah-e Tehran, 1974).

Rashid al-Din Fadl Allah al-Hamadani, *al-Waqfiya al-Rashidiya bi-Khatt al-Waqif fi Bayan Shara'it Umur al-Waqf wa al-Masarif*, ed. Mojtaba Minovi, Iraj Afshar and 'Abd al-'Ali Karang (Tehran: Anjoman-e Athar-e Melli, 1977).

Rashid al-Din Fadl Allah al-Hamadani, *Sawanih al-Afkar-e Rashidi*, ed. Muhammad Taqi Daneshpazhuh (Tehran: Entisharat-i Daneshgah-e Tehran, 1979).

Rashid al-Din Fadl Allah al-Hamadani, *Asar wa Ahya: Matn-e Farsi dar Bare-ye Fann-e Kishavarzi*, ed. Iraj Afshar and Manuchehr Sotudeh (Tehran: McGill University Press, 1989).

Rashid al-Din Fadl Allah al-Hamadani, *As'ila va Ajviba-ye Rashidi*, ed. Riza Sha'bani (Islamabad: Markaz-e Tahaqiqat-e Farsi-ye Iran va Pakistan, 1993).

Rashid al-Din Fadl Allah al-Hamadani, *Jami' al-Tawarikh*, ed. Muhammad Raushan and Mustafa Musavi (Tehran: Alburz, 1994).

Rashid al-Din Fadl Allah al-Hamadani, *Tarikh-e Chin*, ed. Yidan Wang (Tehran: Miras Maktub, 2000).

Rashid al-Din Fadl Allah al-Hamadani, *Tarikh-e Afranj, Papan, va Qayasira*, ed. Muhammad Raushan (Tehran: Miras Maktub, 2005).

Rashid al-Din Fadl Allah al-Hamadani, *Tarikh-e Hind va Sind va Kashmir*, ed. Muhammad Raushan (Tehran: Miras-e Maktub, 2005).

Rashid al-Din Fadl Allah al-Hamadani, *Tarikh-e Oghuz*, ed. Muhammad Raushan (Tehran: Miras Maktub, 2005).

Rashid al-Din Fadl Allah al-Hamadani, *Tarikh-e Aqvam-e Padshahan-e Khitay*, ed. Muhammad Raushan (Tehran: Miras Maktub, 2006).

Rashid al-Din Fadl Allah al-Hamadani, *Tarikh-e Al-e Salchuq*, ed. Muhammad Raushan (Tehran: Miras Maktub, 2007).

Rashid al-Din Fadl Allah al-Hamadani, *Tarikh-e Bani-ye Isra'il*, ed. Muhammad Raushan (Tehran: Miras Maktub, 2007).

Rashid al-Din Fadl Allah al-Hamadani, *Tarikh-e Samaniyan va Buwayhiyan va Ghaznaviyan*, ed. Muhammad Raushan (Tehran: Miras-e Maktub, 2007).

Rashid al-Din Fadl Allah al-Hamadani, *Bayan al-Haqa'iq*, ed. Hashem Rajabzadeh (Tehran: Miras Maktub, 2008).

Rashid al-Din Fadl Allah al-Hamadani, *Tarikh-e Isma'iliyan*, ed. Muhammad Raushan (Tehran: Miras Maktub, 2008).

Rashid al-Din Fadl Allah al-Hamadani, *Tarikh-e Salatin-e Khwarazm*, ed. Muhammad Raushan (Tehran: Miras Maktub, 2010).

Rashid al-Din Fadl Allah al-Hamadani, *Tarikh-e Salghuriyan-e Fars*, ed. Muhammad Raushan (Tehran: Miras Maktub, 2010).

Rashid al-Din Fadl Allah al-Hamadani, *Majmu'a al-Rashidiya*, ed. Hashem Rajabzada (Tehran: Markaz-e Pezhuheshi-e Miras-e Maktub, 2013).

Rashid al-Din Fadl Allah al-Hamadani [sic], *Tarikh-e Iran va Islam*, ed. Muhammad Raushan (Tehran: Miras Maktub, 2013).

Rice, David Talbot, 'Two Islamic MSS in the Library of Edinburgh University', *Scottish Art Review* 7(1) (1959): 4–7.

Rice, David Talbot and Basil Gray, *The Illustrations to the 'World History of Rashīd al-Dīn'* (Edinburgh: Edinburgh University Press, 1976).

Rice, Yael, 'Mughal Interventions in the Rampur *Jāmiʿ al-tavārīkh*', *Ars Orientalis* 42 (2012): 150–64.

Richard, Francis, *Catalogue des Manuscrits Persans* (Paris: Bibliothèque nationale de France, 1989).

Richard, Francis, *Splendeurs Persanes: Manuscrits du XIIe au XVIIe Siècle* (Paris: Bibliothèque nationale de France, 1997).

Richard, Francis, 'Un des peintres du manuscript Supplément persan 1113 de l'Histoire des Mongols de Rašīd al-Dīn', in Denise Aigle (ed.), *L'Iran Face à la Domination Mongole* (Tehran: Institut Français de Recherche en Iran, 1997), pp. 307–19.

Rieu, Charles, *Catalogue of the Persian Manuscripts in the British Museum* (London: British Museum, 1879).

Rieu, Charles, *Supplement to the Catalogue of the Persian Manuscripts in the British Museum* (London: British Museum, 1895).

Riyahi, Muhammad Amin, *Sar Chashmah-ha-ye Firdausi-shenasi* (Tehran: Muʾassasa-ye Mutalaʿat va Tahqiqat-e Farhangi, 1993).

Robinson, B. W., 'Rashid al-Din's World History: the Significance of the Miniatures', *Journal of the Royal Asiatic Society of Great Britain and Ireland* 2(2) (1980): 212–22.

Rohrborn, Klaus, 'Die islamische Weltgeschichte des Rašīduddīn als Quelle für den zentralasiatischen Buddhismus', *Journal of Turkish Studies* 13 (1989): 129–33.

Romaskevitch, A. A., A. A. Khetagurov and Abdulkerim Ali Oǧlu Alizada (eds), *Djami' at-Tavarikh: Volume 1, Part 1* (Moscow: Nauk, 1965).

Rosen, Baron Victor, *Les Manuscrits Persans de l'Institut des Langues Orientales* (St Petersburg: Imperial Academy of Sciences, 1886).

Roxburgh, David J., 'Heinrich Friedrich von Diez and His Eponymous Albums: MSS. Diez A. Fols. 70–74', *Muqarnas* 12 (1995): 112–36.

Rührdanz, Karin, 'Illustrationen zu Rašīd al-Dīn's Taʾrīḫ-i Mubārak-i Ġāzānī in den Berliner Diez-Alben', in Denise Aigle (ed.), *L'Iran Face à la Domination Mongole* (Tehran: Institut Français de Recherche en Iran, 1997), pp. 295–306.

Ryan, James, 'Christian Wives of Mongol Khans: Tartar Queens and Missionary Expectations in Asia', *Journal of the Royal Asiatic Society* 8(3) (1998): 411–21.

Sachau, Edward and Hermann Ethé, *Catalogue of the Persian, Turkish, Hindûstânî, and Pushtû Manuscripts in the Bodleian Library, Part I: the Persian Manuscripts* (Oxford: Clarendon, 1889).

Sadiqi, Gholamhossein, *Zafarnameh Mansub be Shaykh al-Ra'is Abu 'Ali Sina* (Hamadan: Daneshgah-e Abu 'Ali Sina, 2004).

Safadi, Salah al-Din Jalil Aybak, *Kitab al-Wafi bi'l-Wafayat* (Beirut: Orient-Institut der Deutschen Morgenländischen Gesellschaft, 1999).

Salemann, C., 'Das Asiatische Museum im Jahre 1890. Nebst Nachträgen', in *Mélanges asistiques*, vol. 10, St Petersburg, 1894, pp. 274–80.

Saliba, George, 'Horoscopes and Planetary Theory: Ilkhanid Patronage of Astronomers', in Linda Komaroff (ed.), *Beyond the Legacy of Genghis Khan* (Leiden: Brill 2006), pp. 357–68.

Salim, Gholamreza, 'Ta'lim va tarbiyat dar Rab'-e Rashidi', in Said Hossein Nasr, Mojtaba Minovi, Manochehr Mortezavi and Iraj Afshar (eds), *Majmu'a-ye Khatabe-ha-ye Tahqiqi dar Bare-ye Rashid al-Din Fazl Allah Hamadani* (Tehran: Daneshgah-e Tehran, 1971), pp. 167–82.

Salim, Gholamreza, 'Rashid ed-Din Fazlolla's Contribution to the Advancement of Education in His Time with Particular Reference to his Interest in Medical Training', *Journal of the Regional Cultural Institute (Iran, Pakistan, Turkey)* 6 (1973): 137–42.

Sayılı, Aydin, *The Observatory in Islam and its Place in the General History of the Observatory* (Ankara: Türk Tarih Kurumu Basımevi, 1960).

Schmidtke, Sabine, *The Theology of al-'Allāma al-Ḥillī (d. 726/1325)* (Berlin: Klaus Schwarz, 1991).

Schmitz, Barbara and Ziyaud-Din A. Desai, *Mughal and Persian Paintings and Illustrated Manuscripts in the Raza Library, Rampur* (New Delhi: Rampur Raza Library, 2006).

Semenov, Aleksandr, *Sobranie Vostochnykh Rukopisei Akademii Nauk Uzbekskoi SSR: Volume 1* (Tashkent: Izd-vo Akademii Nauk UzSSR, 1952).

Semenov, Aleksandr, *Majmu'a-ye Noskhah-ha-ye Khatti-ye Farsi-ye Farhangestan-e 'Olum-e Jomhuri-ye Uzbekistan: Mujalladat 1–6*, trans. 'Arif Ramazan (Tehran: Saszman-e Madarek-e Farhangi-ye Enqelab-e Eslami, 1996).

Seyed-Gohrab, A. A. and S. McGlinn (eds), *The Treasury of Tabriz: the Great Il-Khanid Compendium* (Amsterdam: Rozenberg, 2007).

Shabankara'i, Muhammad ibn 'Ali, *Majma' al-Ansab*, ed. Mir Hashem Mohaddis (Tehran: Entesharat Amir Kabir, 1984).

Shabistari, Nahid Muhammadiyun, *Talayahdaran-e 'Asr-e Moghul: Khanadan-e Joveyni* (Tehran: Talar-e Kitab, 2007).

Shimo, Satoko, 'Ghâzân Khan and the Ta'rîkh-i Ghâzânî: Concerning its Relationship to the "Mongol History" of the *Jâmi' al-Tawârîkh*', *Memoirs of the Research Department of the Toyo Bunko* 54 (1996): 93–110.

Shimo, Satoko, 'Three Manuscripts of the Mongol History of *Jāmi' al-Tawārīkh* with a Special Reference to the History of Tribes', *Études Mongoles et Sibériennes* 27 (1996): 225–8.

Shiraiwa, Kazuhiko, 'Sur la date du Manuscrit Parisien du *Ğāmi' al-Tavārīkh* de Rašīd al-Dīn', *Orient* 32 (1997): 37–49.

Shiraiwa, Kazuhiko, 'Rashid al-Din Rekishi Shisei Genson Shahon Mokoruku/Rashīd al-Dīn's *Compendium of Chronicles*: a Bibliography of Extant Manuscripts', *Sanko Shosi Kenkyu* 53 (2000): 1–33.

Shiraiwa, Kazuhiko, 'Rashīd al-Dīn's Primary Sources in Compiling the *Jāmi' al-Tawārīkh*: a Tentative Survey', in Anna Akasoy, Charles Burnett and Ronit Yoeli-Tlalim (eds), *Rashīd al-Dīn: Agent and Mediator of Cultural Exchanges in Ilkhanid Iran* (London: Warburg Institute, 2013), pp. 39–56.

Sims, Eleanor, 'The "Iconography" of the Internal Decoration in the Mausoleum of Uljaytu at Sultaniyya', in Priscilla Soucek (ed.), *Content and Context of Visual Arts in the Islamic World: Papers from a Colloquium in Memory of Richard Ettinghausen* (University Park, PA: College Art Association of America, 1988), pp. 139–76.

Sims, Eleanor, 'Thoughts on a *Shāhnāma* Legacy of the Fourteenth Century: Four Injū Manuscripts and the Great Mongol *Shāhnāma*', in Linda Komaroff (ed.), *Beyond the Legacy of Genghis Khan* (Leiden: Brill, 2006), pp. 269–86.

Sims, Eleanor and Tim Stanley, 'The Illustrations of Baghdad 282 in the Topkapi Sarayi Library in Istanbul', in Warwick Ball and Leonard Harrow (eds), *Cairo to Kabul: Afghan and Islamic Studies Presented to Ralph Pindar-Wilson* (London: Melisende, 2002), pp. 222–7.

Sims-Williams, Ursula, *Handlist of Islamic Manuscripts Acquired by the India Office Library, 1938–85* (London: India Office Library and Records, 1986).

Sinor, Denis (ed.), *Proceedings of the Twenty-seventh International Congress of Orientalists, Ann Arbor, Michigan, 13th–19th August, 1967* (Weisbaden: Harrassowitz, 1971).

Smirnov, O. I. (trans.), *Rashid-ad-Din: Sbornik Letopisey: Volume 1, Book 2* (Moscow: Akademii Nauk SSSR, 1952).

Smith, John Masson Jr, '"Ayn Jālūt: Mamluk Success or Mongol Failure?', *Harvard Journal of Asiatic Studies* 44(2) (1984): 307–45.

Smith, John Masson Jr, 'Hülegü Moves West: High Living and Heartbreak on the

Road to Baghdad', in Linda Komaroff (ed.), *Beyond the Legacy of Genghis Khan* (Leiden: Brill, 2006), pp. 111–34.

Sotheby Parke Bernet & Co., *Catalogue of Rashid al-Din's 'World History': Tuesday, 8th July, 1980* (London: Sotheby's, 1980).

Sotudeh, Hosseinqoli, 'The Income and Expenditure of Xājeh Rashid-ed-Din Fazl Ollāh', *Tahqiqat-e Eqtesadi* 8(21) (1971): 86–102.

Soucek, Priscilla, 'Abu'l-Qāsem 'Abdallāh Kašānī', *EIr*.

Soucek, Priscilla. 'An Illustrated Manuscript of al-Bīrūnī's *Chronology of Ancient Nations*', in Peter Chelkowsky (ed.), *The Scholar and the Saint: Studies in Commemoration of Abu'l-Rayhan al-Bīrūnī and Jalal al-Dīn al-Rūmī* (New York: New York University Press, 1975), pp. 103–68.

Soucek, Priscilla (ed.), *Content and Context of Visual Arts in the Islamic World: Papers from a Colloquium in Memory of Richard Ettinghausen* (University Park, PA: College Art Association of America, 1988).

Soudavar, Abolala, *Art of the Persian Courts: Selections from the Art and History Trust Collection* (New York: Rizzoli, 1992).

Soudavar, Abolala, 'Zafarnameh va Shahnameh-ye Firdausi', *Iranshenasi* 7 (1996): 752–61.

Soudavar, Abolala, 'In Defense of Rašid-od-Din and his Letters', *Studia Iranica* 32(1) (2003): 77–120.

Spuler, Bertold, *Die Mongolen in Iran: Politik, Verwaltung, und Kultur der Ilchanzeit, 1220–1350*, 3rd edn (Berlin: Akademie Verlag, 1968).

Storey, C. A., *Persian Literature: a Bio-bibliographical Survey* (London: Luzac, 1927).

Storey, C. A. and Yuri Bregel', *Persidskaya Literatura: Bio-bibliographicheskiy Obzor* (Moscow: Central Department of Oriental Literature, 1972).

Subtelny, Maria and Charles Melville, 'Ḥāfeẓ-e Abrū', *EIr*.

Suhrawardi al-Maqtul, Shihāb al-Din Abu'l-Futuh, *The Philosophy of Illumination (Ḥikmat al-Ishrāq)*, ed. and trans. John Walbridge and Hossein Ziai (Provo, UT: Brigham Young University Press, 1999).

Suleiman, Yasir (ed.), *Living Islamic History: Studies in Honour of Professor Carole Hillenbrand* (Edinburgh: Edinburgh University Press, 2010).

Süleymaniye Umumî Kütüphanesi, *Defter-i Kutubkhane-ye Damad Ibrahim Paşa* (Istanbul: Dersa'adet, 1894).

Takagi, Sanae, '*Akhbār-i Mughūlān* as a Source of Early Ilkhanid History', *Journal of Asian and African Studies* 82 (2011): 95–143.

Takahashi, Hidemi, *Barhebraeus: a Bio-bibliography* (Piscataway: NJ: Gorgias, 2005).

Tauer, Felix, 'Les Manuscrits Persans Historiques des Bibliothèques de Stamboul, Ire Partie', *Archiv Orientální* 3(1) (1931): 87–118.

Tauer, Felix, *Cinq Opuscules Concernant l'Histoire de l'Iran au Temps de Tamerlan* (Prague: Académie Tchécoslovaque des Sciences, 1959).

Tetley, G. E., *The Ghaznavid and Seljuq Turks: Poetry as a Source for Iranian History* (London: Routledge, 2009).

Thackston, Wheeler, *Rashiduddin Fazlullah's Jami'u't-Tawarikh: Compendium of Chronicles. A History of the Mongols* (Cambridge, MA: Harvard University Press, 1998).

Thomas Spalatensis, *History of the Bishops of Salona and Split*, ed. and trans. Damir Karbić, Mirjana Manijević-Sokol and James Ross Sweeney (Budapest: Central European University Press, 2006).

Tirmidhi, B. M., 'Zoroastrians and Their Fire Temples in Iran and Adjoining Countries from the 9th to the 14th Centuries as Gleaned from the Geographical Works', *Islamic Culture: The Hyderabad Quarterly Review* 24(4) (1950): 271–84.

Togan, İsenbike, *On the Miniatures in Istanbul Libraries* (Istanbul: Baha Matbaası, 1963).

Togan, İsenbike, 'Otchigin's Place in the Transformation from Family to Dynasty', in István Zimonyi and Osman Karatay (eds), *Central Eurasia in the Middle Ages: Studies in Honour of Peter B. Golden* (Wiesbaden: Harrassowitz, 2016), pp. 407–23.

Tusi, Nasir al-Din, *Contemplation and Action: the Spiritual Autobiography of a Muslim Scholar*, trans. S. J. Badakhchani (London: I. B. Tauris, 1998).

Tusi, Nasir a-Din, *Zij-e Ilkhani (Noskhah-Bargardan) az ru-ye Noskhah-ye Khatt-e Kitabkhaneh-ye Majles-e Shura-ye Islami, Shomareh-ye 181* (Qom: Majma'-e Zakhar'ir-e Islami, 2012).

Twitchett, Denis, *Printing and Publishing in Medieval China* (London: Wynkyn De Worde Society, 1983).

van den Berg, Gabrielle, 'Wisdom Literature in the *Safina-yi Tabrīz*: Notes on the *pandnāma-yi Anushirvān*', in A. A. Seyed-Gohrab and S. McGlinn (eds), *The Treasury of Tabriz: the Great Il-Khanid Compendium* (Amsterdam: Rozenberg, 2007), pp. 171–82.

van Ess, Josef, *Der Wesir und seine Gelehrten: zu Inhalt und Enstehungsgeschichte der theologischen Schriften des Rašīduddīn Faẓlullāh (gest. 718/1318)* (Wiesbaden: Franz Steiner, 1981).

Verkhovsky, Y. P. (trans.), *Rashid-ad-Din: Sbornik Letopisey: Volume 3* (Moscow: Akademii Nauk SSSR, 1960).

Vivancos, Miguel C., 'Comienza la genealogía del maestro Pedro de Poitiers' / 'The Start of the Genealogy by Master Peter of Poitiers', in Peter of Poitiers, *Genealogia Christi*, ed. Maria del Carmen Catalán Algás and Mònica Miró Vinaixa (Barcelona: M. Moliero, 2000), pp. 93–132.

Vivancos, Miguel C., 'Pedro de Poitiers y su *Genealogia Christi*' / 'The *Genealogia Christi* by Peter of Poitiers', in Peter of Poitiers, *Genealogia Christi*, ed. Maria del Carmen Catalán Algás and Mònica Miró Vinaixa (Barcelona: M. Moliero, 2000), pp. 15–27.

von den Brincken, Anna-Dorothee, 'Zu Herkunft und Gestalt der Martins-Chroniken', *Deutsches Archiv für Erforschung des Mittelalters* 37 (1981): 694–735.

von den Brincken, Anna-Dorothee, 'Martin von Troppau', in Hans Patze (ed.), *Geschichtsschreibung und Geschichtsbewußtsein in späten Mittelalter* (Sigmaringen: Thorbecke, 1987), pp. 155–93.

von den Brincken, Anna-Dorothee, '"In una pagina ponendo pontifices, in alia pagina imperatores": das Kopieren der tabellarischen Papst-Kaiser-Chronik des Martin von Troppae OP (†1278)', *Revue d'Histoire des Textes* 18 (1988): 109–36.

Walbridge, John, *The Science of Mystic Lights: Quṭb al-Dīn Shīrāzī and the Illuminationist Tradition in Islamic Philosophy* (Cambridge, MA: Harvard University Press, 1992).

Ward, Leonard James, 'The Zafar-Nāmah of Hamdallāh Mustaufī and the Il-Khān Dynasty of Iran', PhD dissertation: University of Manchester, 1983.

Wassaf, Sharaf al-Din ʿAbd Allah, *Ketab-e Mostatab-e Wassaf al-Hazrat dar Bandar-e Moghul* (Bombay: Matbaʿ-e Alishan, 1853).

Wassaf, Sharaf al-Din ʿAbd Allah, *Tajziyat al-Amsar wa Tazjiyat al-Aʿsar (Tarikh-e Vassaf)*, ed. Iraj Afshar, Mahmud Omidsalar and Nadir Mottalibi Kashani (Tehran: Talayah, 2009).

Wauchier de Denan, *L'Histoire Ancienne Jusqu'à César ou Histoires pour Roger, Châtelain de Lille: l'Histoire de la Macédonie et d'Alexandre le Grand*, ed. Catherine Gaullier-Bougassas (Turnhout: Brepols, 2012).

Wauchier de Denan, *L'Histoire Ancienne Jusqu'à César ou Histoires pour Roger, Châtelain de Lille: l'Histoire de la Perse, de Cyrus à Assuérus*, ed. Anne Rochebouet (Turnhout: Brepols, 2015).

Wentker, Sibylle (ed.), *Geschichte Wassaf's: persisch Herausgegeben und deutsch Übersetzt von Hammer-Purgstall*, 4 vols (Vienna: Österreichischen Akademie der Wissenschaften, 2010–16).

Wiedemann, E., 'Ḳuṭb al-Dīn Shīrāzī', *EI²*.

Wilber, Donald N., *The Architecture of Islamic Iran: the Il Khānid Period* (New York: Greenwood Press, 1969).

Williams Wynn, C. W., 'Proceedings of the Eighteenth Anniversary Meeting of the Society, held on the 8th of May, 1841', *Journal of the Royal Asiatic Society* 6(2) (1841): i–xxii.

Wing, Patrick, '"Rich in Goods and Abounding in Wealth:" the Ilkhanid and post-Ilkhanid Ruling Elite and the Politics of Commercial Life at Tabriz, 1250–1400', in Judith Pfeiffer (ed.), *Politics, Patronage and the Transmission of Knowledge in 13th–15th-Century Tabriz* (Leiden: Brill, 2014), pp. 301–20.

Woods, John, 'The Rise of Tīmūrid Historiography', *Journal of Near Eastern Studies* 46(2) (1987): 81–108.

Wright, Elaine, *The Look of the Book: Manuscript Production in Shiraz 1303–1452* (Washington, DC: Freer Gallery of Art, 2012).

Yaqut al-Hamawi, *Dictionnaire Géographique, Historique et Littéraire de la Perse et des Contrées Adjacents*, ed. F. Wustenfeld (Paris: Imprimerie Impériale, 1861).

Yastrebova, Olga and Arezou Azad, 'Reflections on an Orientalist: Alexander Kuhn (1840–88), the Man and his Legacy', *Iranian Studies* 48(5) (2015): 675–94.

Yavari, Neguin, 'Mirrors for Princes or a Hall of Mirrors? Niẓām al-Mulk's *Siyar al-mulūk* Reconsidered', *al-Masāq* 20(1) (2008): 47–69.

Yaʿqubi, Abu'l-ʿAbbas, *Les Pays [Kitāb al-Buldān]*, trans. Gaston Wiet (Cairo: l'Institut Français d'Archéologie Orientale, 1937).

Ziai, Hossein, 'Shihāb al-Dīn Suhrawardī: Founder of the Illuminstionist School', in S. H. Nasr and Oliver Leaman (eds), *History of Islamic Philosophy* (London: Routledge, 1995), pp. 434–64.

Ziai, Hossein, 'The Illuminationist Tradition', in Seyyid Hossein Nasr and Oliver Leaman (eds), *History of Islamic Philosophy: Part I* (London: Routledge, 1996), pp. 465–96.

Index

Abaqa (*ilkhan*, 1265–81), 16, 21, 23–4, 31, 33, 35, 36, 68, 169
   depicted by Rashid Khwafi, 144
'Abbasid caliphs, 3, 4–6, 17, 61, 68, 170–1
Abish Khatun (Salghurid, 1263–87), 67
Abraham, 81–2
Abu Bakr b. Sa'd (Salghurid, 1226–60), 67
Abu Sa'id (*ilkhan*, 1316–35), 104, 160
abwab al-birr see Shamb
Account of Truths, 107–9, 111, 114, 154
Accounts of the Mongols, 71–3, 80
Achaemenids, 22, 42, 69–70
Acre, 131–2
administration, 3–4, 6–7, 8–9, 11, 13, 14–15, 19, 49–50
   factions, 13–14, 24, 35, 36–9, 47–9, 156–7, 159
   influence of eastern provinces 22–4, 66–7, 69, 143, 145–6
   joint appointments, 34–5, 49–52
   see also purges, forged letters
Ahmad Teguder *see* Teguder Ahmad
Akhbar-e Moghulan, 71–3, 80
'Ala' al-Din *see* Juvayni, 'Ala' al-Din
Ala Tagh, 60
Alamut, 64
Alan Qo'a, 83, 122, 126
Alexander the Great, 63, 65–6
'Ali b. Abi Talib (d. 661), 52, 59, 74, 92, 104–5
'Alids, 74–5, 104–5, 108
'Alishah, Taj al-Din (d. 1324), 1, 49, 51, 156, 159–60
'Allama al-Hilli (d. 1325), 107
Allocation of Cities and Propulsion of Epochs, 75–7, 154–5, 157–8
Altan Debter, 80–1, 85
analogistic thinking, 164, 167–9

Anatolia, 6, 12, 39, 45–6, 71–2, 159, 163
apocalyptic historiography, 63, 64, 65
Arab conquest, 63, 65–6
Arghun (*ilkhan*, 1284–91), 35–8, 43, 71, 73, 146
   depicted in λ recension, 146–7
Arghun (Oyirad, d. 1275), 11–12, 13–16, 33, 35, 42
Arghuniya *see* Shamb
Aruq (Jalayir, d. 1289), 37–8
astronomy, 20–1
Athar al-Baqiya', 130
Athar wa Ahya' see *Works and Beings*
autobiography of Rashid al-Din, 28, 29, 50–1
'Ayn Jalut (battle, 1260), 18, 171–2
Azargoshnasp, 21–2, 63, 65–6, 69, 92
Azerbaijan, 6, 18–19, 31; *see also* Azargoshnasp, Maragha

ba'urchi (cook), 41–2
Baghdad, 3, 24, 30–2, 34–8, 41, 45–6, 49, 52, 74–6, 92, 105, 110
   Mongol conquest, 17, 64–5, 76, 170–1
Bahram V Gur (Sasanian, 421–38), 59
Baidu (*ilkhan*, 1295), 39, 43–5
Baiju (Besut, d. 1259?), 9, 11, 12
Baljuna, 72
Banakati, Abu Sulayman (d. 1329–30), 75, 142, 147
Bar Hebraeus (d. 1286), 32, 41, 63, 129
Batu (Jochid, d. 1256), 6–7, 12–13
   claim over Middle East, 8–12, 13–17
Bayan al-Haqa'iq see *Account of Truths*
Baydawi, Nasir al-Din (d. 1286), 36, 67–70, 73, 80, 162
Benjamin of Tudela (d. 1173), 31
Berke (Jochid, d. 1266), 17, 34, 64, 65

Blessed History of Ghazan, 60, 62, 76, 78–85, 91, 95, 96, 102–3, 115, 121–49, 180
  additions to, 133–4, 136–40, 142–9
  continuation by Hafez-e Abru, 148–9, 178–9
  dating, 78, 134–5
  genealogical trees, 122–8, 136
  illustrations, 123, 130–3, 136, 137
  recensions, 123–7, 134–40, 142–9
  sources, 121, 133–4, 137
  structure, 83–5, 121
  biography, 160–2
  challenge of Rashid al-Din's 28–9, 31
Biruni, 95, 130, 132
block printing, 140–2
Bolad Chingsang, 40, 74, 82, 85
Book of Clarifications, 106–7
Book of Government, 170
Book of Victory, 50, 164–7, 178, 180
  structure, 168, 170–2
  see also Piruzinamak
book painting, 130; *see also Blessed History of Ghazan*, illustrations
Bozorgmehr, 166–9, 173–4
Buddhism, 45–6, 97, 104–5, 131, 141
Buqa (Jalayir, d. 1289), 13, 35, 37–8, 40, 42, 49, 160
Buzinjird, 74, 140

calendars, 72, 75, 78
Caspian Sea, 60, 73
Caucasus, 6, 12
Chaghadai (Chinggisid, d. 1241 or 1244–5), 4
  descendants, 137–8, 146–7
Chaghadaid Khanate, 11, 17, 42
chancellery prose, 61, 62
chancellor (*chingsang*), 144
chao, 40–1, 43
Chin Temur (Khitan, d. 1235), 7, 8, 14, 23, 35
China, history of, 94–6, 144
Chinggis Khan (d. 1227), 2–4, 64, 75, 76, 80, 83–4, 104–5, 136, 138–40
  army commanders, 133–4
  genealogical tree, 124–6
chingsang, 144
Chormaqun (Sonit, d. 1241), 6–7, 9, 10, 35
chronograms, 145
Chronology of Ancient Nations, 130
Chupan (Suldus, d. 1327), 54, 160

clime *see iqlim*
coinage, 104, 108
Collected Histories of Qashani, 77, 96–100, 102
Collected Histories of Rashid al-Din, 100–3, 106–7, 110–11, 122, 128, 130–2, 134, 142, 147, 162–3
  as model of history, 163, 165–6, 178
Collected Writings of Rashid, 113–15, 127, 142
Collection of Hafez-e Abru, 179
continuation of the *Blessed History*, 148–9, 178–80
conversion
  of Ghazan, 44–5, 47, 97, 104
  of Oljeitu to Shi'ism, 103–7
  of Rashid al-Din, 36, 39, 47
court records, 71–3, 80, 82
Cream of Histories, 98–100, 102
custom, Mongol *see tikishmishi, yosun*

Damascus, 52–4
Dastjirdani, Jamal al-Din, 46–7
descendants of Muhammad *see* 'Alids
Dhayl-e Tarikh-e Mobarak-e Ghazani, 148–9, 178–80
diplomacy, 50, 51–2, 73, 75, 93
discourse on wisdom, 167–8, 172–4
Dobun Bayan, 122, 126

earthquakes, 137, 144
eastern provinces, 19, 33, 35, 42–4; *see also* Khurasan, Mazandaran
Educational History, 129
Eljigidei (Jalayir), 12
endowments, 20, 92, 103, 109–12
  of Rashid al-Din, 110, 159; *see also* Rashidi Quarter
enthronement *see quriltai*
Europe, history of, 94–6, 129

Fakhr al-Din 'Isa ibn Ibrahim, 60–1
Fakhri, 60–2, 73
Fars, 67, 69–70
Firdausi, Abu'l-Qasim (d. 1020), 22–3, 65–6, 68, 78, 132, 155, 162–9
Five Genealogies, 127–9
forged letters, 47, 156–7

Gardizi, Abu Sa'id 'Abd al-Hayy (d. 1061), 68
Gates of Piety *see* Shamb

Geikhatu (*ilkhan*, 1291–4), 39–42
Genealogia Christi, 129
Genealogical trees, 122–30, 137–8
Genealogies of Prophets and Kings and Caliphs
  see *Five Genealogies*
genealogy, 81–3
Genealogy of Christ, 129
Geography of Hafez-e Abru, 179, 181
Ghazali, 106, 108
Ghazan (*ilkhan*, 1295–1304), 42–54, 59–60, 62, 73–8, 85, 91, 92, 95, 97, 104, 110, 142
  campaigns in Syria, 51–4, 59–60, 73–6, 171–2
  compared to Anoshiravan, 169
  depicted by Hamd Alla Mustaufi, 169
  depicted by Qashani, 147
  depicted by Rashid al-Din, 44–5, 59–60, 73–4, 79–80, 81, 84–5, 92–3
Ghazaniya see Shamb
Ghaznavids, 68
Ghiyath al-Din b. Rashid al-Din, 162
Gilan, 93, 103, 105, 107
Golden Register, 80–1, 85
Gushlug (Naiman, d. 1218), 136–7
Guyug (Great Khan, 1246–8), 9–13
  depicted by Rashid al-Din, 136–7

Hafez-e Abru (d. 1430), 147–9, 178–81
Hamadan, 29–32
Hambaqa'i Qa'an, 139–40
Hamd Allah Mustaufi Qazvini (d. 1349), 21, 48, 51, 78, 93, 149, 155, 163–74, 178
Herat, 47, 145
Histoire Universelle see *Universal History* of Wauchier de Denain
Historia Scholastica, 129
historiography
  early Ilkhanid, 60–78
  literary, 155–9
  moralising, 170–2
  regional, 65–79
  Saljuq, 76–8, 85
  Turko-Mongol, 79–81
  verse, 162–3, 165–6, 167–8
History of Hafez-e Abru, 179, 181
History of Oljeitu, 100–1, 104–5, 155–9, 178
History of Prophets and Kings, 98
History of the World Conqueror, 63–6, 73, 75, 76, 84, 143, 145–6

Hulegu (Toluid, d. 1265), 17–21, 24, 34, 64, 67
  campaign of 1256–8, 15–17, 30–2, 62, 64–5, 170–1
  hunting, 52, 59–60, 61, 73–4, 75

Ibn al-Athir, Abu al-Hassan (d. 1233), 61, 76, 112, 134
Ibn al-Fuwati, Kamal al-Din 'Abd al-Razzaq (d. 1323), 32, 138, 160–1
Ibn al-Suqa'i, al-Muwaffaq Fadl Allah (d. 1325–6), 161
Ibn al-Tiqtaqa, Safi al-Din (d. 1310), 60–2, 73; see also *Fakhri*
Ibn Sina, Abu 'Ali (d. 1037), 71, 166–7
Ibn 'Arabi, Abu 'Abd Allah (d. 1240), 70
ideology, 21–3, 51–2
  of Ghazan, 52–4, 59–60, 62, 73–5, 85
  of Oljeitu, 91, 142, 147
ilkhan (title), 16
Ilkhanid family, Rashid al-Din's relation to, 33, 39, 47–8, 50–1, 93, 111–12
*ilkhan*s see names of individual *ilkhan*s
Illuminationism, 70–1, 92–3
'Imad al-Daula, 30, 32, 161
Imperial Book, 107, 127–9
India, history of, 94–6
iqlim, 98
Iran as a political unit, 14, 18–19, 23, 32, 67–9, 71, 94, 96, 166
Islam, history of, 94, 96
Islamisation, 35–8
Isma'ilis, 3, 6, 15, 17, 20, 64, 96–7

Jalal al-Din Khwarazmshah (1220–31), 6
Jamal al-Din Dastjirdani, 46–7
Jami' al-Tasanif al-Rashidi see *Collected Writings of Rashid*
Jami' al-Tawarikh see *Blessed History of Ghazan, World History, Collected Histories*
Jarbadhqani, Abu'l-Sharaf, 62, 78
Jewish heritage of Rashid al-Din, 2, 30, 37, 41–2, 100–1, 106, 144–5, 156–7, 159, 162
Jews 31–2, 37, 38, 45, 46, 82
  in historical writing, 41–2, 94–6, 101, 129, 156–7, 180–1
  see also Sa'd al-Daula al-Abhari
Jochid Khanate, 4, 17, 75
Judeo-Islamic tradition, 22, 69–70, 81–2, 94, 122, 127, 167, 173, 179

Juvayni, Baha' al-Din, 8, 13–14, 23–4, 33, 35, 145
Juvayni, 'Ala' al-Din 'Ata Malik (d. 1283), 4, 13–14, 19, 23, 34–6, 61, 63–7, 71, 73, 76–7, 84, 143, 163; *see also History of the World Conqueror*
Juvayni, Shams al-Din (d. 1284), 14, 34–7, 49, 69, 71, 143, 160, 163
Juzjani, Minhaj al-Siraj, 64

Kamalashri, 97
Kamsun, 97, 99
Ked Buqa (d. 1260), 16, 18, 171–2
Kereyid, 138–9
keshig, 39, 41–2
Key to Commentaries, 106–7
Khosrau Anoshiravan, 166–7, 169
Khudabanda, 93; *see also* Oljeitu
Khurasan, 43, 68, 69
Khwarazm, 1–3, 64, 68; *see also* Muhammad Khwarazmshah, Jalal al-Din Khwarazmshah
Kitab al-Sultaniya see *Imperial Book*
Kitab al-Taudihat see *Book of Clarifications*
klima see *iqlim*
Korguz (Uighur, d. 1241), 8, 11
Kulliyat-e Tarikhi, 179

Lata'if al-Haqa'iq, 109
law, Islamic, 64, 144–5
law, Mongol, 64, 84, 105
Litaji, 97, 99
Lives of Kings, 170

Mahmud Dinawari, 45, 46–7
Mahmud of Ghazna (Ghaznavid, 998–1030), 62, 65, 78
Majd al-Mulk Yazdi (d. 1282), 34–6, 72, 145
Majmu'a Rashidiya see *Rashidi Collection*
Majmu'a-ye Hafez-e Abru, 179
Malikshah (Saljuq, 1072–92), 20, 22
Mamluks, 18, 51–4, 47, 71, 75, 82
manuscripts, 71–3, 130, 131–2, 163–4, 168
  production, 32, 70,71, 112, 114–15, 131, 138–9, 140–2
  of Qashani's work, 77, 96–8, 101–2
  of Rashid al-Din's work, 99–100, 106, 113, 123–8, 132–3, 135–8, 142–4, 146–9
  of Wassaf's work, 158–9

Maragha, 18–21, 24, 32, 63, 70–1, 72, 99, 100, 145, 160–1
Mas'udi, Hasan 'Ali (d. 956), 21, 95
Maymundiz, 31, 64
Mazandaran, 43, 46
medical training
  of Qutb al-Din, 70
  of Rashid al-Din, 32–3, 50, 162
Mengu Timur (Huleguid, d. 1282), 67
Miftah al-Tafasir see *Key to Commentaries*
military (Mongol)
  commanders of Chinggis Khan, 133–4
  in Europe, 9–10
  in Iran and Iraq, 2–4, 6–7, 12, 15–17
  in Syria, 51–4, 59–60, 73–6, 171–2
Mongke (Great Khan, 1251–9), 9, 12–13, 15–18, 19, 31, 64, 66
  depicted by Rashid al-Din, 136–7
Mosul, 60–1
Muhammad Khwarazmshah (d. 1220), 1–3, 67
Munshi Kirmani, Nasir al-Din, 33, 41, 48, 50, 162
Muwaffaq al-Daula, 29–30, 31, 32

Najaf, 52, 104–5
Najib al-Daula, 156–7
Narrative strategy
  of Baydawi, 68
  of Juvayni, 65–66
  of Qashani, 100–2, 155–7
  of Rashid al-Din, 81–2, 83
  of Wassaf, 76–7, 157–9
Nasiri Chapters, 64
Nauruz (Oyirad, d. 1297), 42–7, 51, 74
Nishapur, 8, 43, 137, 142, 144–5
Nishapuri, Zahir al-Din (d. 1187), 85, 172
Nizam al-Din ibn al-Ra'is, 143
Nizam al-Mulk (d. 1092)
  as model for Rashid al-Din, 169–70, 172–4
Nizam al-Tawarikh see *Order of Histories*
Nizam Yazdi, 143
Nizaris see Isma'ilis
Nosal (d. 1241), 8, 10
Nur al-Din al-Rasadi, 145
Nurin Aqa (Qiyat), 43–4

Ogedei (Great Khan, 1229–41), 4, 7–10, 80, 84
Ogedeid court, 17

Oghul Qaimish (Merkit, d. 1251), regent of Mongol Empire, 12
Oghuz Khan, 82–3
Oghuz Turks, history of, 94–6
Oljeitu (*ilkhan*, 1304–16), 1, 32, 46, 52, 77, 93–5, 155–7, 159–60
 birth, 93, 107
 depicted by Qashani, 104–5
 depicted by Rashid al-Din, 102–3, 107–9
Order of Histories, 68–70, 73, 76, 164, 173
Ordo Qiya, 38, 46, 49
Ornament of Histories, 68

pandnameh see discourse on wisdom
paper money *see chao*
patronage, 61, 70, 73, 78, 166
 by Ghazan, 52, 62, 75–8, 92, 97, 142
 by Hulegu, 18–21
 by Isma'ilis, 20, 31
 by Oljeitu, 93–4
 by Rashid al-Din, 93, 115
Persian as language of historiography, 62, 63, 66, 73
Peter Comestor, 129
Peter of Poitiers, 129
Piruzinamak, 166–7
purges (administrative) 13, 17, 34, 36–9, 46–7

Qaidu (Chaghadaid, d. 1303), 43, 134–5, 138
Qaraqorum, 7, 10–19, 21, 31, 63, 66
Qashani, 'Abd Allah, 71–2, 74–5, 77–8, 95–105, 147, 154, 155–9, 162
 attack on Rashid al-Din, 100–2, 155–7
 see also Collected Histories of Qashani, *History of Oljeitu*
Qatran Tabrizi (d. 1072), 22
Qazvin, 15, 40, 103
Qongqur-Oleng *see* Sultaniya
Qubilai (Toluid, d. 1294), 16, 17, 18, 21, 49, 76, 82, 137, 144
quriltai, 6, 10, 12, 13, 52, 54, 73
Quryaquz (Kereyid), 139
Qutb al-Din Shirazi (d. 1311), 70–3, 80, 146
Qutlugh Khan *see* Abu Bakr b. Sa'd
Qutlughshah (Mangqut, d. 1307), 42–4, 49, 54, 60, 104–5, 107

rab'-e rashidi see Rashidi Quarter
Rahba al-Sham, 50, 75

Rashid al-Daula, 32, 157
 Geikhatu's steward, 41–2
Rashid al-Din
 autobiographical information, 28, 29, 50–1
 death, 1, 160
 depicted by Hamd Allah Mustaufi, 173–4
 depicted by Qashani, 100–1, 154–5
 depicted by Wassaf, 154–5, 157–8
 position at court, 41, 48, 50, 52, 91, 93, 108–9
 theological works, 30, 103–9, 127, 129, 141, 168
 writing process, 81, 83
 see also Rashid al-Daula and various topical entries
Rashid Khwafi, 143–6
Rashidi Collection, 112–15
Rashidi Quarter, 72, 109–12, 123, 132, 159, 162
 deed of endowment, 110–12
 manuscript production, 112, 114–15, 132, 135, 140–2, 160, 180–1
Rawandi, Muhammad b. 'Ali, 22
Razi, Fakhr al-Din (d. 1210), 106, 109

Sa'd al-Daula al-Abhari (d. 1291), 38–9, 41–2, 46, 48, 49, 147
Sa'd al-Din Sawaji (d. 1312), 43, 48–52, 75, 93, 109, 112, 154, 159–60
 depicted by Qashani, 155–7
 depicted by Wassaf, 158
Sa'd b. Zangi (Salghurid, 1198–1226), 67
Sadr al-Din Zanjani (d. 1298), 39–42, 45, 46–9, 51, 159–60
Safadi, Salah al-Din (d. 1363), 161–2
ṣāḥib-diwān, 8, 13–14, 23, 46, 49–50
saj' see chancellery prose
Salghurids, 22, 63, 67, 69–70, 76–7
Saljuqnameh, 85
Saljuqs, 3, 62, 92, 169, 172; *see also* Malikshah, Sanjar
Sanjar (Saljuq, 1118–57), 8, 92
Sasanians, 20, 21, 59, 65, 69, 164, 166, 173–4
Sayf al-Din *bitikchi* (d. 1262), 34
sayyids see 'Alids
seasonal camps, 31, 52, 60, 73, 75, 78, 92, 104
Secret History of the Mongols, 3, 80, 139–40
Select History, 164, 167, 170, 171–2, 173
Shabankara'i, 93, 162

Shahnameh, 22–3, 65–6, 68, 69, 130, 155, 162–6, 166–8, 173, 180
Shahrokh (Timurid, 1405–47), 178–9, 181
Shamb, 92, 96, 103, 104, 109, 121, 146
Shams al-Din Juvayni *see* Juvayni, Shams al-Din
Shams al-Din Kart (d. 1278), 145
Shams al-Din Qazvini, 15, 31
Sharaf al-Din Khwarazmi, 9, 11
Sharaf al-Din Simnani, 46
shariʿa see law, Islamic
Shigi Qutuqu (Tatar), 136–7
Shihab al-Din ʿAbd Allah al-Shirazi *see* Wassaf
Shiraz, 162
Shiʿism, 52, 75, 103–8
 of ʿAbd Allah Qashani, 77, 104
Shiz, 21–2
shrines *see* tomb shrines
Shuʿab-e Panjganeh see *Five Genealogies*
sikka see coinage
Siyar al-Muluk, 170
Siyasatnameh, 170
slavery, 144–5
Subtle Truths, 109
Sughunchaq (Suldus, d. 1290), 34–5, 49, 68–9
Sughurluq (summer pasture), 21–2, 92
Suhrawardi, Shihab al-Din (d. 1191), 70, 93
sultan, position of, 91–2, 108, 154
Sultaniya, 103–4, 109–10, 146, 156
summer camps *see* seasonal camps
Syrian campaigns of Ghazan, 51–4, 59–60, 73–6, 171–2

Tabaqat-e Nasiri, 64
Tabari, Muhammad b. Jarir (d. 923), 76, 98
Tabriz, 24, 52, 92, 95–6, 97, 109, 121, 129–30, 132, 162
Taghachar (d. 1296), 40, 45–6, 49
Taj al-Din al-Muʾmini, 106, 109
Taj al-Din Awaji, 156–9
Taj al-Din ʿAlishah *see* ʿAlishah, Taj al-Din
Tajziyat-al-Amsar wa Tazjiyat al-Aʿsar, 75–7, 154–5, 157–8
Takht-e Sulayman, 21–2, 92
Tarikh-e Jahangosha see *History of the World Conqueror*
Tarikh-e Mobarak-e Ghazani see *Blessed History of Ghazan*
Tarikh-e ʿAlam see *World History*

Tatars, 139–40
Tayichiʾud, 139
Teguder Ahmad (*ilkhan*, 1282–4), 35, 71, 73
 depicted by Rashid Khwafi, 144–5
Throne of Solomon, 21–2, 92
tikishmishi, 14, 16
Timurid 'book of histories', 180–1
tomb shrines, 92, 103, 104, 146
 visitation, 52, 74–5
Toregene (Kereit, d. 1246), regent of Mongol Empire, 10–12
translation of Rashid al-Din's work, 113–14
Turko-Mongol tribes, 82
Turks, 79, 82, 94–6, 122
Tusi, Nasir al-Din (d. 1274), 19–21, 23, 29, 71, 72, 99, 137, 145, 155, 160–1

Ujan, 52, 54, 73, 75, 78
ulugh bitikchi, 8–9
Universal History of Wauchier de Denain, 131–2
ʿUtbi, Muhammad ibn ʿAbd al-Jaffar (d. 982), 62, 78
Utrar, 1–3

verse historiography, 162–3, 165–6, 167–8

Wadi al-Khaznadar (battle, 1299), 52–4
waqf see endowment
Wassaf, Shihab al-Din, 75, 78, 114, 134; *see also Allocation of Cities and Propulsion of Epochs*
 writing process, 158–9
winter camps *see* seasonal camps
Works and Beings, 114
World History of Rashid al-Din, 94–5, 107, 122, 127, 173
 compared to Qashani, 99–103
 manuscripts, 148, 180–1
 structure, 94, 100

yasa see law, Mongol
Yazd, 32–3, 48, 143
yosun, 105

Zafarnama see *Book of Victory*
Zayn al-Akhbar, 68
Zoroastrianism, 21–2, 63, 65, 69–70
Zubdat al-Tawarikh, 98–100, 102

EU representative:
Easy Access System Europe
Mustamäe tee 50, 10621 Tallinn, Estonia
Gpsr.requests@easproject.com

www.ingramcontent.com/pod-product-compliance
Lightning Source LLC
Chambersburg PA
CBHW052057300426
44117CB00013B/2165